DICTIONARY OF POLYNESIAN MYTHOLOGY

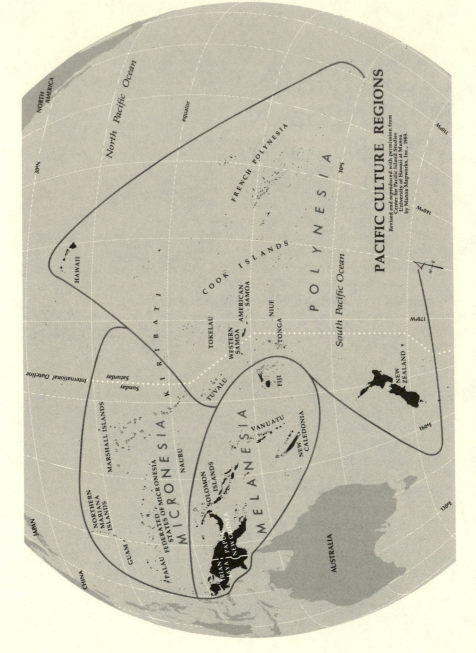

PACIFIC CULTURE REGIONS
Revised and reproduced with permission from
Center for Pacific Island Studies
University of Hawaii at Manoa
by Manoa Mapworks, Inc., 1989.

DICTIONARY OF POLYNESIAN MYTHOLOGY

Robert D. Craig

GREENWOOD PRESS
New York • Westport, Connecticut • London

Library of Congress Cataloging-in-Publication Data

Craig, Robert D., 1934-
  Dictionary of Polynesian mythology / Robert D. Craig.
    p. cm.
  Bibliography: p.
  Includes index.
  ISBN 0-313-25890-2 (lib. bdg. : alk. paper)
  1. Mythology, Polynesian—Dictionaries. I.Title.
BL2620.P6C7 1989
299′.92—dc20   89-7479

British Library Cataloguing in Publication Data is available.

Library of Congress Catalog Card Number: 89-7479
ISBN: 0-313-25890-2

First published in 1989

Greenwood Press, Inc.
88 Post Road West, Westport, Connecticut 06881

Printed in the United States of America

The paper used in this book complies with the
Permanent Paper Standard issued by the National
Information Standards Organization (Z39.48-1984).

10 9 8 7 6 5 4 3 2 1

CONTENTS

PREFACE

Compilation of this reference book began many years ago while I was working as editor of the journal *Pacific Studies* and while developing my previous book for Greenwood Press, *The Historical Dictionary of Oceania*. During that time, I collected thousands of references to Polynesian mythology from books and articles that crossed my desk with an idea that someday I would publish a work that would consolidate and cross-reference the many stories and legends found in these Polynesian islands.

I planned to write entries on every known mythological figure (gods, goddesses, and ancient heroes) found in the extant sources so that comparisons, analogies, and other scholarly studies could be made. As my original research progressed, it became apparent that some decision had to be made whether or not to include references to historical figures (mortals). After much soul searching, I came up with a simple rationale: If a story dealt with mortals and contained no references to gods or to any supernatural intervention, it and its characters were not included. Exceptions were made, however, to those ancient heroes who played a major role in the early history of the islands. Perhaps another publication in the future can supplement this one by including all of those interesting historical figures of ancient Polynesia.

This volume is the result of many years of research, and I hope the entries contained herein will benefit both the scholar and the general reader. Although I have attempted to be thorough in my research, I find even at this late date mythological names that could have been included. A planned publication deadline simply had to be met, and research had to be cutoff at some point. I express my personal appreciation to anyone who may contact me with any other references, and, hopefully, a future edition of this volume will contain those new entries.

ACKNOWLEDGMENTS

A work of this magnitude cannot be completed without the assistance of many other individuals and institutions. Acknowledgments are due to my good friends: Ruby Johnson at the University of Hawai'i for a detailed work she had begun on a similar index for Hawai'i; to Vernice Pere, now senior vice president of the Polynesian Cultural Center in Hawai'i, for her initial inspiration and help in collecting many of the original citations; and to my colleagues at Alaska Pacific University for their many suggestions. A special thanks goes to Lehua Nani Moanaliha Uwekoolani for her invaluable aid in helping with the index.

Special acknowledgments should be made to the various institutions that have assisted in one way or another. To Duncan Ferguson, Academic Vice President of Alaska Pacific University, for the special grant given to assist in the typing of my original manuscript and for the many hours taken from my classes and administrative assignments to complete the work. To the Interlibrary Loan Department of our Consortium Library for the numerous books and articles they ordered without personal cost to me. To the National Endowment for the Humanities for the travel-to-source grant they awarded me to visit the Bernice P. Bishop Museum and the University of Hawai'i libraries during the summer of 1988 to complete my research. Finally, I wish to express my personal thanks to all my predecessors who recorded these legends for posterity. Without their diligent efforts, we would not have the rich Polynesian legacy which this work hopes to elucidate.

Anchorage, Alaska
January, 1989

INTRODUCTION

THE POLYNESIAN RACE

The distinctive Polynesian people, whose mythology provides the basis for this book, were the most widely spread people on the earth prior to A. D. 1500. They settled the area of the Pacific Ocean generally referred to as the "Polynesian triangle" with its three geographical points being Hawai'i to the north, New Zealand to the southwest, and Easter Island to the east, a geographical area twice that of the United States, although its land mass is only a fraction of that of the United States. Within this triangle lies the major island groups of Hawai'i, New Zealand, Western and American Samoa, Tonga, the Cook Islands, French Polynesia (including the Society, Marquesas, Tuamotu, Austral, and Gambier Islands), Easter Island, Phoenix Islands, Line Islands, and Tuvalu (Ellice Islands), as well as numerous small outliers such as Pitcairn, Chatham, Tikopia, Anuta, Rotuma, etc.

A few of the first European navigators, missionaries, and adventurers who visited the Polynesian islands during the eighteenth and nineteenth centuries became interested in the history of their inhabitants and advanced various theories regarding their origins. Most of these early theories, however, were based primarily on conjecture after only a superficial examination of their material culture. Captain James Cook was one of the first of these theorists. In his visit in 1769, he recognized certain close relationships between the cultures of the various Polynesian groups. Because their language and many of their customs were similar to those of the Malay peninsula, he concluded that the various Polynesian groups must have had a common origin in Malaysia, a theory that has stood the test of more than two hundred years of close scholarly examination and scrutiny.

Subsequent writers concluded differently. Based on extremely meager evidence, the Reverend Samuel Marsden (d. 1838), an early missionary to the South Pacific, suggested that the Polynesians were an offshoot of the ancient Hebrews who once lived in Palestine. The Hawaiian missionary, William Ellis, on the other hand, suggested in 1817 that their apparent Asiatic characteristics came about as a result of their migrations from Asia across the Bering Strait down the west coast of the North American continent before sailing out into the Pacific. A third proposal was made by the French trader and scholar Jacques A. Moerenhout (1837) who argued that they were remnants of a large civilization that had at one time existed on a great Pacific continent that had subsequently sunk beneath the sea.

It was not until the twentieth century that serious scholarly efforts attempted to solve this problem by the use of modern research techniques in anthropology and archaeology. The first results of this scientific research were published in the 1920s and 1930s. Since World War II, similar research has been undertaken, and many more publications have appeared. Although variant theories are still advanced regarding the origins of the Polynesians, the summary given below represents the most widely-accepted view today.

Studies in the areas of botany, genetics, language, archaeology, and mythology suggest that the Polynesians descend from the Mongoloid division of the human family, and that they entered the Pacific by way of Malaysia and Indonesia. During their slow migration through Melanesia (perhaps by way of Fiji), the Polynesians intermarried with that group and thus passed on to their progeny the height and heavy build of the negrito Melanesians.

Almost all scholarly evidence points to a southeast Asian origin. Polynesian food stuffs (the taro, yam, coconut, breadfruit and bananas) and animals (the pig, dog, and chicken) are all found to have been first domesticated in southeast Asia, except perhaps the sweet potato that had a South American origin. The cultivation of these crops by Polynesians as well as their fishing methods and social organizations all trace their origins to southeast Asia, and Polyensian legends tell of *westward* migrations not *eastern* migrations into their islands. Linguistic studies also show that the Polynesian languages descend from a single ancestor, a member of the Austronesian family of languages spoken throughout Indonesia, the Philippines, Micronesia, and parts of South Vietnam and Malay, and Polynesian linguists maintain that the first settlement in Polynesia took place in the Tongan Islands about 1300 B.C. or before. (See below, "The Polynesian Languages.")

Summarizing, then, scholars now suggest that the ancestors of the Polynesians pushed through Indonesia into Melanesia by 3000 B.C., then eastward to Tonga and Samoa (western Polynesia) by 1300 B.C., and on to the Marquesas by the second century before Christ (or sooner). From the Marquesas, they settled the eastern Polynesian groups: the Society Islands, parts of the Tuamotus, Hawai'i and Mangareva, and on to Easter Island (Rapanui) about A.D. 500. From the Society Islands, groups sailed to the Cook Islands, to New Zealand (about A.D. 1200), to the southern Tuamotus, to the Austral Islands, and to the island of Rapa. Though American inhabitants may have ventured into the Pacific as Heyerdahl tried to prove by his famous Kon-Tiki raft experiment in 1947, all scholarly research to date has rendered his theory of population from the American continents untenable.

It would have been impossible for the Polynesians to have settled these widely scattered islands had it not been for their expert knowledge of seafaring canoe construction and their ability to navigate by naked-eye observations without the aid of compass, sextant, or chart. No contemporary navigators anywhere in the world could match their bravery and their sailing skills. Without question, the greatest material artifact of the ancient Polynesians is their canoe. These famous double-hulled, outrigger canoes, measuring up to thirty meters in length, could carry up to three hundred people and their cargo. Polynesian legends tell us of vast two-way ocean-going voyages between island groups (between Tahiti and Hawai'i, for example) before the arrival of the Europeans, an almost unbelievable feat. There is general agreement that the various discoveries of the Pacific islands by the Polynesians were deliberately planned, and that their navigational skills allowed them to return to their homeland once they had found a new island on which to settle. The drift theory, in which sailors in their outriggers were blown off course and drifted until by accident they came across new islands, has against it the telling argument that unprovisioned canoes being blown off course would not have survived the long arduous trip between the island groups. Whatever the case may be, their seafaring achievements in settling the vast extent of the Pacific Ocean can only be admired, and they truly earned the title given to them many years ago by Sir Peter Buck, the Vikings of the Pacific.

THE POLYNESIAN LANGUAGES

The thirty some languages spoken by these Polynesian seafarers form a minor branch of a larger Austronesian family of languages that today spreads around two-thirds of the earth's circumference. This minor branch, called Oceanic or Proto-Central Pacific, began to differentiate itself in western Melanesia sometime before 3500 B.C. (see the Polynesian language family tree below), and it too became divided into two different subgroupings, Proto-Fijian and Proto-Polynesian (PPN). All Polynesian languages are considered to be descended from PPN, and to date, some two thousand words have been reconstructed for this ancestor of the Polynesian languages.

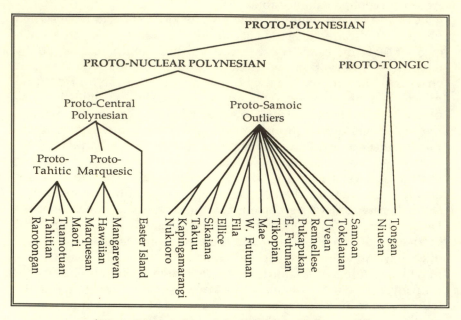

(Fig. 1. Relationship of the Polynesian Languages.)

Because of their common heritage and because of the little or no intrusion of other foreign elements, the languages of each of these subgroupings are fairly homogeneous. Even today, for example, the eastern Polynesians from Hawai'i, New Zealand, Tahiti, and the Marquesas can communicate with each other in their native languages with minor adjustments in the pronunciation of their consonants. The following chart with a sampling of cognates in several of these languages shows these similarities.

English	Tongan	Samoan	Marquesan	Tahitian	Māori	Hawaiian
Love	'alo'ofa	alofa	kaoha	āroha	aroha	aloha
Taro	talo	talo	kalo	taro	taro	kalo
Bird	manu	manu	manu	manu	manu	manu
Old	tefito	tafito	tehito	tahito	tawhito	kahiko
Man	tangata	tane	kane	tāne	tane	kāne
Ancestor	tupu	tupu	tupuna	tupuna	tupuna	kupuna
Fish	ika	i'a	ika	i'a	ika	i'a
Yes	'io	ai	ae	'ae	ae	'ae
Canoe	vaka	va'a	vaka	va'a	waka	wa'a

We must not assume, however, that all words in the Polynesian vocabularies are related. The words above were deliberately selected to show a close relationship between these languages. To show their differences, compare the following phrases:

English	"Hello!"	"Thank You."	"How are you?"	"Good-bye."
Tongan	Mālō e lelei.	Mālō	Fēfē hake?	'Alu ā e.
Samoan	Tālofa.	Fa'afetai.	O ā mai oe?	Tōfā soifua.
Māori	Kia ora.	Whakapai.	Pēhea koa?	Kia ora.
Tahitian	'Ia ora na.	Maurūru roa.	'E aha tō 'oe huru?	Pārahi
Hawaiian	Aloha.	Mahalo.	Pehea 'oe?	Aloha.

Simplified Pronunciation

When the nineteenth-century missionaries created a written language for the Polynesians, they did so by using the Roman alphabet with its Latin pronunciation. Most of the Polynesian consonants (b, f, h, k, l, m, n, p, r, s, t, w) pose no serious problems to the English-speaking reader, and the vowels (a, e, i, o, u), sometimes with both short and long sounds, are pronounced as follows (using Hawaiian as an example):

Long duration vowels (indicated by a macron over the vowel)
    ā . . . . as in "calm"   pāpā (to forbid)
    ē . . . . as in "they"   pēpē (baby)
    ī . . . . as in "bee"   pīpī (to sprinkle)
    ō . . . . as in "lo"   lōlō (stupid)
    ū . . . . as in "rule" or "moon"   'ūha (thigh or lap)
Short duration vowels
    a . . . . as in "around"   papa (board, class)
    e . . . . as in "set"   pepe (flat, as a flat nose)
    i . . . . as in "sit"   pipi (cattle/beef)
    o . . . . as in "obey"   lolo (brain)
    u . . . . as in "put"   lulu (sheltered)

The diphthongs ae, ai, ao, au, ei, eu, oi, ou are always stressed on the first member, and the two vowels are not nearly as closely joined as in the English pronunciation.

Another mark, which is considered a consonant, is the glottal stop and is written as a reverse apostrophe ('). Its pronunciation might be a problem to English speakers. It appears before a vowel or between vowels, and in Proto-Polynesian, it was most likely a k sound which dropped out and was replaced by a glottal sound. The Hawaiian word o'o, for example, is pronounced very much like the English, "Oh, oh."

The macron or the long duration sign (‾) and the glottal stop (') were seldom ever used until recently. Most of the original sources researched for in this study give no indication of either mark. They have made their appearance in recent years, however, as a result of indigenous scholars insisting that their languages be written correctly. In some of the island groups, they still remain unknown, and there are *no* published dictionaries that provide them. I have attempted wherever possible to use these marks correctly, although in some cases the exact translations of these ancient names still remain controversial (in Hawai'i, for example), and thus the use of the diacritical marks on some words remains questionable. Their presence or absence, however, changes both pronunciation and meaning as we have shown above with the use of the macron. A similar situation occurs with the glottal stop. For example, *pau* means "finished," but *pa'u* means "soot," *pa'ū* "moist," and *pā'ū* "sarong;" *koi* means "to urge," but *ko'i* means "adze," and *kōî* "shrill."

Ng and **G** were consonants frequently interchanged by the early missionaries. In most of the island groups, the isolated **G** is pronounced **NG** as in "Tagaloa" (pronounced Tangaloa), or in "Pago Pago" (pronounced Pango Pango). Modern writers are giving up the missionary use of the isolated **G** for **NG**, but we have retained the spellings as found in the original sources.

W and **WH** may also give some confusion. Usually, the **W** is pronounced similar to the English, but in Hawaiian, a **W** after *a, i,* and *e* is usually pronounced like a soft *v*. The Māori **WH** is an interesting combination; the closest approximation is the English **F**. For example, "Tawhaki" is pronounced Ta<u>f</u>akee, and "Whiti" as <u>F</u>eetee.

Selected List of Polynesian Dictionaries and/or Grammars

Those interested in pursuing the richness of the Polynesian languages should consult the following standard references.

Cook Islands - Savage, Stephen. *A Dictionary of the Maori Language of Rarotonga.* Suva: University of the South Pacific, 1980. (460 pp.)

Easter Island - Fuentes, Jordi. *Dictionary and Grammar of the Easter Island Language.* Santiago: Editorial Universitaria, 1960. (1,082 pp.)

Hawaiian - Pukui, Mary K. and Samuel H. Elbert. *Hawaiian Dictionary.* Honolulu: University Press of Hawaii, 1981. 3rd ed. (188 pp.)

Māori - Tregear, Edward. *Maori-Polynesian Comparative Dictionary.* New York: Humanities Press, Inc., 1969. Reprint from the 1891 edition.

Williams, Herbert W. *Dictionary of the Maori Language.* 7th ed. Wellington: R. E. Owen, Government Printer, 1971.

Marquesan - Dordillon, Ildefonse R. *Grammaire et dictionnaire de la langue des îles Marquises.* 2 vols. Paris: Institute d'Ethnologie, 1931-32. (None in English.)

Samoan - Milner, G. B. *Samoan Dictionary.* New York: Oxford
   University Press, 1966. (465 pp.)
Tahitian - Tryon, D. T. *Conversational Tahitian.* Berkeley: Univer-
   sity of California Press, 1970. (177 pp.)
   Lemaitre, Yves. *Lexique du tahitien contemporain.* Paris:
   ORSTOM, 1973. (201 pp.)
Tongan - Shumway, Eric. *Intensive Course in Tongan.* Honolulu:
   University of Hawaii Press, 1971. (723 pp.)
Tuamotuan - Stimson, J. F. and D. S. Marshall. *Dictionary of Some
   Tuamotuan Dialects of the Polynesian Language.* Salem:
   Peabody Museum, 1964. (623 pp.)

THE MYTHS

Polynesian mythology represents one of the richest and most detailed collections of stories relating to gods, demigods, and heroes
that can be found anywhere in the world. These ancient Pacific peoples spent their creative energies in weaving complex, oral narratives that consisted of priestly chants, lengthy legends of gods and
heroes, and love lyrics known to chiefs and commoners alike. Like
other preliterate peoples, Polynesians were far more sophisticated
than our modern literate society in the oral transmission of their
traditional knowledge. The length of some of their chants is incredi-
ble. Some of them take several evenings to recite, especially those
about the popular heroes and heroines, Māui, Laka, Pele, and
Kaha'i, for example. These chants, of course, were meant to be
heard, and when they are, they evoke pleasant mental images in the
minds of the listeners. But when they are read, which is the only way
a modern, non-Polynesian audience may have them, they sometimes
appear to be tedious with their long listings and their repetitious descriptions and phrases.

Everywhere they settled, the Polynesians carried their legends
with them, and when they reached a new land, these traditional
myths were adapted to the local surroundings, enriched, and then
passed down from generation to generation. As time and distance
separated the Polynesians groups from one another, local variations
and even new elements appeared in their traditional narratives. The
stories of the popular demigod Māui, for example, are known from
one end of the Pacific to the other, but the exact details of his exploits
vary significantly from one island to another.

While Greek and Roman mythology has come down to us through
two thousand years of literary embellishment and sophistication,
Polynesian mythology has emerged in written form only within the
last one hundred years. It retains much of its early, pristine character, and as such, its quality differs very little from those Greek leg-

ends that Homer examined when he decided to write his famous epics, the *Iliad* and *Odyssey*. These extant Polynesian legends reveal an exuberance and vitality that rival those found in the earliest of the European national epics such as *Beowulf, The Song of Roland*, etc.

The business of preserving the sacred oral chants of Polynesian gods and heroes as well as the genealogies of their chiefs was generally the function of certain individuals within Polynesian society. In New Zealand, it was the ceremonial priests *(tahunga)*; in Hawai'i, the *haku-mele* (master-of-song); and in Tonga, the *faiva faka-Tonga*. These individuals (usually men) were attached to a chief's court, and it was their duty to aggrandize and glorify the chief's family in hymnlike chants and songs. In Samoa where true ceremonial priests did not exist, the functions of bard, orator, and genealogist were performed by the talking chiefs who passed the traditional lore from one generation to another.

In New Zealand, special houses *(whare wananga)* were sometimes built to instruct young novices in the traditional mythology, genealogy, dance, and chant composition. In Tahiti, a unique Arioi Society, a highly organized traveling "minstrel" group, entertained the people from one island district to another with dance, music, and pantomime. A less organized institution existed in Hawai'i where the hula schools *(hālau)* performed; sometimes the entertainers even used marionettes *(hula ki'i)* to tell their dramatic tales or to make satirical comment on their society.

The training of novices in the sacred lore was rigorous and exact, and great attention was not only given to the memorization of detail, but to the use of voice inflection as well. A breath or hesitation taken at the wrong place could mean ill-luck to those who were being honored.

Precise translations of these ancient chants today requires great skill. A good many of the legends contain archaic words whose exact meanings were already unknown to the common listener a hundred years ago. A good example is the Hawaiian creation chant, the *Ku-mulipō*, a part of which is reproduced below. Numerous English translations of the chant exist, and surprisingly each differs significantly from the others.

Besides the archaic words, another reason for this difficulty is the fact that Polynesian chants are purposely allusive, full of symbolism and analogy, and deliberately ambiguous, using various poetical devices to suggest a deeper meaning within the text than what the words normally would suggest. Polynesians have always had a passion for puns, the double use of words, or the turning of phrases or even verses. They prefer analogies rather than frank expressions. While the ancient audiences understood precisely what the poet meant, it becomes extremely difficult sometimes for the modern translator to give one correct rendition. When we hear the discussion of a canoe, for example, we are not quite sure whether the poet really means a canoe or whether he is using it as a phallus symbol. This symbolistic technique, for example, is still popular in Tonga where it is known as *heliaki*, the hiding of a specific meaning in references to natural objects and places. Verses or even whole chants can be symbolic with various levels of interpretation, and we must continually ask ourselves, "Is this to be taken literally?" Primitive to a certain extent these chants may be, but in meaning and expression, Polynesian chant composition represents a sophistication that challenges the wits of any modern scholar or reader.

Examples of the Extant Chants

Listed below are two sample chants (one in Hawaiian and the other in Samoan) to illustrate the character of our printed Polynesian sources.

Prologue to the Night World, the Kumulipō,
or, the Hawaiian Creation Chant

O ke au i kahuli wela ka honua
O ke au i kahuli lole ka lani
O ke au i kuka'iaka ka la
E ho'omalamalama i ka malama
O ke au i Makali'i ka po
O ka Walewale ho'okumu honua ia
O ke kumu o ka lipo
O ke kumu o ka Po i po ai
O ka Lipolipo, o ka Lipolipo
O ka lipo o ka La, o ka lipo o ka Po
    Po wale ho-i.

At the time that turned the heat of the earth
At the time when the heavens turned and changed
At the time when the light of the sun was subdued
To cause light to break forth
At the time of the night of Makali'i [winter]
Then began the slime which established the earth,
The source of deepest darkness,
Of the depth of darkness, of the depth of darkness,
Of the darkness of the sun, in the depth of night,
    It was night
    So night was born.

This particular English translation was by Queen Liliu'okalani, and her original Hawaiian without accent marks and the translation are found in Beckwith 1951:42–45.

The Battle Song of the Origin of Heaven and Earth
(A Samoan epic recorded by Krämer 1902:395–396.)

'O galu lolo ma galu fatio'o
'O galu tau ma galu fefatia'i,
'O le 'au'au peau ma le sologa a peau,
Na ona fa'afua, 'a e lē fati.
'O le peau lolo ma le peau ta'oto
'O le peau malie ma le peau lagatonu.
'O peau alili'a ma peau la'asia,
'O peau a sisifo mai gaga'e. . .
Tagaloa fia malolō,
Ta lili'a i peau 'o lalō (a lalo)
'Ofea le nu'u na lua'i tupu?
Na lua'i tupu Manue'atele,
Tupu Savai'i, 'a e muli i malae Alamisi
Me le atu Tog ma le atu Fiti
'Atoa le atunu'u itiiti.

Overflowing and violently falling surf,
Fighting and shattering surf,
Leaping sea and incoming sea,
Running high but not shattering.
Going high and running level sea,
Excellent seas coming in from the front.
Dreaded seas, breaking on the beaches of the reef,
Waves from the west and from the east. . .
Tangaloa wishes to rest,
I am alarmed by the waves beneath.
Where is the sport which rose first of all?
Manu'a, the great island, arose first of all,
Savai'i arose, the malae of Alamisi followed,
The Tongan archipelago, the Fiji islands
And all the little islands.

THE PRINTED SOURCES

The individual entries on Polynesian mythology that make up the bulk of this work were gleaned after having examined nearly three hundred sources in English, German, French, and to a lesser extent in the Polynesian languages of Tahitian, Hawaiian, Māori, etc. As you will note from the bibliographic citations, the majority of the entries were extracted from a small number of primary sources that date generally in the nineteenth or early twentieth centuries. The compilers of these records, Grey, Fornander, Henry, White, and Krämer, for example, represent a group of Westerners who felt some affinity toward the dying Polynesian culture and who felt obliged to record their customs and beliefs before all was lost. Unlike the early navigators and missionaries to the islands who were generally unskilled in the scholarly techniques of ethnographic research, these collectors/scholars were in the main better educated and more interested in recording exact details of the ancient cultures they visited. Realizing the fast pace at which Polynesian cultures were changing as a result of their contact with the West, they deliberately set out with a goal in mind of recording this ancient ethnographic data while it was still relatively uncontaminated. Although twentieth century scholars have criticized their methods and their collected materials, we would indeed be poorer had these "amateurs" not preserved for us some of the details given to them by the few survivors of an ancient culture.

Unfortunately, not all of the islands groups were so blessed by having such recorders. The Marquesas Islands, for example, failed in the nineteenth century to attract an ethnographer even though their ancient culture was probably richer in tradition and lore than many of the others. As a result, our knowledge of Marquesan mythology of pre-European times is almost nonexistent. Because of the nature of the source materials, the following study, unfortunately, may appear biased or weighted toward those islands of Hawai'i, New Zealand, Samoa, and Tahiti, homes to the nineteenth-century ethnographers.

Māori Sources

One of the first to begin the task of systematically collecting and publishing ancient Polynesian chants, genealogies, and mythology was Sir George Grey, a British administrator who held the position of governor of New Zealand twice (1845–1853, 1861–1868) and then premier (1877–1879). He is considered the most commanding and influential figure in nineteenth-century New Zealand history. Born in England and after having served as governor of South Australia for three years (1837–1840), Grey arrived in New Zealand during a tortuous period of Māori history. He provided strong leadership because of his proficiency in the Māori language. He insisted that he could do a better job of governing by knowing as much as he could of the Māori people, and, therefore, for eight years, he persuaded chiefs and priests alike to teach him the myths that had been passed down through their generations. Grey observed that even in his day, the individuals responsible for the preservation of traditional knowledge could hardly explain meanings of some of the words. So drastic were the old ways and language changing that he felt pressed to record whatever he could before all had been totally lost. Grey, therefore, represents one of the first scholarly efforts to set down these legends systematically, and the result is one of the finest straightforward accounts published in all of Polynesia. Although his original book, *Polynesian Mythology*, was published first in Māori in 1854, it was translated into English for the first time in 1855. (A new reprint appeared in 1956.) Grey's work provided Europeans with their first popular acquaintance with Pacific mythology.

Although Grey's contribution stands as the first published source of Māori legends, numerous writers and scholars followed with extensive collections of ancient mythology. John White (1826–1891), for example, published his six-volume work, *Ancient History of the Māori*, between 1887 and 1890. White and his parents came to New Zealand in 1835, and after a formal education in England, he returned to New Zealand where he spent much of his time with the learned Māori priests. Because of his excellent command of the Māori language, he became an interpreter for numerous New Zealand administrators, including Governor George Grey. In 1880, the New Zealand government commissioned him to compile a history of the Māori which appeared in six volumes between 1887 and 1891. It remains the richest and fullest account of Māori mythology that has seen print.

Several other contemporaries of Grey and White also provided substantial source materials for this study. Elsdon Best (1856–1931), for example, published more than twenty-five books and fifty papers dealing with the Māori people. Born in New Zealand and after several years of work as a road foreman during which time he took numerous notes regarding Māori customs, he was eventually appointed in 1910 as director of the Dominion Museum in Wellington. His most famous volume, *The Māori*, appeared in 1924.

Edward Tregear (1846–1931), an outstanding public servant and amateur ethnologist, came to New Zealand in 1863. He served in the military during the land wars and later became an important figure in the Labour Movement until World War I. Because of his tireless devotion to Māori culture, he was honored by many scholarly societies for his work. He was one of the founding members of the Polynesian Society, organized in 1892. Although his theory regarding the Aryan origin of the Māori race is not supported today, his major publication, *Maori-Polynesian Comparative Dictionary* (1891), not only ranks as an important linguistic dictionary but serves as a substantial guide to Māori mythology.

Born in England, Stephenson Percy Smith (1840–1922) came to New Zealand with his family in 1850. He became a surveyor and through his work he was able to collect information regarding the Māori way of life. He eventually was appointed Surveyor General in 1889. After he helped organize the Polynesian Society in 1882, he became its first secretary-treasurer and editor, a position he held for thirty years. His production was prodigious although many of his theories regarding the origin of the Māori race were based on flimsy, factual evidence and are discounted today. His most famous work, *Hawaiki: The Original Home of the Maori*, appeared in book form in 1910.

Cook Islands Sources

Closely related to the traditions of the Māoris in New Zealand are those found in the neighboring Cook Islands. The one individual scholar responsible for the first collection of myths and songs from these islands was William Wyatt Gill (1828–1896). Born in Bristol, England, Gill received his bachelor's degree from the University of London. At the age of twenty-three, he sailed to the South Pacific as a London Missionary Society missionary to Mangaia in the Cook Islands where he remained for twenty years. He learned their language and collected their traditional stories and poetry in a manuscript which was published in 1876 as *Myths and Songs from the South Pacific*. His work became an important source for later anthropologists and folklorists.

Tahitian Sources

Without question, the most renowned authority on ancient Tahitian society remains Teuria Henry (1847–1915). Born in Tahiti, Teuria Henry was the daughter and granddaughter of London Missionary Society missionaries to the islands. Her grandfather, the Reverend John Muggridge Orsmond, came to Mo'orea in 1817. From there he journeyed to the other islands of the group until he finally settled on Tahiti in 1831 where he spent the remainder of this life in energetic service to his church. His knowledge of the Tahitian language was prodigious, and the first Tahitian-English dictionary was mainly his work. He spent a great deal of time listening to old chiefs and priests and recording their oral traditions. His manuscript was a source for William Ellis, another LMS missionary who later settled in Hawai'i. Orsmond's handwritten manuscript of ancient Tahitian customs and legends eventually made its way to Paris where it presumably burned in the fire of 1850. His detailed ethnographic work, however, was continued by his granddaughter Teuira who moved to Hawai'i from 1890 to 1905. From her grandfather's surviving manuscripts and from other records gleaned in the Bernice P. Bishop Museum in Honolulu, Henry wrote her scholarly work, *Ancient Tahiti*. It was meticulously edited and posthumously published by the Bishop Museum in 1928. About half of the book's 651 pages contains ancient chants and legends regarding the creation, cosmology, and genealogies.

Marquesan Sources

Although the Marquesas Islands were the first Polynesian Islands to be visited by European navigators (Mendaña in 1595), they failed to attract any significant scholars to their shores until the twentieth century. Early Christian missionary work in the mid-nineteenth century was slow and tedious, and by the time someone became interested in their ancient culture, it was already dead. Disease, firearms, and war had decimated the population. In 1774, Captain James Cook had estimated the population of the islands to be between 50,000 and 100,000. According to the census taken by the French in 1887, there were only 5,246, and by 1920, there remained only 1,500 Marquesans. The first ethnographer to visit the islands was the German scholar Karl von den Steinen who worked in the Marquesas for six months in 1897. He published his work on Marquesan art in 1925–1928, and his twenty-two myths were published posthumously in 1933–1934 in the *Zeitschrift für Ethnologie* (Berlin).

In 1920–1921, the Bernice P. Bishop Museum in Honolulu sponsored an ethnographic expedition to the Marquesas. E. S. Craighill Handy and his wife Willowdean Chatterton Handy were members of that expedition, and both scholars published the results of their collections. E. S. Craighill Handy's work *Marquesan Legends* (1930) provides a primary source of the extant myths in his day, and his wife's work, *Forever the Land of Men*, is an excellent personal account of her stay in the islands.

A significant collection is that of Samuel Elbert whose fifty legends, still in manuscript form, were collected during his residence between March 1934 and May 1935. The collection is one of the richest ones ever made in the Marquesas, but unfortunately it still lies unpublished in the Bernice P. Bishop Museum.

Although most twentieth century scholars maintained that nothing more could be gleaned from the Marquesas, Henri Lavonès, a French scholar living in Tahiti, spent some time in the northern islands of the chain between 1963 and 1966 and gathered two small volumes of additional text materials entitled *Récits Marquisiens*. His collection, however, contains only few references to mythological characters and provided little for our purposes.

Hawaiian Sources

It was well over a hundred years after Captain James Cook's visit to the Hawaiian Islands that a book exclusively devoted to Hawaiian mythology appeared in print. The early navigators to the islands unfortunately recorded only brief references to ancient myths, and the Christian missionaries were more interested in replacing these ancient myths with new religious ones. An exception is William Ellis who toured Hawai'i in 1823. His important book, *A Narrative Tour through Hawaii* contains references to some twenty legends. It is unfortunate that they are not as full as we would like to have seen. Had Ellis been a trained ethnographer, our knowledge of the ancient Hawaiian past would have been much richer.

Three important scholars appeared in the mid-nineteenth century who collected and published ancient Hawaiian legends. The first was Samuel Kamakau (1815–1876) whose writings were published in the Hawaiian newspapers between 1866 and 1871 and provided a source for subsequent Hawaiian scholars. His works were translated into English and published between 1961–64 by the Bishop Museum and the Kamehameha Schools Press. The second scholar was David Malo (1795–1853) who wrote his *Moolelo Hawaii* about 1840. It was translated by N. B. Emerson as *Hawaiian Antiquities* and published in 1903.

The third and perhaps the greatest collector of Hawaiian folklore is Abraham Fornander (1812–1887). Born in Sweden, Fornander first visited the islands in 1838 on a whaling vessel and then returned in 1842 to make them his home. He married Pinao Alanakapu, a member of the Hawaiian nobility from Moloka'i. His three volume work (1878–1885), *An Account of the Polynesian Race*, is an attempt by Fornander to piece together the ancient historical past by using legends, language, and folklore. Fornander's extensive, handwritten collection of Hawaiian legends that he used in his *Account*, however, lay until 1920 when the Bernice P. Bishop Museum printed them it in three volumes as the *Fornander Collection of Hawaiian Antiquities and Folklore*, considered the greatest repository of Hawaiian folklore. Its editor, Thomas G. Thrum, also deserves mention. His name appears in almost every scholarly treatise on Hawaiian folklore. Thrum was born in Australia in 1842 and arrived in Hawai'i in 1853. His famed *Hawaiian Almanac and Annual* appeared regularly until his death in 1932. This publication provided an outlet for numerous translations of legends that normally would have been lost. His first book on Hawaiian legends, *Hawaiian Folk Tales* (1907) and his *More Hawaiian Folk Tales* (1923) contain stories that had appeared in his *Annual*. Because of his tireless industry and dedication, the

Bernice P. Bishop Museum appointed him editor of the Fornander collection.

Subsequent authors of Hawaiian legends include William D. Westervelt (1849–1939) who came to Hawai'i in 1888 and who became an avid student of ancient Hawaiian myth and customs. His three volumes of legends (1915, 1916, and 1923) became best sellers primarily because of his talent of organization and presentation. Another source is William H. Rice. Born on O'ahu in 1846, Rice was active in Hawaiian politics and became the last governor of Kaua'i under Queen Liliu'okalani (1893). Hearing Hawaiian legends from his youth, Rice decided to set them down in writing, and these appeared in 1923 as *Hawaiian Legends,* a brief but important collection.

A twentieth century scholar whose life work is identified with Hawaiian mythology is that of Martha Warren Beckwith (1871–1959). Her prodigious assimilation of Hawaiian legends and myths awards her a special place of honor among all Hawaiians. Although not native born in the islands, she spent her early childhood on the island of Maui where her missionary cousins had lived for many years. She left the islands to study and to work on the mainland. Although she taught for many years at Vassar College until her retirement in 1938, a good amount of her time was spent in the islands at the Bernice P. Bishop Museum. Her *Hawaiian Mythology* and her translation of the Hawaiian creation chant, the *Kumulipō,* acknowledge her as one of the foremost authorities ever on ancient Hawaiian folklore. *Hawaiian Mythology* is not only a scholarly examination of extant Hawaiian traditions, but a comparative study of other South Pacific sources as well. The following reference work owes a great debt to Professor Beckwith's comparative study.

Samoan Sources

One of the first collectors of Samoa ethnographic material was George A. Turner (1818–1891), a missionary for the London Missionary Society, who came to Samoa in 1840 where he spent some nineteen years. His expertise in the Samoan language provided the basis for the translation and publication of the Bible into Samoan. His book, *Nineteen Years in Polynesia,* published in 1861, describes the introduction of Christianity into Samoa, and it became the standard work on Samoan culture. Several years later, his writings on the ancient religion and customs were published as *Samoa, a Hundred Years ago and Long Before* (London: Macmillan & Co., 1884), a work recognized later by the more famous ethnographer Augustin Krämer.

Augustin Friedrich Krämer (1865–1941), a German ethnologist and explorer, studied medicine in Tübingen and Berlin and natural science in Kiel. In 1889, he joined the imperial navy and spent time in the South Pacific (1893–1895 and 1897–1899) where he collected abundant ethnological data on the German Samoan Islands which were published in his two-volume work, *Die Samoa-Inseln*, in 1902 and 1903. This well-documented work provides one of the finest collections of ethnological study ever made of the early Samoan peoples, and his discussion of Samoan myths and legends has never seen an equal. Krämer cites his informants as having been born before the Christian era, and as such, the legends he records claim to be as authentic and as free of interpolations as anyone could ever gather. After spending time in the Micronesian islands to the north, Krämer later returned to Germany where he became the scientific director of the Linden-Museum in Stuttgart.

Other names associated with Samoan ethnographic studies are English writers T. A. Powell, John Fraser, and John B. Stair whose writings were published in the *Journal of the Polynesian Society* (New Zealand) in the 1890s and the German Consul Otto Stuebel, 1889–1891, whose collection was edited and published by the Königlichen Museum für Völkerkunde in 1896.

Tongan Sources

Edward W. Gifford and E. E. V. Collocott compiled the two major collections of Tongan legends. Gifford worked as an ethnographer in Tonga between 1920 and 1921 for the Bernice P. Bishop Museum. His monograph, *Tongan Myths and Tales*, appeared in 1924. After his work in Tonga, Gifford returned to his duties as Associate Curator of the Museum of Anthropology at the University of California. The Reverend E. E. V. Collocott's self-proclaimed "more homely" work, his *Tales and Poems of Tonga*, appeared in 1928 and provides a wealth of local stories and legends. Both scholars published numerous other journal articles regarding Tongan society and culture.

General Collections

Numerous volumes of the retelling of Polynesian stories in various languages have appeared during the past hundred years. Two in English particularly worth mentioning are those written by Johannes C. Andersen and Katharine Luomala. Born in Denmark in 1873, Andersen came to Wellington, New Zealand, where he was appointed librarian in the Alexander Turnbull Library. He became interested in Polynesian folklore and because of his inherent abilities was asked to edited the prestigious *Journal of the Polynesian Society* from 1925 to 1947. He published numerous articles and books regarding Polynesian mythology, the most important for this study is his *Myths and Legends of the Polynesians*, published originally in 1929 and reprinted in 1969. Although not a primary source, his work does rely upon other authoritative sources, and the charming style of retelling the stories makes this a fascinating study. For his outstanding contribution to the discipline, Andersen was awarded the Royal Society Medal for Ethnology in 1944. He died in 1962.

One of the most superb commentaries on the major Polynesian legends remains Katharine Luomala's *Voices on the Wind* (Honolulu: Bernice P. Bishop Museum Press, 1955). Her understanding of the primitive forces that drove the Polynesians to compose their chants appears throughout the volume. No writer surpasses her in her sensitive and entertaining style in retelling the famous stories of the Polynesian heroes of Māui, Tinirau, Tahaki, and Rata. Her lifetime of research and writing in the Pacific has earned her a prominent place among the Polynesian pantheon of scholars.

ORGANIZATION OF ENTRIES

The organization of the following entries is fairly straightforward. The names of all the gods and goddesses (but only the more important mortals) are included in this work. The entries are alphabetically arranged by the major figure within the story, Hina, M āui, Kaha'i, etc., and characters found in the stories who do not warrant a full citation may be found in the index at the back of the book. In many instances, similar characters and stories are found in different island groups (Hawai'i, New Zealand, and Tahiti, for example), and the spelling of the characters' names vary according to the particular Polynesian language. In that case, I have resorted to alphabetizing the main entry according to the Hawaiian spelling with references to spelling variations of the other island groups. For example, the god Kanaloa in Hawai'i is known as Tangaroa in New Zealand, Ta'aroa in Tahiti, and Tagaloa in Samoa, and summaries of all of the stories are found under the Hawaiian spelling, Kanaloa. An entry is made under each variant spelling that refers the reader to the correct Hawaiian entry. An asterisk (*) after a name indicates that a separate entry exists for that character. Short source citations (author, date, and page numbers) are included at the end of each main entry, and the complete bibliographical reference follows next.

SOURCES

Abercromby, John
    1891   "Samoan Stories," trans. G. Pratt, *Folklore* 2:455–467.
    1892   "Samoan Stories," trans. G. Pratt, *Folklore* 3:158–165.
Agostini, J.
    1900   "Folklore de Tahiti," *Revue des Traditions Populaires* 15:65–96, 157–165.
Aitken, Robert T.
    1923   "Mythology of Tubuai," masters thesis, University of Hawai'i.
    1930   *Ethnology of Tubuai*. Honolulu: Bernice P. Bishop Museum Press.
Alpers, Antony
    1970   *Legends of the South Seas*. New York: Thomas Y. Crowell Co.
    1987   *World of the Polynesians Seen Through Their Myths and Legends*. London: J. Murray.
Andersen, Johannes C.
    1928   *Myths and Legends of the Polynesians*. London: Harrap.
    1935   *Tura and the Fairies and the Overworlds and Tu*. Wellington: Watkins.
Ariki-Tara-Are, Te
    1899   "History and Traditions of Rarotonga,"*Journal of the Polynesian Society* 8:61–88,171–178.
    1918   "History and Traditions of Rarotonga," *Journal of the Polynesian Society* 27:178–198.
    1920   "History and Traditions of Rarotonga," *Journal of the Polynesian Society* 29:1–20, 45–69, 107–27, 165–88.
    1921   "History and Traditions of Rarotonga," *Journal of the Polynesian Society* 30:1–15, 53, 70, 129–141, 201–226.
Audran, Père Hervé
    1918   "Legends from the Tuamotus," *Journal of the Polynesian Society* 27:26–25, 90–92, 132–136.
    1919   "Legends from the Tuamotus," *Journal of the Polynesian Society* 28:31–38, 161–167, 232–39.
Baessler, Arthur
    1905   "Tahitische Legenden," *Zeitschrift für Ethnologie* 37:920–924.

Barrère, Dorothy
    1967   "Revisions and Adulterations in Polynesian Creation Myths" in Genevieve A. Highland, ed., *Polynesian Culture History. Essays in Honor of Kenneth P. Emory*. Honolulu: Bishop Museum Press, pp. 103–119.

Barrow, T.
    1967   "Material Evidence of the Bird-Man Concept in Polynesia," in Genevieve A. Highland, ed., *Polynesian Culture History. Essays in Honor of Kenneth P. Emory*. Honolulu: Bishop Museum Press, pp. 191–213.

Bastian, Adolf
    1881   *Die Heilige Sage der Polynesier*. Leipzig: F. A. Brockhaus.

Beaglehole, Ernest & Pearl
    1938   *Ethnology of Pukapuka*. Honolulu: Bernice P. Bishop Museum.

Beattie, J. Herries
    1918   "Traditions and Legends of Murikihu," *Journal of the Polynesian Society* 27:137–161.

Beckwith, Martha
    1919   "Hawaiian Romance of Laieikawai (by S. N. Haleole, 1863)" in the *Thirty-Third Annual Report of the Bureau of American Ethnology*, pp. 285–666. Washington, D. C.: Bureau of American Ethnology.
    1932   *Kepelino's Traditions of Hawaii*. Honolulu: Bernice P. Bishop Museum.
    1940   *Hawaiian Mythology*. New Haven: Yale University.
    1951   *The Kumulipo: A Hawaiian Creation Chant*. Chicago: University of Chicago Press.

Bellwood, Peter
    1978   *Man's Conquest of the Pacific*. Oxford: Oxford University Press.

Best, Eldson
    1893   "Te Patunga O Ngarara-Huorau," *Journal of the Polynesian Society* 2:211–219.
    1894   "The Slaying of Mokonui," *Journal of the Polynesian Society* 3:165–167.
    1897   "Te Rehu-o-Tainui," *Journal of the Polynesian Society* 6:41–66.
    1899   "Notes on Maori Mythology," *Journal of the Polynesian Society* 8:93–121.

1905 "Lore of the Whare-Kohanga," *Journal of the Polynesian Society* 14:205–216.

1906 "Lore of the Whare-Kohanga," *Journal of the Polynesian Society* 15:1–27, 147–163, 183–193.

1907 "Lore of the Whare-Kohanga," *Journal of the Polynesian Society* 16:1–13.

1922 "The Legend of Whiro," *Journal of the Polynesian Society* 31:111–121.

1924 *The Maori.* 2 vols. Wellington: Polynesian Society.

1925 *Tuhoe, the Children of the Mist.* 2 vols. New Plymouth: T. Avery.

1927 "Hau and Wairaka," *Journal of the Polynesian Society* 36:260–282.

1928 "Story of Rua and Tangaroa: Origin Myth," *Journal of the Polynesian Society* 37:257–259.

1928 "Story of Ngae and Tutunui," *Journal of the Polynesian Society* 37:261–270.

1929 "Maui Myths as Narrated by Natives," *Journal of the Polynesian Society* 38:1–26.

Binney, Judith
1984 "Myth and Explanation in the Rangatû Tradition," *Journal of the Polynesian Society* 93:345–398.

Birket-Smith, Kaj
1956 *Ethnological Sketch of Rennell.* Copenhagen: Munksgaard.

Bradley, Diana
1956 "Notes from Rennell and Bellona Islands," *Journal of the Polynesian Society* 65:332–341.

Brown, George
1916 "Folk Tales from Tongan Islands," *Folklore* 27:426–432.

1917 "Some Nature Myths from Samoa," *Folklore* 28:94–99.

Browne, Arthur
1897 "Account of Some Early Ancestors of Rarotonga," *Journal of the Polynesian Society* 6:1–10.

Buck Sir Peter
1932 *Ethnology of Tongareva.* Honolulu: Bernice P. Bishop Museum.

1934 *Mangaian Society.* Honolulu: Bernice P. Bishop Museum.

1938 *Vikings of the Sunrise.* New York: F. A. Stoke.

Bülow, W. von
  1895   "Der Samoanische Sagen," *Globus* 68:139–141, 157–
          159, 365–368.
  1896   "Der Samoanische Sagen," *Globus* 69:322–327.
  1898   "Eine Samoanische Flutsage," *Internationales Archiv
          für Ethnographie* 11:80–82.
  1899   "Die Samoanische Schöpfungssage," *Internationales
          Archiv für Ethnographie* 12:58–78, 129–145.

Burrows, William
  1923   "Notes and Legends of Tokelau," *Journal of the Poly-
          nesian Society* 32:143–173.

Burrows, Edwin G.
  1936   *Ethnology of Futuna.* Honolulu: Bernice P. Bishop
          Museum.
  1937   *Ethnology of Uvea* (Wallis Island). Honolulu: Bernice
          P. Bishop Museum.

Cadousteau, Mai-Arii
  1973   *Dictionnaire Moderne Tahitienne/Française.* Pape-
          'ete: Stepolde.

Caillot, August C.
  1914   *Mythes, légendes et traditions des Polynésiens.* Paris:
          E. Leroux.

Christian, Frederick W.
  1895   "Notes on the Marquesans," *Journal of the Polynesian
          Society* 4:187–202.

Churchward, C. Maxwell
  1937   "Rotuman Legends," *Oceania* 8:104–116, 247–260,
          351–368, 482–497.
  1938   "Rotuman Legends," *Oceania* 9:109–126, 217–231,
          326–339, 462–473.

Clark, Kate M.
  1896   *Maori Tales and Legends.* London: D. Nutt.

Colenso, W.
  1879   "Contributions Toward a Better Knowledge of the
          Maori Race," *New Zealand Institute, Transactions*
          1:77–106.
  1880   "Contributions Toward a Better Knowledge of the
          Maori Race," *New Zealand Institute, Transactions*
          2:108–145.
  1881   "Contributions Toward a Better Knowledge of the
          Maori Race," *New Zealand Institute, Transactions*
          3:57–84.

1882   "Contributions Toward a Better Knowledge of the Maori Race," *New Zealand Institute, Transactions* 4:33–48.

Collocott, E. E. V.
1921   "Notes on Tongan Religion," *Journal of the Polynesian Society* 30:152–163, 227–240"
1928   *Tales and Poems of Tonga.* Honolulu: Bernice P. Bishop Musuem Press.

Cowan, James
1905   "A Canoe of Maui," *Journal of the Polynesian Society* 14:161–162.
1925   *Fairy Folk Tales of the Maori.* Auckland: Whitcombe & Tombs, Ltd.
1930   *Legends of the Maori.* Wellington: Harry H. Tombs, Ltd.
1934   *Maori-Polynesian Historical Traditions.* Wellington: Harry H. Tombs, Ltd.
1945   *Fairy Tales from the South Seas.* Auckland: Whitcombe & Tombs, Ltd.

Davidson, Janet
1975   "Wooden Images from Samoa in the British Museum," *Journal of the Polynesian Society* 84:352–355.

Davies, G. H.
1912   "Tura and Whiro," *Journal of the Polynesian Society* 21:110–116.

Davies, C. O. B.
1855   *Maori Momentos. A Series of Addresses by the Native People to Sir George Grey.* Auckland: Williamson & Wilson.

Dixon, Roland B.
1916   *Mythology of All Races, Vol. 9 Oceanic Mythology.* New York: Cooper Square Publisers, Inc.

Elbert, Samuel H.   "
Ms.   Marquesas Legends. (A manuscript of some fifty legends.) Honolulu: Bernice P. Bishop Museum.
1941   "Chants and Love Songs of the Marquesas," *Journal of the Polynesian Society* 50:53–91.
1959   *Selections from Fornander's Hawaiian Antiquities and Folklore.* Honolulu: University of Hawaii Press.
1964   *From the Two Canoes: Oral Traditions of Rennell and Bellona.* Honolulu: University of Hawaii Press.

Ellis, William
  1825   *Narrative of a Tour through Hawaii.* Boston: Crocker
          & Brewster.
  1829   *Polynesian Researches.* 2 vols. London: Fisher, Son
          and Jackson.
Emerson, J. S.
  1883   "Myth of Hiku and Kawelu," *Hawaiian Annual,* pp.
          36–39.
  1892   "The Lesser Hawaiian Gods," *Hawaiian Historical
          Society Papers* 2:1–24.
  1902   "Some Hawaiian Beliefs Regarding Spirits," *Hawai-
          ian Historical Society Annual Report* 9:10–17.
  1919   "Legends and Cradle Song. A Story of the Hawaiian
          God Ka-ne," *Hawaiian Historical Society Annual
          Report* 27:31–35.
Emerson, Nathaniel B.
  1915   *Pele and Hiiaka, a Myth from Hawaii.* Honolulu:
          Honolulu Star Bulletin. (Page numbers cited in the
          following text are taken from the 1978 reprint by
          Charles E. Tuttle Co., Inc., Rutland, Vermont.)
  1909   *Unwritten Literature of Hawaii. The Sacred Songs of
          the Hula.* Washington, D. C.: Smithsonian Institu-
          tion.
Emory, Kenneth P.
  1924   *The Island of Lanai: Survey of Native Culture.* Hono-
          lulu: Bernice P. Bishop Museum.
  1934   *Stone Remains in the Society Islands.* Honolulu: Ber-
          nice P. Bishop Museum.
  1949   "Myths and Tales from Kapingamarangi," *Journal of
          American Folklore* 62:230–239.
Englert, Sebastian
  1939   *Tradiciones de la Isla de Pascua.* Padre las Casas,
          Chile: San Francisco Publishers.
Feinberg, Richard
  1981   *Anuta: Social Structure of a Polynesian* Island. Laie:
          Institute for Polynesian Studies
  1988   *Polynesian Seafaring and Navigation.* Honolulu:
          University Press of Hawaii
  1988   "Personal Correspondence," August.
Felbermayr, F.
  1948   *Historias y legendes de la isla de Pascua.* Valparaiso.
Firth, Raymond
  1961   *History and Traditions of Tikopia.* Wellington:
          Polynesian Society.

1967   *Work of the Gods in Tikopia.* 2nd ed. New York: Humanities Press.

Fison, Lorimer
1904   *Tales from Old Fiji (Tonga).* London: A. Moring.

Forbes, A. O.
1879   "Origin of Fire," *Hawaii Annual,* pp. 59–60.
1881   "Maui Snaring the Sun," *Hawaii Annual,* p. 59.
1882   "Legend of Kapeepeekauila," *Hawaii Annual,* pp. 36–41.

Fornander, Abraham
1878   *Account of the Polynesian Race.* Vol. 1 London: Trubner.
1880   *Account of the Polynesian Race.* Vol 2. London: Trubner.
1885   *Account of the Polynesian Race.* Vol 3. London: Trubner.
1916   *Collection of Hawaiian Antiquities and Folklore.* Vol. 1. Honolulu: Bernice P. Bishop Museum.
1917   *Collection of Hawaiian Antiquities and Folklore.* Vol. 2. Honolulu: Bernice P. Bishop Museum.
1920   *Collection of Hawaiian Antiquities and Folklore.* Vol. 3. Honolulu: Bernice P. Bishop Museum.

Fraser, John
1890   "Some Folk Songs and Myths from Samoa," *Journal and Proceedings of the Royal Society of New South Wales* 24:195–217.
1892   "Samoan Story of Creation," *Journal of the Polynesian Society* 1:164–189.
1893   "Some Folk Songs and Myths from Samoa," *Journal and Proceedings of the Royal Society of New South Wales,* 26:264–301.
1896   "Some Folk Songs and Myths from Samoa," *Journal of the Polynesian Society* 5:171–183.
1897   "Some Folk Songs and Myths from Samoa," *Journal of the Polynesian Society* 6:19–37, 67–76, 107–123.
1898   "Some Folk Songs and Myths from Samoa," *Journal of the Polynesian Society* 7:15–29.
1900   "Some Folk Songs and Myths from Samoa," *Journal of the Polynesian Society* 9:125–134.

Garcia, M.
1843   *Lettres sur les Iles Marquises.* Paris: Gaume Frère.

Gardiner, J. Stanley
    1898   "The Natives of Rotuma," *Journal of the Royal Anthropological Institute of Great Britain and Ireland* 27:457–524.

Gifford, Edward T.
    1924   *Tongan Myths and Tales*. Honolulu: Bernice P. Bishop Museum.
    1929   *Tongan Society*. Honolulu: Bernice P. Bishop Museum.

Gill, William W.
    1876   *Myths and Songs from the South Pacific*. London: H. S. King.
    1911   "Extracts from William W. Gill's Papers," *Journal of the Polynesian Society* 20:116–151, 189–223.

Goodman, Irving
    1970   *Ancient Polynesian Society*. Chicago: University of Chicago Press.

Goodman, Richard A.
    1971   "Some Aitu Beliefs of Modern Samoa," *Journal of the Polynesian Society* 80:463–479.

Grace, Archdeacon
    1907   *Folk-tales of the Maori*. Wellington: Gordon & Gotch.

Green, Laura
    1926   *Folk-tales from Hawaii*. Poughkeepsie, New York: Vassar College.
    1929   *The Legend of Kawelo*. Ed. Martha Beckwith. Poughkeepsie, New York: Vassar College.

Green, Laura & M. K. Pukui
    1936   *Legend of Kawelo and other Hawaiian Folktales*. Honolulu.

Grey, Sir George
    1854   *Mythology and Tradition of the New Zealanders. Ko nga mahinga a nga tupuna*. London: Willis. (See next entry.)
    1855   *Polynesian Mythology*. Auckland: Brett. (Translation of 1854 edition.)
    1970   *Polynesian Mythology*. New York: Taplinger Press.

Gudgeon, W. E.
    1905a   "Maori Religion," *Journal of the Polynesian Society* 14:107–130.
    1905b   "Maori Superstition," *Journal of the Polynesian Society* 14:167–193.
    1906   "Tipua Kura . . . Spirit World," *Journal of the Polynesian Society* 15:27–58.

Haleole, S. N.
    1863   *Ka moolelo i Laieikawai*. (See Beckwith 1919.) Hono-
            lulu:
Hames, Inez
    1960   *Legends of Fiji and Rotuma*. Auckland: Watterson &
            Roddick, Ltd.
Handy, Edward. S. Craighill
    1927   *Polynesian Religion*. Honolulu: Bernice P. Bishop Mu-
            seum Press.
    1930   *Marquesan Legends*. Honolulu: Bernice P. Bishop
            Museum Press.
Hapai, Charlotte
    1921   *Legends of Wailuku*. Honolulu: Charles Frazier, Co.
Hare Hongi
    1894   "Contest between Fire and Water," *Journal of the
            Polynesian Society* 3:155–158.
    1896   "Tama-Ahua," *Journal of the Polynesian Society*
            5:233–236.
    1898   "Concerning Whare-Kura," *Journal of the Polynesian
            Society* 7:35–42.
    1907   "A Maori Cosmogony," *Journal of the Polynesian So-
            ciety* 16:109–119.
    1920   "Gods of Maori Worship," *Journal of the Polynesian
            Society* 29:24–28.
Hedley, Charles
    1896   *Atoll of Fuanfuti, Ellice Group*. Sydney: Australia
            Museum.
Henry, Teuira
    1928   *Ancient Tahiti*. Honolulu: Bernice P. Bishop Museum.
Hocart, A. M.
    1929   *Lau Islands, Fiji*. Honolulu: Bernice P. Bishop Mu-
            seum.
Johansen, J. Prytz
    1954   *Maori and His Religion*. Copenhagen: Munksgaard.
Johnson, Rubellite K.
    Ms.   "Dictionary of Hawaiian Mythology and Biography,
            A-H," University of Hawaii (n.d.).
    1979   "From the Gills of the Fish: Hawaii's Genealogical
            Ties with the Rulers of Tahiti," *Pacific Studies* 3:51–
            67.
Jourdain, Pierre
    1934   "Légends des trois Tortues," *Bulletin de la Société des
            Études Océaniennes* 5:196–205.

Kaeppler, Adrienne
  1976 *Directions in Pacific Traditional Literature.* Honolulu: Bishop Museum Press.
Kahiolo, G. W.
  1978 *He Moolelo No Kamapuaa.* Honolulu: University of Hawaii Press.
Kalakaua, David
  1888 *Legends and Myths of Hawaii.* Ed. R. M. Daggett. New York: C. L. Webster.
Kamakau, Samuel M.
  1961 *Ruling Chiefs of Hawaii.* Honolulu: Kamehameha Schools Press.
Kararehe, W. Te Kahui
  1898 "Te Tatau-o-te-Po," *Journal of the Polynesian Society* 7:59–63.
Kauika, Wiremu
  1904 "Tutae-Poroporo, the Taniwha Slain by Ao-Kehu at Whanganui," *Journal of the Polynesian Society* 13:94–98.
Kennedy, Donald G.
  1931 "Fields Notes . . . Ellice Islands," *Journal of the Polynesian Society* 39: nos. 6 and 7.
Kirtley, Bacil F.
  1967 "Slain Eel God," in *Folklore International: Essays in Traditional Literature, Belief, and Custom in Honor of Wayland Debs Hand.* Hatboro, Pa.: Folklore Associates, Inc.
  1971 *Motif-Index of Traditional Polynesian Narratives.* Honolulu: University of Hawaii Press.
Krämer, Augustin F.
  1902 *Die Samoa-Inseln.* 2 vols. Stuttgart: E. Schweitzerbart.
Large, J. T.
  1903 "Aitutaki Version of story of Iro," *Journal of the Polynesian Society* 12:133–144.
Lavondès, Henri
  1964 *Récits Marquisiens.* Vol. 1. Pape'ete: ORSTOM.
  1966 *Récits Marquisiens.* Vol. 2. Pape'ete: ORSTOM.
Lessa, William A.
  1961 *Tales from Ulithi Atoll.* Berkley: University of California Press.
Lesson, Pierre Adolfe
  1876 "Traditiones des îles Samoa," *Revue d'Anthropologie* 5:589–604.

Leverd, Armand
>   1911   "Paumotuan Version of Tafa'i," *Journal of the Polyne-
>   sian Society* 20:172–184.
>   1912   "Tahitian Version of Tafa'i," *Journal of the Polynesian
>   Society* 21:1–12
Lieb, A. P., and A. Grove Day
>   1979   *Hawaiian Legends in English.* 2nd ed. Honolulu: Uni-
>   versity of Hawaii Press.
Locke, Samuel
>   1883   "Historical Traditions of the Taupo and East Coast
>   Tribes," *New Zealand Institute, Transactions*
>   15:433–459.
>   1921   "Visit of Pau to Hawaiki . . . Kumara," *Journal of the
>   Polynesian Society* 30:40–47.
Loeb, Edwin M.
>   1926   *History and Traditions of Niue.* Honolulu: Bernice P.
>   Bishop Museum Press.
Low, Drury
>   1934   "Traditions of Aitutaki, Cook Islands, "*Journal of the
>   Polynesian Society* 43:17–24, 73–84, 171–186, 258–
>   267.
>   1935   "Traditions of Aitutaki, Cook Islands," *Journal of the
>   Polynesian Society* 44: 26–32.
Luomala, Katharine
>   1949   *Maui of a Thousand Tricks.* Honolulu: Bernice P.
>   Bishop Museum Press.
>   1951   *Menehune of Polynesia.* Honolulu: Bernice P. Bishop
>   Museum Press.
>   1955   *Voices on the Wind.* Honolulu: Bernice P. Bishop Mu-
>   seum Press.
>   1958   "Polynesian Myths about Maui and the Dog," *Fabula*
>   2:129–162.
>   1973   "Moving & Moveable Images in Easter Island Cus-
>   toms and Myth," *Journal of the Polynesian Society*
>   82:28–46.
MacGregor, Gordon
>   1937   *Ethnology of Tokelau Islands.* Honolulu: Bernice P.
>   Bishop Museum Press.
Malardé, Yves
>   1933   "Légend des Tuamotus-Origine du Cocotier," *Bulletin
>   de la Société des Études Océanienne* 5:498–501,
>   671–674.

Malo, David
    1903   *Hawaiian Antiquities*. Honolulu: Hawaiian Gazette
            Co.
Mariner, W.
    1817   *An Account of the Natives of the Tongan Islands . . .
            compiled by John Martin*. 2 vols. London: Consta-
            ble.
McAlister, J. Gilbert
    1933   *Archaeology of Oahu*. Honolulu: Bernice P. Bishop
            Museum Press.
Métraux, Alfred
    1940   *Ethnology of Easter Island*. Honolulu: Bernice P.
            Bishop Museum Press.
Moerenhout, Jacques A.
    1837   *Voyages aux îles du Grand Océan*. 2 vols. in one.
            Paris: Bertrand.
Monberg, Torben
    1956   "Ta'aroa in the Creation Myths," *Journal of the Poly-
            nesian Society* 65:253–281.
    1965   *From the Two Canoes: Oral Traditions of Rennell and
            Bellona*. Honolulu: University of Hawaii Press.
    1966   *The Religion of Bellona Island*. 2 vols. Copenhagen:
            National Museum.
Morris, G. N.
    1919   "Niue Folk-Lore," *Journal of the Polynesian Society*
            28:226–228.
Moyle, Richard
    1974   "Samoan Medical Incantations," *Journal of the Poly-
            nesian Society* 83:155–179.
Neich, Roger
    1980   "Maori God with Hair," *Journal of the Polynesian
            Society* 89:508, 510.
Nelson, O. F.
    1925   "Legends of Samoa," *Journal of the Polynesian Society*
            34:124–145.
Newell, J. E.
    1895   "Coming of Nareau from Samoa to Tarawa," *Journal
            of the Polynesian Society* 4:231–235
Orbell, Margaret
    1968   *Maori Folktales*. Auckland: Blackwood & Janet Paul.
    1973   "Two Versions of the Maori Story of Te-Tahi-o-te-
            Rangi," *Journal of the Polynesian Society* 82:127–
            140.

1975   "Religious Significance of the Maori Migration Tradition,"*Journal of the Polynesian Society* 84:341–347.

Pakauwera, E. W.
1894   "Story of Hine-Papo," *Journal of the Polynesian Society* 3:98–104.

Pakoti, John
1895   "First Inhabitants of Aitutaki; the History of Ru," *Journal of the Polynesian Society* 4:65–70.

Paulme, J. C., ed.
1931   *Océania: Légends et récits polynésiens.* Paris: Société des Études Océaniennes.

Poignant, Roslyn
1967   *Oceanic Mythology. The Myths of Polynesia, Micronesia, Melanesia, Australia.* London: Paul Hamlyn.

Potae, Henare
1928   "Story of Tawhaki," *Journal of the Polynesian Society* 37:359–366.

Powell, T. A.
1891   "Some Folksongs and Myths from Samoa," *Journal and Proceedings of the Royal Society of New South Wales* 24:195–217.
1892   "Some Folksongs and Myths from Samoa," "*Journal and Proceedings of the Royal Society of New South Wales* 25:70–85, 96–146, 241–286.
1893   "Some Folksongs and Myths from Samoa," *Journal and Proceedings of the Royal Society of New South Wales* 26:274–301.

Pritchard, W. T.
1866   *Polynesian Reminiscences.* London: Chapman.

Pukui, Mary W.
1933   *Hawaiian Folk Tales.* Poughkeepsie: Vassar College.
1981   *Hawaiian Dictionary.* 2nd ed. Honolulu: University of Hawaii Press.

Reed, Alexander W.
1943   *Maui, Legends of the Demi-gods of Polynesia.* Wellington: Reed.
1948   *Wonder Tales of Maoriland.* Wellington: Reed.
1957   *Maori Tales of Long Ago.* Wellington: Reed.
1958   *Legends of Rotorua and the Hote Lakes.* Wellington: Reed.
1961   *Myths and Legends of Maoriland.* Wellington: Reed.

Reiter, F. X.
    1907   "Traditions tonguiennes" *Anthropos* 2:230–240, 438–448, 743–754.
    1933   "Trois récits tonguiennes," *Anthropos* 28:355–382.
    1934   "Trois récits tonguiennes," *Anthropos* 29:497–514.

Rice, William H.
    1923   *Hawaiian Legends*. Honolulu: Bernice P. Bishop Museum Press.

Roberts, R. G.
    1957   "Four Folk Tales from the Ellice Islands," *Journal of the Polynesian Society* 66:365–373.
    1958   "Te Atu Tuvalu: A Short History," *Journal of the Polynesian Society* 67:394–423.

Roosman, Raden S.
    1970   "Coconut, Breadfruit, and Taro," *Journal of the Polynesian Society* 79:219–232.

Ropiteau, André
    1933   "Notes sur l'île Maupiti," *Bulletin de la Société des Études Océaniennes* 5:113–130.

Routledge, Katherine S.
    1917   *Mystery of Easter Island*. London: Sifton.

Russell, W. E.
    1942   "Rotuma: History and Customs," *Journal of the Polynesian Society* 51:229–255.

Rutherford, Noel
    1977   *Friendly Islands: History of Tonga*. Oxford: Oxford University Press.

St. Johnston, Thomas R.
    1918   *Lau Islands and their Fairy-Tales and Folk-Lore*. London: The Times Book Company, Ltd.

Savage, Stephen
    1910   "Rarotongan Version of Rata," *Journal of the Polynesian Society* 19:142–168.

Shortland, Edward
    1856   *Traditions and Superstitions of the New Zealanders*. London: Longmans Green.
    1882   *Maori Religion and Mythology*. London: Longmans Green.

Schultz, E.
    1909   "Samoan Version of the Story of Apakura," *Journal of the Polynesian Society* 18:139–142.

Seurat, Léon G.
    1905   "Légendes de Paumotu," *Révue des Traditions Populaires* 20:433–440, 481–488.

1906   "Légendes de Paumotu," *Révue des Traditions Popu-*
        laries 21:125–131.
Shand, Alexander
1894   "Moriori People of Chatham Islands," *Journal of the*
        Polynesian Society 3:76–92, 121–133.
1896   "Moriori People of Chatham Islands," *Journal of the*
        Polynesian Society 5:195–211.
1898   "Moriori People of Chatham Islands," *Journal of the*
        Polynesian Society 7:73–88.
Shortland, Edward
1882   *Maori Religion and Mythology.* London: Longmans
        Green.
Sibree, James
1923   *A Register of Missionaries.* London: London Mission-
        ary Society.
Sierich, O.
1900   "Samoanische Märchen," *Internationales Archiv für*
        Ethnographie 13:223–237.
1901   "Samoanische Märchen," *Internationales Archiv für*
        Ethnographie 14:15–23.
1902   "Samoanische Märchen," *Internationales Archiv für*
        Ethnographie 15:167–200.
Skinner, W. A.
1897   "Legend of Para-hia," *Journal of the Polynesian Soci-*
        ety 6:156–157.
Skinner, H. D.
1923   *The Moriories of Chatham Islands.* Honolulu: Bernice
        P. Bishop Museum Press.
Smith, S. Percy
1903   "Some Paumotu Chants," *Journal of the Polynesian*
        Society 12:221–242.
1905   "Story of Ngarara-Huarau," *Journal of the Polynesian*
        Society 14:202–204.
1907   "History and Traditions of the Taranaki Coast,"
        "Journal of the Polynesian Society 16:203.
1909   "Story of Kataore," *Journal of the Polynesian Society*
        18:210–216.
1910   *Hawaiki, Original Homeland of Maoris.* Wellington:
        Whitcombe & Tombs.
1911   "Story of Te Rapuawai & Kuhui-Tipua," *Journal of*
        the Polynesian Society 20:12–14.
1911a   "Ngati-Whatua Traditions," *Journal of the Polynesian*
        Society 20:78–100.

1921   "Rarotongan Story of Ta'aki," *Journal of the Polynesian Society* 30:1–13.

South Sea Islander

1820   *South Sea Islander; Containing many intersting facts relating to the former and present state of society in the island of Otaheite; with some remarks on the best mode of civilising the heathen.* (No author's name.) New York: W. B. Gilley.

Stair, John B.

1892   *Old Samoa or Flotsam and Jetsam from the Pacific Ocean.* London: Religious Tract Society.

1895   "Samoa: Whence Peopled," *Journal of the Polynesian Society* 4:47–58.

1895   "Flotsam and Jetsam . . . Early Samoan Voyages," *Journal of the Polynesian Society* 4:99–131.

1896   "Jottings on the Mythology and Spirit Lore of Old Samoa," *Journal of the Polynesian Society* 5:32–57.

Steinen, Karl von den

1933   "Marquesanische Mythen," *Zeitschrift für Ethnologie* 65:1–44, 326–373.

1934   "Marquesanische Mythen," *Zeitschrift für Ethnologie* 66:191–240.

Stevenson, Robert Louis

1912   *South Seas and Other Papers.* New York: Vailima Edition.

Stimson John F.

Ms.   Collection of Tuamotuan Myths. Salem, Mass.: Peabody Museum archives.

1933   *The Cult of Kiho-tumu.* Honolulu: Bernice P. Bishop Museum Press.

1934   *Legends of Maui and Tahaki.* Honolulu: Bernice P. Bishop Museum Press.

1937   *Tuamotuan Legends: Island of Anaa.* Honolulu: Bernice P. Bishop Museum Press.

1957   *Songs & Tales of the Sea Kings.* Ed. D. Marshall. Salem: Peabody Museum.

Stimson, John F., and S. Marshall

1964   *Dictionary of Some Tuamotuan Dialects of the Pololynesian Languages.* Salem: Peabody Museum.

Stübel, Otto

1896   "Samoanische Texte," ed. F. W. K. Müler, *Veröffentlichungen aus dem Königlichen Museum für Völkerkunde* 10:59–246.

Tahiaoteaa
    1933   "Légende Marquisienne," *Bulletin de la Société des Études Océaniennes* 5:490–498.

Tama-Rau and Tutaka Ngahau
    1899   "Story of Hape, the Wanderer," *Journal of the Polynesian Society* 8:51–57.

Tarakawa, T.
    1899   "Mahu and Taewa-a-Rangi," *Journal of the Polynesian Society* 8:127–134.

Taylor, Richard
    1870   *Te Ika a Maui.* 2nd ed. London: Macintosh.

Taylor, C. R. H.
    1965   *A Pacific Bibliography.* 2nd ed. London: Oxford University Press.

Taylor, Alan
    1981   *Polynesian Tattooing.* Laie, Hawaii: Institute for Polynesian Studies.

Te Aro
    1894   "Slaying of Mokonui," *Journal of the Polynesian Society* 3:166–167.

Thornton, Agathe
    1984   "Story of the Women Brought Back from the Underworld," *Journal of the Polynesian Society* 93:295–314.

Thrum, Thomas G., ed.
    1905   *Hawaiian Almanac and Annual.* Honolulu. Numerous articles.
    1907   *Hawaiian Folk Tales.* Chicago: McClurg.
    1923   *More Hawaiian Folk Tales.* Chicago: McClurg.

Travers, T. L.
    1887   "Notes on Customs of Mori-oris," *New Zealand Institute, Transactions* 9:15–27.

Tregear, Edward
    1891   *Maori-Polynesian Comparative Dictionary.* Wellington: Government Printer.
    1893   "Asiatic Gods in the Pacific," *Journal of the Polynesian Society* 2:129–146.
    1900   "Creation Song of Hawaii," *Journal of the Polynesian Society* 9:38–46.

Tu-Whakawhakia, Kerehoma
    1896   "Story of Whaki-Tpuia and Tu-Taia-Roa," *Journal of the Polynesian Society* 5:155–170.

Turei, Mohi
  1912   "History of the *Horouta* Canoe," *Journal of the Poly-*
          nesian Society 11:152–163.
Turner, Geroge
  1861   *Nineteen Years in Polynesia.* London: J. Snow.
  1884   *Samoa a Hundred Years Ago and Long Before.* Lon-
          don: Macmillan & Co.
Westervelt, William D.
  1910   *Legends of Ma-ui.* Honolulu: Hawaiian Gazette Co.
  1915a   *Hawaiian Legends of Ghosts & Ghost-Gods.* Boston:
          G. H. Ellis.
  1915b   *Hawaiian Legends of Old Honolulu.* Boston: G. H.
          Ellis.
  1916   *Hawaiian Legends of Volcanoes.* Boston: G. H. Ellis.
Whetu, Karipa Te
  1897   "Kame-Tara and His Ogre Wife," *Journal of the Poly-*
          nesian Society 6:97–106.
White, John
  1885   "Maori Customs and Superstitions," in T. W. Gud-
          geon, *History and Doings of the Maoris from 1820*
          to 1840. Auckland: Brett, pp. 97–225.
  1887   *Ancient History of the Maori.* 6 vols. Wellington: G.
          Disbury. (Volume numbers are listed in the follow-
          ing text as **a**, **b**, **c**, **d**, **e**, or **f**.)
Wickman, Frederick B.
  1985   *Kauai Tales.* Honolulu: Bamboo Ridge Press.
Williams, John
  1895   "Legend of Honoura," *Journal of the Polynesian Soci-*
          ety 4:256–294.
Williams, Herbert W.
  1971   *Dictionary of the Maori Language.* 7th ed. Wellington:
          R. E. Owen, government printer.
Williamson, Robert W.
  1933   *Religious and Cosmic Beliefs of Central Polynesia.* 2
          vols. Cambridge: Cambridge University Press
Wilson, Rathmell
  1905   *Hinemoa and Tutanekai. A Maori Legend.* London:
          Elkin Matthews.
Wohlers, J. F. H.
  1874   "Mythology and Tradition of the Maori," *New*
          Zealand Institute, Transactions 6:45.
  1875   "Mythology and Tradition of the Maori," *New*
          Zealand Institute, Transactions 7:3–53.

1876   "Mythology and Tradition of the Maori," *New Zealand Institute, Transactions* 8:108–123.

Wyatt, William W.

1855   *Jottings in the Pacific.* London: Religious Tract Society.

Young, J. L.

1898   "Origin of the Name Tahiti," *Journal of the Polynesian Society* 7:109–110.

1919   "Paumotu Conception of the Heavens and of Creation," *Journal of the Polynesian Society* 28:209–211.

DICTIONARY OF
POLYNESIAN
MYTHOLOGY

–A–

Ā, the name for god in the Tuamotus and in New Zealand; also refers to endless space surrounding the universe. As a prefix, **a** frequently refers to rule: for example, **ao** in Hawaiian means to regard with reverence; in Samoan and Tongan **aoao**, to be supreme. (Pukui 1971:1; Stimson 1964:41; Tregear 1891:1.) See also **Ao**.

'Ā'AIA-NUI-NŪKEA-A-KĀNE, a white-beaked bird with white feathers belonging to the Hawaiian god Kāne.* In one story of the creation, Kumu-honua,* the first man, and Lalo-honua,* the first woman, lived happily until she met the Great White-Beaked Seabird of Kāne who persuaded her to eat the sacred apples of Kāne. She turned into a seabird, and both she and Kumu-honua were driven out of their ancestral paradise. (Fornander 1880: 16,18; Fornander 1916:14–17, 24–35, 42–47.) On Rarotonga, Cook Islands, the *kakaia* is a native white tern (*Gyqis candida*) with black markings burned by the demigod Māui* from the rear corner of each eye to the back of the head, hence, the white-tern-singed-by-Māui, *kakaia-tungi-a-Māui*. (Gill 1876: 81; Johnson ms.) See also **Creation; Hema; Kaha'i**.

'ĀEATOSO, a young boy from Uea island, off the northwest coast of Rotuma, who, with his sister Rakitefurusia, were orphaned because their father, Titimoteao, was eaten by the ghosts (*'atua*) of his grandparents and because their mother, Sinetearoia, deserted them to marry another man from another island. The two children had to stave off numerous attacks by ten-headed ghosts, and they survived only through the help of an old Tongan from Rā'esea who had befriended them. Eventually 'Äeatoso was captured from people from heaven, and as he was making his way skyward, his sister Rakitefurusia followed as far as she could. On top of mount Sarafui, she set down and in anguish rubbed her heel into the soil until she had made a deep hole. Her tears quickly filled it up, and it became a mountain spring. She died there of a broken heart. Meanwhile Äeatoso looked from heaven and threw down several plants to her which took root and grew nearby. He descended from heaven, but he was unable to revive his sister. In anguish, he returned to heaven. (Churchward 1938:109–126.)

AEMANA, the name of a sacred chant to the god Lono* in the Tuamotus. (Stimson 1964:42.)

AEOOA, a god of Atafu, Tokelau Islands. (Macgregor 1937: 61.)

AEWA, the ancient name of the Rarawa tribe as well as the name of the living water of Kāne* in Māori myth. (Shortland 1882:25; Tregear 1891:2; White 1887a:142.) See also Waiora.

AFĀ, a demigod from the island of Fakaofo, Tokelau, who was one-half devil. Also known as Toikia, he often visited the island where he captured and devoured the souls of mortals. A priest finally trapped him, cut open his dead body, rescued all the mortal spirits, and returned them to their relatives. Afā, however, came to life again and returned to the sea. (Burrows 1923:172.)

'AHA-ALI'I, a ruling body of sacred chiefs in ancient Hawai'i. Those of highest rank were considered gods, and at death their bones were carefully preserved and worshipped as family deities. Names of the most famous chiefs were handed down from one generation to another. Primary among those was Haho, the traditional founder of the class. (Beckwith 1948:378; Fornander 1880:28–30.)

ĀHAEHAE, a rainbow god in New Zealand. His appearance usually signifies an ensuing battle. (Tregear 1891:2.) See also Kahukura.

AHĀTEA, a Tuamotuan god who created the heavens. (Stimson 1964:43.) See also Creation; Heavens.

AHEITENGENA, one of the numerous district gods of the Kaitu'u clan on Bellona Island, the son of the principal god, Tehu'aingabenga.* (Monberg 1966:67.)

'AHIFA-TŪ-MOANA, a sea serpent in the Tahitian Rata (Laka*) story which was so large it could destroy war canoes. When killed by Rata, its spirit went to the underworld.* (Henry 1928:494.)

AHĪMŪ, a god worshipped by female chiefs in ancient Hawai'i; a reptile (mo'o) or lizard goddess; also known as Wahīmū. (Malo 1903:83.)

'AHO'EITU, son of the Tongan god Tagaloa 'Eitumatupua (Kanaloa*) and the mortal woman 'Ilaheva (daughter of chief Seketoa*). As a young boy, 'Aho'eitu inquired from his mother about his father. She told him where his father lived, anointed him with coconut oil, wrapped him in a loin cloth, and set him on his way to heaven. Once there, his father welcomed him, but his jealous sky brothers killed and ate him. He was brought back to life, however, and he returned to earth, displaced the old Tu'i Tonga,* and ruled the Tongan Islands. His son Lolofakagalo succeeded him. (Beckwith 1948:482–483; Gifford 1924:25–29, 38–43; Reiter 1933:355–363; Rutherford 1977:27–28.)

AHOLOHOLO, oldest son of Ka-lani-Menehune, renowned for his swiftness in Hawaiian legend, ancestor of the Menehune,* the little people who were the first settlers of the Hawaiian Islands before the arrival of the Polynesians. (Beckwith 1948:322, 337.)

AHU, in Hawaiian legend, a son of Kumu-honua,* killed by his famous brother Laka.* (Fornander 1878:35n.) An *ahu* is a pie-shaped land division with its point beginning inland at the tops of the mountains. The island of O'ahu was named after the good chief Ahu, son of the goddess Papa* and her husband Luanu'u.* (Beckwith 1948:302, 305.) Also the name of a mythical land in Tuamotuan legend. (Stimson 1964:45.)

ĀHUA, the Māori name of the twelfth age of the existence of the universe. (Tregear 1891:5.) See also **Creation; Heavens, Kore.**

AHU-I-MAI'A-PĀ-KANALOA, a brother to the Hawaiian goddess Pele,* literally banana-bunch-of-Kanaloa's-field. The only one of Pele's brothers living in the legendary Nu'umealani* homeland who could appease

Pele and cause her to cease her angry fires. (Fornander 1916: 106; Johnson ms.) See also **Kanaloa**.

AHU-ROA, the father of Tiki* in the Tuamotuan legends. He and his wife, One-rua,* were demigods. (Stimson 1937:3–8.)

'ĀHURU-NU'U-RĀRĀ, one of the hosts of heaven that dwelt with the god Tāne (Kāne*) in the Tahitian creation story. (Henry 1928:371.)

AHUTARA, a mythical Tuamotuan *marae** (temple) whose exact location is unknown. (Stimson 1964:45.)

'AI'AI, son of the Hawaiian fishing god Kū'ula-kai* and his wife Hina-puku-i'a.* Upon his deathbed, Kū'ula-kai gave to 'Ai'ai four magical fishing tools: a decoy stick, a cowry lure, a magical fishhook, and a fish-attracting stone. Following his father's instructions, 'Ai'ai traveled around the Hawaiian islands establishing fishing grounds and building fishing shrines (*ko'a*) and altars (*kūula*) for offerings to the gods (*'aumākua*) consisting of two fish from each catch. (Beckwith 1948:19–23; Fornander 1916: 554–558, 1920:172–175; Thrum 1907:215–249.)

'AIĀRU, an old Tahitian goddess who acts as one of the guardians of the world. The other guardians were Fa'aipu, Fa'aīpō, Nihoniho-tetei, 'Ōrerorero, Tahu'a, and Tamaumau-'ōrere. (Henry 1928:416.)

'AIFA'ARUA'I, a fearful monster who once lived on the islet of Motue'a, near Taha'a in the Society Islands (French Polynesia). (Andersen 1928:145–146.)

AIHU-MOANA, a sea god, ancestor to the Māori hero Paikea.* (Andersen 1928:105.)

'AI-KANAKA, in Hawaiian means man-eater and generally the term refers to the man-eating shark, a symbol of the high chiefs. In Hawaiian legends, 'Ai-kanaka is the husband of the volcano goddess Pele.* (Beckwith 1948:214.) It is also the name of the last ruling cannibal chief on O'ahu at a place called Hale-manu* (Hale-mano) near the towns of Wahiawā and Hale'iwa. His band of followers was regarded as foreign because of their dark skin, different speech, and no *kapu* (sacred) laws. 'Ai-kanaka (sometimes called Ka-lo-aikana or Ke-ali'i-ai-kana) was finally killed in a struggle with Hoahānau, the brother of one of his victims. (Beckwith 1948:340–342, 524; Fornander 1917:238; Westervelt 1915b:194–203.) Another 'Ai-kanaka, son of Haleipawa, was a Maui chief who married the goddess Hina* and was unsuccessful in stopping her as she leaped into the moon.

(Beckwith 1948:241–242; Pukui 1971:381; Thrum 1907:69–71.)

'AI-KANAKA-A-MAKO'O, father of the famous Hawaiian heroes Puna* and Hema.* (Fornander 1878:249.)

'AI-KANAKA-LAKA, same as Laka.*

'AI-KE'ĒHIALE, bird-man in Hawaiian, a messenger of 'Aiwohi-kupua* (a legendary hero on the island of Kaua'i). (Beckwith 1948:526–528.) See also **Lā'ie-i-ka-wai.**

'AI-LĀ'AU, the Hawaiian fire god before the arrival of the more famous volcano goddess Pele.* (Pukui 1971:381.)

'ĀINA-A-KĀNE-HŪNĀ-MO-KU, the hidden-land-of-Kāne* in Hawaiian legend. It is a mythical island paradise located midway between heaven and earth that receives the spirits of departed mortals into everlasting, youthful life. Numerous references are made to it affixed with "-Kāne." For example: 'Āina-hūnā-a-Kāne, 'Āina-kaimelemele-a-Kāne, etc. (Beckwith 1948:67–72, 77–80.) See also **Kāne-huna-moku.**

ĀIO-TE-REA, the son of Tiki* and Io-wahine,* the first mortals in Māori legends. (Tregear 1891:6; White 1887a:165.)

AITU, the second mortal man according to Tuamotuan creation chants, was born to Tumu* and Papa* after his elder brother Matata* had died. Aitu was born without one arm and without legs, and similar to his elder brother, he did not survive. The third son, Hoatea,* was born perfectly formed, and he and Hoatu* became the progenitors of the human race. (Henry 1928:347.) Aitu is also named as a Māori god (White 1887a:116) and a Tuamotuan god of hurricanes and severe weather (Stimson 1964:46); a word meaning god in other Polynesian languages. (Stair 1896:37–38; Tregear 1891:6.)

AITUĀ, the Māori god of death, the first-born son of Rangi* (sky father) and Papa* (earth mother.) (Tregear 1891:6.) See also **Creation; Heavens.**

AITU-I-PAVA, a Samoan war god worshipped at Fa'asalele-anga. (Stair 1896:41.)

AITU LANGI, Samoan name for the gods of heaven who supposedly fell from the heavens and became village gods in Samoa. An earthly representation was a sea shell erected in a large temple. Tupai was the name of the high priest and prophet. The owl was the god incarnate, and various acts of the bird foretold certain fortunes. (Turner 1884:23–24.)

AI-TŪPUA'I, an ancient Tahitian goddess of healing, the daughter of the warrior god 'Oro* and his wife Tū-fe'ufe'u-mai-i-te-ra'i.* (Henry 1928:145, 231, 375.)

AITU-TAO-MIRA, a Tuamotuan god. (Stimson 1964:46.)

'AI-WOHI-KUPUA, a semidivine Hawaiian chief who unsuccessfully wooed the beautiful goddess Lā'ie-i-ka-wai* in the legendary land of Pali-uli on the island of Hawai'i. (Pukui 1971:381.) At Hāna, Maui, he was attracted to the lovely Hina*-i-ka-lama whom he observed surfing at Puhele, but she defeated him at Hawaiian checkers (*kōnane*). He then courted and wed the mountain goddess Poli-'ahu* on Hawai'i, and they returned to Kaua'i where Hina went to claim him. Hina and 'Ai-wohi-kupua embraced, but an angry Poli-'ahu enveloped them in heat and cold, forcing them to separate, whereupon Hina returned home. Poli-'ahu then departed with her three companions, Lilinoe, Waiaie, and Ka-houpo-kāne, leaving 'Ai-wohi-kupua deserted by both goddesses. (Beckwith 1918:378–383, 402–407, 474; Beckwith 1948:222.)

AKA, one of the two Hawaiian women in the Pele* legend who watched over the cave where chief Lohi'au* had been buried. (Fornander 1920:344.) See also

Hi'iaka. Aka (Laka*) is also known in the Marquesas as a great voyager, the grandson of the hero Kaha'i,* who made an historic voyage to the island of Aotona in the Cook Islands some thirteen hundred miles to the southwest to obtain the highly prized red parrot (*kula, kura, ula*) feathers for his son and daughter as they reached puberty. They set out in a huge outrigger canoe named Va'ahiva with 140 rowers, a hundred of whom die of hunger before they reached their destination. Once there, however, they set lairs for the birds, captured them, filled 140 bags with feathers, and returned home. (Handy 1930:130–131; Steinen 1933:9–21.)

AKAAKA-TAPU-A-TĀNE, Māori name of the heavenly home of Punga (Puna*) in the legend of Tāwhaki (Kaha'i*). (Tregear 1891:6–7; White 1887a:16.)

'AKĀHI, a bird in Hawaiian legend whose nest and eggs continually fall and thus annoy Po'opapele. (Fornander 1917:342; Johnson ms.)

AKALANA, husband of the Hawaiian goddess Hina,* father of the famed demigod Māui*-ki'iki'i-a-kalana. (Beckwith 1948:220, 227; Fornander 1917:536–539; Westervelt 1910:x, 3–5.) Tradition records that Akalana returned to the island of Kahiki (Tahiti?) and other lands to the south. (Fornander 1878:191, 199, 249; Johnson ms.)

AKATAURĪA, one of the three principal gods of Mangaia and progenitor of the Mangaian tribes through his wife Ruānge.* (Gill 1876:15–18.) See also **Mokoiro; Rangi.**

AKAUFAKARAVA, the rock base of Havaiki* (ancestral homeland) and personified as one of the demon servants of king Puna* in the Tuamotuan epic of Rata (Laka.*) (Stimson 1964:47.)

ĀKEA, see **Ātea** and **Wākea.**

AKI, name of the mortal used as bait on Māui's* fishhook when he pulled up the Pacific islands from the ocean floor in Māori legends. (Tregear 1891:8; White 1887b:91.)

AKU-AKU, name for supernatural beings (both male and female) on Easter Island. They supposedly came to the island with the first settlers (Hotu-Matua*), consisted of approximately ninety in number, and were generally cannibalistic in character. One famous female *aku-aku* by the name of Uka-o-hoheru married a mortal, Tupahotu, lived with him at Mahatua, and bore a child. Once in a heated argument between the two, Uka-o-hoheru fled in a whirlwind and was never seen again. Two other female *aku-aku*, Kava-ara and

Kava-tua, captured a mortal, Uré-a-hohové, and imprisoned him in a cave on the hillside. Another old *aku-aku* saved his life, and he was eventually rescued from the cave by a woman from his village. Two other *aku-aku*, Mata-wara-wara and his wife Papai-a-taki-vera, captured human souls as they wandered at night in sleep. The next morning, their victims became ill and eventually withered away. Mortals who communed with *aku-aku* were called *koromaké* or *ivi-atua*. (Routledge 1917:236–239.)

AKUA (ATUA), a generic name in most Polynesian languages meaning god, spirits, devils, ghosts, or any other supernatural being. Many suffixes with this name are found throughout the islands. On some islands, there were various classes or rankings of these *atua*, the lowest class being that of mortal spirits.

'ALAE-A-HINA, the sacred bird (mud hen) of the goddess Hina* in Hawaiian legend that guarded the secret of making fire. Māui* wrested the knowledge of fire-making from her. One legend relates that Māui baited his magical hook with an *'alae* in order to fish up the Hawaiian islands. (Fornander 1920:104; Westervelt 1910:18–19, 62–64.) 'Alae-a-hina is also a goddess on Moloka'i (Hawai'i) whom Hawaiians invoke along with Maka-kū-koa'e* and Uli* to bring about the death of an enemy. (Beckwith 1948:115.)

'ALALĀ, father of the rat man, Pikoi-a-ka-'alalā,* on the island of Kaua'i, Hawai'i. (Beckwith 1948:426; Kamakau 1961:40; Fornander 1916:450.)

ALALAHE, the Hawaiian goddess of love, sometimes referred to as Laka,* the shining one, the beloved. (Beckwith 1932:182–183; Beckwith 1948:186.)

'ĀLANA-PŌ, the name of a Hawaiian temple (*heiau*) on the island of Kaua'i at Humu'ula where tradition says the great warrior Palila* was born as a piece of cord. He was rescued by his grandmother Hina* and then reared by the priests at 'Ālana-pō. (Beckwith 1948:414–415; Fornander 1917:144, 372.)

ALEIPATA, a Samoan subdistrict on the island of 'Upolu which claims to have been settled by a couple from heaven, Alei and Pata. They were so beautiful that their children originated the practice of embalming to preserve them even after death. (Krämer 1902:279–281.)

ALELE, mythological people in ancient Samoan legends who lived far to the east of the islands and who could fly from one island to another by means of wings on their backs. Their king's name was also Alele, and he and his people were notorious in plundering food from neighboring tribes. They were once followed by the hero Lele'a-sapai* who forced them to give up the yams they had stolen from his grandfather and to promise that they would never invade Samoa again. (Fraser 1890:203–206.)

'ALELE-KĪ-NANA, see HA'A-LELE-KĪ-NANA.

ALELOLOA, a god from the island of Niue who licked up mortals' food with his long tongue. His colleagues were Futimotu,* Futifonua,* and Fuluhimaka. (Loeb 1926:161.)

ALIHI (ARII, KARIHI, KARIKI, KARIHI ALISE), brother to the famous demigod Kaha'i* (Tāwhaki), who accompanied Kaha'i on his journeys to revenge the death of their father Hema.* In Samoa, Karihi Alise accompanied Tafa'i to heaven to woo the goddess Sina (Hina*).

ALII-O-FITI, chief-of-Fiji, a benevolent household god of Samoa, who takes the form of an eel. (Turner 1884:70–71.)

ALII TU, a Samoan god whose earthly representation in the form of a *ve'a* (rail) bird designates good fortune when observed during battle. (Turner 1884:24.)

'ALO'ALO, the son of the Samoan sun god Tagaloa (Kanaloa*) or Lā (Rā*) through his wife Magamagaifatua (or Ui* ?). He married Sina (Hina*), the daughter of the Tuifiti (king of Fiji), and when she became pregnant, 'Alo'alo set out to heaven to obtain a gift for her—a lucky fishhook belonging to his ancestors. Disobeying the instructions of the gods regarding opening the package before he returns home, he broke the tapu, fell into the ocean near Fiji, and lost the fishhook. (Beckwith 1948:25; Krämer 1902:411–416.) Another legend states that the fishhook was found by another Sina from Samoa whose son I'umagatunu used it for numerous years before it was lost in the bay of Falealili, near the island of Nu'usafe'e where it is still today. (Krämer 1902:415.) Another tradition tells that after the death of 'Alo'alo, the fishhook was given to the fisherman La'ulu* by the Tuifiti for safe keeping, and it passed down into that family. See also **Kalokalo-o-ka-la; Tautini.**

ALOIMASINA, an inferior household god of Samoa, a moon god who cures sickness. (Turner 1884:67.)

'AMARA, one of the artisans in the Tahitian creation chant who helped the creator god Ta'aroa (Kanaloa*). Others mentioned are Fa'a-tae, Huri-'aro, Huri-tua, Nana, and Rauti. (Henry 1928:356.)

AMA-TAI-ĀTEA, king of the ocean in the Tahitian story of Māui* and the creation of the islands. (Henry 1928:464.) See also **Creation; Heavens.**

AMETO, the lowest division of the underworld* (*pō**) in Māori legend where the soul becomes nonexistent. (Tregear 1891:9.)

'AMOKESE, the creator of darkness at daytime (solar eclipses ?) on Bellona Island. (Monberg 1966:83.)

'AMOTONU, one of the many district gods of the Kaitu'u clan on Bellona Island, the son of the principal god Tehu'ainga-benga.* (Monberg 1966:67.)

ANA'E-MOE-OHO, one of the sea demons in the Tahitian Rata (Laka*) legend, killed by Rata and his brave men. (Henry 1928:470–495.)

'ANA-HEUHEU-PŌ, one of the pillars of the sky in the Tahitian creation story that became a twinkling star. He took to wife Tere-e-fa'a-ari'i-mai-i-te-ra'i, and they begat the planet Jupiter. (Henry 1928:361–362.) See also **Creation; Heavens.**

'ANA-HOA, one of the pillars of the sky that became a star in the Tahitian creation story. (Henry 1928:361.) See also **Creation; Heavens.**

ANAHULU, older brother of Hale-mano* in Hawaiian legend. (Beckwith 1948:523–524; Fornander 1917:228–263.)

ANA-ITA, a night demon in the Tuamotus. (Stimson 1964:49.)

'ANA-IVA, one of the pillars of the sky that became a star in the Tahitian creation story of the heavens; the star Phaet in the southern constellation of Columba. (Henry 1928:362.)

'ANA-MUA, the entrance pillar of the dome of the sky in the Tahitian creation chant; also Antares, the brightest star in the constellation Scorpio. (Henry 1928:361. See also **Creation; Heavens.**

'ANA-MURI, originally one of the pillars of the Tahitian sky that became the god of blackening or tattooing; also Aldebaran, the brightest star in the constellation Taurus. (Henry 1928:361.) See also **Creation; Heavens.**

'ANA-NI'A, Polaris or the north star in the Tahitian legend of the creation. (Henry 1928:362.) See also **Creation; Heavens.**

'ANA-ROTO, one of the pillars of the sky in the Tahitian creation story that became the star Spica in the constellation Virgo. (Henry 1928:361.) See also **Creation; Heavens.**

'ANA-TAHU'A-TA'ATA-ME-TUA-TE-TUPU-MĀVAE, one of the pillars of the sky in the Tahitian legend of the creation that became Arcturus, the brightest star in the constellation Boötes and in the northern sky. (Henry 1928:361.) See also **Creation; Heavens.**

'ANA-TAHU'A-VAHINE-O-TOA-'E-MĀNAVA, one of the pillars of the sky in the Tahitian legend of the creation that became Procyon, the brightest star in the constellation Canis Minor and one of the nearest to our sun. (Henry 1928:361.) See also **Creation; Heavens.**

'ANA-TIPU, one of the pillars of the sky in the Tahitian legend of the creation that became the star Dubhe in the constellation Ursa Major. (Henry 1928:361.) See also **Creation; Heavens.**

ANAUNAU, name of a mythical land in Tuamotuan legends. (Stimson 1964:49.) See also **Underworld.**

'ANA-VARU, one of the pillars of the sky in the Tahitian creation chant that became the star Betelguese in the constellation Orion. (Henry 1928:361–362.) See also **Creation; Heavens.**

ANGABANGU, a malevolent god on Bellona Island who steals spirits from mortals' souls. (Monberg 1966:78.)

ANOANOTAU, a god of Niue Island. (Loeb 1926:161.)

ANUA, an old goddesses named in the Tahitian creation chant. (Henry 1928:416.) See also **Creation.**

'ĀNUENUE, a rainbow goddess, a sister to the Hawaiian gods Kāne* and Kanaloa.* Her descendants were of chiefly rank. (Wickman 1985:158.)

ANU-MĀTAO, the legendary wife of Tangaroa (Kanaloa*) in Māori legends. Her children were the fish gods Whatukura, Poutini,* Te Pounamu,* etc. (Tregear 1891:12.)

AO, recognized as the god of light in Māori legends, the god of the upper world, the visible world, one of the first unborn forces in the universe throughout eastern Polynesia; another name for the god Ātea (Wākea.*) (Pukui 1971:24; Stimson 1964:50; Tregear 1891:14–15.) See also **Creation; Heavens.**

AO-ĀO-MĀ-RA'I-Ā, the first Tahitian who discovered how to make fire. After the separation of day from night, humans unsuccessfully attempted to make fire by various methods of fric-saw a large red fly light on a dry fau branch. "Fire must be in that branch," he mused. He then split the branch open, rubbed the dry branches together, and after several attempts finally produced a roaring fire. His wife Mahuie* was responsible for caring for the fire so that it would not go out. Āo-āo-mā-ra'i-ā was also the first human to cook his food. (Henry 1928: 427–429.) See also **Māui.**

AOKEHU, powerful Māori hero or *tohunga* (priest) who slew the great water monster Tū-tae-poroporo.* (Kauika 1904:94–98; Tregear 1891:15.)

AO-MARAMA, the world of light according to Chatham Island mythology, the son of Rongo-mai-whenua, and the first ancestor of all the Chatham Islanders; also the ancestor of the Hiti* or giant people. (Shand 1894:122.)

AO-MŌTEA, the upper world of light and day in Tuamotuan legends. (Stimson 1964:50.) See also **Creation; Heavens.**

AO-NEI, the upper world or earth where man dwells in Tuamotuan legends. (Stimson 1964:50.) See also **Creation; Heavens.**

AO-O-MILU, the Hawaiian underworld,* ruled over by the tion. One day Āo-āo-mā-ra'i-ā Hawaiian god Milu.* (Beckwith 1948:114, 118, 155, 159.)

AO-PIKOPIKO-I-HITI, the name of Rata's (Laka's*) ship in the Tuamotuan epic. (Stimson 1964:51.)

AOPOTO, Tuamotuan name of the land formed during the creation. (Stimson 1964:51.) See also **Creation; Heavens.**

AOROA, the name of the heavenly residence of the god Tāne (Kāne*) in Māori legends. (Tregear 1891:15.)

AOTANGI, the Tuamotuan heaven where winds originate. (Stimson 1964:51.)

AOTEA, the Māori designation of the first level of the lower world (Papa*). Also the name of one of the great outrigger canoes in the original migration of the Polynesians to New Zealand, commanded by chief Turi.* (Tregear 1891:15.) See also **Canoes, Māori Migration.**

APA, a companion to the god Tāne (Kāne*) in Tuamotuan legends. (Stimson 1964:51.)

APAAPA, a deified ancestor of New Zealand Māoris, a descendant of the first man Tiki,* and the son of Whātonga. (Tregear 1891:15.) See also **Ruatapu; Tupufua.**

APAKURA (APA'ULA, APEKUA), the Māori wife of Tūhuruhuru* (nephew to Rupe*) whose son Tū-whakararo* was jealously slain by an enemy. Tū-whakararo's younger brother Whakatau-pōtiki gathered a war party and killed the chief's family involved in the murder. (Grey 1970:77–83.) In another Māori story she was the wife of Tū-whakararo (son of Rata) and mother to Whakatau* who was born miraculously from her girdle when she threw it into the depths of the ocean. He was nurtured there by the sea god Rongo-takawiu* (Grey 1970: 91–92; Tregear 1891:15.)

In the **Marquesas**, Apekua (also called Pei-kua) sought revenge for the murder of her son Pota-a-te-mau. Her brother E-tia-i-te-toua gained the service of the long-armed god beneath the sea who stretched his arm and snatched the enemy despite numerous monstrous obstacles. Apekua, however, was finally avenged. (Handy 1930:74–78; Steinen 1933:364–365.)

The **Samoans** tell of their Apa'ula who set out to revenge the murder of her son Tui-o-savalalo by her brothers. She found his body, and his head told her to gain the stretching services of his brother, Va'atausili. She and Va'atausili set out for Fiji, and killed the murders. (Krämer 1902:268–270; Schultz 1909:139–142.) The Moriori from the Chatham Islands tell of Apukura's revenge upon the death of her son Tū by her powerful relative Whakatau who leaped over mountains. (Krämer 1902:268–179; Stair 1895:161–176.) See also **Kana; Kinilau; Laka.**

APANOA, the Tuamotuan name of the round entrance to Tāne's (Kāne's*) sky residence; also a name of a land in the underworld.* (Stimson 1964:51.) See also **Pō.**

APAPA-LANI, name of the Hawaiian heavens* as versus the underworld* called Apapa-nui.* (Emerson 1915:230.)

APAPA-NUI, name of the Hawaiian underworld* as versus the heavens called Apapa-lani.* (Emerson 1915:230)

ĀPARANGI, the New Zealand god of peace and mediation. (Tregear 1891:16.)

APATAHI, the Tuamotuan final resting place for the souls of the dead. (Stimson 1964:52.) See also **Underworld.**

APELESA, an inferior household god of Samoa who cures illness. (Turner 1884:67–69.)

API-TA'A-I-TE-RA'I, one of the monsters of the deep in the Tahitian story of Rata (Laka.*) (Henry 1928:477.)

APORAU, a messenger for the god Tāne's (Kāne's*) in Tahitian legend. (Henry 1928:369.)

'ĀPUA, brother to the Hawaiian hero 'Au-kele-nui-a-iku.* (Beckwith 1948:490–493.) He introduced the coconut* to humans. (Fornander 1917:590–594.) Also the same as Kāne-'āpua,* a brother to the volcano goddess Pele.* (Beckwith 1948:170.)

'ĀPUA-KEA, she and her mother Muliwai'ōlena were slain at Kāpua in Ko'olau on the island of O'ahu because she compared herself to the beauty of the Hawaiian goddess Hi'iaka.* (Fornander 1920:373, 429.)

APŪHAU or APŪMĀTANGI, a Māori storm god, a son of Tāwhiri-mā-tea* (the lord of storms). (Tregear 1891:17; Grey 1855::8.)

ARA-'ĀRAHU, a Tahitian god created from coral taken from a land called Pau-tere-fenua.* (Henry 1928:341.) See also Creation.

ARAHURA, the name of one of the great outrigger canoes in the original migration of the Polynesians to New Zealand, commanded by chiefs Pekite-tahua, Rongokahe, Rangitatau, and chiefess Hineraho. (Tregear 1891:20.) See also Canoes, Māori Migration.

ARAHUTA, daughter of the Māori lightning god Tāwhaki (Kaha'i*) and his wife Tangotango.* (Tregear 1891:18-19.)

ĀRAI-ARA, wife of Whiro-nui* and mother of Hutu-rangi,* who emigrated to New Zealand in the Nukatere canoe. (Tregear 1891:19; White 1887c:41.) See also Canoes, Māori Migration.

ĀRAITEURU, name of one of the great canoes in the Polynesian migration to New Zealand; also the mother of all the great water monsters such as Waihou, Waima, Orira, Mangamuka, Ohopa,* and Wairere. (Tregear 1891:19.) See also Canoes, Māori Migration; Tāniwha.

ARAKAU, name of a ghost ship (canoe) in the Tuamotus. (Stimson 1964:53.)

ARAMATIETIE, the dwelling place of the sun in the Tuamotuan legend of Māui.* (Stimson 1964:53.) See also Creation.

ARATIERE, an axe belonging to the Tuamotuan god Tanaroa (Kanaloa*). (Stimson 1964:54.)

ARAURI, god of all black birds in New Zealand, the son of Tāne-mahuta.* (White 1887a: App.)

ARAWA, name of the most famous canoe used in the great migration of the Polynesians to New Zealand. See also Canoes, Māori Migration.

'ARE-MATA-PŌPOTO, one of the great demons of the sea, a tidal wave in the Tahitian story of Rata (Laka.*) (Henry 1928: 470–495.) See also **'Are-mata-roroa.**

'ARE-MATA-ROROA, one of the demons of the sea, a long wave, in the Tahitian Rata (Laka*) story. (Henry 1928:469–495.) See also **'Are-mata-pōpoto.**

ARI, a primeval god of New Zealand, son of Rangi-pōtiki* (prop of heaven) and Papa* (earth mother), twin brother to Hua.* (Tregear 1891:23; Shortland 1882:17.) See also **Creation; Heavens; Rangi.**

ARIKIMAITAI, the name of one of the great outrigger canoes in the original migration of the Polynesians to New Zealand. One of the first to land in New Zealand. (Tregear 1891:20; White 1887b:177.) See also **Canoes, Māori Migration.**

ARIKINOANOA, the New Zealand god of ferns. (Tregear 1891:24; White 1887c:95.)

ARIKU-TŪA-MEA, a Tuamotuan god of superior rank. (Stimson 1964:55.)

ARIMATA, sister of Huauri* and aunt to Tahaki (Kaha'i*), the famous legendary figure in the lengthy Tuamotuan epic by that name. Arimata had a son Niu-kura* to whom she chanted of his exploits when he was born. Huauri became jealous and repeated the same chant for her son Tahaki. The jealousy between the two families ended when Niu-kura killed Tahaki and cut him into pieces. Through her magical powers, Huauri was able to restore life to her son. She had her revenge by making the ocean swallow up the sons of Arimata, and they became porpoises. (Stimson 1934:50–53.)

ARIOI SOCIETY, a peculiar social order that existed among the Tahitians and found in no other Polynesian group. The *arioi* consisted of a select group of Tahitians organized into what could generally be called a fraternity, guild, or an association of selected entertainers whose main function in the society was to provide music, dances, tabloids, satirical jests and acts in exchange for extensive hospitality and lavish gifts from the recipients. It is estimated that approximately one-fifth of the population belonged to this sect.

Legend tells us that the origin of the *arioi* dates back into primeval times when the god 'Oro* took to wife a beautiful maiden from Bora-Bora. For a gift to his bride, he turned his two companions into pigs. One of the sacred pigs was given to Tamatoa I, high chief of Ra'iātea, who supposedly originated this semidivine cult dedicated to 'Oro and whose principal *marae** (temple) was at Opoa (Taputapuātea) on

Ra'iātea. From Ra'iātea it spread to the other islands where representatives from Opoa were authorized to initiate newcomers into the society. Abortion or infanticide was widely practiced since no *arioi* member could be encumbered with menial domestic duties associated with family life. Any member allowing children to live, therefore, was degraded and looked upon with contempt by the other members of the order.

Theoretically, the head of the group was the chief priest at Opoa on Ra'iātea, called the *Taramanini*. Each district on each island had its own grand master who controlled the inner workings of the association within his own lodge. There were seven to eight ranks or grades within the society. Although they were generally opened to all social classes, the vast majority of the top ranks were made up of the *ari'i* (noble class). Novices advanced in degrees by mastering the complex techniques of the dance, music, story telling, and acting. The highest ranks were jealously guarded by the older members; and, as a result, novices spent most of their time doing most of the entertaining as the group traveled from one district to another. Ranks were visibly recognized by unique tattoo patterns reserved only for them. The top ranking individuals were called black legs because of the heavy tattooing on these limbs.

According to sources, their entire life was one *upa upa* (festivity). Having privileges held by no other social class, they enjoyed a type of perpetual youthfulness with full time devoted to entertaining and unrestricted love making. When lodge members moved from one district to another, they were greeted by great shouting and applause by the entire populace. Lavish gifts were presented to them after which a large feast would begin. Amusements, dancing, story telling, and lampooning would last for days. These wandering entertainers were free to satirize even the highest social classes with an accompanying use of sexual and copulative imagery and gestures. Explicit sex acts were not uncommon. After the district had been practically stripped of its food supply, the group either went to another lodge in another district or returned home until another day.

These *arioi* (both men and women) were highly privileged; they were immune from ghostly attacks generally made upon everyone else; they could make unreasonable demands on most of the society; and in death, they alone had immortality—one continual *upa upa* in the spirit world which lingered over the sacred island of Ra'iātea. (Ellis 1829a:312–315; Moerenhout

1837b:131–132; Henry 1928: 231–234.)

ĀROHIROHI, wife of the sun god Rā* and mother of the first woman Kau-ata-ata* in Māori legends. (Tregear 1891:25, 136; White 1887a:App.)

ARU, name of a demon or demigod in Tuamotuan legends. (Stimson 1964:57.)

ARUTARUTA-TĀMAUMAU-AUAHI, an old goddess in early Tahitian myths whose eyes are red from tending her ever firey furnaces. (Henry 1928:416.) See also **Pele.**

ASOMUA, an inferior household god of Samoa who detects and names thieves. (Turner 1884:69.)

ATA, one of the powers of light in Māori legend. (Tregear 1891:26.) An epithet of the supreme deity in the Tuamotu islands. (Stimson 1964:58.) Also the god of thieves in Marquesan legends. (Christian 1895:189.) See also **Kore.**

ATAHIKURANGI, a daughter of Rangi* (sky father), and Atatuhi,* the goddess of light or full day in Māori legends. (Tregear 1891:27.) See also **Hiku-rangi.**

'ATAITEKABA, one of the many district gods of the Kaitu'u clan on Bellona and Rennell Islands, the son of the principal god Tehu'aingabenga.* (Monberg 1966:67.)

'ATAITENGENGA, one of the many district gods of the Kaitu'u clan on Bellona and Rennell Islands, the son of the principal god Tehu'aingabenga.* (Monberg 1966:67.)

ATAITENO'A, one of the many district gods of the Kaitu'u clan on Bellona and Rennell Islands, the son of the principal god Tehu'aingabenga.* (Monberg 1966:67.)

ATAKIARO, name of a mythical island in the Tuamotuan legend of Te Makehu-tumu. (Stimson 1964:59.) See also **Atakitua.**

ATAKITUA, name of a mythical island in the Tuamotuan legend of Te Makehu-tumu. (Stimson 1964:59.) See also **Atakiaro.**

ATAMAI, in Māori legend, the thirteenth age in the existence of the universe. (Tregear 1891: 27.) See also **Kore.**

ATARAGA, father of the great Tuamotuan demigod Māui* and husband to Hava.* Ataraga raped Huahega* and she delivered a boy, Māui-tikitiki-a-Ataraga. (Stimson 1934:5–8.)

ATARAHI, the name of an ancient New Zealand Māori who supposedly died and returned to life five days later. (Shortland 1882:45; Tregear 1891:27.)

ATARAPA, the dawn goddess in Māori legends, the daughter of Rangi* (sky father) and Ata-tuhi.* (Tregear 1891:27.)

ATARI-HEUI, a chief artisan for the Tahitian god Ta'ere* in the center of the earth, who was commanded to take his stone adze and attempt to cut away at the sky god Ātea (Wākea*). Looking upon his majesty, Atari-heui and companions fled back to their homes. (Henry 1928:374, 407.)

ATATUHI or **ATUTAHI**, the star Canopus, the wife of the sky god Rangi* in Māori legends, and therefore the mother of the moon, the stars, and daylight. (Tregear 1891:27; White 1887a: 7.) See also **Creation; Heavens.**

ĀTEA, vast space as personified as a supreme god. A story from Rarotonga, Cook Islands, maintains that Ātea was once a man who argued with the god Tangaloa (Kanaloa*) over the parentage of his newborn son. The two divided the child and threw its remains into the heavens where one part became the sun and the other became the moon. (Fraser 1892:76–77.)

In **Marquesan** legends, Atea is the god of husbandry, the patron god of agriculture and planting, who brings refreshing rains. One wife Uene gave birth to the kava plant, and Puoo bore Mako, the shark. (Christian 1895:189.) See also **Wākea.**

ĀTEA-NUKU-MAU-ATŪA, father of Ngāti-Pui, one of the Tuamotuan gods. (Stimson 1964:59.) See also **Wākea.**

ĀTEA-NUKU-MAU-TAN-GATA, ancestor god of all humans according to Tuamotuan belief. (Stimson 1964:59.) See also **Wākea.**

ĀTEA-TEA-ATŪA, a Tuamotuan god. (Stimson 1964:59.) See also **Wākea.**

ATELAPA, a god of Niue Island. (Loeb 1926:163.)

ATIOGIE or **LEATIOGIE**, an ancient Samoan chief, a direct descendant from Pili,* whose sons Le Alali, Savea, Tuna, Fata, Maau, and Va'etauia freed Samoa from Tongan domination and established the ruling families in Samoa. The story is somewhat reminiscent of the ancient Greek conflict with the Trojans. About A.D. 1200, Tongans invaded Samoa and for the next four hundred years dominated the country. As a result, there grew up in Samoa a hero class of men who fought against the Tongans. Among those were the sons of Atiogie (especially Tuna and Fata) who organized a revolution called Matamatame. They gathered an army, defeated the Tongans, and as the Tongans sailed away they cried back "*Malie tau, malie to'a*" (Well fought brave warriors). Tuna and Fata adopted the name Malietoa* as a joint title and established the most important ruling houses in Savai'i and 'Upolu. (Krämer 1902:83, 238–241, 258–260; Stübel 1896:84–88; Turner 1884:253–254.)

Ā-TORO-I-RA'I, Tahitian god of everlasting work, responsible for the growth of food and trees. (Henry 1928:377–378.)

ATU or **ATUA**, a general term meaning god, lord, or master; the Tuamotuan primordial one. (Stimson 1964:60; Tregear 1891: 30–31.) See also **Akua**.

ATUA-ANUA, a goddess mentioned in the Easter Island creation chant as the god mother. (Métraux 1940:321–322.) See also **Atua-Metua**.

ATUA-I-KAFIKA, the supreme god of the island of Tikopia. Also known as Atua-i-raropuka.* (Firth 1961:53.)

ATUA-I-RAROPUKA, the supreme god of the island of Tikopia. He and his wife Atua-Fafine were first recognized when the islands emerged from the bottom of the ocean. Atua-i-raropuka was seen braiding sinnet while Atua-Fafine was seen weaving pandanus mats— the traditional labors of man and woman. (Firth 1961:26.) See also **Atua-i-kafika.**

ATUAKIKOKIKO, Māori legends say that these are demons who haunt and torment the sick and mentally ill people. (Tregear 1891:31.)

ATUA-MANGUMANGU, an emaciated god of the underworld* on the island of Futuna. (Burrows 1936:105–108.)

ATUA-MATA-LUA, a two-eyed god of the underworld* on the island of Futuna. (Burrows 1936:105–108.)

ATUA-MATARIRI, a god mentioned in the Easter Island creation chant, the god with the angry face, suggesting a relation with the god Tū (Kū*) in the other Polynesian islands. (Métraux 1940:321–322.)

ATUA-MATA-TASI, a one-eyed god of the underworld* on the island of Futuna. (Burrows 1936:105–108.)

ATUA-METUA, a god mentioned in the Easter Island creation chant as the god parent. (Métraux 1940:321–322.) See also **Atua-Anua.**

ATUANGAU, demons in Māori legends who are supposed to cause internal pains in humans. (Tregear 1891:31.)

ATUA-NOHO-IRANGI, another name for the god Tāne (Kāne*) in Tuamotuan legends. (Stimson 1964:60.)

ATUASOLOPUNGA, a cannibal spirit in Tuvalu who assumed the form of the mortal man named Tokalalanga to seduce his wife Tapulei. He was found out and cooked in an oven, and the husband and wife were reunited. (Roberts 1957:365.)

ATUATORO, another name for Kāhukura,* the Māori god of the rainbow, the spying god. (Grey 1970:129–130; Tregear 1891:31.)

ATUGAKI, a Tongan god of the creation, son of the goddess Touiafutuna* (metallic stone), twin to Maimoa'alognona* whom he married and gave birth to Vele-lahi* (mother to the sky god Tagaloa (Kanaloa*). (Reiter 1907:230–240.) See also Creation; Heavens.

ATŪHENŪA, according to Tuamotuan legend, the name of the first land created, rock foundation. (Stimson 1964:60.)

ATUA TAFITO, a god of Fakaofu, Tokelau Islands. (Macgregor 1937:61.)

ATU-TAHI, in the Tahitian creation chant, the star Piscis-Australis who mated with his wife Tū-i-tū-moana-'urifa, and they become the parents of more sky and stars. (Henry 1928:360–361.) See also Atatuhi; Creation; Heavens.

'AU-KELE-NUI-A-IKU, is one of the oldest and most renown of all Hawaiian romances. 'Au-kele-nui-a-iku ('Au-kele) was the youngest and favorite son of Iku and Ka-papa-i-ākea who lived in Kū'ai-he-lani, a mythical land which belonged to his grandmother, the lizard goddess Ka-mo'o-i-nanea.* 'Au-kele was hated by his brothers because his father made him heir of his kingdom, consequently, they attempted to get rid of him. They threw him in a great pit belonging to his grandmother, but she rescued him and told him to go to a vacant land ruled over by the goddess Nā-maka-o-kaha'i.* She gave him magical implements to help him in his journey—a food-providing leaf, an axe, a knife, part of her tail, her pā'ū (skirt), and a box containing the god Lono-i-ka-'ou-ali'i.*

'Au-kele and his brothers set out on the journey southward, and the food-providing leaf saved them from starvation. When they landed, his brothers were killed in an ensuing battle, and 'Au-kele used his magical implements to marry Nā-maka-o-kaha'i and to become ruler over the land.

His other adventures include being rescued from a huge bird called Halulu* and sailing to a distant land in search of the water of life to restore the life of his brothers. Not long after, 'Au-kele's son Ka-uila-nui-makaeha-i-ka-lani became involved in a family feud with his cousins, and in anger all of 'Au-kele's brothers set out to sea where they met their death. As time passed, 'Au-kele became enraptured by his wife's cousins (sisters ?), Pele* and Hi'iaka.* In a jealous range, Nā-maka-o-kaha'i drove her cousins from one island to another until Pele and Hi'iaka finally made their way to the Hawaiian chain. 'Au-kele eventually followed them and became chief of the island of Kaua'i. (Beckwith 1948:51,79, 264, 490–497; Fornander 1878:40–42, 78, 100–101; Fornander 1916:32–111, 1919: 10n; Johnson ms.; Pukui 1971: 381.)

AULIALIA, the name of the supreme god on Nui, Tuvalu, who created the first man (Tepapa) and woman (Tetata). (Turner 1884:300.)

AUMĀ, an inferior household god of Samoa, represented in the form of a wild pigeon. (Turner 1884:69.)

AURAROTUIA, the name of Māui's* canoe in Māori legends. (Tregear 1891:33; White 1887b:91.)

AURU, the Māori god who presides over the western sky. (Tregear 1891:34.)

AUTĀ, Tuamotuan name for the land of the dead, the underworld,* a land of lamentation and despair. (Stimson 1964:62.)

AVARO, a Tahitian god invoked to cause skin blemishes to disappear. (Henry 1928:382, 378.)

AVATELE, name of the underworld* in Niuean traditions. (Loeb 1926:157.)

AVE-AITU, god in the shape of a meteor with a long tail according to Tahitian mythology, a messenger for To'a-hiti* sent to be a guide for Tāne's (Kāne's*) hosts in time of war. (Beckwith 1948:114; Henry 1928:379.) See also **Fakakonaatua; Kālai-pā-hoa; Rongomai.**

AVE-I-LE-TALA, a Samoan god of childbirth who supposedly predicted the arrival of the powerful Christian god and the destruction of the old gods of Samoa. (Turner 1884:24.)

AWA, see **Kava.**

ĀWHIOWHIO, the Māori god of whirlwinds, son of Ranga-mao-mao,* descendant of the sky father Rangi.* (Tregear 1891:36; White 1887a:28.)

–B–

BAABENGA, a goddess of the island of Bellona and daughter of the god Mauloko, her brother was Teangaitak and her sister was Tehahine'angiki, capable of appearing either as male or female and playing mischievous tricks on humans. She is vaguely associated with sharks. On the island of Rennell, she is identified as the daughter of Sikingimoemore* and Tehainga'atua. As a male, he was a malevolent god, and the interior of the island, the bush, and the trails were sacred to him. (Monberg 1966:56, 65, 77.)

BAEIKA, one of the many district gods on Bellona Island. (Monberg 1966:71.)

BANYAN TREE, Origin of the. The shadows on the moon were considered by the ancient Tahitians to be the tree from which the goddess Hina* obtained bark to make tapa. Once while Hina was climbing the tree, one of the branches broke off and fell to earth, landing at Opoa on the island of Ra'iātea (French Polynesia.) It struck root and from there spread throughout the islands of the Pacific.

BIRD CULT OF EASTER ISLAND, see **Makemake.**

BIRDS. Birds are regarded by the Tahitians to be shadows of the gods. Different birds repre-

sent different gods. The light-yellow thrush of Tahiti, for example, is the shadow of the god 'Oro-i-te-maro-tea ('Oro-of-the-yellow-girdle), and the albatross is considered to be the shadow of Ta'aroa.* (Beckwith 1948:92; Henry 1928:384.)

BREADFRUIT, Origin of the. Legends regarding the origin of breadfruit, the staple food throughout the Pacific, are told everywhere. The **Tahitian** legend tells the story of a father's selfless devotion to his family. During the reign of chief Nohoari'i,* a great famine raged on the island of Ra'iātea. One man called Rūa-ta'ata and his wife ached because of the suffering of their starving children. They decided to flee into the mountains where they could possibly survive on a few edible ferns. Finally, Rūa-ta'ata became desperate and called to his wife. He told her that when she awoke the next morning, he would be gone. Outside their dwelling she would find that he had turned into a great tree. His legs would be the roots, his torso the trunk, and at the top of the tree she would find fruit which would represent his head. He told her to take the fruit, roast it, soak it in water, beat off the skin, and feed some of its insides to his children so that they would no longer be hungry.

Sure enough, the next morning the wife found exactly what the husband had pre dicted. The weeping wife did as her husband had told her. While she was washing the roasted breadfruit, particles broke off and floated down the stream where others found them, tasted them, and took the new food to their chief. The family was brought before the chief, and the wife told him of the story of her husband. Henceforth, the breadfruit became the staple food on Ra'iātea. From there it spread to the neighboring islands of Taha'a and Bora-Bora (introduced there by a beautiful maiden called Teiti), and then to all the other islands of the Pacific. The valley on Ra'iātea today is called Tua-urua (place-of-breadfruit.) (Henry 1928: 423–426; Roosman 1970:219–232.) See also **Ka-ha'i**.

In **Hawai'i**, the first breadfruit grew from the testicles of a man who had died for his family. When the gods tasted the fruit, they found it desirable, but when they heard where it had come from, they vomited it up and spread the fruit over the islands. (Beckwith 1948:98; Fornander 1917:676–679.)

On **Rarotonga**, Cook Islands, Tangaroa takes a wife who prepares him food he does not like. Her mother, Vai-takere, dies and becomes the first breadfruit which they mash and prepare with coconut. (Ariki-Tara-Are 1899:65–66; Beckwith 1948:101.)

BUATARANGA, wife to the god Rū, supporter of the heavens, in Mangaian legends, and mother to the great demigod Māui. It was Buataranga who introduced Māui to the secret of fire from the god Mauike (Mahuika*). (Gill 1876:51–58.)

–C–

CANNIBALISM. The practice of eating human flesh (anthropophagy) is found to have been practiced at various times over much of the world, and Polynesian mythology makes frequent reference to this particular phenomenon.

In **Samoan** legend, the cannibal god Maniloa* dwelt in a deep ravine over which he had constructed a spidery bridge for humans to pass. Frequently, he would shake the bridge, and the unsuspecting traveler would fall to his death, whereupon Maniloa would devour him. As time passed, a group of Samoans decided on revenge. They found an alternative path to his dwelling, fell upon him, and killed him. In doing so, Maniloa's spirit entered into his avengers, and as a result, they acquired his taste for human flesh. (Krämer 1902:247, 275.)

Cannibalism to the Polynesian was the supreme act of defiance and obscenity, an act difficult for Westerners to comprehend fully. Human flesh was not eaten as a regular source of protein or food, but rather as an act of superiority over the one being eaten. Bodies of the slain enemy, for example, would be cooked and then eaten by the victors. Revenge was not complete until at least some parts of the slain had been devoured. Cooked food lacked all sacredness and dignity. To do that to another human being would bring the desired revenge and would thus bring to the living an immense release. "I will roast you" was the greatest insult spoken by a Samoan.

Although cannibalism was abhorred in Tahiti and apparently was not practiced in Hawai'i, investiture ceremonies of high-ranking chiefs in both island groups retained what might have once been a more common practice. They newly-invested chief would swallow the left eye of a human sacrifice so that he might receive a rejuvenation of strength. There are also Tahitian and Hawaiian references in mythology to cannibalism, but there is no evidence that it was actually practiced in these two island groups.

The most legendary cannibal in Polynesian mythology is Whaitiri,* goddess grandmother of the great hero Tāwhaki (Kaha'i.*) [In Tahiti, her name is Rona-nihoniho-rora, Rona-of-the-long-teeth.] In **New Zealand**, Ue-nuku,* a deified ancestor, killed his wife Takarita* because of her infidelity and then fed her heart to his son Ira. Takarita's family swore revenge and came to meet Ue-nuku in a famous battle called Rotorua. In Rarotonga, Cook Islands, an extant dirge reflects the stoic feelings of Rao, who watches as preparations are made for her fate by her husband: "Oh, weep for me! The sun goes down behind our lands. Have you no pity, none for me? There stands our well-used cooking place. He is splitting up the firewood: Aue! It is to cook this flesh of mine! O, weep, o, weep for me. Farewell we-two, we-two farewell!" (Alpers 1970:295, 351; Beckwith 1948:339–343; Goodman 1970: 33, 128, 150, 328, 330.) See also **Sacrifices, Human.**

CANOES, MĀORI MIGRATION. According to Māori tradition, their ancestors set sail from Hawaiki* in great ocean-going outrigger canoes to find new lands in which to settle. Kupe* was the first great chief from Hawaiki to discover New Zealand (c. A. D. 950?). Supposedly, he eloped with Kura-maro-tini,* wife of Hoturapa,* owner of a great canoe called *Matahorua*, whom Kupe murdered. To escape the vengeance of Hoturapa's family, Kupe and Kura fled across the sea in the ship navigated by Riti. Kupe named their newly-discovered island Aotearoa (long-white-cloud.) After exploring its coast lines and killing the sea monster Te Wheke-a-Muturangi,* they eventually returned to Hawaiki where they publicized the finding of their new land.

Centuries later (c. A. D. 1250?), other relatives left Hawaiki because of famine, over population, adventure, or intertribal warfare to settle in the new land. Although several great canoes are generally remembered today, there are many more that can be identified. The most famous are the seven: *Arawa, Tainui, Aotea, Kura-haupō, Toko-maru, Takitimu,* and *Matatūa*.

The *Arawa* was formed from a great tree in Rarotonga, supposedly on the other side of Hawaiki, by such mythological characters as Rata (Laka*), Wahie-roa, and others, but the canoe belonged to Tama-te-kapua,* son of Houmai-tāwhiti.* A series of battles broke out between Tama's family and the high chief Ue-nuku.* Tama's father and brother were killed, and Tama then gathered up what goods and family he could, kidnapped Ngātoro-i-rangi,* navigator/priest of the *Tainui* canoe, and his wife Kearoa, and set out in the *Arawa*. During the voyage, Tama seduced Kearoa, and in revenge Ngātoro-i-rangi created a great whirlpool which almost pulled them down into oblivion. The *Arawa* finally landed in New Zealand near Cape Runaway. After his death, Kama was buried on Mount Moehau* so his spirit could gaze far over the ocean and over the land of Aotearoa. He was later deified by his descendants as a god of thievery.

Tainui was one of the largest canoes and was the first to land in New Zealand in the great migration. Its high priest navigator Hotu-roa* was a distant relative of Tama-te-kapua* of the *Arawa* canoe. When Hotu-roa learned of the tribal conflict and that relatives were leaving Hawaiki for new lands, he decided to follow suit. Hotu-roa had two wives, Marama-kiko-hura and Whakaotirangi,* who brought the sweet potato (*kumara*) to New Zealand. Many of the *Tainui* descendants settled in the present-day Auckland area and along the west coast.

The great double canoe *Aotea* was built by Toto* from one half of a huge tree grown on the banks of the Wai-harakeke river in Hawaiki. Toto gave the canoe *Aotea* to his daughter Rongo-rongo,* wife of Turi,* and the other half of the tree he made into the canoe *Matahorua* and gave to his daughter Kura-maro-tini.* In the fight against chief Ue-nuku, Turi killed the chief's son Hawe-pōtiki, and similar to Tama and Hotu-roa, set out for New Zealand with thirty-three passengers from three different families. Turi stashed away on board some sweet potatoes, *karaka* berries, edible rats, swamp hens, and green parakeets. During their rough voyage, they stopped at the island of Rangitahua (Raoul Island, Keremedic Group) and picked up the shipwrecked passengers from the *Kura-haupō*, navigated by Ruatea (some legends say Pou or Te Maunganui). After some disagreement regarding direction of navigation, they finally arrived at Aotea Harbor and settled around the Patea River near Whanganui on the west coast of New Zealand.

The *Tokomaru*, commanded by Manaia,* was originally owned by his brother-in-law in Hawaiki. While Manaia was away, a group of friends raped his wife Rongo-tiki. When he returned home, Manaia slew his friends including chief Tū-penu, fitted out the *Tokomaru*, offered up his brother-in-law as a sacrifice, and set sail with his family for New Zealand. They landed at Whangaparaoa but finally settled in Taranaki county.

Legends regarding the *Takitimu* (or *Takitumu*) also include chief Ue-nuku. Ruawharo, commander of the canoe, and his companions fled Hawaiki on the *Takitimu* after having stolen fish from Ue-nuku and raping the wife of high priest Timu-whakairihia. They brought the god Kāhukura on board and his presence made the canoe extremely *tapu* (taboo or sacred.) No food could be cooked during its crossing, and as a result, the destitute crew resorted to cannibalism before they finally reached their destination. Their descendants settled along the northeast coast of the North Island.

The *Matatūa*, commanded by Toroa (or Ruaauru), brought the staple food taro and landed at Whakatane (Bay of Plenty.) Other migration traditions include stories of numerous other canoes—the *Arahura*, the *Arai teuru*, the *Kirauta*, the *Horouta*, the sacred *M āhangaatua-matua*, etc. A re-examination of the legends and a study of their origins lead scholars to surmise that rather than a single fleet of canoes as once supposed, that the migration extended over several centuries after Kupe's original discovery. (Grey 1970: 106–127; Tregear 1891:20–22; White 1887b:176–184; White 1887d:28, 58.)

COCONUT, Origin of the. Legends of the origin of the coconut are widespread throughout all of Polynesia (except Hawai'i), and almost all tell similar stories. The most popular **Tahitian** myth is the one about Hina,* the princess of Papeuriri in southern Tahiti, who was the daughter of the sun and moon. She was engaged to the king of Lake Vaihira, located in the mountains of central Tahiti. As Hina ascended the mountain to meet her new bridegroom, she saw that the king was an immense eel. In terror she fled for protection to the cave of the demigod Māui at Vairao, Tai'arapu (southern Tahiti.) Māui cast his fishhook into the sea, caught the eel, and hacked it to pieces. He then wrapped its head in breadfruit leaves and instructed Hina to put it down only when she got to her home. Thoughtlessly, Hina placed the bundle down to cool herself in a nice stream of water, whereupon, the bundle sprouted roots and grew into a coconut tree. The stream of water belonged to Ruroa and her two sons. Because of their kindnesses to her, Hina granted them the status of nobility, married the two sons, and had children. One day while holding coconuts in their hands, Hina's two daughters were caught up in a rainbow and transported to the island of Ana'a in the Tuamotus. This was the origin of the first coconut on the island of Ana'a. (Henry 1928:421–423; 615–619.)

In **Samoa** and **Tonga**, the story is told of the eel god, who fled to the islands of Samoa where he took up residence in a particular pool that belonged to the princess Sina (Hina.) By and by Sina became pregnant, whereupon, the vengeful people of the village drained the pool and hacked the eel to death. Sorrowful, Sina carefully buried its head. Five days later, a new form of a tree spouted from its burial place. Upon maturing, the new tree provided leaves for plaited baskets, thatching for houses, and numerous other daily needs. Its fruit provided food and oil, and when scooped out provided containers and cups. The husks were used to make sennit (twine.) (Gifford 1924:181–183; Kirtley 1967; Roosman 1970:219–232.)

CREATION. Throughout Polynesia, the central theme of the creation of the universe is that of genealogy, the union of male and female that gives birth to new forms of life, and many variant texts exist from island to island to explain specific details. A less common account, and one purportedly of more modern origin, is that of a supreme god of creation without father and mother who creates the world out of himself and by himself. (Monberg 1956:253–281.)

In **Hawai'i**, the Kumulipō chant of some 2,077 lines tells the birth of all forms of life out of chaos (slime) through union of male and female. "Slime was the source of the earth, the source of darkness. . .Born was Kumulipō in the night, a male, Born was Po'ele in the night, a female. . ." In this manner all forms of life on the earth and all the gods were created. The Kumuhonua chant, however, gives predominance to the creator god Kane,* although he is assisted by the gods Kū* and Lono* (a trilogy called *lahui akua*, union of gods). (Beckwith 1948:42–46, 310–313; Beckwith 1951; Fornander 1920:267, 273–276, 335.)

In **New Zealand**, the genealogical creation chant begins with a recitation of the vast ages of Te Po* (The Night), Te Ao (The Light), and Te Kore* (The Emptiness) and continues to the union of Rangi* (sky father) and Papa* (earth mother) from whom are born seventy sons, the six most important being the gods Tāwhiri (winds, storms), Tangaroa (sea, fish),

Rongo (sweet potato, cultivated food plants), Haumia* (fern root, wild food plants), Tū (fierce Man), and Tāne (forest, birds). The children are frustrated because of their parents' union and the darkness and restrictions it has created. Five of them decide to separate their parents with Tāne as the dominant force. Tāwhiri-matea disagrees and is angered over their action. He gathers his forces (wind, thunder, and lightning) and rages against them. Most of the gods go into hiding, and it is only Tāne who stands strongly against him. Rangi is forced upward and his reaching arms to Papa were severed by the adzes of Tāne and Tū. Their blood can be seen to this day in the red glow of the sky and in the red ocher of the earth. After their separation, Rangi's tears drop to earth in the form of rain, and Papa's sighs rise heavenward in the form of mists. (Grey 1970:1–11; White 1887a:17–53.)

There also exists in New Zealand a tradition of a supreme being or creator of all things by the name of Io-take-take (Io*), the primal ancestor without father or mother. The chant is no doubt of pure Māori origin, but certain aspects may have been influenced by Christianity (Gudgeon 1905:109–119; Monberg 258; Best 1924:40). "Io dwelt in the open space of the world, The world was dark, water was everywhere. There was no day, no light, no place of light, Only darkness and water everywhere. And it was he who first pronounced this word. . ." (Johansen 1954:18.)

The **Samoan** creation stories are based on genealogical backgrounds. The High Rocks (Papatu) unite with Earth Rocks (Papa'ele) and children are born, including the power demons Saolevao* and Saveasi'uleo* (god of the underworld* or Pulotu*). In the seventh generation, Tagaloa (Kanaloa*), the creator of human beings, is born (Turner 1884:3–5, 10; Krämer 1902:7).

Tagaloa had two children, a son Moa and a daughter Lu. Lu bore a son also named Lu who argued with his uncle Moa and fled to earth which he called Samoa. Various versions of the story exist. In eastern Samoa in the Manu'a group, Tagaloa created man by sending down a vine to earth that begot maggots who in turn formed human beings. In other words, man was not formed by genealogical union (copulation) but by command of the god Tagaloa. (Fraser 1890:207–211; Krämer 1902: 392, 396; Stair 1896: 35–36.)

Another story maintains that a married couple in the underworld* by the names of Si'usi'uao (end of the day) and Uluao (beginning of the day) had four children: Ua (Rain), Fari (Long Grass), Langi (Heavens), and Tala (Story), who were ill treated on a trip to Papatea. In revenge, king Elo*

of the underworld waged war against Papatea, and everything was killed except four couples who fled to the upper world and peopled Samoa: Ma and Nu'a (Manu'a), Tutu and Ila (Tutuila), U and Polu ('Upolu), Sa and Vai'i (Savai'i). (Krämer 1902:106; Turner 1884: 222–223.)

A story narrated by Tauanu'u to T. A. Powell in 1871 tells of Tagaloa creating the first man (Fatu-ma-le) and woman ('Ele-'ele) from Spirit, Heart, Will, and Thought, and it is they who first peopled the island of Manu'a in Samoa. From Manu'a, their descendants moved to the other Samoan islands with this parting command from Tagaloa, "Always show respect to Manu'a." (Fraser 1892:268–285.)

Tongan creation stories are rare. One that survives (Caillot 1914:239–241; Reiter 1907:230–240) is genealogical in nature. In it Limu, "Seaweed" (male), united with Kele, "Slime" (female), and they begot a child called Touiafutuna,* a large metallic stone, which frequently rumbleed, opened up, and each time produced twins, one male and one female form, both gods. These intermarried and produced another generation of offspring until eventually there were three categories of beings, Hikuleo* (god of the underworld), Tagaloa*(god of the heavens) and Māui* (god of the earth).

Another Tongan story tells of the creation of land. The king of heaven, Tama-pouli-ala-ma-foa, and his Tagaloa assistants sent their bird Kiu to earth to see if it could find land. When Kiu returned and gave a negative report, Tagaloa-tufuga threw wood chips to earth and the island of Eua emerged. The gods came to earth, cut open a rock and three mortal men emerged, Kohai, Koau, and Momo. When the Māui brothers set out on their fishing expedition, they met the three mortal men, saw their plight of having no women, and set out to Lolo-fonua (earth) and obtained wives for them. They then peopled the earth.

Another manuscript tells of the creation as being the result of the sexual intercourse between the twin deities Tau-fulifonua (male) and Havea Lolofonua (female). Human beings were created from maggots or worms. The first woman was called Kohai and the man Momo. (Collocott 1921:152–153; Gifford 1924:14–15.)

The recurrent theme throughout the **Marquesas** legends is again genealogical, intercourse between Ātea* (sky father) and One-u'i (earth mother), and there exists no single god of creation (Handy 1923:328–329). One Marquesan legend, however, describes how Papa-uka (world above) and Papa-oa (world beneath) produced numerous progeny including the gods Tāne, Ātea, Tokohiti, etc., before their was light. Ātea finally stamped his foot, a hole appeared, and the gods climbed out, each settling in the land that pleased them. (Christian 1895:187–202.)

Two neighboring island groups, the **Tuamotus** and the **Society Islands**, have the same fundamental story of the creation—the beginning of the universe in the form of an egg. In the Tuamotuan version, the bottom layer of the egg contains Tū-Tumu and Tū-Papa who create earth life, the first human beings (Hoatea* and Hoatu*), animals, and plants (Henry 1928:347–349). The Tahitian version maintains that the supreme god Ta'aroa, without father or mother, dwelt in the egg for eons of time before he broke out of his shell and began the act of creation. From the two parts of the shell he created the heavens and earth, and from parts of his body he created various life forms of the earth (Henry 1928:336–344).

In **Mangaia** (Cook Islands), the world and creation are referred to as a growing plant, or the hallow of a vast coconut divided up into six layers (See drawing in Gill 1876:2–3). In the lower portion of the coconut lies the goddess Vari-ma-te-takere* (fertile mud or slime) and from her own body she plucks her six children, Avatea (Vatea or first man), Tumu-te-ana-ao (echo), Tinirau (Kinilau*), Raka, Tango (wind god), and Tū-metua. From the union of Vatea and Papa, several children were born: Tangaroa, Rongo, Tonga-iti, Tāne-papa-kai, Tangiia, and Te Rā-kura-iti, the ancestors of all created beings. (Buck 1934:9–18, 23.) See also **Heavens; Kore; Man; Woman.**

–D–

DELUGE. Numerous Polynesian stories of a great flood have been recorded by Westerners, but most are considered by modern scholars as being spurious or of questionable origin. The **Ra'iāteans** tell the story of two friends, Te-aho-roa and Ro'o, who went fishing. They happened upon the sleeping place of the ocean god Rua-hatu. When they drop their fishhooks into the deep, they hit his head, and he became enraged. Rising to the surface, he swore he would cause Ra'iātea to sink below the sea before the night was over. The two mortals repented of their mistake, and Rua-hatu warned them that they can escape only if they bring their families to that spot (the islet of Toa-marama.) The two friends convinced their families as well as members of the royal family to set sail with them that evening.

During the night while they are sleeping, the whole island of Ra'iātea slipped under the ocean and then rose again the next morning. Nothing was saved except the two friends and their families. Within a month, however, new buds and growth sprang forth and provided food for those who had escaped the flood. Afterwards they erected sacred *marae* (temples) and dedicated them to the god Rua-hatu. Rua-hatu is also the god responsible for opening passages in the reefs around the islands so that humans can navigate safely. (Henry 1928: 445–452.)

On the island of **Tahiti**, a legend relates a similar story of a great deluge. No reason for the tragedy is given, but the whole island, save Mount Pito-hiti, sunk beneath the waves. One human couple gathered up their domesticated animals and together fled to Mount Pito-hiti where they spent ten days until the flood subsided. For a great while, the family had little or no food, but soon plants sprouted, and the human family flourished once again. (Henry 1928: 448–452.)

In **Hawai'i**, Nu'u and his wife Lili-noe (or Nu'u-mealani) survived a great flood and found themselves atop Mauna Kea on the Big Island. He made sacrifices to the moon who he thought has saved him, but the creator god Kāne* descended to earth on a rainbow, explained Nu'u's mistake, and accepted his offerings. (Beckwith 1948: 314–315; Fornander 1878:34–43, 91–95; Fornander 1920:269–270, 335.)

In **New Zealand**, Rua-tapu* became angry because his father Ue-nuku* elevated a more noble, but junior brother ahead of him in seniority. In revenge, he took a boat load of noble sons far out into the sea and drowned them. He called upon his gods to bring a great flood and to destroy all of his enemies. Only Paikea's* family survived. (Beckwith 1948:319; White 1887c:9–13, 23–31, 36–41, 48–58.)

The **Marquesans** tell of how the great war god Tū* became distressed because of the disparaging remarks made by his sister Hii-hia. His tears bore straight through the floor to the world below. Clouds developed, and a torrent of rain rushed down into the valleys where it carried away everything in its path. Only six people were saved. (Handy 1930:110.)

–E–

'E'EKE, husband of Līhau and father of Pu'u-laina. According to Hawaiian legend, 'E'eke fell in love with his sister-in-law, Pu'u-wai-o-hina, and the goddess Hina-i-ka-'uluau placed a *kapu* on the two lovers. When they broke the *kapu*, they were changed into two mountain features. In west Maui, the summit crater is named 'E'eke and the peak by Olowalu is named Līhau. (Beckwith 1948: 189.)

EEL GOD, see **Coconut, Origin of; Hina; Tuna.**

EHO, a god of the Chatham Islands. (Shand 1894:90.)

EIKIMOTUA, a Tongan god who, along with Eikitufunga* (craftsman) and Vaeuka (well-formed leg) transformed the brother of Vaenuku* into the most handsome man ever seen. The jealous Vaenuku, however, killed his brother, and the gods swore they would never create such a handsome man again. (Collocott 1928:51.)

EIKITUFUNGA, craftsman, a Tongan god. See **Eikimotua.**

EITUMATUPUA, another name for the Tongan god of creation, Tangaloa (Kanaloa*).

EKEITEHUA, also called Singano,* brother to the god Tehainga'atua,* was originally born of a mortal couple on Bellona Island. He and his sister Teu'uhi* were adopted by the goddess 'Iti'iti and her father Sikingingangi, sky deities of Bellona. His two wives were Moeanga (no children) and Teungitaka, mother of all of his children. According to another tradition, Ekeitehua as a sister goddess to the god Ekeitehua, possesses people and makes them mad. (Monberg 1966:57, 78.) See also **Sikingimoemoe.**

ELEILAKEMBA, the god of Thenu, Lau Islands (Polynesian outliers in Fiji). (Hocart 1929: 197.)

'ELE'IO, a swift runner on the island of Maui whose primary task was to bring fresh fish daily from Hāna (East Maui) to the chief of Lahaina (West Maui). Three times during one of his trips, he was pursued by a spirit named Ka-ahu-'ula (red cape), and once 'Ele'io's sister, Pōhākū-loa, frightened the spirit away by exposing her body to it. When 'Ele'io changed his route from north to south to avoid the annoying spirit, he encountered the departed spirit of the high chiefess Kanikani-a-'ula.* He took time from his duties to restore her to life. Upon his late arrival in Lahaina, 'Ele'io found an oven prepared for his death. He was saved, however, when he presented the restored Kanikani-a-'ula to the chief for his wife. (Beckwith 1948:151–

152). **Hiku-i-ka-nahele; Hutu; Kena; Milimili; Pare.**

'ELEPAIO BIRD, a Hawaiian flycatcher (*Chasiempis sandwichensis*), worshipped as a goddess of canoe makers. When a canoe is to be constructed, the priest selects a tree in the forest. He then waits for an flycatcher to land on the tree. If it runs up and down on it, the trunk will be sound, but if it stops to peck at a spot, then surely the inner part of the tree is rotten and not suitable for a canoe. (Beckwith 1948:91; Fornander 1916:458, 462; Westervelt 1915b:100.)

ELO, Samoan ruler of the underworld* (Pulotu*). (Turner 1884:222–223.) See also **Milu; Nafanua; Saveasiuleo.**

ELVES AND FAIRIES. Traditions common throughout the Pacific tell of bands of small, supernatural characters who inhabit the islands and who sometimes appear to mortal beings. In **Hawai'i**, they are called the Menehune,* in **New Zealand** the Ponaturi* or the Patupaiarehe.* Though they do not bear names dialectically related to each other, they share characteristics that are common from one island group to another. These little folk generally live in caves in the interior of the islands. They are the islands' original inhabitants, and since the coming of the Europeans, they have almost totally vanished. These elves or fairies are active only at night during which time they toil in building large stone works, canoes, or islands, while singing or chattering noisily away. They are usually friendly to humans, but they do possess magic that could cause them ill. Sometimes they annoy others by stealing objects, performing tricks, or telling jokes. More often, they frighten humans during their nocturnal peregrinations.

In the Laka* legends, for example, these sprite, woodland spirits appear nightly to restore the tree that was felled by Laka during the day. On the third night, Laka remains awake and captures their leader, Toahiti, who promises to build Laka's canoe if he is released. The spirits set to work, and the next morning they sail the completed canoe into Lake's bay where they then accompany him on his great journey of adventure. (Andersen 1928:115–156.)

In **New Zealand**, numerous stories are told of elves and fairies. For example, Kahukura* comes upon a troop of Patupaiarehe at night while they are pulling in their fish nets. He gives them some help, but when they find out he is mortal, they flee and leave their nets behind. Kahukura takes the nets home, and since then, mortals have known the art of making fish nets.

On **Mangaia**, elves or fairies are called Tapairu, named after the four daughters of Miru (Milu*), deformed goddess of the underworld.* Their brother Tautiti presides over dancing, and they delight in making their appearance whenever mortals perform the dance named after him. These nocturnal fairies are also associated with the worship of the god Tāne. (Gill 1876: 256–257.)

In **Hawai'i**, stories of the Menehune are legion. They have been specially collected together in works by William Rice, Thomas G. Thrum, and Abraham Fornander. Other delightful children's books continue to appear to show the strong belief yet today of these small pixies. (Beckwith 1948: 321–336; Luomala 1951; Rice 1923; Thrum 1907.) See also **Mu People.**

ENEENE, a Mangaian mortal who successfully visited the underworld* to rescue his wife, Kura,* who had fallen through a hole and captured by the spirits who caught her. (Gill 1876:221–224.)

'ERE'ERE-FENUA, a powerful Tahitian goddess, wife of Tuatapuanui and mother of numerous other deities. She is accompanied by storms and/or war. (Henry 1928:359.)

−F−
(See also Wh)

FĀ, the feather plume of red feathers worn in the Tuamotus, invested with the sacred spirit of the gods. Also refers to the altar of a *marae** (temple) formed of four upright slabs of coral set in a square and open at the top. (Stimson 1964:69.)

FA'AHOTU, the mother of the gods Ro'o* (a defier of magicians and evil spirits—a disenchanter), Tahu,* and many other Tahitian gods and goddesses; the wife of Ātea (Wākea*) in the Tuamotuan legends; also the wife of Te-fatu* who gave birth to Hina,* and thus mother-in-law to Ti'i (Tiki*), the first man. (Henry 1928:210, 349, 372, 373, 402.)

FA'A'ĪPŌ, an important Tahitian household god. Possibly the same as Fa'a'ipu.* (Henry 1928: 377.)

FA'A'IPU, one of the old goddesses in Tahitian legends who are guardians of the world. Possibly the same as Fa'aīpō, Nihoniho-tetei,* 'Ōrerorero,* Tahua,* and Tāmaumau-'ōrere.* (Henry 1928:416.)

FAAMALU, a Samoan god to whom prayers are addressed to avenge thievery; also a Samoan war god whose earthly representations in the form of a fish or cloud foretells the outcome of the adventure. (Turner 1884:26–27.)

FAAOLA, a Samoan war god who bestows bravery upon those who worship him. (Turner 1884:27–28.)

FA'ARAVA'I-TE-RA'I, a handsome blue shark, a messenger for the Tahitian god of creation Ta'aroa (Kanaloa*). (Henry 1928:356, 361, 404.)

FA'ARUA, the Tahitian wind from the north created by the god Te-fatu-tiri* (the god of thunder and lightning). (Henry 1928:394.)

FA'A-TAE, one of the artisans who helped the Tahitian creator god Ta'aroa (Kanaloa*). Others mentioned are 'Amara,* Huri-'aro,* Huri-tua,* Nana,* and Rauti.* (Henry 1928:356, 406.)

FA'ATUPU, an important Tahitian household god. (Henry 1928:377.)

FĀFĀ, one of the learned artisans for the Tahitian god Tāne (Kāne.*) (Henry 1928:370, 455.)

FAFIE, a patron god of ocean voyaging of Fakaofu, Tokelau Islands. He can take the form of a great canoe and travel to distant islands. Possibly he is a deified high chief who once lost a wrestling match to the god Toikia* and was worshipped even before his death. (Macgregor 1937:60, 62.)

FAI, a Tahitian ocean god in the creation chant, the son of Tiki* and Kahu-one. (Henry 1928:356.) Also the name of the first human being in Marquesan legends who obtained fire for use by humans. He obtained it from the gods Natia-i-te-pu, Māhuike,* and Iike, who lived in a cave on the top of the mountain. Fai returned with it and taught the people how to use it. (Handy 1930:103–104; Steinen 1934:213–218.)

FA'IFA'IMALIE, a Samoan god in Tongan myth who was the first to cultivate the yam from which the Tongan goddess Fe-huluni* stole some of its fruit to transport to her own islands of Tongan. (Gifford 1924:178–180; Krämer 1902:203.)

FAIMALIE, an old Tongan goddess who visited the underworld* (Pulotu*) with four other gods (Haveatoke,* Faka-fuumaka,* Haelefeke,* and Lohi*), successfully defeated the forces of the underworld in drinking, eating, and sporting games, and secretly brought back the yam to the upper world for food. (Gifford 1924:155–170; Reiter 1934:497–514.)

FAINGAA, a Tongan goddess who was in love with Pasikole,* a Samoan who once lived in Tonga. (Gifford 1924:197–199.)

FAKAFOTU, a god of storms and hurricanes from Fakaofu, Tokelau Islands. He also appears in the form of a great tree. (Macgregor 1937:60.)

FAKAFUHU, god of the village of Kanokupulu, Tonga. (Collocott 1921:231.)

FAKAFUUMAKA, a Tongan god who once visited the underworld* (Pulotu*) with three other gods (Haveatoke, Haelefeke, and Lohi*) and goddess (Faimalie*) and collectively defeated the forces of the underworld in drinking, eating, and sporting games. (Gifford 1924: 155–170.)

FAKAHOKO, a war god and one of the five major gods of the island of Niue. (Loeb 1926:157–159.) See also **Faō; Huanaki; Lageiki; Lagiatea.**

FAKAHOTU, wife of the sky god Ātea (Wākea*) in Tuamotuan legends; also the goddess of feasting mats who holds authority under Tonga, the god of the forest and its creatures. (Stimson 1964:73.) As queen of the eight heavens in the Hiro* epic, she became the mistress of Hiro and became pregnant. When Hiro sets out on his long adventure, nothing more is heard of her. (Stimson 1957; Smith 1903:232.)

FAKAKONAATUA, a god of Niue Island associated with meteors and thunder, prayed to before battle to poison the gods of the enemy. (Loeb 1926:161.) See also **Ave-aitu; Rongomai.**

FAKALAGALAGA, a war god of Niue Island. (Loeb 1926:161.)

FAKAPAETE, a god of Niue Island invoked in order to be protected against the enemy's stones. (Loeb 1926:161.)

FAKAPATU, a Tongan god who dwells in an ocean cave on Mo'unga'one island. Once the shark god Tui Tofua visited Fakapatu to put an end to the continual noise coming from his cave. Fakapatu, however, was not at home, so Tui Tofua entered and made himself at home. When Fakapatu returned, Tui Tofua opened his wide mouth ready to swallow Fakapatu. Fakapatu turned himself into a small fish called the *meai* and entered Tui Tofua's stomach. There he began swelling larger and larger until Tui Tofua could stand it no longer. He offered Fakapatu all types of rewards if he would stop his torment. He finally promised that he would molest none of the people of Mo'unga'one as they traveled from one island to the another. This promised satisfied Fakapatu, and he shrank in size and left Tui Tofua's stomach. This is why the people of Mo'unga'one say they are never bitten by sharks. (Gifford 1924:81–82.) A variant story states that it was the giant Taufatahi, lord of fishes, who swallowed Faka-patu and who thus swore never to bother the people of Mo'ungan'one ever again. (Gifford 1924:82–83.) See also **Tui Tofua.**

FAKAPOLOTO, a god of Niue Island invoked in making neck-laces. (Loeb 1926:164.)

FAKATAFETAU, a war god of Liku, Niue Island. (Loeb 1926:160.)

FAKAVELIKELE, an ancestral god worshipped on Futuna. (Burrows 1936:105–108.)

FALEKAHO, a malevolent god of Makefu, Niue Island, who kills people. (Loeb 1926:160.)

FALE'ULA, a house on the is-land of Manu'a, Samoa, the first residence of the gods on earth that later became the home of the high-ranking chiefs, the Tui Manu'a.* (Krämer 1902: 392.)

FANONGA, a Samoan war god, usually represented in the form of an owl, to whom Samoans offer food sacrifices. (Turner 1884:25–26.)

FĀO, one of the first two gods (mortals ?) to swim from Tonga to settle Niue. (Turner 1884: 304.) Also named as one of the

five principal gods of Niue. He came up from beneath the earth at a pool in the reef and established a residence at Toga-liulu. (Loeb 1926:157–159; Smith 1903:1–31.) See also **Fakahoko; Huanaki; Lageiki; Lagiatea.**

FAOA, the Tuamotuan word for ancient lore, records, sayings, discourses, or spells. (Stimson 1964:78.)

FARE-ATA, the name of Māui*-karukaru's house in the nether-world according to Tuamotuan legends. (Stimson 1964:80.)

FĀRO, an artisan for the Tahi-tian god Ta'ere-ma-'opo'opo,* who dwells in the center of the earth. (Henry 1928:374, 406.) See also **Creation; Heavens.**

FAROA, a sacred, red-feathered plume of a Tuamotuan priest that represents the supreme de-ity. (Stimson 1964:81.)

FARUIA, an ancient navigator, giant, and warrior who is ven-erated on the island of Fakahina in the Tuamotus. (Audran 1919: 235–236.)

FATAA-KOKA, a Marquesan sorceress whose grandson, Puhi-nui-aau-too, was born in the shape of an eel to his mother, Hina-ooi-fatu, and fa-ther, Au-too. His grandmother nurtured him to maturity. After seducing his sisters, Kua-nui and Kua-iti, and fighting with his brothers ,Tai-mumuhu and Tai-vavena, he was finally reunited with his parents and family. (Handy 1930:78–81.)

FATALEVAVE, an ancient Fijian chief and demigod, the son of Tuifiti and Sinafiti, who sailed to 'Upolu, Samoa, married Maugaoali'i of Vaimaga, and had a son named Puatau. He then married the daughter of Sitagata and had sons, Leu and Tauiliili, and a daughter, Talalaufala. Tauiliili became the ancestor of the rulers of Amaile, Samoa. (Krämer 1902:303.)

FATITIRITAKATAKA, a minor god in the Tuamotus, one of the leaders of the spirit legions of Kiho* (the supreme god). (Stimson 1964:83.)

FATUKURA, one of two stars rising over the horizon in November said to be evil gods in Tuamotuan legends. (Stimson 1964:84.)

FATU-KURA-A-TĀNE, one of the leaders of the Tuamotuan spirit legions of the god Kiho* (the supreme god). He acts as Kiho's messenger to his followers. (Stimson 1964:84.)

FATU-NU'U, a Tahitian god of the adze, invoked by the hero Rata (Laka*) to aid him in the construction his famous canoe. (Henry 1928:484.)

FATUPUAA-MA-LE-FEE, an inferior household god of Samoa. (Turner 1884:72.)

FATU-TIRI, the god of thunder in Tahiti from whom the god Tāne (Kāne*) obtained thunderbolts (Fatu-'ura-tāne*) in his fight against the great god Ātea (Wākea.*) (Henry 1928: 350.)

FATU-'URA-TĀNE, the name of the thunderbolt used by the Tahitian god Tāne (Kāne*) to destroy the great god Ātea (Wākea*). (Henry 1928:351.) See also **Futu-tiri**.

FAUMEA, an eel-woman in the Tuamotus, who had eels in her vagina. The god Tangaroa (Kanaloa*) visited her island to court her, and she taught him how to entice the eels outside. He slept with her, and they had two children, Tū-nui-ka-rere and Turi-a-faumea. Turi-a-faumea took Hina-a-rauriki to wife, but she was kidnapped by the demon octopus Rogo-tumu-here and taken to the bottom of the sea. Tangaroa and Turi launched their boat while Faumea caught the wind in her armpit. The octopus was slain, and Hina was rescued. (Stimson Ms.) See also **Haumea.**

FE'E, a Samoan war god, brought to the island of Manu'a by the god Tagaloa (Kanaloa*) who found him floating on a piece of coral. He became the father of the gods, Sinā-sa'umani* and Sasa'umani,* and ruled the underworld* (Pulotu) for a while. When he departed, his son Saveasi'uleo* became ruler. A festival to his honor was held at Leulumaega on the north coast of Aana. According to another legend, he created the large hole in the reef of Apia harbor when he came to visit his bride at Vaimauga (outside of Apia) where a temple called Faleopouma'a was built in his honor. His earthly representation is that of the cuttlefish or octopus, and their actions foretell the outcome of battles. (Krämer 1902:45, 152–153, 229–231; Turner 1884:28–32.)

FEHULUNI, a Tongan goddess who journeyed to Samoa to obtain starts of the yam in order to introduce it into Tonga. (Gifford 1924:178–180.) See also **Faifaimalie.**

FEHUNUI, a Tongan god. See **Tui Haatala.**

F E K E, an octopus god responsible for the creation of the island of Tikopia. (Firth 1967:38–40.)

FENU, a spirt spirit who resides on Nukunono, Tokelau Islands, and who once chased away a similar spirit from Fakaofu who had invaded his territory in the search of fresh water. (Macgregor 1937:62–63.)

FENUA, the earth goddess in the Tuamotuan story of the creation. (Henry 1928:347.) Also a god of Nukunono islet, Tokelau Islands. (Macgregor 1937:61.) See also **Creation; Heavens.**

FE'U, one of the many artisans for the Tahitian god Ta'ere-mā-'opo'opo,* who dwells in the center of the earth. (Henry 1928:374, 406.)

FIALELE, a god of Niue Island, who lives in and governs the cliffs. (Loeb 1926:161.)

FINAU-TAU-IKU, a Tongan god worshipped in the form of a lizard in east Tongatapu. (Collocott 1921:227.)

FINELASI, an ancestral god worshipped on Futuna. (Burrows 1936:105–108.)

FIRE, DISCOVERY OF. See **Āo-āo-mā-ra'i-ā; Fai; Mafui'e; Matuku; Māui.**

FIRIFIRI-'AUFAU, a Tahitian goddess, a genealogist, who is one of the old guardians of the world. The other guardians are 'Aiaru,* Fa'a'ipu,* Nihonihotetei,* 'Ōrerorero,* Tahu'a,* and Tāmaumau-'orere.* (Henry 1928:417.)

FITI, an ancient god of Avetele, Niue Island, famous for his fishing exploits. (Loeb 1926:162.)

FITIAUMUA, a ancient Samoan who conquered the entire chain of island and who became the first king of Samoa. According to the legend, he was born to his parents, both named Veu, in exile on the Rose Atoll because they had eaten from the breadfruit trees belonging to chief Tufulemata'afa. When Fitiaumua was grown, he made two strong ironwood clubs, and with the aid of the god Tagaloa (Kanaloa*) waged war on Samoa. He returned to his native island of Manu'a where he became the first king of all of Samoa, the Tui Manu'a.* (Krämer 1902:434–436.) Another legend says that he first conquered all of Fiji before he invaded Samoa. (Turner 1884:224.)

FITIHULUGIA, a god of Niue Island. (Loeb 1926:161.)

FITI-KAI-KERE, gods responsible for erecting stone walls in various places around the island of Tikopia by using their supernatural powers. This activity annoyed the gods Pua* and Ma,* who were afraid that their reputation and prestige would suffer by comparison. They, therefore, drove the Fiti-kai-kere from the island by digging a hole in the ground and forcing them into it until they disappeared. One Fiti-kai-kere by the name of Singano* survived, however, and he married a relative and became the ancestor of the group of Tikopians called Nga Faea. (Firth 1961:41, 91.)

FITIKILA, a war god of Hakupu, Niue Island. (Loeb 1926:160.)

FITU, an ancestral god worshipped on Futuna. (Burrows 1936:105–108.)

FOGE, a Samoan rain god from the island of Savai'i. He and and the god or goddess Toafa* are represented in the form of two oblong, smooth stones and are said to be the parents of the rain goddess Saato.* (Krämer 1902:23, 58; Stübel 1896:149–150; Turner 1884:24–25.)

FOILAPE, one of the two principal gods on the island of Nukufetau, Tuvalu. (Turner 1884:285.) See also Tevae.

FO'ISIA, an ancient Samoan chief, the Tui'ofu, who waged war against Tui'olosega. When he saw that the village might be defeated, he relinquished his title, and jumped into the sea where he was changed into a tall black rock located on the southwest corner of 'Ofu. (Krämer 1902:451.)

FONO-KI-TANGATA, a Tongan god worshipped by chief Valu in Utulau, central Tongatapu. (Collocott 1921:232.)

FONOLAPE, a principal god on the island of Nukulaelae, Tu

valu, represented by a stone. (Turner 1884:280–281.)

FOLAHA, one of the principal gods on Nanumea, Tuvalu. (Turner 1884:291.)

FONU, turtle god of Futuna. (Burrows 1936:105–108.)

FOTOGFURU, a malevolent god of Rotuma. (Gardiner 1898: 468.)

FOTOKIA, a reef god of Niue Island. (Loeb 1926:161.)

FOUMA, Rotuma's greatest ancient warrior. Once, a giant from Tonga named Serimana walked across the sea to Rotuma with his beautiful daughter Sulmata, who met and married Fouma. Eventually a large continent of Tongans came looking for Serimana, and when they arrived, a conflict broke out between them and Fouma. After numerous attempts on his life, Fouma's friend Onunfanua arrived and in one swoop cut through a large tree with his left hand. The splinters killed more than half the Tongans, and the remainder rushed to their canoes and set sail for home. Knowing that Serimana was behind the entire conflict, Fouma crushed him and his house in one blow of his club. (Gardiner 1898:510–512.)

FUAILAGI, the creator of the heavens according to Samoan tradition who dug up the earth and created a new island, but a debate between him and chief Niuleamoa caused them to go from one place to another to place it. They finally wound up anchoring the island between 'Ofu and Ta'ū, the island now called Olosega because chief Sega married the girl Olo. Also, Fuailagi is known in Samoa as a fierce war god who takes the form of a sea eel. (Krämer 1902:450–451; Turner 1884:32.)

FUTIFONUA, one of the gods on Niue Island invoked in time of hunger. (Loeb 1926:161.) See also **Futimotu.**

FUTIMOTU, one of the gods on Niue Island invoked in time of hunger. (Loeb 1926:161.) See also **Futifonua.**

–G–
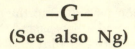
(See also Ng)

GA'E, a Samoan war god whose earthly representation is a plaited coconut basket. (Turner 1884:32–33.)

GAI'O, a Samoan god in the creation that gave life to a rock from the depths of the turbulent sea that became wife to the creator god Tagaloa (Kanaloa*) and mother to the messenger Tuli.* (Krämer 1902:395.) Also the god sent down to earth to the island of Manu'a to create human life from the maggots born from Tagaloa's creeping plant. (Krämer 1902:396–397.) He was assisted by the gods Gaitosi and Gaiva'ava'ai. (Stair 1892:212.)

GALUMALEMANA, an ancient Samoan chief responsible for the introduction of the custom of giving fine mats to the chief's servants upon his death. All descendants of Galumalemana are nobles (*aloali'i*). (Krämer 1902:29.)

GAUGANO, a primeval god of Bellona Island, represented in the form of a smooth, dolerite stone approximately two feet high, brought to the island by the first immigrant, Kaituu, along with another smaller stone representing the goddess Gauteaki.* They two were set up at a sacred spot called Gavenga and were later smashed with the introduction of Christianity. (Bradley 1956:333.)

GAUTEAKI, a primeval goddess of Bellona Island. (Bradley 1956: 333.) See also **Gaugano**.

GEGĒ, a Samoan god who lived at Falealili, island of 'Upolu. He once killed the demons from the island of Savai'i by changing them into stone. (Krämer 1902:288; Stübel 1896:81.)

GHOSTS. To the ancient Polynesians, there existed a distinction between the departed spirit of an individual and its ghost. Spirits who had entered the underworld* were invisible, but those who remained on earth for one reason or another could appear visible to mortals. These ghosts were generally malevolent and did physical harm. Such ghosts, for example, were warriors slain in battle or those who had met an untimely or violent death. Often these ghosts became demons mentioned in many of the Polynesian myths. There are instances of ghosts returning from the dead and making unprovoked attacks upon the living, or tearing their eyes out or causing sickness. Even cannibalistic spirits were known to have terrified the ancient Polynesians.

It was also believed that not until the proper treatment of the corpse could the spirit of the deceased settle comfortably in the next world. As a result, bodies were preserved by the living until all the flesh had disappeared, and the bones were then properly buried in secret places. In Hawai'i, for example, the ghost of Pūmai'a visited his wife and revealed where his body had been thrown so that she could give it a decent and proper burial. In the Hi'iaka* legend (see also Pele*), a drowned man's ghost wanders aimlessly until Hi'iaka forces it back into its body, whereupon, the body slowly returned to life.

Not all ghosts, however, were evil in intent. There were frequent references to ancestral spirits who returned to protect or to give advice to their progeny. And there were always the guardian spirits who came at death to meet the soul and to accompany it on its journey to the underworld. In all, stories of ghosts provided entertainment to the ancient Polynesians much as they have to other cultures throughout the world.

GIANTS. Many Polynesian legends mention giants having lived in the islands, some purely fictional but others may have been historical characters whose extreme heights have been expanded with time.

In **Hawai'i**, the most renown is Kana,* a giant 2,400 feet tall, whose limbs can stretch and return similar to a telescope. The Hawaiian kings 'Umi,* Lano, Līloa,* and Kihu were supposedly eight or nine feet tall. See also **Kanaloa-huluhulu.**

The **Samoans** tell of a giant race whose friendly leader Tafai (Tarohaki*) could throw a coconut tree as a spear and whose steps crushed prints into solid rock. Losi,* the famous fisherman who instigated the war in heaven, was one of these individuals. Another was Tele.

Many giants appear in **Māori** legends. The South Island of New Zealand supposedly was once inhabited by a group called Kāhu-tupua. They could step from one mountain range to another, swallow whole rivers in a single gulp, and transform themselves into any form they wished. (Tregear 1891:465; White 1887c:189.) One named Ka-whara was twenty four feet tall, and Rau-kawa (ancestor of the Ngāti-Rau-kawa tribe) was over thirty. The bones of chief Tahourangi were nine feet and were used for a long time in sacred ceremonies. Tama-te-kapua* was defeated in a single battle by Ruaeo,* both nine feet tall.

Moke, the son of Tavare in the **Cook Islands** (Mangaia) was sixty feet tall, and his foot prints in the rocks today measure two feet eight inches in length. Te Manavaroa's graves supposedly covers the whole island, with his two arms forming two mountain ranges two and three miles in length.

The giants in the **Tuamotus** are called Hīvas or Tavas, a

foreign race, and several stories tell of them landing on the islands and causing all kinds of destruction. When two Hivas landed at Ngake (Marokau Island), they were slain by Te Huo and Mati,* but not after their struggle had formed an immense hole in the ground. Two others, Tapuae-huritini and Te Mangareva, were formed on Takaora Island by Rumaere. Another story relates that three Tavas, Te Taukup, Ru,* and one unnamed, arrived on Hao and took refuge in the *marae** (temple) where they stayed for some time. When they were fed a roasted dog, they were furious and went into a rage. They tore up the reef, broke down coconut trees, and threatened the lives of all on the island. One Tava was particularly interesting. It was Hitiraumea, a giant who had gills under his ears, which he could use while swimming. (Audran 1918:90–92.)

GUTUFOLO, a god of Niue Island, invoked when fishing. (Loeb 1926:161.)

–H–

HĀ, the name of the supreme god in the Tuamotu Islands. (Stimson 1964:101.)

HA'A, a class of hairless dogmen in ancient Hawaiian legends. Sometimes called *'ōlohe** (cannibals), they had supernatural powers and human form with tails like dogs. They were professionals who killed and robbed travelers along the roads. The most famous *ha'a* in Hawaiian legend is Kū-'īlio-loa.* See also **Kaupẹ Puapua-lenalena.**

HAAHAU, a pool in Felema (island of 'Uiha, Ha'apai, Tonga) turned bitter because the Tongans disregarded the command of the gods to keep it covered. (Collocott 1928:11.)

HA'AKAUILANĀ, servant of the god Wākea* and progenitor of the slave class (*kauwā*) in Hawaiian legend. After divorcing Wākea, Papa* lived with Ha'akauilanā, and their offspring become the ancestors of the *kauwā* class. (Beckwith 1948:300; Malo 1903:69, 96–100.)

HA'ALELE-KĪ-NANA or **'ALE-LE-KĪ-NANA**, the first idol known to ancient Hawaiians. Ha'alele-kī-nana was a son of Hoa-make-i-ke-kula,* a chiefess of high rank from Kohala. When he was born, he was in the form of a wooden image. It was this first image that gave the Hawaiians the idea of carving the forms of gods out of wood. (Beckwith 1948:515–516; Fornander 1916:538, 540.)

HAAMATA-KEE, a Marquesan goddess who instructed her artisans to fashion great idols out of stone. (Christian 1895:189.)

HA'APUA-'INANEA, a lizard woman and companion of Up-oho in Hawaiian mythology. Both are servants of the goddess Nā-maka-o-kaha'i* who befriended the romantic hero 'Au-kele-nui-a-iku.* (Beckwith 1948:490–493; Fornander 1917: 42, 54, 58.)

HAELEFEKE, a Tongan god responsible for first bringing the *ava* (milk fish) from Samoa to Tonga. (Gifford 1924:84, 86.) A Tongan god who visited the underworld* (Pulotu*) with three other gods (Fakafuumaka, Haelefeke, and Lohi) and goddess (Faimalie*) and collectively defeated the forces of the underworld in drinking, eating, and sporting games. (Collocott 1921:231; Gifford 1924:155–175.) Also a Samoan god who unsuccessfully attempted to steal some of the Tongan islands. (Gifford 1924:89–90.) See also **Heimoana; Moso.**

HAENŌ-VAIRURA, or **HAE-NŌ-VAIURUA**, also known as Oā-hī-vari,* a Tahitian god of marshlands who takes on a human form, dwells in the depths of the mud, and shoots up into the air at night. (Henry 1928:376–377.)

HAERE, a Māori god who resides in rainbows or clouds. (Tregear 1891:41.) See also **Kahukura.**

HAERE-AWAAWA, mother goddess of the rail and kiwi birds in Māori legends. (White 1887a:1943; Tregear 1891:41.)

HAHA-POA, a Marquesan who killed his wife because of her infidelity. After her spirit had gone to Havaiki (Hawaiki*) or the underworld,* Haha-poa set out to bring her back. He followed the instructions of a diviner who told him to carry seven candlenuts for light and a cloth to cover his wife's eyes. Once he reached the depths of the underworld, he found his wife's spirit, covered her head with the cloth, and packed her off in a basket. His wife pleaded to be let go, but Haha-poa kept strictly to his orders. Finally his wife promised him sexual intercourse should he let her go. Haha-poa gave in, released his wife, and as they made love, the last candlenut burned out leaving them in the dark. They became separated, and Haha-poa finally made his way back home, but he had lost his wife forever. (Handy 1930:121–122.)

HAHO, a Maui chief, the son of Paumakua* and grandson of Hua-nui-ka-la'ila'i, considered the traditional founder of the sacred class of chiefs in ancient Hawai'i called the *'aha-ali'i*,* who were deified upon death. (Beckwith 1948:378; Malo 1903: 322–323.)

HA'I, abbreviated form of Ha-'ina-kolo,* a Hawaiian goddess of tapa makers and bird catchers. (Beckwith 1948:506–510; Pukui 1971:381)

HA'INA-KOLO, the daughter of Kū-waha-ilo and his wife Hina* (sometimes referred to in chants as Ha'i-wahine* or simply Ha'i.) The Hawaiian romance of Ha'ina-kolo relates the tragic story of close intermarriage between members of a family living in Waipi'o Valley on the island of Hawai'i. Ha-'ina-kolo married her nephew Keaunini (Keanini), who lived in a distant land called Kū'ai-he-lani.* A son, called Leimakani, was born to them there, but after seven years, Keauanini left Ha'ina-kolo for the love of a former sweetheart.

Ha'ina-kolo and her son set out for her home in Hawai'i. In route, they were shipwrecked, but she and her son swam to shore. In shock, she headed inland at Waipi'o and left her son on the shore where he was found by Lu'ukia, his aunt. Not knowing his true identity, she took him home, and when he was grown, she married him.

When Lu'ukia discovered Leimakani was having an affair with her younger sister, she killed their son Lono-kai-olohi'a. Meanwhile, Ha'ina-kolo returned, and Leimakani's sorrowful chant restored his mother's sanity while both of their prayers bring Lono-kai-olohi'a back to life. Soon after, Keaunini returned to his family in Hawai'i, and they lived happily ever after. (Beckwith 1948:506–507; Emerson 1915: 143.)

HAI-PUKA, a Marquesan demigod who once lived under the sea. His sister, however, lived in a valley on the island with her son. When the boy was slain by his enemies, the mother called for Hai-puka's aid. He rose up out of the water, bathed in magical water prepared by his sister, and became a handsome man. Hai-puka then set out and avenged the death of his nephew. (Handy 1930:136.)

HA'I-WAHINE, also known as Ha'ina-kolo,* an Hawaiian goddess, symbolized by a ti leaf worn around the neck of the hula instructor. (Emerson 1909: 20; Fornander 1880:49, 56–57.) Also the name of a shark god who transported Laka's* body from Kualoa, O'ahu, to Maui. (Beckwith 1948:264; Fornander 1878:191; Malo 1903:323.)

HAKALANILEO, father of the Hawaiian demigods Kana* and Nīheu* by his wife Hānai-a-ka-malama* (sometimes called Hina*). (Beckwith 1948:464–466; Fornander 1917:436–449, 1917:518–521, 1920:158, 489–491.)

HAKAMOE-NUKU, a Tuamotuan god who supposedly destroyed Hawaiki,* the ancient homeland of the Polynesians, by making it sink beneath the sea. (Stimson 1964:109.)

HAKAOHO, a Marquesan god, principally worshipped on Nuku Hiva, the son of Papa-Uka and Papa-Ao in the creation. (Christian 1895:187–202.)

HAKASAOHENUA, one of the many district gods of the Kaitu'u clan on Bellona and Rennell Islands, the son of the principal god Tehu'aingabenga.* (Monberg 1966:67.)

HAKAU, see **'Umi.**

HĀKAWAU, a legendary Māori sorcerer who heard of the reputation of a magician named Puarata* and of his talisman, a magical wooden head on Sacred Mountain, that killed all who came near. Gathering his spells and enchantments, he set out to destroy the power of the wooden image. Arriving at Sacred Mountain, guarded by Puarata and Tautōhito, Hākawau let loose his benevolent genii who attacked and utterly destroyed the evil spirits of the

mountain. (Grey 1855:176; Grey 1970:216–220.)

HAKE, according to Tuamotuan legends, the human used as bait for Māui's* fishhook when he pulled up the islands from the ocean depths. See also **Aki.**

HAKIRERE, the Māori canoe used by Whakatea in his expedition to revenge the death of his friend Tūwhakaro.* (Grey 1855:62; Grey 1970:79.)

HAKIRIMAUREA, wife of the ancient Māori chief Tū-whakaraoa.*

HAKUMANI, a patron goddess of tapa making on Niue Island. (Loeb 1926:164.)

HAKUTURI, Māori fairies or elves, the offspring of the god Tāne (Kāne*) in the Rata (Laka*) epic. Each night when Rata fell a tree to build his great canoe, they righted it again, eventually, though, they finally agreed to complete his canoe for his great expedition. (Grey 1855:57; White 1887a:68.) See also **Elves and Fairies; Ponaturi.**

HALA-ANIANI, an interloper from Puna, island of Hawai'i, who through the aid of his sorceress sister prevented the marriage of Lā'ie-i-ka-wai* to her intended husband, Kekalukalu-o-ke-wā, a ruling chief on the island of Kaua'i. (Beckwith 1919; Beckwith 1948:527.)

Also the name of a woman transformed by the volcano goddess Pele* into a prominent rock on the Puna coast of the island of Hawai'i. (Emerson 1915.)

HALĀLI'I, chief of the malevolent spirits who once inhabited the island of O'ahu, Hawai'i. They cannibalized visitors from the island of Kaua'i who retaliated by substituting wooden images for human bodies, and then they burned the spirits as they feasted. (Beckwith 1948: 430, 444; Fornander 1916:476–482; Johnson ms.) See also **Hana'aumoe.**

HALAPOULI, a god of Niue Island, invoked when throwing the spear. (Loeb 1926:161.)

HALE-LEHUA, an allusion to the Hawaiian goddess or mermaid Moana-nui-ka-lehua* (a relative of the volcano goddess Pele*) whose home lies deep beneath the ocean channel between the islands of O'ahu and Kaua'i. (Pukui 1971:394.)

HALE-MANO, a romantic Hawaiian from the island of O'ahu who wooed the beautiful Kāma-lālā-walu from Puna (the Big Island). He died of grief from her rejection but was restored to life twice by his sorceress sister Laenihi. He finally won her affections, however, by mastering the art of the hula and the *kilu* (a sexual game). He eventually wearied of her infidelity, though, and left her to her lovers. (Beckwith 1948:523–425; Fornander 1917:228–263.)

HALE-MA'U-MA'U, name of the pit at Kī-lau-ea volcano on the island of Hawai'i, home of the goddess Pele* and her family.

HALEVAO, a god of Niue Island. (Loeb 1926:163.)

HĀLI'A-'ŌP U A or H A I L I-'ŌPUA, name of a Hawaiian sky god, piling-up-of-cloud-portents. (Emerson 1915:117.)

HALIUA, a god of Niue Island. (Loeb 1926:163.)

HĀLOA, son of Wākea* (first man) by his own daughter Ho-'ohoku-i-ka-lani* in Hawaiian legend. The first offspring of this union between father and daughter was in the form of a taro root. After being discarded, it sprouted into a taro plant, the origin of the plant in Hawai'i. When a normal child was born to them, they named him *Hā* (stalk) *loa* (length) after the plant. Wākea's angry wife Papa* (Haumea*) returned to Kahiki (Tahiti ?) where she miraculously became a young girl again. She took Hāloa, her grandson, as a husband, and from this union sprang the ruling chiefs of Hawai'i. (Beckwith 1948:280–281; 297–298; For nander 1878:190; Fornander 1920:319, Malo 1903:244.)

HALULU-I-KE-KIHI-O-KA-MOKU, a large man-eating bird from Kahiki* (Tahiti ?), said to have been born from the shoulder of his mother, Hau-mea,* and able to take human form. He was killed by the Hawaiian hero 'Au-kele-nui-a-iku.* (Beckwith 1948:91–92, 492, 496; Fornander 1916:64–67, 422; Emory 1924:12–13.)

HALULUKO'AKO'A, an Ha-waiian god who lives in the rainbow and who takes the form of the wind. Halulu-ko'ako'a is also the name of a *heiau* (temple) at Lahaina, Maui, where the demigod Māui* was taken prisoner by the priests looking for human sacrifices. (Fornander 1917:540.)

HAMA, an ancient Tongan sorcerer or clairvoyant who lived on the island of 'Eua. Through his divination, he discovered 'Ata, a small island southwest of 'Eua, reported the outcome of a fight that occurred many miles away on Tongatapu, and informed the high chief to what lands his pet bird had flown and the day of its return. (Collocott 1928:52–54.)

HAMI-KERE, a fish who received its black skin through the exploits of the great Tuamotuan hero Tahaki (Kaha'i.*) (Stimson 1937:89-90.)

HĀ-MURI, one of the first three coconuts born to Rā-tā'iri (sun god) and Pito-'ura in Tahitian legends. Hā-muri only bore very small coconuts called *ra'ita* while her brothers Pā-rapu and Toerau-roa bore the larger green and brown ones. (Henry 1928:421.) See also **Coconut, Origin of.**

HANA'AUMOE, one of the malevolent spirits on the island of O'ahu, Hawai'i, gifted in flattery. When all the spirits on O'ahu were slain by vengeful warriors from Kaua'i, Hana-'aumoe was the only spirit who managed to escape. (Beckwith 1948:444; Fornander 1916:476–483, 1917:428–435.) See also **Halāli'i.**

HĀNAI-IA-KA-MALAMA, another name for the Hawaiian goddess Hina.* (Beckwith 1948:220; Fornander 1880:17.) A benevolent goddess, the wife of Hakalanileo* and the mother of the demigods Kana* and Nī-heu* who presides over certain chiefly taboos. (Malo 1903:227; Emerson 1915:138.)

HANA-KAHI, an ancient Ha-waiian chief synonymous with profound peace and whose name is associated with the city of Hilo on the Big Island. (Pukui 1971:382 Emerson 1909:60.)

HANAKĀMĀLU, another name for the Hawaiian underworld*

found in the chant of Kāwelu.*
Before Kāwelu strangled herself, she chanted that "Kāwelu
shall henceforth live in Hanakāmālu, Where the *ko'olau-
wahine* winds waft there below,
For I shall henceforth belong
there below." (Fornander 1917:
184.)

HANAKE or **NIHO-OA**, a malevolent Marquesan god who
inflicts paralysis and other
wasting sicknesses upon humans. (Christian 1895:190.)

HĀNAU-A-RANGI, name of
supernatural beings in the Tuamotus who help populate the
underworld* (*pō*). (Stimson
1964:117.)

HĀNEO'O, a fish pond on Maui
where the Hawaiian lizard
goddess Kiha-wahine* sits and
combs her long hair on a rock
called Lauoho Rock in the center
of the pond. (Beckwith 1948:126;
Thrum   1923:185–196;
Westervelt 1915a:152–162.)

HANGAROA, one of the ancient
gods brought to New Zealand
from Hawaiki* by the first
Māori settlers. (Gray 1855:102,
104; Tregear 1891:47.) See also
Manaia.

HANITEMAU, goddess of Rotuma, patron of trees and vegetation. The first mortal immigrants to Rotuma were chief
Raho* and his granddaughter
Maiva from the island of

Savai'i, Samoa. They brought
soil with them and with it created the island of Rotuma. They
returned to Savai'i, and while
they were gone the goddess
Hanitemau* appeared and
claimed the island for herself.
When Raho and his contingent
returned, there was a quarrel
for control of the island. They
met and settled the matter, and
they lived happily ever after.
(Russell 1942:229–255.)

HĀ'OA'OA, sister goddess to
the Tahitian god 'Oro* (god of
war) who descended to earth to
find a wife for him. Searching in
vain on the islands of Hu'ahine,
Ra'iātea, and Taha'a, she and
her sister Te-'uri* found a
choice mate for him on Bora-
Bora. They were enchanted
with the princess Vai-rau-mati
whom they took into heaven to
become 'Oro's bride. (Henry
1928:231, 375.)

HĀPAI, a heavenly goddess
(sometimes called Tongo-
tongo*) who became enchanted
with the exploits of the Māori
hero Tāwhaki (Kaha'i*) and
came to earth to be his wife.
After bearing a daughter, Arahuta, she returned to heaven.
Tāwhaki and his brother Karihi
then set out on their great
adventure to find Hāpai and
Arahuta. (Grey 1855:41; Grey
1970:52; Tregear 1891:47–48.)

   In the **Tuamotuan** legends,
Princess Hapai lived near
Tahaki's grandparents, Ituragi*

and Hina.* They informed Ta-haki of Hapai 's beauty, where-upon, he secretly tried to seduce her on three consecutive nights, but she refused. On the morning of the fourth day, however, she finally saw him in daylight and realized who he is. She sub-mitted. She returned to her parents who told her that Ta-haki had first to complete three tests before they would allow him to have her. He succeeded and Hapai became his. After Tahaki died, Hapai sang a long lament for him. (Stimson 1934: 70–77.)

HĀPOPO, a Māori god who folded up the sun during the great deluge.* (Tregear 1891:49; White 1887a:181.)

HA-PU'U, a Hawaiian goddess of necromancy. (Emerson 1915: 78, 80) See also **Ka-lei-hau-ola.**

HARATAUNGA, daughter of Mangamanga-i-atua and one of the two wives of the Māori hero Tinirau (Kinilau*) before he took Hina* to wife. Hara-taunga and her sister Horo-tata* jealously abused Hina, and both were slain through Hina's incantations. (Grey 1970: 63.)

HĀ-ROA, a brother to the young Māori chief Hatupatu* who arrived in New Zealand aboard the famous *Arawa* ca-noe from Hawaiki.* (Grey 1855: 115; Tregear 1891:51.)

HARONGA, a heavenly god, a prop of heaven in Māori leg-ends, son of Hina-ahu-papa and Rangi-pōtiki,* who mar-ried Tongotongo* and gave birth to the sun and to the moon. (Shortland 1882:17; Tregear 1891:51.)

HATONA, a Marquesan god mentioned in the story of Ta'a-pō* in her journey to the un-derworld.* (Handy 1930:85.)

HATUMANOKO, a god of Bellona Island, who went on a fishing trip with the goddess Nguatupu'a* and her brother, but was eaten by the two. (Monberg 1966:89–90.)

HATUPATU, an ancient Māori hero responsible for avenging the burning of the *Arawa* ca-noe which had brought the first Polynesians to New Zealand. Being the youngest of four brothers (Hā-nui, Hā-roa,* and Karikā), Hatupatu was denied privileges of going birding with them and of eating the niceties of their catch.

One day when his brothers went hunting, Hatupatu de-cided to feast upon the larder and to make it appear that rob-bers did the deed. The brothers eventually learned of the deceit and in anger killed their younger brother. In distress, their father sent a spirit named Tamumu-ki-te-rangi* to search for his young son's body.

Tamumu's enchantment brought him back to life.

On his way home, he encountered Kūrāngaituku, an old ogress, half woman, half bird, who captured and imprisoned him. One day while she was out hunting, Hatupatu gathered up all of her beautiful feather cloaks and weapons and fled. When she heard of his escape, she raced after him only to meet her death in the hot springs at Roto-rua. He successfully made it home, but his brothers continued their hostility.

Finally, their father decided that they must channel their energies toward the revenge of the great *Arawa* canoe which was burned by chief Raumati. The sons prepared for the long trip, and the three oldest set out in their canoes without Hatupatu. Hatupatu, however, was not to be outdone. He swam the great distance and arrived with all his gear before his brothers. In dividing the warriors for battle, the brothers again denied support to Hatupatu. Ingenuously, however, Hatupatu disguised tree roots as men by using his feather cloaks.

During the next day's battle, the enemy feared Hatupatu's "army" because it appeared as though it consisted mainly of brave chiefs, something which his brothers' armies did not possess. When his brothers' men turned and fled before the enemy, Hatupatu rose up and encouraged the men to return to battle. Hatupatu killed chief Raumati, and the enemy was routed. When Hatupatu returned home, his father raised him to the status of senior son. The burning of the *Arawa* canoe was thus avenged. (Grey 1970: 143–157; Tregear 1891:51–52.) See also **Canoes, Māori Migration**.

HAU, a Tahitian god of peace. (Henry 1928:384.)

HAUHAU-TE-RANGI, a sharp jade axe made by Ngahue* for the construction of the *Arawa* * canoe in the Māori legend of migrations to New Zealand. (Grey 1855:83; Grey 1970:107–108; Tregear 1891:54.) See also **Canoes, Māori Migration**.

HAU-HUNGA, the Māori god of bitter cold, son of Tāwhiri-matea* (god of winds and storms.) (Grey 1970:2–10; Tregear 1891:54; White 1887a: App.)

HĀ-U'I, a sea dragon in the legend of Pele* and Hi'iaka.* (Emerson 1915:xxx.)

HAU-LANI, Hawaiian plant goddess, daughter of Hina,* sister to Haunu'u* and Kamapua'a.* (Beckwith 1948:207.)

HA'ULILI, Hawaiian god of speech. (Pukui 1971:382.)

HAUMAKAPU'U, Hawaiian god, protector of fish ponds. (Malo 1903:82; Pukui 1971:382.)

HAU-MĀ-RINGIRINGI, one of the Māori gods of mists, an offspring of the sky god Rangi.* (Grey 1855:15; Grey 1970:18; Tregear 1891:54.) See also **Hau-maro-tō-roto**.

HAU-MARO-TŌ-ROTO, one of the Māori gods of mists, an offspring of the sky god Rangi.* (Grey 1855:15; Grey 1970:18; Tregear 1891:54.) See also **Hau-mā-ringiringi**.

HAUMEA, a Hawaiian fertility goddess from Nu'umealani,* the sacred land of the gods, the daughter of Kāne-hoa-lani.* Numerous stories tell of her mysterious character. By rebirths, she changes her age to marry her children and grandchildren. She transforms herself into a tree to save her husband. She is the patroness of natural childbirth. She is the mother of numerous progeny including the volcano goddess Pele* (who was born from her armpit) and of the Hawaiian people themselves. She owns a magical stick (Makalei) that attracts fish, and thus she is never without food. She embodies the power of creation as well as destruction. In the story of Ka-ulu,* she causes a famine to fall upon the land, and her daughter Pele destroys everything in her path. She marries Puna,* the chief of the island of O'ahu, and fights the goddess Kiha-wahine* for possession of him. (Beckwith 1948:

276–290; Westervelt 1915a: 152–162.)

In **New Zealand**, she is identified as Haumia-tikitiki,* the goddess of food production and as an ogress who devours her own children. (White 1887b:167–172.) The **Marquesan** god Haumei is a cannibalistic deity who especially enjoys the eyes. (Garcia 1843:42–43.) In **Tahiti**, she is the ogress Nona.* (Leverd 1912:1–3), and in the **Tuamotus**, she is identified as Faumea,* the eel woman. (Beckwith 1948:289; Stimson Ms.)

HAUMIA, ancestress of Paikea,* a Māori water monster (*tāniwha**) (Grey 1970:10; Shortland 1882:77); also mother of the Hawaiian war god Kekauakahi. (Tregear 1891:54.) See also **Ureia**.

HAUMIA-TIKITIKI, Māori god of all growing vegetable foods for humans, son of Rangi* (sky father) and Papa* (earth mother), who agreed with his brothers Tū-matauenga,* Rongo-mātāne,* Tāwhiri-matea,* and Tangaroa to the separation of their parents in the creation (Grey 1855:7; Grey 1970:3, 7–10.) According to another legend, Haumia-tikitiki (god of the fern root) is the son of Tama-nui-a-rangi, son of Rangi and Hekeheke-i-papa. (Tregear 1891:54; White 1887a:20.)

HAU-NGANGANA, Māori god of blistering winds. (Shortland 1882:13; Tregear 1891:55.)

HAUNGA-ROA, daughter of Manaia* and Kuiwai* in the Māori legend of the curse of Manaia. (Grey 1855:102; Grey 1970:129–130; Tregear 1891:55.)

HAUNU'U, Hawaiian plant goddess, daughter of Hina* and sister to Haulani* and Kamapua'a.* (Beckwith 1948:207.)

HAU-ORA, the seventeenth age of the universe according to Māori traditions; the fourth of the ten heavens presided over by the demigod Tāwhaki (Kaha'i.*) (Tregear 1891:55; White 1887a:App.)

HAURAROTUIA, name of Māui's* canoe in Māori legends. (Tregear 1891:55.)

HAU-TI'A, a Tahitian god to whom prayers are offered in order to ward off evil spells. (Henry 1928:213.)

HAU-WAHINE, lizard goddess of the Ka'elepule and Kawainui ponds found in the Ko'olau district of O'ahu (Hawai'i). She protects people from sickness, provides plentiful catches of fish, and punishes whoever owns the pond if they do not help the poor. (Beckwith 1948:126.)

HAU-WHENUA, an offspring of Rangi* (sky father) and Papa* (earth mother), the god of gentle breezes in Māori legends. (Grey 1855:15; Grey 1970:18; Tregear 1891:56.)

HAVA, wife of the Tuamotuan god Ataraga,* the father of the hero Māui* by Huahega.* (Stimson 1934:5–8.)

HAVAIKI, see Hawaiki.

HAVAIKI-NOHI-KARAKARA, a Tuamotuan god prayed to by One-kura (wife of Tiki*) to become pregnant. She gave birth to the famous goddess Hina.* (Stimson 1937:4–6.)

HAVAIKI-NUI-A-NA-EA, land of the Tuamotuan deities, presided over by Ahu-roa and his wife One-rua, parents of Tiki,* the first man. (Stimson 1937:3–4.)

HAVAIKI-TE-ARARO, legendary land in Tuamotuan stories where One-kura and her father Mati live. One-kura traveled to the land of Havaiki-nui-a-na-ea and became Tiki's* wife. (Stimson 1937:4.)

HAVEA-LOLO-FONUA, the Tongan creator goddess, the daughter of Piki* and Kele, who cohabited with her twin brother Taufulifonua* and gave birth to Hikuleo* (god of the underworld*). (Gifford 1924:14–15; Reiter 1907:230–240.) See also Creation; Heavens.

HAVEATOKE, a Tongan god who once visited the underworld* (Pulotu*) with three other gods (Fakafuumaka, Haelefeke, and Lohi) and goddess (Faimalie*) and collectively defeated the forces of the underworld in drinking, eating, and sporting games. (Gifford 1924:155–170; Reiter 1934:497–514.)

HAVILIA, a god of Niue Island. (Loeb 1926:161.)

HAWAI'I-LOA, an ancient navigator responsible for the discovery of the Hawaiian islands. According to the Kumuhonua* legend, four brothers, sons of Aniani-ka-lani, named Kī, Kanaloa,* La'a-kapu,* and Hawai'i-loa, were responsible for the discovery and peopling of the Pacific islands. Kī settled the Society Islands (Tahiti, etc.), Kanaloa the Marquesas, and La'a-kapu the islands west. After having settled the Hawaiian Islands, Hawai'i-loa made several trips to Tahiti where he obtained spouses for his children from his brother Kī's family. On one voyage, he discovered that Kī had abandoned their old gods, Kū, Kāne, and Lono, and thus he stopped all further communication between the two island groups. From Hawai'i-loa and Kī descend the high chiefs of Hawai'i, and from Hawai'i-loa's navigator, Makali'i,* descend the commoners. (Beckwith 1948:363–375; For-nander 1878:23–24, 132–159.) See also **Hawaiki.**

HAWAIKI (HAVAIKI), a word used to indicate the original homeland of the Polynesians, and in some cases, the term has passed into the realm of poetic expression referring to the underworld* or Hades. Almost every island group has a Hawaiki. Both the islands of Fakarava (Tuamotus) and Ra'iātea (French Polynesia) were once called Havaiki. The Māoris and Marquesans have their Havaiki, the Samoans their Savai'i, the Rarotongans their Avaiki, the Tongans their Habai, and the Hawaiians their Hawai'i. When the Polynesians were first asked by Westerners from whence they had come, they answered "from Hawaiki," simply meaning from a motherland. Confusion arose, therefore, when Westerners used these Polynesian expressions in their attempt to reconstruct Pacific migration patterns.

Polynesian legends also confuse Hawaiki (their distant homeland) with nomenclature of their current dwelling place. For example, the Māoris claim that Māui first fished up their islands of New Zealand and that this chain was the first homeland of their ancestors, yet they also claim that they sailed from those original islands (Hawaiki) to settle the new lands of New Zealand, uninhabited until they arrived.

Other examples could be given. The name was very popular, and story tellers would frequently use the term to give authenticity and other worldly character to their tales. (Smith 1910:46–62.)

HAWE-PŌTIKI, a young Māori boy killed by Turi* in revenge for a murder committed by Hawe-pōtiki's father, Ue-nuku* (high priest in Hawaiki*). (Grey 1855:126, Grey 1970:158–164; Tregear 1891:59.) See also Canoes, Māori Migration.

HEAUORO, a war god on the Chatham Islands. (Shand 1894: 89.)

HEAVENS. Central to the creation* stories found among the various Polynesian islands is the concept of the heavens and the underworld.* Numerous variations in these descriptions exist from one island to another, and we can only summarize the most detailed account of the extant sources. The common Polynesian view of the universe is that of an egg or coconut with a major division between the world of humans (earth), the upper world of gods, and the underworld, each subsequently divided into divisions, very much reminiscent of Dante's nine levels of heaven and of purgatory in his Divine Comedy. These heavenly degrees or rankings of the Polynesians were perhaps created to give sanction to the elaborate social and political rankings on earth which dominated the everyday life of the Polynesians.

According to several important Māori accounts (Tregear 1891:168 and White 1887a: App.), the heavens are divided into ten separate realms. Counting from the lowest upward, they are (1) Kiko-rangi, presided over by the god Toumau; (2) Waka-maru, the heaven of rain and sunshine; (3) Ngā-roto, the heaven of lakes, presided over by the god Maru;* (4) Hau-ora, or the Living Waters of Tāne, the place of origin of the spirits of newborn children; (5) Ngā-Tauira, home of the inferior or servant gods; (6) Ngā-atua, ruled over by Tāwhaki (Kaha'i*); (7) Autoia, where the human soul is created; (8) Aukumea, where spirits live for a time; (9) Wairua, residence of the spirit gods who wait upon those in the tenth heaven; and (10) Naherangi or Tūwarea, the highest heaven inhabited by the great gods, presided over by Rehua.* (Other Māori accounts, however, number the heavens from two to as many as fourteen.)

The heavens are supported either by gods as in Hawai'i (Rice 1923:33), by columns or pillars as in Tahiti (Henry 1928:342) and New Zealand, by an octopus as in another Tahiti legend (Henry 1928:338), or even by humans along the edge of the earth as in the Ellice Islands (Kennedy 1931:165).

Pillars of Heaven (Tahitian)
'Ana-heuheu-pō
'Ana-hoa
'Ana-iva
'Ana-mua
'Ana-muri
'Ana-roto
'Ana-tahu'a-ta'ata-metua.
'Ana-tahu'a-vahine. . .
'Ana-tipu
'Ana-varu
Ra'i-pua-tātā
Ti'ama-ta'aroa

Props of Heaven (Māori)

Haronga
Rangi-pōtiki
Ruatipua
Toko
Toko-maunga
Tokomua
Toko-pā
Tokoroto
Tūrangi

Ten divisions of the Māori underworld equally exist. They are (1) the place of grasses, trees, etc., presided over by Tāne-Mahuta; (2) the realm of Rongo-ma-tāne and Haumia-tikitiki; (3) Te Reinga, presided over by the supreme goddess Hine-nui-te-pō;* (4) Au-Toia, dwelling place of Whiro (Hilo*); (5) Uranga-o-te-Rā, (6) Hiku-Toia, and (7) Pou-Turi, the residence of Rohe,* wife of the demigod Māui,* who kills all the spirits she can; (8) Pou-Turi,

(9) Toke, and (10) Meto (extinction), presided over by the chief goddess of the underworld, Mero or Miru (Milu*).

A similar notion of the universe is believed in the Tuamotus, where in 1869, chief Paiore made a famous drawing which was eventually printed in 1919 in the *Journal of the Polynesian Society*, volume 28, opposite page 210, as below.

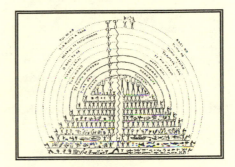

HEI, a legendary Māori chief who sailed in the *Arawa** canoe from Hawaiki* to settle New Zealand. (Grey 1970:117, 125–126; Shortland 1882:51; Tregear 1891:60.) See also **Canoes.**

HEI-AO, the upper world, the world of humans, the world of light in Tuamotuan legends. (Stimson 1964:127.)

HEIAU, an ancient religious edifice (temple) where Hawaiians could worship their gods with prayers and offerings presided over by properly qualified priests. These structures are common throughout eastern Polynesia, and in all areas serve

similar purposes. They are called *marae* in French Polynesia,
tohua or *me'ae* in the Marquesas, and *ahu* on Easter Island.

Most *heiau* or *marae* a r e
open air structures that usually
contain altars, shelters for religious paraphernalia, pits for
discarding sacred objects, and
temporary burial sites. Numerous drawings of these structures
were made by the early European navigators or Christian
missionaries to the islands. Unfortunately, most of the temples
were destroyed as "paganism"
was abolished in the islands.
Some structures were no larger
than a few feet square (private)
while others (national) were
thousands of square feet. They
usually were rectangular in
form, bounded by continuous
stone walls of several feet high.
Inside and at one end, stood the
altar (the *ahu*) where the spirits
or gods dwelt when they visited
the sacred edifice. The altars
were not primarily used for
offerings as might be expected
in other cultures. A slab to the
side of the altar served as a
resting place for the images of
the gods. Other upright stones
in the structure served as
leaning posts for the officiating
priests, backrests for the titled
nobility, or memorial stones for
departed chiefs' spirits. Many of
these structures contained
special houses where the religious paraphernalia were
stored and where the priests
might sleep. Sacred trees of
various sorts were usually
planted around the holy
grounds.

The *marae* in New Zealand,
malae in Tonga and Samoa,
were open, public places within
the common living area rather
than sacred temples. The religious structures in western
Polynesia were usually houses
(*fale aitu*) built especially for the
gods or as in the case of New
Zealand merely shrines at se-
cluded spots marked by stones
or posts. (Emory 1934; Bellwood
1978:331–360.)

HEIKAPU, a name for the Milky
Way in Tuamotuan mythology.
(Stimson 1964:127.)

HEIMA, the Tahitian god of
winter. (Possibly a corruption of
the French *hiver*.) (Henry 1928:
377, 394.)

HEIMOANA, a Tongan eel god
responsible for first transport-
ing the *ava* (milk fish) from
Samoa to Tonga. (Gifford 1924:
85.) Also the mother of the
Tongan demigod Māui and his
sister Hina* by her husband
Malekulaulua.* (Gifford 1924:
19.) See also **Haelefeke.**

HEIVA, a type of eulogy chant
that, according to Tuamotuan
legends, was brought from the
netherworld in their distant
past; thus, ancient or sacred
songs and dances (the *kotaha*,
for example). (Stimson 1964:
128.)

HEKE, name of a legendary octopus in the Tuamotu Islands. (Stimson 1964:128),

HEKEHEKE-I-PAPA, name of Turi's* farm after arriving in New Zealand from Hawaiki.* (Grey 1855:136; Grey 1970:171; Tregear 1891:61.)

HEMA, the celebrated father of the Māori heroes Tāwhaki (Kaha'i*) and Kariki, the son of Kaitangata and Whaitiri (a cannibal goddess), and husband to Uri-Tonga. According to Māori legends, Hema was slain by the wicked goblins (the Ponaturi*), whereupon, Tāwhaki and Kariki began their great adventure to avenge their father's death. (Grey 1970:46, 48; Tregear 1891:61; White 1887a:54, 120, 121, 128.) In **Hawai'i**, Hema, a chief on the island of Maui, is the father of Kaha'i-nui and is captured by the 'Ai'aia* bird and taken to Kahiki (Tahiti ?). (Beckwith 1948:248.)

HEMOANA, a primeval Tongan god, son of Toki-langa-fonua* by his daughter Topukulu,* abandoned in the sea by his mother, and became a sea snake. (Collocott 1921:237.)

HERE, an obscure god's name in the Tuamotu Islands. (Stimson 1964:132); a Māori god, the son of Rangi*-pōtiki (prop of heaven) and Papa-tū-a-nuku, twin brother of Punga* (a god of lizards.) (Shortland 1882:17; Tregear 1891:62.)

HEREKOTI, Tuamotuan god, one of the nine children of the sky god, Ātea (Wākea*), and his wife, Fakahotu. (Stimson 1964: 133.)

HETA, name of the Māori chief who fought against Ue-nuku* in the battle of Ratorua. (Tregear 1891:182.)

HIHIRI, seventh of the ages of the existence of the universe in Māori legends. (White 1887a: App.) See also **Kore.**

HI'IAKA, younger sister to the Hawaiian volcano goddess Pele,* heroine of the epic story of Pele and Hi'iaka, patroness of the hula. She was born of an egg from the mouth of her mother, Haumea,* and carried under Pele's armpit until she matured. Having established her home in Kī-lau-ea crater on the island of Hawai'i, Pele desired to send someone to Kaua'i to escort her lover, chief Lohi'au,* back to Hawai'i. The only one she could trust is Hi-'iaka whom she sent out with magical powers to aid her against the dangers that would confront her and with certain instructions. She had to return within forty days, and she should not touch (kiss) or embrace Lohi'au on the way. Hi-'iaka, on the other hand, left her dearest friend Hōpoe* in Pele's care.

Crossing the island of Hawai'i, Hi'iaka and her party encountered evil lizard monsters (*mo'o*) who unsuccessfully tried to prevent their journey by means of fog, sharp rain, and dense jungle growth of vines. The shark in Waipi'o Valley was also slain, and the ghost god Hinahina-kū-i-ka-pali was put to route.

On Maui, Moloka'i, and O'ahu, the party encountered numerous adventures that slowed its journey and delayed its arrival on Kaua'i. Once there, Hi'iaka learned that Lohi'au had died out of grief for the woman (Pele) who had danced before him. Hi'iaka was able to restore his spirit and life. Now they had face the return voyage, and already the forty days had passed. From atop a ridge on O'ahu, Hi'iaka looked toward her home on the Big Island and saw her beloved forests in flames and her friend Hōpoe encircled with scorching lava. Pele was angry! In spite of bitterness and despair, Hi'iaka continued her voyage through all kinds of miserable weather.

Nearing home Hi'iaka sent two messengers on ahead to present themselves before Pele at the crater of Kī-lau-ea. Pele could not be contained, nor could any explanation for the long delay satisfy her. At her command, the messengers were put to death. Hi'iaka and Lo-

hi'au made it alone to the top of the crater where now, defiantly, she accepted Lohi'au's love, and they embraced in full view of Pele and her retinue.

Pele's servants withdrew from the command to destroy the couple, whereupon, Pele furiously engulfed them in flames. Hi'iaka's magical power prevented her destruction, but Lohi'au's body was consumed. Again, Hi'iaka sought after his spirit through the innermost bowls of the earth and restored him to life. Together they returned to Lohi'au's home on Kaua'i, the most remote part of the Hawaiian chain from Pele's mountain home. The legend of Hi'iaka comes to a close. (Emerson 1915.)

HI'IAKA-I-KA-'ALE-'Ī, Hi'iaka-in-the-giant-billow, one of the sisters to the Hawaiian goddess Hi'iaka.* (Pukui 1971:383.)

HI'IAKA-I-KA-'ALE-MOE, Hi-'iaka-in-the-low-lying-billow, one of the sisters to the Hawaiian goddess Hi'iaka.* (Pukui 1971:383.)

HI'IAKA-I-KA-'ALE-PO'I, Hi-'iaka-in-the-breaking-wave, one of the sisters to the Hawaiian goddess Hi'iaka.*(Pukui 1971:383.)

HI'IAKA-I-KA-'ALE-'UWEKE, Hi'iaka-in-the-uncovering-billows, one of the sisters to the

Hawaiian goddess Hi'iaka.*
(Pukui 1971:383.)

**HI'IAKA-I-KA-PUA-'ENA-
'ENA**, one of the sisters to the
Hawaiian goddess Pele,* who
prepared leis and *kava* for Pele.
Also known as Kuku-'ena-i-ke-
ahi-ho'omau-honua, a healer
and a guide to lost travelers.
(Beckwith 1948:168; Pukui 1971:
383.) See also **Hi'iaka.**

HI'IAKA-NOHO-LAE, Hi'iaka-
guarding-point, one of the sisters to the Hawaiian goddess
Hi'iaka,* also the name of a
rock beyond the seawall at
Kailua, Kona, Hawai'i. (Beckwith 1948:168; Pukui 1971:383.)

HII-HIA, sister to the Marquesan war god Tū* whose disparaging remarks about her
brother brought about the great
deluge.* (Handy 1930:110.)

HI'I-LAWE, son of Kākea and
Kahola, brother to Lau-ka-
'ie'ie,* Hawaiian goddess of the
wildwood. Upon his death, his
body was transformed into a
stone, and his spirit became the
mist of the Hi'i-lawe waterfall
in the Waipi'o Valley, Hawai'i.
(Beckwith 1948:17, 522.)

HIKA-ITI, Māori god of tides.
(White 1887c:49; Tregear 1891:
66.)

HIKUERU, a Tuamotuan sea
monster, a demigod. (Stimson
1964:140.)

HIKU-I-KA-NAHELE, an Hawaiian from the Big Island who
fell in love with the beautiful
Kāwelu* who tempted him into
her home for six days without
giving herself to him. Frustrated, he left her, whereupon
Kāwelu followed, but Hiku now
rejected her love. Kāwelu
strangled herself, and her spirit
went down to Milu* in the underworld.* After a change of
heart, Hiku descended from a
vine, captured her spirit, and
the two were pulled up to the
earthly world where her spirit
was reunited with her body.
They lived happily ever after.
(Beckwith 1948:147–148; Fornander 1917:182–189; Wes-
tervelt 1915a:224–240.) Also the
name of the hero son of Kū-
'ōhi'a-a-laka* and Hina.* (Pukui 1971:383.) See also **Hutu;
Kanikani-a-'ula; Kena; Milimili;
Pare.**

HIKULEO, Tongan god or
goddess of the underworld*
(Pulotu*). (Gifford 1924:153–
175.) In one legend, he is the son
of Tau-fuili-fonua* and thus
half-brother to the god Tagaloa
(Kanaloa*) and to the demigod
Māui.* Sometimes known as
Havea. (Reiter 1907:234.) See
also **Creation; Fehuluni; Moso;
Tui-Haatala; Vele-lahi.**

HIKU-RANGI, known as the
holy mountain in Māori legends, it was the first land of
Hawaiki* which appeared

lands, the mountain on which mortals took refuge during the great deluge.* (Tregear 1891:68; White 1887a:43, 50, 148; 3:11, 31, 37, 51.) See also **Pukehapopo; Rutapu.**

HIKUTOIA, the sixth level of the Māori underworld.* (Tregear 1891:68; White 1887a: App.) See also **Reinga.**

HILO (HIRO, IRO, WHIRO), a principal Polynesian god, particularly identified as the patron god of thieves and the god of misfortune.

The most elaborate cycle comes from the **Tuamotus**. Here, Hiro was a tall, mighty warrior, endowed with certain magical powers. Once coming upon an island called Upper Havaiki,* Hiro entered a dance contest to gain the hand in marriage of Tiaki-tau, the king's daughter. He won, but the king demanded a certain deed be successfully performed before Hiro could be accepted by the royal family. He had to fetch the gourd of sweet-scented oil that belonged to the ogress Nona.* Hiro set out, successfully stole the oil, returned home, and presented himself before the king.

Just as the marriage festivities began, the young princess was carried off by a demon-monster in a whirlwind to the bottom of the ocean. Hiro sought the demon, killed him, and rescued Tiaki-tau, whereupon the king made Hiro

sovereign over all his lands.

Hiro's favorite son Tautu* became an overseer in the service of King Puna,* and because of the misadventures of Tautu's servants, the king imprisoned him in a tree. When Hiro learned of the tragedy, he swore to avenge his son. He began the construction of a great outrigger sailing ship. But while construction of the ship was underway, Tiaki-tau enraged her husband by making disparaging remarks about his phallus to her neighbors! In heat of anger, Hiro snatched up his great mallet, clubbed her to death, and buried her in the sand near the ship.

When Hiro's son heard of the tragedy, Marama* exhumed his mother and took her far away for a decent burial. Hiro decided to get revenge on his son by tricking him. He instructed his daughter Piho* to find her brother and in disguise dance nude before him. When she did, Marama grabbed and raped her. When she took off her disguise, Marama saw what he had done and was distraught over his father's trick.

Returning home through King Puna's lands, Piho and Marama found their brother Tautu, released him from the tree, and then told him of their father's prank.

When they arrived home, they killed all of their father's warriors, and then found out that their father had fled in his canoe. Marama returned to his mother's body, and through magical and mysterious means persuaded her spirit to return to her body in the upper world where they lived together happily.

Hiro's next adventure involved his sister Hina,* who had just married Prince Te Rogo-mai-hiti without Hiro's consent. Hiro set out to see his sister. Far out to sea, Hiro's crew killed a sacred bird belonging to the god Tāne (Kāne.*) Tāne was furious and sank their ship. The tragedy awoke Hiro who regained his vessel and continued his voyage.

When Hiro and Hina finally met, the two are reconciled, and each sheds tears of joy. They story concludes with Hiro winning the hand of Princess Mongi-here,* but not without some real opposition at first on her part. The couple finally returns to the land of Hiro (Toganui) where they live together. (Stimson 1957:137–190.)

Hiro in the **Tahitian** legends resembles those found in the neighboring Tuamotu islands, but with less detail. In Tahiti, Hiro was more of the trickster. As a young man, he attended his grandfather's school at 'Uporu on Tahiti. He absorbed everything, and then decided to become a thief under the protection of the god Hiro. He stole breadfruit, coconuts, special kava trees, and pigs.

Once while sailing to Ra-'iātea, he and his brothers experienced the same problem with the cherished bird of Tāne. Finally reaching Ra'iātea, Hiro fell in love with the beautiful Vai-tū-mārie* who was already married. Hiro killed her husband, married her, and became the king of Ra'iātea. The couple had two children, Marama and Piho. When they were grown, their mother was slain by their father because she made derogatory remarks to her neighbors regarding her husband's foul smell.

Hiro's exploits are many. For example, he discovered fire by friction, he struck mountains, and caused devastating landslides. A rock on Hu'ahine is called Hiro's paddle. His last great exploit was the building of a huge ocean-going canoe (*Hohoio*), the most beautiful one ever constructed. It was provisioned with all sorts of foodstuff, and Hiro and his friends' families set sail never to return again to Tahiti. (Henry 1928: 537–552.)

In **New Zealand**, the god Whiro played a prominent role in the creation when he bitterly opposed the plan of his brother Tāne (Kāne*) to separate their parents, Rangi* (sky father) and Papa* (earth mother.) A battle (known as Te Paeranti) between the two forces ensued, and in the end Whiro was defeated. His forces were driven down to earth and to the underworld* where he was responsible for all the ills of mortal beings.

Whiro, the patron god of thieves in **New Zealand**, was originally a mortal voyager and adventurer. Having formed an illicit union with the wife of his nephew Taomakati, Whiro was forced into battle in which he killed his brother Hua* as well as his nephew. In fear of his life, Whiro proposed to Tura,* another brother, to flee to Wawau (Vavau ?), an ancient homeland of the Polynesians. Heading out to sea, the voyagers experienced many wonders on their journey. When they neared the island of Otea, the frightened Tura landed, leaving Whiro to continue the voyage to Wawau without him. (Reed 35–36, 62–68, 79–82.)

Very little is known of Hilo (Hiro) in Hawai'i and Easter Island. The town and district of Hilo on the Big Island of Hawai'i may have been named after this infamous Polynesian navigator. On Easter Island, the name of Hiro is considered a rain god, and on the northeast coast a rock is called Pu-o-Hiro (the trumpet of Hiro) which is pierced by a natural hole and sounds as a trumpet when the wind blows. (Métraux 1940: 310.)

On Aitutaki, **Cook Islands**, the story is told of Iro, the son of Moe-Terauri and Akimano-ki-a-tū, whose childhood pranks caused all kinds of changes in the topography of the island. He brewed beer and drank it all, he stole pigs and ate them all, he overturned mountains, and brought about all kinds of changes. He set out on a distant voyage to the mythical land of Vavau to the west (Hawaiki*) and then on to other voyages with his friend, chief Makea, a thief. (Large 1903:133–144.) See also **Fire, Discovery of.**

HINA (INA, SINA), the most popular goddess in Polynesia, resides in the moon and is the patron of *kapa* (tapa) beating. **Tahitian** legends say that Hina was the daughter of Ātea (Wākea*) and Hotu and lived on the island of Ra'iātea. There she and her brother Rū* planned a great voyage of discovery to New Zealand. They stationed their canoe at Motu-tapu (Sacred Island) and left through the pass called Te-ava-o-Hina. Not far from there is a place called Tutura'a-ha'a-a-Hina where she supposedly spread her tapa cloth out to dry. A breadfruit tree stands nearby from which it is said she made her white tapa cloth, and upon the ground lies a long stone which resembles the beater that Hina used in her cloth making.

One evening when the moon was full, she set sail alone to visit it. Arriving at her destination, she stepped into the moon and let her canoe drift away never to return to earth again. From her unique position, she watches over travelers at night. When the moon is full, she is seen beating her tapa cloth under the limbs of the banyan tree.

It is said that once while she was climbing the tree, a branch broke off and fell to earth at Opoa on the island of Ra'iātea. It took root and was the first tree of its kind ever seen by humans. Its fruit provides the staff of life throughout the Pacific.

Hina is also the wife of the Tahitian demigod Tafa'i (Kaha'i*), whose marvelous exploits are eulogized in almost every Polynesian group. After his many adventures, Tafa'i returned to Tahiti and married Hina, a chiefess from the north famed for her long black hair.

Once Tafa'i returned home to find that his beloved Hina had just died. In great grief, he inquired of the priests as to the direction her spirit would take on its way to paradise. They replied that it would travel from Tahiti to Mo'orea and then to Ra'iātea from which it would make its final ascent to paradise. Swiftly, Tafa'i set sail in his canoe to Ra'iātea, and as Hina's spirit made its final departure, Tafa'i leapt into the air and grabbed her long flowing hair in his hands. As they struggled, the god Tū-tā-hora told her that her time had not come and to remain on earth with her husband. So they returned to Tahiti where they lived a long and happy life together. Their son Vahieroa became the father of the famous hero Rata

(Laka.*) (Henry 1928:407–408, 462–464, 563–565.)

In the **Tuamotus**, Hina is the sister of Hiro (Hilo*), the mighty warrior from the land of Marama. Without her brother's consent, she set out on her own to find the handsome prince Te Rogo-mai-Hiti* on Motu-tapu (Sacred Island.) She hoped to gain the services of several sea creatures to carry her there, but each failed in its attempts. The flounder sank under her weight, and in anger she beat it flat and took out one eye and placed it on the same side as the other. That is why the flounder is flat with both eyes on the same side. She hit the rock cod on the head and crumpled it in. She knocked the turtle on the back with her coconut and thus caused the lump on the upper end of the turtle's back. She finally climbed aboard her friend, the whale, cracked her coconut open on its tail, and thus divided it into two.

She finally reached Motu-tapu, found her handsome prince, married him, and had a son, Tāne*-the-third-god. When the angry Hiro heard of his sister's marriage, he set out to find and to punish the couple. After many great adventures, Hiro finally arrived in Marama where he was reconciled with his beloved sister and her husband Te Rogo-mai-Hiti. (Stimson 1957:137–190.)

In **New Zealand**, Hina is the sister to the famed hero Māui.*

When her husband Irawaru displeased Māui during a fishing expedition, he turned him into a dog. Distraught, Hina threw herself into the sea and was swept away to Motu-tapu. After being rescued by her two brothers, Hina married Tinirau (Kinilau*), the god of fishes. When Hina's brother Rupe* learned that Hina was at Motu-tapu, he transformed himself into a pigeon, flew to the island, and carried off his sister and her new-born son. (Grey 1855:32–34; Grey 1970:62–66; Tregear 1891:69.)

Some **Samoan** legends claim that Sina is the daughter of the great creator god Tagaloa (Kanaloa.*) As Tagaloa created the Samoan Islands, he sent Sina in the form of the bird Turi (Tuli) to find dry land. Again and again she returned until finally she saw dry land appearing from among the crashing waves. Sina was sent down once again with creeping vines that eventually turned into mortal beings. (Fraser 1897:19–33, 1890:206–217.)

Other legends state that Sina was the beautiful daughter of Tafitofau and Ongafau who refused all proposals of marriage for their daughter, even from the king of Fiji (the Tuifiti). When they received a proposal from the highest chief of Samoa, the Tupu-o-le-fanua, they were delighted, but the young girl, being in love with the handsome Tigilau (Kinilau*), refused the match. She was carried away against her will to Tupu-o-le-fanua's home where Tigilau followed in the form of a bird. That night in Sina's bedroom, he resumed his own form, and the couple escaped to Tigilau's home where they lived thereafter. (Fraser 1890:197–199; Lesson 1876:591.)

Numerous stories of Hina (with many appellations) appear in **Hawai'i**. Hina-i-ke-ahi was the wife of Akalana* and thus the mother of Māui.* One of Māui's greatest feats was snaring and slowing down the sun so his mother's tapa cloth might dry sufficiently. While he was away, Hina was visited by Lono-ka-'eho (Lono-kaheo) and some say Kuna (Tūna*) the eel. When she rejected his advances, he threw a mass of lava across the stream, and the rising water threatened her life. Hina called for Māui who rescued her by using his magical snares on his mother's suitor. Lono-ka-'eho was turned into a rock. (Beckwith 1948:226–237; Elbert 1959:196–203.)

Another Hina is the mother of the legendary Kama-pua'a,* half man and half hog. In these stories, Hina is the daughter of the chiefess Ka-maunu-a-niho who came to Hawai'i from Kahiki (Tahiti ?.) On the island Maui, Ka-maunu-a-niho married chief Kalana and gave birth to Hina. Becoming an adult, Hina first married 'Olopana,* chief of O'ahu, and then his younger brother Kahiki-'ula. Various legends mention Hina-i-ka-malama (Hina-in-the-moon) who is born in the undersea world of Kahiki-hon-ua-kele,* who became a gourd bailer, and who makes tapa in the moon. (Beckwith 1948:201–213; Fornander 1880:43–44; Elbert 1959:196–203, 242–249.)

In **Mangaia**, Cook Islands, Ina is the daughter of Vai-tooringa and Ngaetua and the sister to Tangikūkū and Rupe. Once, she was left at home to air out their valuable possessions, but in doing so, she was attacked by the thief Ngana, and their articles stolen. Ina set out to locate them on the back of the shark Tekea who took her to the home of the god Tinirau (Kinilau*). Ina became his wife and the mother of a son, Koromau-ariki, and a daughter, Ature. Eventually Ina's brother, Rupe, came to visit her, and they have a grand celebration. (Gill 1876:88–97.)

On **Mangareva**, Hina is the goddess of the underworld and presides over the captive souls of deceased mortals. (Caillot 1914:154.) See also **Coconut, Origin of the.**

HINA-'EA, Hawaiian goddess of sunrise and sunset, a healer, and an expert *kapa* maker. (Pukui 1971:384.) See also **Hina.**

HINA-HĀNAI-A-KA-MALA-MA, see **Hina-i-ka-malama.**

HINA-HELE, the Tahitian and Hawaiian goddess of fishes. (Henry 1928:467–468.) See also **Hina-puku-'ai.**

HINA-I-KE-AHI, daughter of Hina-i-ka-malama, wife of Akalana,* and thus mother to the demigod Māui.* (Beckwith 1948:227.)

HINA-(I)-KE-KĀ or **HINA-KE-KA'Ā**, Hawaiian goddess of canoe bailers, the beautiful and shy sister to Hina-i-ke-ahi (mother to Māui*), sometimes equated with Hina-'ōpū-hala-ko'a* (the goddess of coral). (Beckwith 1948:219; Hickman 1985:159.)

HINA-LAU-LIMU-KALA, the most beautiful of the Hawaiian Hinas, a goddess who lives at the bottom of the sea and is the patron goddess of the *kahunas* (priests) skilled in medicines from the sea. (Pukui 1971:384.)

HINA-OIO, a goddess of Easter Island, wife of Atua-metua,* who became the mother of all water animals. (Métraux 1940:321–322.)

HINA-NUI-TE-'ARA'ARA, a goddess invoked by Tahitian fire walkers. (Henry 1928:407–408.)

HINA-NUI-TE-PŌ, see **Hine-nui-te-pō.**

HINA-'ŌPŪ-HALA-KO'A, Hawaiian goddess of coral and spiny creatures of the sea. From her shells, Māui* made his fa mous fishhook for fishing up the Pacific Islands. (Beckwith 1948: 219; Pukui 1971:384.)

HINA-PUKU-'AI, Hawaiian goddess of vegetable food, sister to Hina-puku-i'a,* also known as Hina-hele.* (Beckwith 1948:69; Pukui 1971:384.)

HINA-PUKU-I'A, Hawaiian goddess of fishermen, wife to Kū-'ula-kai, mother of 'Ai-'ai,* and sister to Hina-puku-'ai.* (Beckwith 1948:69; Pukui 1971: 384.)

HINA-TE-'IVA'IVA, conjured forth to become the wife of the Tahitian god Rua-tapua-nui (source-of-the-great-growth) in the creation. (Henry 1928:358.) See also **Creation.**

HINA-TUAFUAGA, a Tongan goddess sent from heaven to be the wife of Tokilagafanua,* the first ruler of 'Eua, Tonga, who also was her brother. Their daughters Topukulu* and Nafanua,* rain goddesses, also gave birth to children by their father, and the entire family was turned into volcanic stones. (Reiter 1907:743–754.)

HINA-'ULU-'ŌHI'A, patron goddess of the *'ōhi'a-lehua* trees on the Big Island of Hawai'i, the mother of the famous voyager Kā-'ulu,* and wife of Kū-ka-'ōhi'a-laka.* Her blossoms are sacred, and no one dares to pluck the flowers on their journey to the volcano except through proper invocations. She also goes by the name Nahinahi-ana, the patron goddess of printing and coloring tapa. (Beckwith 1948:17; Emerson 1915:139; Green 1936:146–149.)

HINE-ĀHUA, one of the Māori goddess seen floating on the waters during the great deluge.*(Tregear 1891:71; White 1887a:175.) See also **Hine-rakatai; Hine-apohia.**

HINE-AHUONE, see **Hine-nui-te-pō**

HINE-AHUPAPA, first wife of the Māori god Rangi-pōtiki* (prop of heaven), mother of several sky gods and goddesses, and grandmother of the sun (Rā*) and the moon (Marama*). (Tregear 1891:71.)

HINE-APO-HIA, one of the Māori goddess seen floating on the waters during the great deluge.* (Tregear 1891:71; White 1887a:175.) See also **Hine-āhua; Hine-ahuga; Hine-rakatai.**

HINE-ATEREPō, a daughter of the goddess Hina* and Tūna-roa-te-tupua (an eel god) in Māori legends. (Tregear 1891: 61.)

HINE-HĒHĒHEIRANGI, a Māori god invoked by those

deep sea fishing. (Colenso 1882: 8; Tregear 1891:71.)

HINE-HUARAU, name of the water monster killed by the Māori chief Tara* at Wairarapa. (Tregear 1891:474.)

HINE-IKUKUTIRANGI, same as **Hine-hēhē-irangi.***

HINE-ITAITAI, Māori wife of Rakurū (first thief in the world) and thus mother of the ancient hero Tau-tini,* who constructed a ship and went on a famous voyage that lasted two months. (Tregear 1891:71; White 1887a: 171.)

HINE-ITEIWAIWA, wife of Tinirau (Kinilau*) in Māori legends, who helped in the capture of the old sorcerer Kae* after he had murdered Tinirau's pet whale, Tutu-nui. (Grey 1970:72, 74, 93–98; Tregear 1891:71) See also **Hina.**

HINE-KŌRAKO, a Māori spirit who lives in lunar rainbows. (Tregear 1891:71.)

HINE-MAKURA, Māori goddess who drank the flood waters at the time of the great deluge,* thereby saving mortal life. (Tregear 1891:71; White 1887c: 31.)

HINE-MĀRU, mother of the beautiful maiden Hine-moa* in the Māori romance. (Grey 1855:146; Grey 1970:184; Tregear 1891:71.)

HINE-MOA, heroine of the Māori romance of Hine-moa and Tūtānekai. Tūtānekai, the illegitimate son of Rangi-uru and her lover Tū-whare-toa, lived with his mother, his stepfather, Whakaue-kaipapa, and his four stepbrothers on the island of Mokoia. Tūtānekai and his brothers sought the hand in marriage of Hine-moa, a young maiden of rare beauty, daughter of high chief Umu-karia and his wife Hine-maru, who lived on the mainland.

Often the young people mingled during tribal festivities, and Tūtānekai and Hine-moa secretly fell in love. All the eligible young bachelors desired Hine-moa as a wife, but her family remained adamant that she should marry only one worthy of her beauty and station. The two lovers secretly planned to be united. At the appropriate time, Tūtānekai was to play music upon his *putorino* (flute), and hearing it from her mainland home, Hine-moa would come to him.

One evening, Tūtānekai gave his signal, but unfortunately Hine-moa's family had secured all the canoes so that she could not venture out. Undaunted, Hine-moa gathered six empty gourds to use as floats and swam the great distance to Mokoia.

Exhausted, she arrived on the island, warmed herself in the nearby hot springs where she was met by Tūtānekai, and was then taken to his village to become his wife. Their descendants still tell the story of the beautiful Hine-moa and of her swim to Mokoia. (Grey 1970: 183–191; Tregear 1891:71–72; Wilson 1907.)

HINE-NGARO, name of the ninth age of the universe according to Māori legends. (Tregear 1891:72; White 1887a: App.) See also **Kore.**

HINE-NUI-O-TE-KAWA, wife of the Māori god Paikea* who dwells in the heavens. Leaving her husband once, she fell in love and married the great hero Tāwhaki (Kaha'i*). (Tregear 1891:72; White 1887a:54.)

HINE-NUI-TE-PŌ,   Māori goddess of the underworld* or the night (pō*), a daughter of the god Tāne (Kāne*) and Hine-ahu-one (earth maiden). Ignorant of her own parentage, Hine-nui-te-pō (originally called Hine-a-tauira) had several children by her father. On discovering her relationship to Tāne, she fled to the underworld in shame and despair to become the goddess of the night.

In her new domain, she drags down the souls of mortals to their destruction. When the great demigod Māui* tried to gain immortality for humans, he entered the underworld of Hine-nui-te-pō where he met his own death. (Tregear 1891: 72; Grey 1970:8, 23, 42–44; White 1887a:131, 146.)

HINE-PIRIPIRI, wife of the great Māori hero Tāwhaki (Kaha'i*), who rescued Tāwhaki when he was attacked by his cruel brothers; also the mother of Wahieroa (Wahieloa*). (Grey 1855:63; Grey 1970:46; Tregear 1891:72.)

HINE-PŪPŪMAINAUA, mother of the great Māori heroes Tāwhaki (Kaha'i*) and Karihi, also known by Karenuku and Pūpū-mai-nono. (Tregear 1891:72; White 1887a:54, 121.)

HINE-RAKATAI, one of the Māori goddess seen floating on the waters during the great deluge.* (Tregear 1891:72; White 1887a:175.) See also **Hine-āhua; Hine-apohia.**

HINE-RUAKI-MOE, Māori goddess of night, visited by the god Tāne (Kāne*) when he was searching for his wife Hine-a-tauira. (Tregear 1891:72.; White 1887a:146.)

HINE-TE-KĀKARA, daughter of the Māori chief Kohu, who married chief Ihenga* of the great *Arawa** canoe. (Shortland 1882:63, 76; Tregear 1891: 72.)

HINE-TENGARUMOANA, wife of the Māori hero Tinirau (Kinilau*), known also as Hine-te-iwa-iwa. (Tregear 1891:72; White 1887b:136.)

HINE-TĪTAMA, also known as Hine-nui-te-pō,* wife of Tāne-nui-a-rangi, and thus ancestress of the Māori people. (Tregear 1891:72; White 1887a:117, (3), 123.)

HINE-TĪTAMAURI, daughter of the Māori god Tāne (Kāne*) and Hine-a-tauira. (Shortland 1882:23; Tregear 1891:73.) See also **Hine-nui-te-pō**.

HINE-TŪ-A-HŌANGA, a Māori priestess and sorceress, granddaughter of the great hero Tāwhaki (Kaha'i*), and sister to Rata (Laka.*) When Rata was unable to fell a tree to make his famous canoe, Hine told him to sharpen his axe on her sacred body. Once done, Rata was able to accomplish his task. (Grey 1855:69; Grey 1970:106, 108; Tregear 1891:73; White 1887a:69.)

HINE-TŪ-A-MAUNGA, ancestress of the Māori god Tāne (Kāne*), also the wife of Tāne who forsook her when she bore only rusty waters and mountain monsters as children. (Shortland 1882:21; Tregear 1891:73.)

HINIHINI, name of a Tuamotuan demon-god. (Stimson 1964:141.)

HĪRAUTA, name of one of the great Māori canoes used in the migration to New Zealand by the Polynesians, commanded by chief Kiwa. (Tregear 1891:20, 72; White 1887b:191.) See also **Canoes, Māori Migration.**

HIRIVARI, a Tahitian god of land development in Havai'i (Hawaiki.*) (Henry 1928:375.)

HITI, name of the original inhabitants of Bellona and Rennell Islands before the arrival of the Polynesians. They were short with long hair that reached to the soles of their feet, and they taught the newcomers various arts of survival. Geographical features of the landscape are attributed to them. Similar to the Menehunes* in Hawai'i, their modern-day descendants are considered supernatural. (Monberg 1966:92–95.) See also **Elves and Fairies; Moriori.**

HĪTĪ-MĀRAMA, a legendary island in Tahitian mythology, supposedly north-northeast of Pitcairn Island, that sank beneath the ocean and confronted the hero Rata (Laka*) in his legendary voyage. (Henry 1928:70, 505.)

HĪVA, Tuamotuan name of the warrior-giants who anciently inhabited the islands. (Audran 1918:90–92; Stimson 1964:147.)

See also **Elves and Fairies; Giants.**

HIVAITI, name of a land mentioned in Tuamotuan legends as being on the way to Easter Island, possibly Pitcairn Island. (Stimson 1964:147.)

HIVA-KARERE, a benevolent Easter Island demon. (Métraux 1940:317.)

HIVA-RŌ-TAHI, a mythical land in the Tahitian Rata (Laka*) legend. The two witches, Nua and Mere-hau, disguised as ducks, held as hostage Vāhi-vero, the young son of Kui and Puhehueue. King Hoka of Hiva-rō-tahi captured the two giant lizards that fled from the land of Puna and used them as door keepers. (Stimson 1937:99–100.)

HOA-MAKE-I-KE-KULA, daughter of Ho'oleipalaoa and his wife Pili* in Hawaiian mythology, who was born in the shape of a taro plant and thrown away. Her grandmother Makapailu rescued her, wrapped her in a cloth of red bark, and after twenty days, Hoa-make-i-ke-kula emerged faultless in beauty.

Once while stringing flowers, she was visited by the *'elepaio** bird who carried her off to his master, a young chief named Kalama-'ula (red-torch.) Hoa-make-i-ke-kula dreamed of a handsome chief higher in rank than Ka-lama-'ula and fell in love with the vision.

One day during a fog, she ran away and hid in the uplands of Pahulumoa. While there, she was found by Pu'uhue, the chief of Kohala and the object of her love. The two were united in marriage, and from that union was born a son, 'Alele-kī-nana* (or Ha'alele-kī-nana*), in the shape of a wooden image. 'Alele-kī-nana's birth began the idea of worshipping of wooden god images in the Kohala district. (Beckwith 1948:515–516.)

HŌ-ANE, a god mentioned in Tahitian legends as a colleague of the god Tāne (Kāne.*) Possibly the same as Hō-ani.* (Henry 1928:356.)

HŌ-ANI, a crafty artisan and bosom friend of the Tahitian god Ta'ere* who dwells in the center of the earth. Numerous suffixes are added to his name to describe his particular personality as a tempter. Possibly the same as Hō-ane.* (Henry 1928:374.)

HŌ'ATA-MEAMEA, the only son of the Tahitian god 'Oro* and his wife Tū-fe'ufe'u-mai-te-ra'i,* also called Ho'a-tapu (sacred friend) and Ho'ata-tino-rua. (Henry 1928:376.)

HO'A-TAPU, son of the Tahitian god 'Oro.* (Henry 1928:

231, 238, 376.) See also **Ho'ata-meamea**.

HŌ'ATA-TINO-RUA, son of the Tahitian god 'Oro.* See also **Hō'ata-meamea**.

HOATU, the first mortal female in Tuamotuan legend, the wife of Hoa-tea (or Haotu), first mortal male, and from them descend the human race. (Henry 1928:347.) See also **Creation**.

HOIE, the patron god of Matusa, a sting-ray, on the island of Rotuma. (Gardiner 1898:468.)

HOI-MATUA, a Māori chief of Hawaiki* whose son was murdered by the high priest Uenuku.* (Grey 1970:158.)

HOI-TINI, the Marquesan goddess of the yam and ti plants. (Christian 1895:190.)

HOKA, ruler of the legendary netherworld called Hiva-ro-tahi (near the land of Puna*) in the Tuamotuan epic of Rata (Laka*). Hoka captured two giant lizards from Puna and used them to guard his front door. (Stimson 1937:146.)
    In **New Zealand**, a legend of Murihiku states that the mortal man Rona went fishing each day leaving his wife at home. While he was away, she called Hoka down from the heavens to be her lover. Being suspicious of her acts, Rona hid and, as a result, discovered the deception.

He killed Hoka, but he and his children had to flee the wrath of his wife. He took flight to the moon where he can still be seen today, and the children hid in a cave in the cliffs. When anyone shouts out before the cliffs, the children return their call, and this is the origin of the echo in Māori legends. (Beattie 1918: 161.)

HŌKEO, a Hawaiian god who assisted the god Lono* in bringing winds to Hawai'i. (Pukui 1971:384.)

HOKĪO, a bird in New Zealand whose night cry *kakao, kakao* is an omen of war. Supposedly, its cry results from its choking on the hair of warriors who will fall in the coming battle. (Tregear 1891:76; White 1885: 166.) See also **Kakao; Tarakakao**.

HOKOHOKO, a goddess of Niue Island, wife to Tia. (Loeb 1926:162.)

HONO-A-LELE, a Hawaiian wind god who causes mad love and sleeplessness and is associated with the god Makani-ke-oe.* (Pukui 1971:384; Beckwith 1948:93.)

HONO'URA ('ONO-KURA), a giant of telescopic powers in Tuamotuan legend who could lengthen or shorten himself, the eldest son of chief Aua-toa-i-tahiti of Ta'aroa and Te-more-ari'i-vahine of the district of Puna'auia on the island of Tahiti. Hono'ura was born to the happy couple in the form of a great clod which his father took and buried in a cave on the side of mount Tahu'a-reva. From this clod sprang Hono'ura who, having no other food, lived on the stones in the cave.

He grew to gigantic proportions, but remained hidden from everyone's view. Eventually he was discovered by Tautu, a friendly neighbor from Tautira, who informed his parents of his existence. His mother prepared a huge loin cloth to hide his nakedness, and his brothers carried it and other presents of food to the cave. They tried to persuade him to return home with them, but he refused. On the following day, he stood up with his head above the clouds and showed his full stature to the people.

Meanwhile, Tuamotuan warriors attacked the district of Tautira, killed chief Tui-ha'a, and carried his body back to Takume island. Hono'ura decided to come out of seclusion and to declare war upon the Tuamotuans. Before going to battle, however, he decided to make a tour around the island of Tahiti during which time he performed remarkable feats of strength, and then he returned back to his mountain.

After the required period of mourning, Hono'ura carved a spear (Rua-i-pao'o) out of a single ironwood tree and pre-

pared for battle. He and his men traveled to Ra'iātea and then to Hiva where they met the enemy in a bloody battle. Chief Tūtapu was slain, and Hono'ura and his followers set sail to take his widow taken back to Tahiti to become the wife of chief Ta'ihia.

En route, they stopped at Fakaau (Fa'au) where they engaged in a dance contest in which Hono'ura won. There he married the beautiful Ra'i-e-ho-ata-nua who bore him a son 'Aitu-ta-ata-matata'i-te-'aro-'aua. The war party continued its journey, but not without difficulty. It encountered spirits and demons along the way, but the death of chief Tui-ha'a was eventually revenged and his body returned to Tahiti. The Tahitians offered Hono'ura sovereignty over the island, but he refused. He lived the rest of his life in retirement. (Henry 1928:516–537; Williams 1895: 256–294.)

The **Mangaian** version from the Cook Islands blends the Tuamotuan story of Hono'ura with that of the Polynesian hero Rata (Laka*) in the felling of the great ironwood tree. The legend states that once a group of Tongans brought the first ironwood tree to Mangaia and planted it deep within a valley. The tree was possessed by an evil spirit that guarded it from being used by mortals. Many brave Mangaians unsuccessfully attempted to cut the tree down to make spears and weapons.

One day there appeared 'Ono-kura (Hono'ura), a stranger to the island, in possession of a magical adze (Rua-i-para), which had been given to him by his father. He pounced upon the tree and dug at its roots. He cut away the tributary roots until he came to the tap root itself. He hacked it in two, and when the tree crashed to the ground, the demon Vao-tere became visible and engaged in a terrible battle with 'Ono-kura. He split open the skull of the demon with one blow from his magical adze, thus freeing Mangaia from the malicious forest god. The trunk of the tree was made into spears and other weapons, and the roots cut up and planted throughout the island. (Gill 1876:77-87.)

HO'OHOKU-I-KA-LANI, beautiful daughter of Wākea* and Papa* (Haumea*), the progenitors of the Hawaiian people. Wākea instituted tapu nights so that he could sleep with his daughter (a custom of intermarriage common in Polynesia). From this union rose the chiefly class (ali'i) in Hawai'i. When Papa learned of her husband's infidelity she spit in his face and left him. (Beckwith 1918:37–40; Beckwith 1948:296–297; Fornander 1920:319; Malo 1903:314–315.)

HOPE-KOU-TOKI, a Marquesan god of house building and carpentry. (Christian 1895:190; Steinen 1933:43.) See also **Motu-haiki.**

HŌPOE, favorite friend of Hi'iaka* in the Hawaiian legend of Pele* and Hi'iaka. Hōpoe first danced the hula for Hi'iaka and Pele in the Puna district on the Big Island. The red and white forests of Lehua trees in that area were planted for Hōpoe by Hi'iaka. When Hi'iaka was sent on a mission by her sister Pele, Hōpoe was left in Pele's care. Hi'iaka was given forty days to complete her mission. When she returned late, she climbed a ridge at Pōhākea and saw that her sister Pele had covered Hōpoe with lava in retaliation. Near Kea-au in Puna is a fallen rock that once had the shape of a dancing figure. According to legend, the rock represents the figure of Hōpoe caught by the lava while dancing. (Beckwith 1948:173, 176, 181.)

HOPU-TŪ, the sixteenth age in the existence of the Māori universe. (White 1887a: App.) See also **Kore.**

HORAHORA, a beautiful maiden seduced by the great Tuamotuan hero Tahaki (Kaha'i*) in his attempts to locate his father Hema.* A daughter

Mehau* was born from this union. (Stimson 1934:60–62.)

HOROAUTA, one of the great canoes of the Māori migration to New Zealand. (Tregear 1891: 85.) See also Canoes, Māori Migration.

HORO-FANA'E, a messenger for the Tahitian god Ta'aroa (Kanaloa.*) (Henry 1928:356, 364, 405.)

HOROMATANGI, a famous water monster of Lake Taupō, New Zealand; also a reptile goblin who resides in an underwater cave on Motutāiko Island. (Tregear 1891:85; White 1885:119.)

HOROTATA, daughter of Mangamanga-i-atua and one of the two wives of the Māori hero Tinirau (Kinilau*) before he took Hina* to wife. Horotata and her sister Harataunga* jealously abused Hina, and both were slain through Hina's incantations. (Grey 1970:63; Tregear 1891:85.)

HOROUTA, another named for Takitumu,* one of the great canoes in the Māori migrations to New Zealand, so named for its swiftness. (Turei 1912:152–163; Tregear 1891:20, 85.) See also Canoes, Māori Migration.

HOTU, a Tahitian goddess, daughter of Te-fatu (lord of the skies) and Fa'ahotu. She became the wife of the god Ātea (Wā-kea*) and the mother of numerous other deities. (Henry 1928: 373–374, 404.)

HŌTŪĀ, the first mortal man ever killed according to Māori legend. He was slain by Rau-riki who was jealous of his good looks and admiration by women. (White 1887a:41–42.)

HOTUKURA, name of a Tuamotuan goddess. (Stimson 1964:161.) Also a Māori chiefess of Hawaiki* mentioned in the legend of Turi* and Ue-nuku.* (Grey 1970:159.)

HOTU-MATUA, the first immigrant to Easter Island. He and his followers left the island of Maraerenga because of war with Oroi,* a rival chief on the island. An exploratory expedition set out and found Easter Island. When Hotu-Matua landed, his son Tu'u-ma-heke was born. Oroi, however, had hid himself in the canoe and found shelter in the caves near the beach. As time passed, Hotu-Matua's six sons came to bathe near the beach cave, and when they did, they were slain by Oroi. Hotu-Matua eventually captured Oroi and slew him. Hotu-Matua's eldest surviving son, Tu'u-ma-heke, succeeded him as chief although his youngest, Hotu-iti, was his favorite. (Alpers 1970:237–241; Routledge 1917:277–289.)

HOTU-NUI, famous chief of the *Tainui** canoe in the great

Māori migrations to New Zealand. (Tregear 1891:86.) See also **Canoes, Māori Migration; Hotu-roa.**

HOTU-PUKU, a Māori lizard monster. (Tregear 1891:86.)

HOTU-RAPA, a Māori chief in Hawaiki* in the Turi* legend of the migrations to New Zealand. (Grey 1855:192, Grey 1970:161–162; Tregear 1891:86.)

HOTU-ROA, commander of the famous *Tainui*ronomy canoe in the great Māori migrations to New Zealand. (Tregear 1891:86.) See also **Canoes, Māori Migration; Hotu-nui.**

HOTU-TĀIHI-NUI, Tuamotuan name of the two ships built by Marama* and his father Hiro (Hilo*). (Stimson 1957.)

HOUMAI-TĀWHITI, an ancestral hero of the Māori who lived in the legendary land of Hawaiki.* His dog Pōtaka-tāwhiti was murdered by the great high priest Ue-nuku.* The revenge that followed sparked off an intertribal war that resulted in the migration of the Māoris to New Zealand. (Grey 1855:76; Grey 1970:99, 104, 127; Shortland 1882:56; Tregear 1891:87.) See also **Canoes, Māori Migration.**

HOU-MEA, an ancient Māori ogress known for devouring her own children. She was destroyed by hot stones being thrown down her open mouth; also a name given to all evil women. (Tregear 1891:87; White 1887b:171.)

HOVA, an Easter Island god mentioned in the creation* myth as being formed by the supreme god Makemake;* a name not known in other Polynesian islands. (Métraux 1940:315.)

HUA, an ancient Māori god of tides, a son of the god Rangi-pōtiki* and Papa-tū-a-nuku,* and a twin brother to the god Ari.* (Tregear 1891:88; White 1887c:49.)

HUA-ARIKI, name of an ancestral god in the Tuamotus. (Stimson 1964:163.)

HUAHEGA (HUAHENGA), mother of the famous demigod Māui* according to Tuamotuan legend. As a young maiden, she was seduced by Ataraga* who had gone inland in search for food. The child born of this union was the famous Māui-tikitiki. His four older half-brothers lived with their father, Ataraga, and his wife, Hava. Māui, however, lived with his mother, Huahega, and she played a dominant role in his many exploits in this Tuamotuan chant. (Stimson 1934:5–8; Stimson 1964:163.)

HU'AITEKONGO, a malevolent district god on Bellona Island. (Monberg 1966:65, 76.)

HUAKA'I-PŌ, or **OI'O**, Hawaiian marchers of the night, spirits of gods or departed relatives who march on certain nights in procession, chanting, drumming, or playing musical instruments and are to be avoided by humans. (Beckwith 1948:164; Westervelt 1915a:251; Malo 1903:152, 154.)

HUANAKI or **HUNANAKI**, one of the five primary gods of Niue. Huanaki and Fāo were the first two gods to swim from Tonga to settle Niue island. Upon reaching the atoll, they stamped their feet and the land rose higher, and they then created mortals from the ti plant. Huanaki rules over the ocean with his ten children. (Smith 1903:1–31; Turner 1884:304.) Also known as Tuanakinoa, a lazy god and a great robber. According to another tradition, these gods fled from the netherworld, called Fonuagalo, because they had been slighted at feasts. The god Fāo began the creation of the island, but was unable to complete it until Huanaki appeared. Afterwards, the other gods, Fakahoko, Lage-iki, and Lagi-atea, settled on the island. Another story maintains that Huanaki and Fāo fled the underworld* (Avatele) because the children there were lazy. Fāo came to the upper world and unsuccessfully tried to make the tides disappear. It was only when Huanaki came forth that dry land appeared. (Loeb 1926:157–159.)

HUĀ-NGA, a collective name of the first mortals, the offspring of the gods, according to Tuamotuan traditions. (Stimson 1964:162.)

HU'A-NU'U-MARAE, one of the many ingenious gods and goddesses living with the Tahitian god Tāne (Kāne*) in the sky. (Henry 1928:371.)

HUA-TINI, the Marquesan god of dance. (Christian 1895:190.)

HUAURI, mother of the famous Tuamotuan hero Tahaki (Kaha'i*) and the wife of Hema* whom the goblins of Matuauru captured and enslaved in their kingdom. (Stimson 1937:60–68; Stimson 1964:164.)

HUHURA, one of the many ingenious gods and goddesses living with the Tahitian god Tāne (Kāne*) in the sky. (Henry 1928:371.)

HULI-HONUA, a mythical ancestor of the Hawaiian people, more popularly known as Kumu-honua.* (Beckwith 1948:41–46; Kamakau 1961:433.)

HULU, a Hawaiian god wrapped in tapa who assists in

childbirth; also a mythical bird who pecked a hole through Kalalea hill (Kaua'i) so he might look through to the other side. (Pukui 1971:385; Malo 1903:139.)

HUNA-KIKO, or Huno-kiko, an enchanted red cloak owned by the great Māori hero Turi.* (Grey 1970:170; Tregear 1891: 94.)

HUNANAKI, see **Huanaki.**

HURA-VĀNANGA, a Tuamotuan word meaning to expound or to reveal any ancient religious lore. (Stimson 1964:169.)

HURIANGA-I-MATAAHO, the name given to the great deluge* in Māori legends. (Grey 1855: 47; Tregear 1891:96.)

HURI-'ARO, one of the many artisans in the Tahitian creation chant who helped the creator god Ta'aroa (Kanaloa*). Others mentioned are Amara, Fa'a-tae, Huri-tua, Nana, and Rauti. (Henry 1928:356, 365.)

HURI-MAI-TE-ATA, the patron goddess of the ti plant (*manuka*) in New Zealand. (White 1887a: 27.)

HURI-TUA, one of the many artisans in the Tahitian creation chant who helped the creator god Ta'aroa (Kanaloa*). Others mentioned are Amara, Fa'a-tae, Huri-'aro, Nana, and Rauti. (Henry 1928:356, 365.)

HURU, a Māori reptile god. (Tregear 1891:96; White 1887a: App.)

HURUKOEKOEĀ, name of one of the numerous Māori gods dwelling with Miru (Milo*) in the underworld.* (Tregear 1891:97.)

HURU-MĀNU-ARIKI, a Māori god of the ocean. (Tregear 1891:97; White 1887c:56.)

HUTU, an ancient Māori chief who was courted by the beautiful chiefess Pare.* Humiliated by not gaining his approval, she hanged herself. Her tribe held Hutu responsible, and to save his own life, he had to follow her spirit to the underworld* where he offered his priceless jade club to the goddess Hine-nui-te-pō* for directions to the home of the spirits. At first Pare would not see him, but after Hutu attained honors in a new sport he invented (bending down a tree and swinging up on it), she finally emerged from her retreat. She then accompanied Hutu back to the upper world of the living where he forced her soul back into her body through the soles of her feet. (Tregear 1891:98; White 1887b:164–167.) See also **Hiku-i-ka-nahele; Kanikani-a-'ula; Kena; Milimili; Pare.**

HUUTI, name of a Marquesan man who tamed the evil ogress

Te-mo'o-nieve, and the two became the parents of the several
children, the progenitors of the
Marquesans who live in Taaoa
valley, Hivaoa. When Huuti
was a young man playing
games with his colleagues, he
threw his *teka* (a reed shaft) and
hit the ogress Te-moo-nieve in
the ear, and she became vexed.
Huuti then went hunting for a
proper tree for a canoe, and
found one outside of Te-moo-
neve's cave. He fell the tree, but
in so doing, Te-moo-neve pulled
him into her cave and threatened to eat him. He persuaded
her to let him return to his own
people to obtain food. She discovered his deception (to remain with his people), captured
him again, and returned to the
cave. Huuti finally persuaded
her to give up her evil ways and
to return to his people with him.
They lived their final days in
Taaoa valley where they became the parents of Fifa, Paoe,
and Hina (born posthumously).
(Handy 1930: 21–25; Orbell
1968; Thornton 1984:295–314.)

–I–

IA, the principal epithet of the
supreme deity in the Tuamotus.
(Tregear 1891:99.) Also the
name of malevolent gods (reef
eels) of Rotuma who live in a
cave called Anhufhuf or in an
underwater land called Fali-
anogo off the coast of Solkopi.
(Gardiner 1898:468.)

I'AULUALO, an ancient Samoan who, along with his two
sons, was swallowed by a great
fish which had threatened the
passage into the bay at Safata,
'Upolu, Samoa. Once inside the
fish, I'aulualo and his sons
hacked away at its sides with
bamboo knives until the fish in
anger broke through the reef
and landed on shore. The
thrashing of the huge fish created the ideal harbor at Safata.
(Krämer 1902:233; Turner 1884:
245.)

IGO (INGO), a Tuamotuan
word meaning to initiate into
the sacred mysteries or to or-
dain a priest by initiation and
ceremonies. (Stimson 1964:173.)

IHENGA, the Māori god of the
sweet potato, the son of Rongo-
ma-tāne* (White 1887a:App.);
also a chief of Hawaiki* who
traveled in the *Arawa** canoe in
the great migrations to New
Zealand. He saved the high
priest Ngātoro-i-rangi* when
the canoe was being engulfed in
the great whirlpool. Ihenga

married Hine-te-kākarau, daughter of chief Kahu. (Shortland 1882:63; Tregear 1891:100; Grey 1855:87, 96.)

IHI, the Tahitian goddess of wisdom and learning, daughter of the supreme god Ta'aroa (Kanaloa*) and his wife, Paparaharaha* (Henry 1928:374); also the name of a water monster who lives in Lake Taupo, New Zealand. (Tregear 1891:100.) The Marquesan god of the breadfruit tree. (Christian 1895:190.)

IHI-AWAAWA, a Hawaiian goddess of lightning. (Emerson 1915:198.) See also Ihi-lani.

IHIIHI, another name for the goddess Hina* in New Zealand, sister to the demigod Māui,* wife to Irawaru* (who was turned into a dog by Māui), and mother of Pero.* (Tregear 1891:100; White 1887a:App..)

IHI-LANI, a Hawaiian goddess of lightning. (Emerson 1915:198.) See also Ihi-awaawa.

IHIMATŌA, name of the tree from which Hiro's great outrigger canoe was made in Tuamotuan legends. (Stimson 1964:174; Stimson 1957.) See also Hilo.

IHINGĀ, a Māori chief who visited the underworld* of Miru (Milu*) and brought back charms, songs, and games.

(Tregear 1891:100.) See also Rongomai.

IHO-O-TE-RANGI, a god from Hawaiki* (ancient homeland of the Polynesians) who, according to Māori legends, assisted Ngātoro's* niece in crossing the ocean to New Zealand. (Grey 1855:102, Tregear 1891:101.) See also Kuiwai; Manaia.

IHU-ATA, Tahitian god of the mountains above the clouds to whom the hero Rata (Laka*) went to obtain a tree from which to make his canoe for his great journey. (Henry 1928:483, 489.)

IHUATAMAI, one of the two brothers in Māori legend who found the body of the goddess Hina* when it was washed up on the shores at Wairarwa after her long swim in the ocean. Ihuatami* and his brother, Ihuwareware,* became the husbands to Hina, but eventually she became the wife of the great hero Tinirau (Kinilau*), the god of fishes and the son of Tangaroa (Kanaloa*). (Grey 1855:49; Shortland 1882:110; Tregear 1891:102.)

IHU-GATA, a sacred valley on the island of Vavau-nui (Mangareva?) where the great hero Rata (Laka*) spent his last days until his death. (Stimson 1937:146.)

IHUNGARU, an ancient god from Hawaiki* (ancient homeland of the Polynesians) whom the Māori settlers first brought with them to New Zealand. His physical representation was a lock of human hair entwined in a sennit rope. According to accounts, the representation of this god was destroyed in a intertribal war in A. D. 1823. (Shortland 1882:135; Tregear 1891:102.)

IHU-NGARU-PAEA, name (stranded-log-of-timber) assumed by the goddess Hina* after being found on the beach by the two brothers Ihuatamai* and Ihuwareware.* (Grey 1855: 49; Tregear 1891:102.)

IHUNGATA, a Tuamotuan god who resides in the underworld.* (Stimson 1964:175.)

IHUPUKU, goblins (Ponaturi*) in the Māori legend of Tāwhaki (Kaha'i*) who captured Hema,* Tāwhaki's father. (Tregear 1891:102.)

IHU-WAREWARE, one of the two brothers who saved Hina* from drowning and who became her husband. (Grey 1970: 62.) See also Ihu-atamai.

IKA-TAU-KI-RAGI, name given to the Milky Way in Tuamotuan mythology. (Stimson 1964:176.)

IKA-TERE, the Māori god of fishes, the son of Punga,* and grandson of Tangaroa (Kana-loa*). He fled to the ocean to escape the wrath of Tāwhiri-matea* (god of storms and tempests) in the battle to separate the great gods Rangi* (sky father) and Papa* (earth mother). (Grey 1970:6; Tregear 1891:103; White 1887a:App.)

IKIIKI, a demigod from the island of Fakaofo, Tokelau, husband to Talaga, whose son Lu pushed up the sky and secured fire from Mafuike (Mahu-ika,* god of the underworld*). See also Māui.

'ILAHEVA, a mortal Tongan woman, daughter of chief Seketoa,* who became the wife of the god Tagaloa (Kanaloa*), and thus mother to 'Aho'eitu,* the first Tu'i Tonga* (king of Tonga). (Gifford 1924:25–28.)

ILOILOKULA, goddess of the Sau clan in Yandrana, Lau Islands (Polynesian outliers in Fiji), feared by the men of that island. (Hocart 1929:196.) See also Rā Marama.

'IMOA, appears as the first living being (female) in the Samoan evolutionary scale as reported in the pedigree chart of the Tui A'ana, the high ranking chief on 'Upolu, Samoa. (Krämer 1902:168.) See also Creation; Ma'ata'anoa; Tui Manu'a.

INA, see Hina.

INA-ANI-VAI, the wife of the god Tangaroa (Kanaloa*) in Mangaian legends and mother of Tarauri and Turi-the-Bald. (Gill 1876:118.)

INSECTS. In Tahitian legends, insects are commonly agents of the gods or spirits. The spider, moth, and butterfly are the shadows of the god Tū (Kū*); the dragon fly, the shadow of Hiro (Hilo*), god of thieves; and centipedes, the shadows of Tama-teina,* the god of medicine. (Henry 1928:391–392.)

IO (IHO, IHOIHO), widely believed by some of the New Zealand Māori to be the supreme creator, although modern research shows that the idea most likely emerged from attempts of two priests, Te Matorohanga and Nepia Pohuhu, in the 1870s to reconcile ancient tradition with Christian theology. (Barrère 1967:103–119; Buck 1949:535–536; Hare Hongi 1907:109; Poignant 1967:40–41; Tregear 1891:106; White 1887a:32, 2:4.)

'IO-I-TE-AO-NUI-MARAMA, one of the Tuamotuan gods named in the Rangiroa creation* chant. (Stimson 1964:177.)

'IO-ULI, an Hawaiian bird god, a dark hawk. (Malo 1903:186; Pukui 1971:385.)

IO-WAHINE, name of the first woman in Māori legends, formed by the god Tāne (Kāne*) and given to Tiki*-au-aha, the first man. (Tregear 1891:106; White 1887a:158.)

IPO-KINO, a Marquesan woman put to death because of her infidelity to her husband, Tue-ato, a chief fisherman of Hiva Oa. Tue-ato's four spirit sisters who had caused Ipo-kino's death took pity on their brother and set out to Havai'i (Hawaiki*) or the underworld.* They caught Ipo-kino's soul, and when they arrived in the upper world, her spirit entered a wooden image (*tiki**), and became human again. Ignorant of the taboo against sexual relations for thirteen days, the couple slept together that night, and the wife's spirit once more returned to the underworld. The spirit sisters returned again to Havai'i and rescued her spirit. The taboo was acknowledged, and all was well. The happy couple had several children born to them, one of whom was Pohu,* a demigod of great power. (Handy 1930:113.)

IRAWARU, the Māori god of dogs, the husband to Hina* (sister to Māui*). According to one legend, Irawaru and Māui went fishing together. Māui became jealous of Irawaru's successful catch and turned him into a dog, the first of its kind. When Māui's sister Hina saw what has happened to her husband, she threw herself into the sea, but her two brothers, Ihuatamai* and Ihu-wareware,* rescued her. (Grey 1855:32.) In another Māori legend, Irawaru is called Owa, and he and his wife Ihiihi (Hina) were the parents of Pero,* the first dog. (White 1887b:77, 86, 119.) See also **Ri**.

IRE, a messenger god to Ta'aroa (Kanaloa*) in Tahitian legend (Henry 1928:356, 369.) Also the name of a pet shark of the gods Tū (Kū*) and Ta'aroa who rescued it from death at the hands of mortals and who then gave it to the god Tāne (Kāne*). It was taken to heaven where it became the Milky Way. (Henry 1928:403–404.) See also **Sharks**.

IRI, Tuamotuan name given to a medium who is spiritually possessed. (Stimson 1964:178.)

'IRI-NAU, a messenger for the Tahitian gods, especially Tūpapa.* (Henry 1928:163–164, 357.)

ITA-NGATA, a vindictive, Samoan spirit (god) who can enter his earthly priests and bring calamity upon his enemies. (Stair 1896:37.)

ITI, a principal god of Aitutaki, Cook Islands. (Pakoti 1895:65–70.)

'ITI'ITI, a goddess from the island of Bellona. (Monberg 1966: 57.) See also **Ekeitehua; Tehainga'atua**.

ITI-ITI, named as the sister to Rupe* in the Māori legend of Tinirau (Kinilau*), most likely another name for their sister Hina.* (Grey 1855:57; Tregear 1891:108; White 1887a:85.) See also **Kae**.

ITO, a Tahitian god who guards the earth during dark nights when there is no moonlight. (Henry 1928:376.) Also a Tuamotuan word for demon. (Stimson 1964:180.)

ITUPAOA, an ancient Māori god brought to New Zealand from Hawaiki.* (Grey 1855:102; Taylor 1870:31); also name of one of the chief gods on the island of Ana'a in the Tuamotus. (Stimson 1964:180; Tregear 1891:109; White 1885:171.)

ITU-PAWA, one of the gods brought to New Zealand by Kuiwai,* her sister Haungaroa,* and three other women. They were borne over the vast ocean only by the power of these gods. According to legend, they landed at Tāwhiuwhiu on the North Island of New Zealand. (Grey 1970:129, 130; Tregear 1891:109.)

ITURAGI, grandfather of the Tuamotuan hero Tahaki (Kaha'i*), husband to the goddess Hina,* who lives in the netherworld called Tuaraki-i-te-pō. (Stimson 1934:68–70.)

IULAUTALO, a minor household god of Samoa to whom all tips of leaves were sacred. (Turner 1884:70.)

'IWA, a famous trickster in Hawaiian legend, a master thief from birth. Once he entered a particular contest between six other professional thieves. The object was to fill a house with stolen goods in a single night. He waited until all the others had filled their houses and had gone to bed, whereupon, he slipped into their houses, stole everything from them, and filled his own. He also stole a magic cowry squid lure from chief 'Umi* and a sacred adze tied between the necks of two old ladies. (Elbert 1959:18–31; Pukui 1971:385.) See also **Kana; Kawelo; Ono.**

–K–

KA'AHUA, name of a legendary Marquesan canoe, captained by chief Te-heiva, that sailed from Paumau on the island of Hiva Oa to a mythical land toward the east called Tefiti. The double-hulled, outrigger canoe contained several houses, a large number of people from Hiva Oa, and great quantities of provisions for the long journey. Some of the explorers remained, and the others returned. (Handy 1930:131.)

KA-'AHU-PĀHAU, a friendly shark goddess in Hawaiian legend, who lives with her brother (or son?) Ka-hi'u-kā in a cave at the mouth of Pearl Harbor (O'ahu). Having been born of human parents, they are always benevolent to humans and protect O'ahu from man-eating sharks. (Beckwith 1948: 138–140). See also **Sharks.**

KA-'AINA-I-KA-HOUPO-A-KĀNE, a continent once believed by the Hawaiians to have connected all the land masses, but was divided during the great deluge.* (Beckwith 1948: 328.)

KA-'ALAE-NUI-A-HINA, an Hawaiian sorcery god. (Malo 1903:82). See also 'Alae-a-Hina.

KĀ'ANA-E-LIKE, a beautiful Hawaiian goddess, the grand

daughter of the cannibal, tongue-stretching god Kū-waha-ilo,* who lives on Ulu-ka'a (or Uala-ka'a), a floating island of the gods, with her parents and eleven sisters. She married chief Ke-awe-a'oho of Waipi'o, Hawai'i, whom she rescued from a certain death at sea. After a while Ke-awe-a'oho returned to Hawai'i, and when his son, Nā-ku'emake-pau-i-ke-ahi, became of age, he set out to visit his father. He persuaded him to return to Ulu-ka'a. Once there, Ke-awe-a'oho was attracted to Kā'ana-e-like's younger sister, and in anger, Kā'ana-e-like sent a fiery flood that destroyed everything on the island except herself and her son. Her son left, and she was left alone on the burning island. (Rice 1923:19–31; Green 1928: 115–118.)

KA-AO-MELEMELE, maid-of-the-golden-cloud, daughter of the Hawaiian gods Kū* and Hina,* reared in a mythical land called Ke-'aloha-lani.* She is taught the graceful movements of the hula by Kapo, sister to the poison god Mauna-loa. She took her brother Kau-mā'ili-'ula as a husband (highest form of Hawaiian marriage), and together they ruled the islands. The romance tells of the lore of the ever-changing clouds, the appearance of the stars in the sky, the motion of the swaying leaves and blossoms as depicted in the hula, and numerous other allusions to ancient Hawaiian culture. (Beckwith 1948:519–523; Westervelt 1915a:116–151.)

KABA'EHA, one of the many district gods of the Kaitu'u clan on Bellona Island, the eldest son of the principal god Tehu-'aingabenga.* (Monberg 1966: 67.)

KAE ('AE), name of the magician in the Māori legend of Tinirau (Kinilau*) who killed Tinirau's pet whale Tutunui. (Best 1928:261–270; Grey 1970:69–76; Tregear 1891:110.) The **Marquesan** version tells that Kae was shipwrecked on Vai-noki (Puamau), an island of women. He met and married the beautiful chiefess Hina* and had a son, Kae-te-tama. Eventually, Kae became homesick and returned to his native land on the back of the whale Tunua-nui, Hina's brother. Once home, Kae's people killed and ate Tunua-nui. Meanwhile Kae's son decided to visit his father on the back of another large fish, Tunua-iti. When he arrived, Kae's people attempted to seize it and drag it ashore. Instead, it was they who were dragged out to sea and drowned. The death of Tunua-nui was avenged. (Handy 1930:56–63; Steinen 1933:353–365.)

In one **Samoan** story, 'Ae (Kae) is represented as a Tongan who accompanied Tinilau on his journeys on the back of two turtles. When Tinilau learned that 'Ae had killed his pets, he called upon the gods to transport the sleeping 'Ae to his home. Once there, 'Ae was slain, cooked, and eaten in revenge for his deed. (Bülow 1900:13, 67; Krämer 1902:1:128–130; Turner 1884:110.) Another Samoan story (Brown 1917:94–99) parallels the following Tongan narration.

In **Tonga**, Kae survived the perilous journey taken by king Lo'au to the edge of the horizon. He grasped the leg of a huge bird (*kanivatu*), and he was carried to Samoa. There, Sinilau (Kinilau*) welcomed him and provided further transportation to Tonga on the back of his pet whales, Tonga and Samoa. When Kae arrived home, his people killed and ate Tonga. Sinilau ordered the gods to go to Tonga to collect the remains of his pet whale and to bring Kae back to him. Kae was killed, and Tonga (the whale) was reconstituted and brought back to life. (Gifford 1924:139–152.)

KA-'EHU-IKI-MANŌ-O-PU'U-LOA, a little brown shark god who guards the entrance to Pearl Harbor (O'ahu) but originally from Puna, Hawai'i. Born of human parents, he was reared on kava mixed with mother's milk. He befriended all of the king sharks in Hawai'i except a threatening one on Māui whom he killed following a journey that took him throughout the Pacific islands. Ka-'ehu then returned via

O'ahu where he encountered Pehū, a man-eating shark, off Waikiki. He lured Pehu to shore where the Hawaiians killed the brute. Ka-'ehu then returned as a hero to his home in Puna. (Beckwith 1948:139–140; Thrum 1923:293–308.) See also **Sharks**.

KAHA, a Tuamotuan image of a god made of feathers and fish bone and bound with sennit. (Stimson 1964:183–184.)

KAHA'I (KAHAKI, TAFA'I, TAHAKI, TAVAI, TĀWHAKI), a handsome, red-skinned Polynesian demigod whose exploits and widespread legends are second in popularity only to those of Māui.* In **N e w Zealand,** Tāwhaki was the grandson of a cannibalistic goddess Whaitiri* who married a mortal, Kaitangata, and who had two sons, Hema* and Punga.* Having gone blind and disliking her motherly role, Whaitiri left her family to return to her heavenly abode. Hema, her oldest son, married a goddess, and they had two children, Tāwhaki and Kariki. While looking for an adequate gift for his newborn son, Hema trespassed on lands belonging to the wicked goblins, the Ponaturi.* They seized him, gouged out his eyes, threw him into a dung heap, and then captured his wife, Uru-Tonga.

The subsequent legend centers around Tāwhaki's exploits in rescuing his parents from such disgusting circumstances. In his journeys, he met and married Hine-piripiri from whom was born their son Wahieroa (Wahieloa*). Tāwhaki's four brothers-in-law unsuccessfully attempted to slay him, whereupon he aroused the wrath of the gods who sent a great flood (Mataaho*) to destroy them. Tāwhaki and his brother Kariki then set out again to revenge their father. They reached the lands of the Ponaturi and found their enslaved mother. She told them that light was fatal to the Ponaturi who slept in a dark hut on land during the night and who roamed under the sea during the day. Tāwhaki, Kariki, and their mother closed out all rays of light in their hut and thus the goblins slept until after day break. Upon awakening, they found themselves trapped within their hut. Meanwhile, the brothers found their father, burned down the hut, destroyed the goblins, and escaped together.

In his search for his third wife Hāpai (sometimes Tangotango), Tāwhaki set out again with Kariki. They encountered their blind grandmother, Mataerepō* or Whaitiri,* who guarded the vines to heaven. They stole her taro, and she thrashed about trying to slay the thieves. When the brothers hit her eyes and magically restored her sight, she agreed to help them reach the heavens. Forgetting to use his

magic, Kariki was unable to weather the strong winds he encountered and thus returned to earth. Tāwhaki safely succeeded in reaching the celestial world where he disguised himself as an old man and as an assistant to the canoe makers. Tāwhaki finally revealed his true self and was reconciled with his wife and his daughter, Arahuta. He decided to remain in the sixth heaven, Ngātaatua, where he became the god of lightning and thunder. (Grey 1970:46–61; Potae 1928:359–366.) The **Rarotongan** story of Ta'aki and Harii is found in Smith 1921:1–13.

In the **Tuamotuan** story, Tahaki and Karihi are twin brothers, but only Tahaki was endowed with magical powers. One day, Tahaki's father, Hema, went crabbing on lands belonging to the goblins of Matuauru who captured and carried him off to their home. In their search for their father, Tahaki and Karihi encountered their blind and bewitching grandmother, Kuhi. When Karihi got caught on her fish line and was tied up, Tahaki climbed the nearest tree and threw coconuts down at the old woman. When they hit her eyes, she miraculously became well and rejoiced in seeing her grandson. After seeking directions from the star maidens, Tahaki set out to find his father. He reached Matuauru where he pulled his father from the pit and restored his sight. Leaving his father with the star maidens, he returned to Hiva-nui, the land of the goblins, made a strong net called Tukutukuraho-nui (great spider), threw it over them, and beat them to death. On his voyage home, he stopped in the land of the fish and gave his dark skin to the Hami-kere fish. After his death, Tahaki ascended to the sacred sky of Tāne (Kāne*), where he was set apart as regent for the gods over Havaiki-nui. (Stimson 1937:60–96; Stimson 1934: 50–100.) Another Tuamotuan version of Tafa'i and Ariki is given by Leverd 1911:172–184.

In one **Tuamotuan** legend from the island of Fagatau, the young Tahaki was killed by his jealous cousin Niu-Kura,* but was brought back to life through the magical powers of his mother, Huauri.* After his lengthy exploits which gain him fame, he received the hand in marriage of princess Hāpai, but when he took Hapai's sister as a mistress, trouble followed, and Tahaki fled to the land of the Manono clan where he was slain. His wife, Hapai, sang his long lament, "you have gone far away to the night realm of Kiho, the last heaven of repose, this tale of Tahaki is concluded." (Stimson 1934:50–77.)

In **Samoa**, Tafa'i, his brother 'Alise, and sister Ifiifi are children of Pua and Sigano.* In hopes of getting a suitable bride for his master, their servant Lauamatoto ascended to the skies where he entreated the goddess Sina-tae-o-i-lagi, the daughter of Tagaloa-lagi, to receive the two brothers. She agreed. When they heard this, Tafa'i and Alise disguised themselves as dirty, ugly men so that they might safely pass by the people of heaven. Upon seeing them in this filthy condition, Sina ordered them to another end of the house. The next morning, the two brothers took on their normal, handsome appearance and prepared to leave. Seeing them as their true selves, Sina was distraught and ran after them. On the way to earth, Tafa'i threw Sina down into a chasm out of which she was rescued by his parents and was taken to their earthly home to live. Eventually, Tafa'i falls in love with her, but she alludes his advances and flees to her home in the sky. Eventually, she is persuaded by her family to return to earth and to marry Tafa'i. From this union was born La (Rā*), the sun, who went to live with his mother in the skies. (Krämer 1902:455–456).

In **Tahiti**, Tafa'i was the son of Hēmā* and the goddess Hina*-tahu-tahu. After a serious quarrel between the two parents, Hēmā left and went to the underworld ($p\bar{o}$*), where he was captured, degraded, and made a prisoner. After a childhood marred by the pranks of his cousins, Tafa'i grew to masculine size, admired for his wisdom, bravery, generosity, and love. Tafa'i's first task consisted of cutting the sinews of the of the island of Tahiti (originally a large fish) to render it stable. He later fished up the atolls in the Tuamotuan archipelago, then moved northward where he fished up the Hawaiian chain. He and his companions originally had planned to drag the entire Hawaiian chain back to Tahiti with them. The magic spell to accomplish this was broken when they looked back to check on the islands. The line broke, and as a result the Hawaiian islands remain forever in the northern Pacific. Tafa'i then rescued his father from the underworld and returned him to the world of light and to his family. Tafa'i and his five brothers then competed in several contests for the hand in marriage of the beautiful Hawaiian princess Te-'ura-i-te-ra'i. After the usual feasting and merriment, the Hawaiians were astonished that Tafa'i and his brothers decided to return to Tahiti to marry from among their own. Tafa'i married Hina, famed for her beautiful long black hair. Once on returning from one of his exploits, Tafa'i found that Hina was dead and that her spirit was making its way to its final resting place in the spirit world. He sped away in his canoe, snatched her spirit by the hair, and restored her spirit to her body. There was much rejoicing and the two lived happily ever after. (Henry 1928:552–565; Leverd 1912:1–12.)

The **Hawaiian** Kaha'i legends are fragmentary. Kaha'i-nui (Kaha'i-the-great) was the son of Hema, a chief on the island of Maui, and of his wife, Luamahehoa. Kaha'i and his brother Aliki (Kariki) followed the path of the rainbow to seek their father who had been captured by the 'Ai'aia* bird near the borders of Kahiki (Tahiti ?). Successfully returning home, Kaha'i landed on the island of Hawai'i and married Hina-'ulu-'ōhi'a. (Beckwith 1948:248; Malo 1903:323; Fornander 1880:16–18.)

KA-HA'I, Hawaiian grandson of the famed voyager Mo'i-keha* who is responsible for the introduction of the breadfruit into the Hawaiian Islands. Tradition says he sailed to 'Upolu, Samoa, and returned to Hawai'i where he planted the breadfruit starts at Pu'u Loa, Kohala. (Beckwith 1948:97; Fornander 1880:54; Fornander 1916:392–393.)

KAHA-KAEKAEA, a residence of the Hawaiian gods in the romance of Lā'ie-i-ka-wai.* (Beckwith 1948:530.)

KAHAKĀUAKOKO, mother of the Hawaiian goddess Papa* (wife of Wākea*). (Beckwith 1948:307, 309; Fornander 1878:181–185.)

KAHA-KURA, Tuamotuan name for the crimson girdle (loin cloth) associated with the god Ātea (Wākea*). (Stimson 1964:184.)

KA-HALA-O-MĀPUANA, the youngest Maile* sister, also a sorceress in the Hawaiian romance of Lā'ie-i-ka-wai.* She restores the dead and entangles her enemies in growing vines. (Beckwith 1948:527, 533–534.)

KA-HALA-O-PUNA, a young Hawaiian beauty sometimes called the rainbow maiden on the island of O'ahu who was slain by her fiancé Ka-uhi* because he was lead to believe that she had been unfaithful to him. Her spirit cried out to passers-by who told her parents, and they found her body and restores her to life. One account tells of her being brought back to life by her guardian owl Pueo. (Beckwith 1948:152–153; Fornander 1917:188–193; Westervelt 1915a:84–93.)

KAHEKAHE, Tuamotuan word meaning a superior god such as Tāne (Kāne*), Tū (Kū*), etc. (Stimson 1964:185.)

KAHIKI-HONUA-KELE, a legendary land, a land of origin in Hawaiian mythology, a paradise made by the gods where they placed the first man and woman. (Beckwith 1948:43, 45, 73; Malo 1903:208.) Also the name of the brother to Kama-pua'a* (hog man). (Beckwith 1948:202; Fornander 1880: 43–44.)

KAHIKINA-O-KA-LĀ, Hawaiian god invoked to cure sickness. (Beckwith 1948:12.)

KAHIKO-LUA-MEA, the ancestor of all the Hawaiian people, the father of Wākea,* Līhau-'ula, and Maku'u, and husband to Kūpūlanakēhau. (Beckwith 1948:294–298; Fornander 1878: 112.)

KAHI-KONA, a Hawaiian god of fishermen. (Emerson 1915:121.)

KAHINALI'I, father of the Hawaiian volcano goddess Pele* according to one Hawaiian tradition. (Beckwith 1948:170–171, 315; Thrum 1907:36–38; Westervelt 1916:7.)

KA-HINIHINI, a Hawaiian god of war, a relative of the goddesses Hi'iaka* and Pele.* (Emerson 1915:43.) See also **Ka-maiau**.

KA-HI'U-KĀ, see **Ka-'ahu-pāhau**.

KA-HOA-LEI, a chief on Kahiki (Tahiti ?) in the legend of the Hawaiian stretching god Kana.* (Rice 1923:102–105.)

KA-HŌ-ĀLI'I, a Hawaiian god associated with the underworld,* an ancestral god of the

Pele* family represented by a naked man (a priest) during the *makahiki* * festival and at dedications of important temples (*heiau*) at the end of which the priest swallows the eyeball of a fish (*bonito*) and of a human victim. He accompanied Pele to Hawai'i from their ancient homeland in Tahiti. (Beckwith 1948:49–51, 106, 110, 130; Emerson 1915:145; Malo 1903:206.) See also **Ka-hoa-lei.**

KA-HOLI-A-KĀNE, a shark god worshipped by the Hawaiian chief Ka-lani-'ōpu'u at the time of king Kamehameha I (d. 1819). (Pukui 1971:385.) Also a powerful shark god of Ka'ū, Hawai'i, who attempted to prevent the marriage between the volcano goddess Pele* (his relative) and the mortal chief Lohi'au* from Kaua'i. (Pukui 1971:389; Emerson 1915:160–162.) See also **Kua; Sharks.**

KAHORIŪ, Tuamotuan word for a familiar spirit, household or ancestral god, or a defied ancestor. (Stimson 1964:185.)

KA-HUILA-MAKA-KEHA'I-I-KA-LANI, a Hawaiian god of thunder and lightning and an ancestor of the goddess Pele.* (Beckwith 1948:48, 108, 192.) Also son of the Hawaiian hero 'Au-kele-nui-a-iku.* (Beckwith 1948:492–495; Fornander 1916: 32–111.)

KA-HUILA-O-KA-LANI, see **Kālai-pāhoa.**

KĀHUITARA, the Māori goddess of seabirds, the daughter of Kikiwai.* (Tregear 1891:113; White 1887a: App.)

KĀHUITOKA, name of the original inhabitants of New Zealand before the arrival of the Polynesians, discovered by the great Māori voyager Kupe.* (Tregear 1891:114.) See also **Kāhuitupua.**

KĀHUITUPUA, name of the original inhabitants of the South Island of New Zealand before the arrival of the Polynesians. (Tregear 1891:114.) See also **Tupua; Hītī; Kāhuitoka.**

KĀHUKAKANUI, illegitimate son of Manaia* (a powerful Māori chief living in Hawaiki*). (Grey 1970:175, 198; Tregear 1891:114.)

KĀHUKURA, the Māori god of travelers, the Māori rainbow god, also known as Atuatoro, brought to New Zealand aboard the *Takitūmu* * canoe by Ruawhārō (Grey 1855:84; Grey 1970:129–130); the first mortal who learned the art of making fishnets from fairies (Grey 1855:180); a Māori who brought the sweet potato to New Zealand from Hawaiki* (Tregear 1891:114; White 1887c:98–104).

KAHU-MATANGI, an ancient Tuamotuan god. (Stimson 1964: 186.)

KĀHURAKI, a sacred place in the heavens (blue skies) where the Māori gods Tū (Kū*) and Rongo (Lono*) made war. (Tregear 1891:114; White 1887a: 37.)

KĀHU-RERE-MOA, also known as Te Kāhu-rere-moa, beautiful daughter of the great Māori chief Paka,* son of Ho-tunui* (chief of the *Tainui** canoe in the great migration to New Zealand). Kāhu-rere-moa married Takakōpiri and bore a daughter Tūpara-haki* from whom sprang the famous Ngātipaoa tribe in New Zealand. (Grey 1855:168; Grey 1970:198–209; Tregear 1891: 115.)

KĀHUTIATARANGI, same as Paikea.* (Tregear 1891:116.) See also **Ruatapu.**

KAIHAGA, a god of Niue Island. (Loeb 1926:163.)

KAIHAMULU, a god of Niue Island. (Loeb 1926:163.)

KAI-HERE, Māori wife of Tūtakahinahina.* (Tregear 1891:116.)

KAI-HEWA, the place in heaven where the rebellious spirits were driven by the Māori god Tāne (Kāne*). (Tregear 1891: 116; White 1887a:38.)

KAIKAIPONI, an ancient, brave warrior of Rotuma, but originally he was from Tonga. He married a girl from Rotuma and because of his bravery was appointed chief. During his reign, kava (from Samoa) was introduced into Rotuma. One day his son went out to play and found two goddesses, Opopu and Rara, who had come down from heaven. The young boy was injured while playing in their swing, but when the two goddesses ascended to heaven, a rain shower poured down upon the young boy and miraculously cured him. The spot is called Vakoi. (Gardiner 1898: 515–517.)

KAIKAPU, a cannibalistic lizard (*mo'o*) who lives in a cave on the island of Hawai'i, and whose granddaughter, Ninole, attracts travelers to her cave to be eaten for food. (Beckwith 1948:264.) In the Laka* epic, she guards the cave where Laka's grandfather's bones are thrown. She is slain by Laka and his companions. (Beckwith 1948: 263). In the romance of 'Au-kele-nui-a-iku,* she is the blind relative whose eyesight is restored and who guides 'Au-kele to the water of life. (Beckwith 1948:264.)

KA-IKI-LANI, beautiful wife to the Hawaiian god Lono* in whose memory Lono institutes the harvest festival called the *makahiki*.* (Beckwith 1948:36–37; Fornander 1880:115–119; Thrum 1907:108–116.)

KĀ'ILI, Hawaiian war god worshipped by Līloa* (a ruling chief on Hawai'i), represented in the form of feathers, became the war god Kū-kā'ili-moku* in the days of king Kamehameha I (d. 1819). (Beckwith 1948:28–29, 113, 396; Pukui 1971:395.)

KA-ĪLIO-HAE, a Hawaiian warrior whose soul visited the underworld, but the spirit of his departed sister allowed him to pass through the guards and return to earth. (Beckwith 1948:146; Westervelt 1915a:100–107.) See also **Hiku-i-ka-nahele; Hutu; Kanikani-a-'ula.**

KAĪNA, Tuamotuan name for the little people who dwell in Vai-tea, a land beneath the earth in the underworld.* Originally, mortals could visit the land by passing through a gate guarded by Tū-ki-hiui, but after he was slain by Ta-Haki, the gateway was permanently closed to mortals. (Stimson 1964:188.) See also **Elves and Fairies.**

KAINONO, a god of Niue Island who eats insects off trees but not invoked for this purpose. (Loeb 1926:161.)

KAIRAURUA, a legendary Tuamotuan woman from the islet of Hao who was captured by a group of men from Mokorea who had hairy bodies and long fingernails. They took her to Vaiari where she remained for a long time. She taught the men the secret of cooking their food and the women the method of giving birth naturally rather than by their caesarian method. She eventually returned to her native land with samples of red coconuts to prove that she had been to this legendary land. (Caillot 1914:57–60.)

KAITANGATA, son of the Māori god Rehua,* accidentally killed by the demigod Rupe* (brother to Māui*) in his search for his sister Hina.* It is Kaitangata's blood that tinges the evening sky. (Grey 1970:67–68; Grey 1855:53; Tregear 1891:118.) Also the grandfather of the Māori hero Tāwhaki (Kaha'i*).

KAITANGO, a nonworshipped god on Bellona Island, brought anciently from their homeland, 'Ubea. (Monberg 1966:75.)

KAITOA, an evil god who dwells in the Māori underworld* with Miru (Milu*). (Tregear 1891:118.)

KAKAO, also known as Tara-kakao,* a malevolent Tuamotuan bird whose voice is heard the night prior to a battle. Its choke comes from the hair of the men soon to be slain in battle being caught in its throat. (White 1887b:17.) See also **Ho-kio.**

KAKAUFĀNUI, Tuamotuan name for Rata's magical adze. (Stimson 1964:191.) See also **Laka.**

KĀKUHIHEWA, a famous Hawaiian chief of O'ahu who aided Ka-welo* in his invasion of the island of Kaua'i. (Pukui 1971:386; Elbert 1959:62–63.)

KĀLA'E-PUNI, a fearless Hawaiian demigod who in his youth killed sharks with his own hands and pulled trees up as if they were sticks. He was treacherously slain by the ruling chief Ka'ewe-nui-a-'umi and priest Mokupane. (Fornander 1916:488–497; Beckwith 1948:421.) Similar stories are told of Kāla'e-hina, Kālai-kini, and Kalei-kini. (Beckwith 1948:421–423; Fornander 1917:198–211; Green 1928:11–15.)

KĀLAI-PĀHOA, a renown Hawaiian sorcery god, or poison god, from the island of Moloka'i. An image of this god was first formed by a man on Moloka'i named Kāne-iā-kama who prayed to the god Kāne* for gambling success. Kāne answered his prayers, and Kāne-iā-kama carved on image from the *nioi*, a poisonous pepper tree, which became the property of the ruling chiefs on Moloka'i. The god was subsequently wor-

shipped throughout the islands after the unification by king Kamehameha I (d. 1819). He is often seen as a streak of light through the heavens similar to the gods Ave-aitu* and Rongomai.* (Beckwith 1948:109, 111–118.) See also **Ma'i-ola.**

KA-LAMA-I-NU'U or **KA-LANI-MAI-NU'U**, a Hawaiian lizard (*mo'o*) goddess from Lā'ie, O'ahu, who lured a lover (Puna-ai-koa'e) to her cave in the Wai'anae mountains. After several months, he longed to go surfing again. Ka-lama-i-nu'u gave him her surf board, but warned him not to talk to anyone. Disregarding her advice, he talked to his friends who informed him of his lover's true nature. Puna returned to the cave, saw Ka-lama-i-nu'u in her true form, but showed no fear. Ka-lama-i-nu'u sought after the informants and eventually captured and killed them at the bottom of the sea. (Beckwith 1948:193–194, 200.) See also **Haumea; Nona; Puna.**

KALAMA-'ULA, *mo'o* (lizard) grandmother to Manini-holo-kuāua* (the noted Hawaiian thief on Moloka'i). She lived in a cave where her grandson stored his stolen goods. (Beckwith 1948:339; Fornander 1917:164–167.)

KALANA-I-HAU'OLA, the Hawaiian paradise where the first man and woman were placed by the gods. The Māori equivalent is Taranga-i-hau-ola. (Beckwith 1948:43, 73; Fornander 1920:267, 268, 273–276.)

KALANIMANUIA, a Hawaiian "rat" son of the chief Kū and the beautiful Kauno'a. Ignorant of his son's parentage, Kū had him thrown into the sea. His spirit returned and was snared by Kū's men. It first took the form of a rat, and when he successfully competed for his sister's hand-in-marriage, he then became human. (Beckwith 1948: 479–480; Fornander 1920:548–553.)

KA-LAU-MĀKI, a younger brother to the Hawaiian hero Ka-welo* from Kaua'i. (Beckwith 1948:405–407.) See also **Kamalama.**

KA-LEI-HAU-OLA, a Hawaiian goddess of necromancy. (Emerson 1915:78, 80.) See also **Hapu'u.**

KA-LELE-A-LUA-KĀ, a Hawaiian demigod of supernatural powers, the son of 'Opele (Ka-'opele-moemoe), the sleeper (sleeps for six months) from the Big Island of Hawai'i. He can jump over great precipices and run on water like a duck. Once, he sailed to the island of O'ahu, reunited with his father, and befriended the chief of the island and helped him defeat his enemies with numerous daring feats. He eventually became the ruling chief over O'ahu. (Beckwith 1948:415–418; Fornander 1916:464–471, 1917:168–171; Thrum 1907:74–106.)

KALOAFU, father of the eel god Tuna* in the Tongan story of Hina* and the origin of the coconut.* (Gifford 1924:181.)

KALOKALO-O-KA-LA, son of the sun god on Fakaofo atoll, Tokelau, he set out to visit his father and to obtain a lucky fishhook as a present for his bride. Encountering an old woman with eight taro sprouts, he restored her eyesight (reminiscent of the legend of Kaha'i*), climbed the tree to heaven, and found his father. He was given the fishhook but was told not to open the package it was in until he returned home. Disregarding the warning, he fell into the sea but was saved by a shark. His son, Tautini,* inherited the hook and was successful in fishing until he lost the hook once more. (Beckwith 1948:25; Burrows 1923: 168–170.) See also **'Alo'alo.**

KA-MAIAU, a Hawaiian war god, a relative of the goddesses Hi'iaka* and Pele.* (Emerson 1915:43.)

KAMA-I-KA-'ĀHUI, a Hawaiian guardian god, who once lived in the Hāna district of Maui, part man, part shark, and who warned people going to the ocean against man–eating sharks. He would devour those who continued on their way. He eventually was expelled to O'ahu where he became the ruling chief of 'Ewa until he was slain by the god Palila.* (Beckwith 1948:140–141; Fornander 1917:140–144, 372–374.) See also **Ka-welo; Nanaue; Nenewe; Mano-niho-kahi; Pauwalu; Sharks.**

KA-MAKA-NUI-'AHA'ILONO, a Hawaiian sorcery god who introduced the art of healing by first causing Lono's * foot to swell and then teaching him how to cure such wounds. (Beckwith 1948:119; Pukui 1971: 386.)

KAMALAMA, younger brother to the Hawaiian hero Ka-welo* from Kaua'i. (Beckwith 1948: 405–407.)

KAMA-PUA'A, a popular Hawaiian demigod in the form of half man and half hog, tall and handsome with sparkling eyes, the son of Hina* and Kahiki-'ula. The narrative of his four major adventures is said to take sixteen hours to recite (Emerson 1892:13–14). His first adventures tells of his conflict with his stepfather 'Olopana,* chief of Ko'olau on O'ahu. 'Olopana sent his men four times to capture Kama-pua'a because of his depredations against him. Each time, his grandmother, Kaumanua-niho rescued him with her chants, and he killed his

captors. Finally he and his family retired to Wahiawa as farmers, but once again 'Olopana's men captured him and returned him to Kailua for sacrifice. He was rescued, however, through the intercession of the priest Lonoaohi and decided to leave O'ahu for the island of Kaua'i.

On Kaua'i, he married the chief's daughter and became involved in their family feuds against his own uncle. His parents entered the conflict, invaded Kaua'i, and declared they have no other son than Kahiki-honua-kele. It was only after reciting all of his name songs and then revealing himself naked to his mother Hina do they finally believe him. From here Kama-pua'a swam to the southeast coast of Kaua'i, changed into a pig, and rooted up the growing crops. He befriended Lima-loa,* and the two married the beautiful daughters of the ruling chief. Again, he became involved in their wives' family feuds, and in retaliation confiscated all the chief's share of the booty. When discovered, Kama-pua'a was banished from the island.

From Kaua'i, Kama-pua'a fled to Kahiki (Tahiti ?) where again he became involved in intertribal warfare against Lono-ka-'eho* with the eight stone foreheads. Kamapua'a called upon his plant bodies who strangled Lono-ka-'eho, and then his hog bodies ate up Lono and all his men. His second struggle was with Kū-'īlio-loa, the dog-man, whom he stuffed with weed bodies which killed him from within.

Kama-pua'a's last exploit involves the wooing of the volcano goddess Pele* at Hale-ma'uma'u Crater on the Big Island. Pele refused his advances, called him a son of a pig, and hurled flames at him. Kama-pua'a retaliated by sending a deluge of water to engulf the crater. Finally, Pele yielded, and the two divided the island between them. Pele took Puna, Ka'ū, and Kona (the districts overrun with lava), and Kama-pua'a took Kohala, Hāmākua, and Hilo (the windward, rainy districts). The two eventually had a son named 'Ōpelu-nui-kau-ha'alilio who became the ancestors of the chiefs and commoners of Hawai'i. (Beckwith 1948:201–213; Fornander 1917:342–363, 1917:326–343; Pukui 1971:386.)

KAMA-UA, a Hawaiian rain god, the son of rain. (Emerson 1915:79c.)

KA-MAUNU-A-NIHO, a Hawaiian sorceress who immigrated to Hawai'i from Kahiki (Tahiti ?), grandmother to Kama-pua'a* (hog man), who nurtured him until he was grown. (Beckwith 1948:115–116, 201–204, 496–497.)

KĀMEHA'IKANA, name of the Hawaiian goddess Haumea* in her rebirth as a woman who turned into a breadfruit* tree to save her husband Mākea from being killed by chief Kumu-honua. The tree was later carved into an image and taken to Maui to become a god of king Kamehameha I (d. 1819). (Beckwith 1948:281–283.)

KAME-TARA, a Māori who took an ogre for his third wife. Once the wives went fishing, and the ogre left the other two to drown, however, they were transported to another island by water nymphs. Twin boys were born to the older wife, and when they grew up, they built a canoe and set out to find their father. They found their homeland, rescued the remainder of their family, but left Kame-tara to his ogre wife. (Whetu 1897: 97–106.)

KA-MOHO-ALI'I, most famous and fearful of the Hawaiian shark gods, a god of steam and elder brother to the volcano goddess Pele,* who once gave refuge to his sister in her conflict with Kama-pua'a.* When Ka-moho-ali'i assumes human form, he appears nude, a mark of the gods. (Beckwith 1948: 129–130, 167; Emerson 1915: xxv.) See also **Sharks**.

KA-MO'O-'INANEA, an ancient *mo'o* (lizard) goddess of the Hawaiians before their migration to Hawai'i, the man-eating ancestress of 'Au-kele-nui-a-iku.* (Beckwith 1948:127,

490–492; Fornander 1916:38–43; Westervelt 1915a:116, 122.)

KANA, a stretching god of Hawai'i, a hero of numerous legends that explain gashes, rock ledges, and footprints on the islands. When the Moloka'i chief Kapepe'e-kauila and his forces abducted Kana's mother, Hina,* Kana pressed after them, stretched up into the sky like a spider web, defeated them, and brought Hina back to her husband. (Fornander 1916: 436–449; 1917:518–512; 1920: 158, 489–491.) Another legend tells how Kana saved the stars, moon, and sun from being permanently abducted to Kahiki by its ruling chief Ka-hoa-ei. Kana stretched from Hawai'i to Kahiki and rescued them. (Rice 1923:102–105.) Various physical sites on the islands are attributed to Kana—a foot print on Kaua'i, the hill Haupū and the Rocks of Kana on Moloka'i, and a notch in the crater of Hale-a-ka-lā on Maui where he leaned across the majestic mountain. (Beckwith 1948:464–477.) See also **Apakura; Hono-'ura; Hilo; Lima-loa; Ono; Toouma.**

KANAE, sea demons in the Māori story of Tāwhaki (Kaha'i*) who emerged with the Ponaturi* from the water to their house. The Ponaturi were slain by Tāwhaki and Karihi in revenge for the death of their father Hema,* but the Kanae were able to escape and return to the sea. (Grey 1855:40; Tregear 1891:122.)

KANAEMOEHO, a giant mullet, a demon henchman for king Puna* in the Tuamotuan legend of Rata (Laka*). (Stimson 1964:193.)

KANALOA (TA'AROA, TAGALOA, TAKAROA, TANAOA, TANGAROA), although referred to as one of the major gods of Polynesia, his position in the Polynesian cosmology varies from one island group to another. His highest rank as the supreme god of creation appears in **Tahiti** where Ta'aroa, having no father or mother, is the ancestor of all the gods, the creator of all existence. He was born of a egg or shell (*rumia*) from which he made heaven and earth. These two then united and gave birth to a succession of creatures. (Beckwith 1948:336–346; Monberg 1956: 253–281.)

In **Samoa,** Tagaloa, a minor deity, was born in human form from "cloudless-heaven" and the "spread-out-heaven" in the seventh generation of creation. He created the heavens and the earth (Lalolagi). He threw stones from heaven that became the numerous Samoan islands. He sent his daughter Sina (Hina*) to earth in the form of the bird Tuli to find dry land upon which he created all living things including man and wo man. He is worshipped under several names prefixed with Tagaloa, and the moon is one of his chief places of residence, especially during the month of May. One wife was named Lagimafola from whom he also had a son named Pili.* The Tagaloa title of nobility in Samoa traces its origin back to the union of Tagaloa and a mortal woman, Sinaaláua (daughter of Lafaisaotele and Sinafagaava), whom he desired very much. In return for the favor, he gave his name to Funefe'ai (Sinaaláua's husband) for a ruling title in Samoa. (Krämer 1902:89–90, 394; Fraser 1890:207–211.) The Tagaloa family occupies a prominent position in Samoan mythology. Another wife, Ui,* sat on the sun with her legs opened, became pregnant, and gave birth to Tagaloaui who had four sons (Taeotaloga, Leganoga,* Lele, and Leasiasilogi) and two daughters (Muiu'uleapai and Moatafao) by his demon wife Sināsa'umani. Another wife, Magamagaifatua, gave birth to 'Alo'aloolelā (sunbeam). (Krämer 1902:392–393.)

The ancient **Tongans** worshipped Tagaloa (Eitumatupua) as a great god who dwelt in the heavens, the god of thunder and lightning, the god of carpenters, of arts, and of inventions. Tagaloa fished up the Tongan islands (see also the story of Māui*). His son Tubo became the ancestor of the Tongan people while his son Vaka-akau-uli became the ancestor of the Europeans. (Collocott 1921: 152–153; Gifford 1924:14–15.)

In the **Tuamotus**, Takaroa, born of Te-Tumu and Te-Papa, is a malevolent god and sets fire to the highest part of heaven in order to destroy everything. (Handy 1928:377.)

The **Māoris** of New Zealand believed Tagaroa to be the son of Rangi* (sky father) and Papa* (earth mother). He and his brothers rent apart their parents to allow light to enter their creation. When his brother Tāwhiri attacked him for his actions, Tangaloa fled to the ocean where he became god of the seas and all of its creatures. (Grey 1970:1–11.) The Moriori of the Chatham Islands regard Tangaroa as a god of fish and of no great importance. (Shand 1894:89–90.)

Kanaloa in **Hawai'i** represents only a minor god, the god of the squid as well as the god of the underworld* where he is called Milu.* He is frequently coupled with the god Kāne* in the opposing attributes of good and evil. (Beckwith 1948:60–66.)

KANALOA-HULUHULU, a Hawaiian giant* of ancient times who, when looking for his head, tore up the grassy area around Kōke'e near Waimea Canyon on the island of Kaua'i. (Wickman 1985:161.) See also **Giants.**

KĀNE (TĀNE), one of the most popular and widely worshipped gods throughout all of eastern Polynesia, as the god of creation and the god of light. In Hawai'i, Kāne is recognized as the supreme god who emerged from the eternal *pō* (darkness) to form the heavens and earth. In numerous accounts, he was aided by the powerful gods Kū* and Lono,* and the earth is called the great earth of Kāne (*Ka-honua-nui-a-Kāne*). He planted the sun, moon, and stars in the heavens, and with his co-creators he formed man and woman in the image of Kāne. Biblical allusions in the Polynesian creation stories apparently are attempts to reconcile truly native traditions with the newly introduced Western religion. Kāne worship was widespread and every family invoked him under the name of it is own family Kāne god (*'aumakua*). Thousands of descriptive references to him are found in Hawaiian prayers:

O Kāne-of-the-great-lightning.
O Kāne-the-render-of-heaven,
O Kāne-the-rolling-stone,
O Kāne-of-the-whirlwind,
O Kāne-of-the-rainbow,
O Kāne-of-the-atmosphere,
O Kāne-of-the-rain,

and no human sacrifices were ever made to him because life is sacred to Kāne. (Beckwith 1948: 42–66.)

In **New Zealand**, Tāne is the son of Rangi* (sky father) and Papa* (earth mother). Among his brothers are the powerful gods Rehua,* Tū (Kū*), Rongo (Lono*), Tangaroa (Kanaloa*), Tāwhiri-matea,* and others. It is only Tāne, the god of the forests, who is able to separate his parents to allow light to enter the creation. As a god of goodness and light, Tāne drove Tū, Rongo, and the rebellious spirits down from heaven to the darkness of Kai-hewa. Tāne created man (Tiki*) and woman (Hine-hau-one*), and because of the wickedness of mortals, he sent the great deluge.* (Grey 1970:1–11; Tregear 1891:461–462; White 1887a:29, 38, 44, 158–165, 166.)

In **Tahiti**, Tāne is the son of the god Ātea and his wife, Papa-tu'oi. He was without form or shape, and thus messengers were sent forth to obtain artisans to shape his body, but no one dared approach the majesty of Ātea. Finally, the supreme god Ta'aroa (Kanaloa*) sent his spirit to do the work. With the aid of Ātea, he caused skin to grow, and finally, Tāne was made whole. He stood up and proclaimed, "It is I, great Tāne, god of all things beautiful, with eyes to measure the skies." Tāne is the god of artisans in the world, the bailer of the sea, and his pet bird (the white sea swallow) is a good omen to sailors at sea. Tāne's wife is 'Aruru, and his messenger is

'Aporau. Once war ranged in heaven between Te-tumu* and Tāne. Te-Tumu caused heavy rain from heaven, but Tāne became furious and turned it into dry, clear weather. Te-Tumu caused famine and death everywhere; Tāne in anger cast down everything good to eat. Te-Tumu conjured up the night, and Tāne turned it into day. A vigorous battle continued between the two. Once Tāne, his friends, and his wife set out on a journey in their canoe to reach the dome of the sky (Ātea) in order to rend it in two. Being unsuccessful in approaching the powerful Ātea, they went to the underworld* (Ta'ere*) where they learned new tactics. Even with his magic stick, his lightning bolts, and the other inventions he had learned in Ta'ere, he could not defeated Ātea, and Ātea has stood unmoved in his place to this day. A peace offering–a shooting star–became a token of his deference to Ātea, and the saying "When strife arises in the morning, let there be peace in the evening" resulted. (Henry 1928:353–354; 364–369.)

In the **Tuamotus**, Tāne is the son of Te-hau (peace) and Metua (parent), and Ātea is the shapeless being mentioned in the Tahitian legend. Ātea became the god of the expanse just above the earth. While still a youth, Tāne came down with a large retinue to wage war against Ātea. They were unsuc-

cessful. Some were slain, and Tāne fled to earth to live with humans who treated him kindly. Ātea learned of Tāne's flight and sent messengers to all corners of the earth to find him. Tāne finally escaped through the keeper of the gate into his own heaven once again. Tāne, who had become accustomed to eating earthly foods, finally resorted to killing one of his ancestors to eat. This was the beginning of cannibalism. His cravings lead him to desire Ātea himself. He gathered his thunderbolts, cast them upon Ātea, so that he died. After disposing of Ātea, Tāne made his home on the large cliff-bound atoll called Fakarava (formerly called Havaiki) and from there distributed the languages on the earth in the following manner. "From the rat came the human language; from the grasshopper came the language of birds; variable sounds was the language of the gods; whistling was the language of kings." (Henry 1928:349–352.)

KĀNE-'ĀPUA, a demigod of Hawai'i whose numerous legends refer to him as the younger brother of the volcano goddess Pele,* as one of the four bird brothers in the romance of 'Aukele-nui-a-iku,* or as a fish god worshipped on Lāna'i. In the legend of Waha-nui,* Kāne-'apua angers his brothers Kāne* and Kanaloa* by urinating in their water. They fly away, leaving him alone on Lāna'i. The Hawaiian voyager Waha-nui approaches the island in a canoe, and Kāne-'āpua convinces him to take him aboard. His powers prove useful in their trip to Kahiki (Tahiti ?). When Waha-nui sets out to return, Kāne-'āpua gives him an image to take back with him. Disregarding Kāne-'āpua's instructions, Waha-nui displays the image on Kaua'i whose chief kills him for it. His death is revenged, however, when his successor on Hawai'i massacres many of the people on Kaua'i. (Beckwith 1948:448–454; Fornander 1916:516–523.) Also reference is made to him in Hawaiian cosmology as the sacred cycle of time, the Lua-nu'u. (Beckwith 1948:321; Emerson 1915:xxv–xxvii.)

KĀNE-'AUKAI, a swimming stone god in the Hawai'i legends of Hina*-i-ka-malama who is found and worshipped by the fishermen on the Waialua coast of O'ahu. (Beckwith 1948:215; Fornander 1917:266–273.)

KĀNE-HEKILI, Hawaiian god of thunder, brother to the volcano goddess, Pele*; when seen by humans, he stands on the earth with his head touching the clouds. One side of his body is black (tattooed ?) and the other white. (Beckwith 1948:48, 167; Westervelt 1915a:69–71, 124.)

KĀNE-HOA-LANI, a Hawaiian god who rules the heavens, husband to Haumea* (earth mother), ancestor of the Mū* and Menehune* people, and father of the volcano goddess Pele* who chanted her love for him when she left O'ahu on her famous voyage. (Beckwith 1948:170, 307, 321; Fornander 1878:97–99.)

KĀNE-HULI-HONUA, brother to the Hawaiian volcano goddess, Pele,* perhaps the same as Kāne-hekili.* See also **Kumu-honua.**

KĀNE-HULI-KOA, brother to the Hawaiian volcano goddess, Pele,* perhaps the same as Kāne-hekili.* See also **Kumu-honua.**

KĀNE-HŪNĀ- M O K U , a mythical land in Hawaiian legend, sometimes called Ulu-koa, where the gods Kāne* and Kanaloa* live, the middle land between heaven and earth presided over by the god by the same name who carries away the spirits of his worshipers when they die. (Beckwith 1948: 67–72, 77–80.) Also an ancestral shark god of the Hawaiian people. (Beckwith 1948:129.) See also **Sharks.**

KĀNE-I-KA-PUALENA, a Hawaiian god worshipped by the great hero-warrior Ka-welo,* literally Kāne-of-the-yellow flower. (Beckwith 1948:406.)

KĀNE-I-KAULANA-'ULA, one of the Hawaiian sorcery gods, a descendant of the goddess Pahulu,* banished to Moloka'i where he created new trees on the island where none had been before. Red is his sacred color, and he sometimes appears as a flaming fireball in the heavens. (Beckwith 1948:118; Thrum 1907:50–57; Westervelt 1915a: 95–98; Emerson 1965:33.) See also **Kālai-pāhoa.**

KĀNE-I-KŌ-KALA, a friendly Hawaiian shark god who saves people from shipwrecks; the *kokala* fish is sacred to him. (Beckwith 1948:129.) See also **Sharks.**

KĀNE-KA-POLEI, the Hawaiian god of flowers and shrubs. (Emerson 1915:141.)

KĀNE-KAUWILA-NUI, a Hawaiian god, brother to the volcano goddess, Pele.* Perhaps the same as Kāne-hekili.* (Beckwith 1948:167; Westervelt 1915:69–71.)

KĀNE-KOA, a Hawaiian fish god. (Beckwith 1948:90.)

KĀNE-KOKALA, a Hawaiian fish god. (Beckwith 1948:90.)

KĀNE-KUA'ANA, a Hawaiian lizard goddess (*mo'o*) who lives on various parts of the island of O'ahu. She especially brings abundant fish and pearl oysters and wards off sicknesses. (Beckwith 1948:126.)

KĀNE-LA'A-ULI, name given to the first Hawaiian, Kumu-honua,* after his disobedience and ejection from paradise. (Beckwith 1948:45; Fornander 1920:24–35, 42–47.)

KĀNE-LAU-'ĀPUA, Hawaiian god of the goby (*'o'opu*) fish, a healing and benevolent god from Lāna'i. (Beckwith 1948: 136, 452; Emerson 1915:194c.)

KĀNE-LU-HONUA, a Hawaiian sea god who destroyed the monster Pana-'ewa* in the Hi'iaka* and Pele* legend. (Emerson 1915:45.)

KĀNE-LULU-MOKU, Hawaiian god of earthquakes. (Beckwith 1948:46.)

KĀNE-MAKUA, a Hawaiian fish god. (Beckwith 1948:90.)

KĀNE-MILO-HAI, the elder brother to the Hawaiian volcano goddess Pele,* who accompanied her from Kahiki to Hawai'i, and who was left as a guard of the outlying island of the group. In the Hi'iaka* legend, he caught the spirit of Lohi'au* before it left the earth, and returned it to Hawai'i, where it was restored to life. (Beckwith 1948:170, 177, 452; Emerson 1915:xxv–xxvi, 237.)

KĀNE-NUI-ĀKEA, the name of a Hawaiian stone image, originally from Kaua'i, but in modern times (1800s) found at Pua-pua'a in Kona, Hawai'i. (Beckwith 1948:46; Ellis 1825: 88.)

KĀNE-POHĀ-KA'A, an important Hawaiian god who presides over sacred stones. (Beckwith 1948:88.)

KĀNE-PUA'A, a Hawaiian god of agriculture in the legend of Makua-kau-mana*; he brings rain and an abundance of crops. (Beckwith 1948:69, 207; Fornander 1917:116–132.)

KĀNE-PŪNIU, a Hawaiian demigod who assumes the form of a coconut. (Pukui 1971:388.)

KĀNE-WAHINE-I-KIA-'OHE, warrior wife to the Hawaiian hero Ka-welo.* (Beckwith 1948: 406–408.)

KĀNE-WAWAHI-LANI, Hawaiian god of thunder and lighting, ancestor of the volcano goddess Pele.* (Beckwith 1948: 48, 192.)

KANGOKANGONGA'A, an ancient hero of Bellona Island whose voyaging colleagues were turned into porpoises, and the fragments of his canoe were turned into constellations in the heavens. (Monberg 1966:89.)

KANIKA'A, paramount chief spirit on Hawai'i, worshipped as a spear god by Kapunohu (a famous riddler). With Kanika'a as his god and with his magical spear (Kani-ka-wī), Kapunohu was able to defeat all of his family's enemies. (Beckwith 1948:419, 430; Fornander 1917: 214–225.)

KANIKANI-A-'ULA, a Hawaiian god who accompanies Mokuleia (or Mokulehua) to the underworld* in search of the spirit of his departed wife, Pueo, who has just hanged herself. (Beckwith 1948:146; Fornander 1878:83, 1920:337.) See also **Hiku-i-ka-nahele; Hutu; Kena; Milimili; Pare.**

KANI-KA-WĀ, a Hawaiian sprite who inhabits the *hokeo* (a type of whistle), and who attempted to lure the goddess Pele* away from her intended trip to Kaua'i. (Emerson 1915:4.)

KANI-KA-WĪ, a Hawaiian sprite who inhabits the nose flute, and who attempted to lure the goddess Pele* away from her intended trip to Kaua'i. (Emerson 1915:4.)

KANI-LOLOŪ, a Hawaiian with an eel body who once visited Kahiki (Tahiti ?) and boasted of the superior beauty of his own land. When he returned, he found the islands of Kaua'i, Maui, and Hawai'i covered with lava from the jealous fire goddess, Pele.* (Beckwith 1948:190; Fornander 1917:534; Westervelt 1916:31–32.)

KANIOWAI, wife of Rata (Laka*) in Māori legend. (Tregear 1891:123; White 1887c: 5.)

KANI-UHI, a Māori goddess who answers the prayers of the mortal priests Tupu-nui-a-uta* and Para-whenua-mea* to send the great deluge* for vengeance on the wicked. (Tregear 1891:123; White 1887a:172–180.)

KA'ŌHELO, sister to the Hawaiian volcano goddess Pele,* from whose body, upon her death, grew the 'ōhelo bush (vaccinium reticulatum, a member of the cranberry family) so abundant on the volcanic mountains of Hawai'i, noted for its red or yellow edible berries. (Beckwith 1948:99, 187–188; Fornander 1917:576–580.)

KA-O-MEA-LANI, a Hawaiian rain god whose massive white clouds indicate his presence. (Emerson 1915:118.)

KA'ŌNOHI-O-KA-LĀ, eyeball-of-the-sun, divine husband to the Hawaiian chiefess Lā'iei-ka-wai.* His unfaithfulness caused his banishment to earth as a wandering ghost (Beckwith 1948:527–528); also a sky-dwelling Hawaiian god who lives in the sun and who guides the souls of deceased chiefs to

their final resting places. (Beckwith 1948:83, 109–110.)

KA'ŌNOHI-'ULA, wife to the Hawaiian god Kāne-hūnā-moku* (sacred, hidden land of Kane). (Beckwith 1948:71.)

KA-PAPA-I-A-KEA, mother of the Hawaiian hero 'Au-kele-nui-a-iku.* (Beckwith 1948:491, 494; Fornander 1916:32–111.)

KAPI-RARO, lower half of the underworld* according to Tuamotuan legends. (Stimson 1964:196.)

KAPI-RUA, the Tuamotuan name for that part of the universe where mortals or human heroes can venture. Only the gods can go above or below. (Stimson 1964:197.)

KAPI-RUNGA, the upper one-half of the upper world, the region where human beings could venture according to Tuamotuan legends. (Stimson 1964:197.)

KA-POHĀ-I-KAHI-OLA, a Hawaiian god of explosion, identified as the brother to the volcano goddess, Pele.* (Beckwith 1948:168; Westervelt 1915a:69–71.)

KAPO-'ULA-KĪNA'U, one of the daughters of the Hawaiian goddess Haumea* and thus a sister to the volcano goddess Pele,* Laka* (the female fertil ity goddess), and Hi'iaka.* When Kama-pua'a* (hog-man) and Pele* declared war, it was Kapo who intervened, and with her detached vagina deferred Kama-pua'a's attacks. On Maui, Kapo is worshipped as a goddess of sorcery, and her mediums are able to foretell the future. Her husband is Pua-nui. (Beckwith 1948:185–187, 212–213; Emerson 1915:67.)

KAPUA'I-'AIA, see **Makani-ke-oe.**

KAPULANAKEHAU, mother to the ancient Hawaiian chief Wākea,* wife to Kahiko-lua-mea, ancestress to all the Hawaiian people. (Beckwith 1948: 294–295.)

KAPUNOHU, a Hawaiian from the Big Island who obtained the use of the magical spear of his ghost god Kanika'a.* He avenged an insult made to his brother-in-law by slaying the warrior Paopele at a place called Lamakēe. After he allied with 'Olopana* on O'ahu and killed the chief, he made his way to Kaua'i and settled at Kōloa. There he entered into a throwing contest with the strong man Kemamo. Kapunohu cast his spear so strongly that it pierced through the cliff at Kalalea and finally landed in Hanalei (northern tip of the island). (Beckwith 1948:419; Fornander 1917:214–225, 428.)

KA-PŪ-O-ALAKA'I, a Hawaiian forest goddess who presides over the lines (ropes) stretched to guide canoes safely from their mountain origins to the sea. (Beckwith 1948:16; Pukui 1971:388.)

KARAGFONO, the Rotuman god responsible for introducing chickens to mortals. He is sometimes called Sunioitu. In return for the warm hospitality he received by the mortal To Noava, Karagfono invited him to visit his home in the underworld.* There he was given a present of a pair of chickens that he was allowed to bring back to earth with him. Once here, they became the progenitors of all the chickens on earth. (Gardiner 1898:512–514.)

KARE-NUKU, one of the Māori goddesses seen by the survivors floating upon the waters after the great deluge.* (Tregear 1891:130; White 1887a:175.) Also the wife of Hema* and the mother of the legendary Māori heroes Tāwhaki (Kaha'i*) and Karihi. (Tregear; White 1887a: 121.) See also **Kare-rangi; Tu-putupuwhenua.**

KARE-RANGI, one of the Māori goddesses seen by the survivors floating upon the waters after the great deluge.* (Tregear 1891:130; White 1887a: 175.) See also **Kare-nuku; Tu-putpuwhenua.**

KARIHI-NUI, the brother to Tahaki (Kaha'i*) in the Tuamotuan legend. (Stimson 1937: 60–95.) See also **Alihi.**

KARU-AI-PAPA, an ancient Māori instructor of religious incantations and ceremonies. (Tregear 1891:132; White 1887a: 169.)

KĀTAKA, the Tuamotuan name for the realm of the underworld.* (Stimson 1964:205.)

KATOTIAE, a monster encountered by the first Polynesian explorers, Te Erui and his brother Matareka, to Aitutaki, Cook Islands. (Gill 1911:149–150.) See also **Mokoroa; Uika.**

KAUAKAHI, Hawaiian war god, son of the goddess Haumea.* (Beckwith 1948:276–282, 309.) See also **Kūkauakahi.**

KA-UA-KU'ĀHIWA, Hawaiian rain goddess. See also **Kū-ka-'ōhi'a-laka.**

KAU-ATA-ATA, name of the first woman in Māori legends. She was the daughter of the sun god, Rā,* and his wife Rikoriko (Ārohirohi*). (Tregear 1891:136; White 1887a: App.) See also **Kauika.**

KA-UHI, a Hawaiian demigod chained to a cliff at Kahana (O'ahu) by the volcano goddess Pele.* When Pele's sister Hi'iaka* refused to free him, he tore himself loose but was frozen in stone in a crouching position similar to a lion. Today, the landmark is well known since the construction of the Crouching Lion Inn restaurant. (Emerson 1915:93–94; Pukui 1971:388.) Another Ka-uhi is the jealous husband of Kahala-o-puna* who beat her to death and hid her body. Her spirit, however, revealed the truth to her parents who found her body and restored it to life. (Beckwith 1948:151–152.)

KAUHUHU, a malevolent Hawaiian shark god of Māui. (Beckwith 1948:129, 134–135.)

KAUIKA, the first man in Māori legends, created by the god Tiki,* also called One-kura* (red-earth). (Beckwith 1948:114; Tregear 1891:136.)

KAUKAUGOGO, a (mortal ?) woman of Bellona Island who became the wife of Tehu-'aingabenga,* the primary god of the island, and from them descend the other secondary gods of the island. (Monberg 1966:63.)

KAUKAU-MATUA, a celebrated ear ornament made from the sacred greenstone, Whaiapu, by the ancient Māori hero Ngahue,* brought to New Zealand from Hawaiki* by the first Polynesians, supposedly lost only in 1846. (Grey 1855:95; Grey 1970:107, 121.)

KAUKAUTUTU, a porpoise god of Futuna. (Burrows 1936:105–108.)

KA-'ULA-HEA, a Hawaiian goddess, mistress to the god Wākea* after his divorce from his wife Papa.* Also a high chief of Maui who unsuccessfully attempted to thwart Hi'iaka's* voyage to Kaua'i to obtain chief Lohi'au* for her sister, the volcano goddess Pele.* (Emerson 1915:78–81, 115.)

KAULANA-IKI-PŌK I ' I , the youngest sister to the four Hawaiian Maile* sisters. Kaulana was endowed with magical powers, and when her brother-in-law killed her five brothers, she turned in vengeance against him, and killed him. She joined her brothers' ashes with their bones and restored them to life. (Beckwith 1948:517–518; Fornander 1916:560–569.) Also the younger sister to Ka-ao-mele-mele* (maid of the golden cloud) and hula expert. (Beckwith 1948:520.) Also known as Ka-'ula-wena and Ka-hala-o-māpuana.

KA-'ULU, a Hawaiian demigod known for his travels and for being a trickster, the youngest son of Kū-ka-'ōhi'a-laka and Hina-'ulu-'ōhi'a. He was born as a rope but then took human form to search for his lost brother Kaeha. He smashed waves with his strong hands and thus formed the surf; he broke the dog Kū-'īlio-loa into pieces and thus formed the small dogs of today; he played tricks on the gods and spirits. He tore a shark to pieces in rescuing his brother and hurled him up into the Milky Way. He finally returned home where he killed Haumea* and Lono-ka-'eho* and assumed the title of chief over Ko'olau. (Beckwith 1948:436–437; Fornander 1916:522–533; 1917:364–371.)

KAUNATI, an ancient Tuamotuan who possessed great magical powers. (Stimson 1964:208.)

KAUNOLU, the chief of all the spirits on the island of Moloka'i. (Beckwith 1948:430.)

KAUPĒ, a cannibalistic dogman who once lived on O'ahu, Hawai'i. He sailed to the Big Island where he captured the chief's son and held him for a sacrifice. The father sought the advice of a *kahuna* (priest) who lead him to implore the power of the gods Kū,* Lono,* and Kāne.* His prayers were answered, he sailed to O'ahu, killed Kaupē, and the two returned to their island of Hawai'i. (Beckwith 1948:345; Westervelt 1915b:90–96.)

KĀURA, a Tuamotuan supernatural being, a demon. (Stimson 1964:209.)

KAUTU, Tuamotuan name for the lands and people belonging to the eel god Tuna* in the legend of Hina* and Tuna. (Stimson 1937:6–8.)

KAUTUKU-KI-TE-RANGI, the Māori name of the famous paddle in the *Aotea** canoe in the great migrations to New Zealand. (Grey 1855:131; Tregear 1891:139.) See also **Canoes, Māori Migration.**

KAVA, Origin of. Sometimes referred to as the drink of the gods. Made from the chewed or pounded roots of the *Piper methysticum*, kava is widely drunk throughout Polynesian (except New Zealand and Easter Island). It is made nowhere else in the world, and both ancient Tonga and Samoan societies developed elaborate ceremonies surrounding its preparation and consumption. Unlike alcohol, kava is not fermented, brewed, or distilled, and its physiological effects are very different from alcohol. Heavy indulgence makes it difficult to walk and induces sleep. (See J. P. Buckley, "The Pharmacology of Kava," *Journal of the Polynesian Society* 1967, vol. 76:101–102.)

Tongan legends tell that once chief Lo'au visited his servants Fefafa and Fevanga on the island of Eueiki at a time when there was a scarcity of food. The couple could find no meat to prepare for their lord, whereupon they decided to kill their own daughter Kava-onau and prepare her in the underground oven. When the food was brought before Loau, he told them to take it away and give it a decent burial. From the daughter's head grew the first kava plant. (Gifford 1924:71–75.)

KAVE-AU, the Marquesan god of the breadfruit tree. Known also as Ihi.* (Christian 1895: 190.)

KĀWALAKI'I, a stone image from the Big Island of Hawai'i once worshipped by king Kamehameha I (d. 1819). (Beckwith 1948:392.)

KAWEAU, a Māori lizard god, son of Tū-te-wanawana* and Tū-pari.* (White 1887a: App.)

KA-WELO, a popular Hawaiian warrior whose exploits are recited in great detail. Born at Hanamā'ulu, Kaua'i, Ka-welo grew up to become an expert spear thrower. He and his two brothers traveled to O'ahu where they became proficient in the arts of warfare. Here he married Kāne-wahine-iki-'a-'ohe who gained her father's unique snaring stick (a *pikoi*). Ka-welo and his men returned to Kaua'i to aid his deposed father in his conflict against 'Ai-kanaka.* They met in battle, and just as Ka-welo was about to give up, his wife advanced and by using her snaring stick was able to turn the battle. For her courage, she was given the district called Hanalei. Ka-welo was pressed into battle once again, almost slain, but revived himself, and killed everyone. Ka-welo retired and lived out his life at Wailua. Other accounts of Ka-welo vary, but all present rich details of Hawaiian culture. (Beckwith 1948:404–414; Green 1929.)

KA-WELO-MAHAMAHA-I'A, elder brother to the Hawaiian hero Ka-welo.* Another legend claims him as grandfather to Ka-welo and chief on Kaua'i who was turned into a shark and worshipped at death. (Beckwith 1948:410.)

KĀWELU, wife of the Hawaiian hero Hiku-i-ka-nahele,* who strangled herself and whose spirit was rescued from the underworld* by her lover. (Beckwith 1948:147–148; Westervelt 1915a:224–240.)

KEA, see **Nu'a-kea.**

KE-AKA-HULI-LANI, the first woman created in Hawaiian legend, wife to Kāne-huli-honua.* See also **Kumu-honua; Lalo-honua.**

KE-ALI'I-KAUA-O-KA'Ū, a shark god of Hawai'i, born to a beautiful maiden at Ka'ū, who protects humans against man-eating sharks, a cousin to the volcano goddess Pele.* Numer-ous stories relate his protection by sailors and people swept out to sea. (Beckwith 1948:132–135.) See also **Sharks.**

KE-ALI'I-WAHI-LANI, a Hawaiian god who descended from heaven, took the first mortal woman (La'ila'i*) to wife, and begot the first man named Ki'i (Tiki*). (Beckwith 1948:42, 276–277.) See also **Creation; Tiki.**

KE-'ALOHI-LANI, a land in the Hawaiian heavens called the shining heaven, located just below Nu'umealani* (the sacred land of the gods.) (Beckwith 1948:80, 520, 530.)

KEAROA, wife of the Māori priest Ngātoro-rangi* who boarded the famous canoe *Arawa* to offer proper sacrifices for its safety on its journey to the new land of New Zealand. When he heard of Kearoa's affair with Tama-te-kapua,* the ship's captain, Ngātoro cast a spell that forced the canoe into a great whirlpool, but at the last minute, he recanted and saved the ship and all its passengers. (Grey 1970:109–112; Tregear 1891:142.)

KE-AU-HELE-MOA, a Hawaiian demigod from Maui who appears as a rooster in the legend of Lepe-a-moa.* (Beckwith 1948:428–429; Thrum 1923:164–184.)

KE-AU-KĀ, ocean current, brother to the Hawaiian volcano goddess, Pele.* (Beckwith 1948:169; Rice 1923:7–10.)

KE-AU-LAWE, the tide, brother to the Hawaiian volcano goddess, Pele.* (Beckwith 1948:169; Rice 1923:7–10.) See also **Ke-au-miki.**

KE-AU-MIKI, the tide, brother to the Hawaiian volcano goddess, Pele.* (Beckwith 1948:169; Rice 1923:7–10.) See also **Ke-au-lawe.**

KEHA, an ancient Tuamotuan god. (Stimson 1964:213.)

KE-KA-KO'O, a Hawaiian god who guided the war party of Hi'iaka* through the dense forest trails on her way to Kaua'i to obtain Lohi'au* for her sister, the goddess Pele.* (Emerson 1915:43–44.)

KE-KALUKALU-O-KE-WĀ, a chief from Kaua'i, a wooer of the Hawaiian chiefess Lā'ie-i-ka-wai,* who lost her to a young rascal from Puna through the efforts of his sorceress sister. (Beckwith 1919; Beckwith 1948:527.)

KEKAUAKAHI, a Hawaiian war god. (Tregear 1891:54.)

KELE, the Tongan goddess of all creation,* who united with Limu,* "seaweed," to bring forth the goddess Touiafutuna.*

Also the name of her granddaughter who married her twin brother, Piki.* (Reiter 1907:230–240.)

KE-LI'I-KOA, a brave chief of ancient Hawai'i whose life was made miserable by a magical coconut tree on the island of Kaua'i. (Wickman 1985:163.)

KENA, a Marquesan hero who traveled to the underworld* (Havaiki, under the sea) to seek the spirit of his beloved wife, Tefio. After having successfully defeating ogres, sirens, and crushing rocks, he was allowed to carry his wife's spirit back to the upper world in a basket, but only on the condition that he not open the basket until he arrived at his destination. Not being able to contain himself on his journey, he inadvisably opened the basket, whereupon, his wife's spirit returned to the underworld. Kena once again journeyed to Havaiki to regain his wife, and this time he obeyed the tapu. (Handy 1930:117–20; Poignant 1967:64; Steinen 1933: 34, 38; 1933–34:212.) **Hiku-i-ka-nahele; Hutu; Kanikani-a-'ula; Milimili; Pare.**

KE-O-AHI-KAMA-KAUA, brother to the Hawaiian volcano goddess, Pele.* (Beckwith 1948:167; Westervelt 1915a:69–71.) See also **Kumu-honua.**

KE-OLO-'EWA, chief on the island of Moloka'i (Hawai'i), husband to the goddess Nu-akea* (goddess of nursing mothers), who after his death was deified as a rain god. (Beckwith 1948:32; Fornander 1880:31–32; Emerson 1915:79b.) Also a sorcery goddess on Maui, ruler of all the spirits on the island. A wooden image of Ke-olo-'ewa dressed in tapa, wicker, and feathers was observed in a temple on Maui by the missionary William Ellis during his tour of the island in 1823. (Beckwith 1948:114, 430; Ellis 1825:66–67.)

KE-O-WAHI-MAKA-O-KA-UA, a Hawaiian messenger god so closely related to the goddess Pele* that she called him brother. (Emerson 1915:3.)

KEPĀKĀ-ILI-'ULA, a Hawaiian demigod, born to Kū* and Hina* in the form of an egg and nurtured to birth by his uncles. He became the ruling chief at Kohala (Hawai'i) and of the islands of Maui and O'ahu. (Beckwith 1948:423–424; Fornander 1916:498–517, 1917:384–405.)

KERERŪ, Māori god of pigeons. After coming to earth and eating some bitter berries, he became hoarse and could only say *ku, ku,* hence the Māori name *kuku* and *kukupa* for the pigeon. (Tregear 1891:143.)

KE-UA-A-KE-PŌ, Hawaiian god, rain-of-fire, brother of the volcano goddess, Pele.* (Beck-with 1948:167; Westervelt 1915a:69–71.)

KEUHEA, a Tuamotuan bird who is possessed by the souls of the dead; a harbinger of news. (Stimson 1964:222.)

KĪ, one of the four brothers (Kī, Kanaloa,* La'a-kapu, and Hawai'i-loa*) who Hawaiian legends claim peopled the South Pacific islands. Kī peopled French Polynesia (Tahiti, Bora-Bora, Hu'ahine, Taha'a, Ra-'iātea, and Mo'orea). Hawai'i-loa settled the Hawaiian Islands and intermarried with Kī's family to produce the highest-ranking chiefs in Hawai'i (the *ali'i*). (Beckwith 1948:363–365; Fornander 1878: 23–24, 132–159; Thrum 1923:1–19.)

KIHA, a Hawaiian lizard monster, a follower of Pana-'ewa* who opposed the forces of the goddess Hi'iaka* in her journeys to Kaua'i. (Emerson 1915: 45.)

KIHA-NUI-LULU-MOKU, a Hawaiian *mo'o* (lizard) god who crouches on tops of trees to observe the approach of enemies and who once fought against the supernatural dog (Kalahu-moku) owned by chief 'Ai-wohi-kupua* of Kaua'i in the romance of Lā'ie-i-ka-wai.* The dog ran home stripped of both ears and tail. (Beckwith 1919:472–475; Beckwith 1948: 348, 350.)

KIHA-WAHINE, the most famous of the Hawaiian lizard (*mo'o*) deities; originally, she was a chiefess on Maui who became a goddess and was worshipped upon her death. An image of her was erected in the *heiau* (temple) by king Kamehameha I (d. 1819) who conquered the islands in her name. Everyone must prostrate before her. She occasionally takes the form of a chicken, a fish, or a spider. (Beckwith 1948:125–126, 195, 200; Malo 1903:114, 155; Westervelt 1915a:152–162.)

KIHIA, name of a famous weapon owned by the ancient Māori chief Manaia* in Hawaiki.* (Grey 1970:182; Tregear 1891:147.)

KIHO, Tuamotuan name for the supreme creator, perhaps known only to a few learned priests, perhaps spurious. (Stimson 1964:224.) Also the night realm, the last haven of repose where departed spirits go in the Tuamotuan legend of Tahaki (Kaha'i*). (Stimson 1934:50–53.) See also **Io; Kiho-tumu.**

KIHO-TUMU, a supreme Tuamotuan god, whom Māui visits and where he is tested by Kiho-tumu in order to gain equal powers with the gods. Māui's task is to pursue and return an illusive floating island called Nuku-tere. (Stimson 1933:39–41.) See also **Kiho.**

KI'I, the first mortal man according to the Hawaiian Kumulipō* genealogy. The first mortal created was a woman called La'ila'i.* Her husband was Ke-ali'i-wahi-lani,* who descended from the heavens, took her to wife, and begat Ki'i, the progenitor of the Hawaiian people. (Beckwith 1948:42, 276–277, 293.) See also **Creation; Kumu-honua; Tiki.**

KIKI, an ancient Māori sorcerer whose shadow withered shrubbery. He was slain by the incantations of a more powerful wizard named Tamure. (Grey 1855:168.)

KIKI-PUA, a Hawaiian witch, a chief lizard monster on Moloka'i who attempted to thwart Hi'iaka's* trip to Kaua'i to obtain chief Lohi'au* for her sister, the volcano goddess Pele.* Her husband was Haka-a'ano. (Emerson 1915:83–85.)

KIKIWAI, son of the Māori chief Tahu and grandson of Tiki,* father of Kāhuitara, the goddess of sea birds. (Tregear 1891:147; White 1887a: App.)

KIKO-RANGI, Māori name of the lowest heaven nearest the earth, one of the three heavens presided over by the war god Maru.* (Tregear 1891:148; White 1887a: App.)

KILA, son of the Hawaiian hero Mo'i-keha,* and great grand son of Māweke, the first settlers in the Hawaiian islands from Kahiki (Tahiti ?). When Moʻi-keha died, he entrusted his son the task of returning to Kahiki to escort the high chief Laʻa to Hawaiʻi to supervise the proper disposition of his bones. After his father's death, Kila became the ruling chief on Kauaʻi. (Beckwith 1948:355–358; Fornander 1916:128–153, 160–173.)

KILI-NOE, an expert hula teacher on Kauaʻi in the legend of Hiʻiaka* and Pele.* (Beckwith 1948:181; Rice 1923:14.)

KILIOE, a patron god of the chiefs on the island of Kauaʻi (Hawaiʻi) in the legend of Hiʻiaka* and Pele.* (Beckwith 1948:175; Emerson 1915:41–46.) In some versions, Kilioe is the sister to Lohiʻau* (chief of Kauaʻi and Hiʻiaka's lover). (Beckwith 1948:176; Rice 1923: 14, 119.)

KILIOE-I-KA-PUA, a son to the Hawaiian volcano goddess Pele* who aided Hiʻiaka* in her trip to Kauaʻi to get Lohiʻau for her sister Pele. (Emerson 1915: 41–46.)

KINILAU (TIGILAU, TIMIRAU, TINGILAU, TINILAU, TINIRAU, SINILAU), a romantic hero of innumerable tales known throughout most of Polynesia as well as Micronesia. In eastern Polynesian, he is the god of the ocean and fish while in western Polynesia, he is a handsome, charming, island chief who falls in love with the beautiful Hina* (Ina, Sina).

In **Tahiti**, he is known as Ru-ahata-tinirau, the god of fishermen, the ruler of the sea. According to their legends, he became enraged when two mortals, Te-aho-roa and Roʻo, accidentally dropped their fish sinkers and hit him on the head while he was sleeping. He warned the fishermen to gather their families together, for he planned to send a great deluge* to destroy all living creatures. His great flood lasted for one day and night, and only the families of Te-aho-roa and Roʻo were saved. Since then, Rua-hata-tinirau is also known as 'Oro-paʻa, the great engulfer. (Henry 1928:148, 165, 358, 448–450.)

In **New Zealand**, Tinirau not only ranks among the pantheon as the god of fishes who dwells on Motu-tapu (sacred island) but also as the most handsome hero of his time. Upon the death of Hina's husband (see the story of Hina), she threw herself into the sea and floated to Motu-tapu where she was rescued by Tinirau's two wives, Ihu-ata-mai and Ihu-wareware. Tinirau was enchanted with Hina's beauty and married her. When she became pregnant, Hina cast a spell upon the other jealous wives and killed them. She now had Tinirau all to herself. Meanwhile, Hina's devoted brother Rupe set out to find his long-lost sister. He visited the heavens (Rehua*) where he was informed that Hina now resided on Motu-tapu. He turned himself into a pigeon, flew to the island, and carried his sister off to heaven. On earth, Tinirau looked for a skillful priest to insure a bright future for his son Tū-huruhuru. The sorcerer Kae* arrived and performed the necessary rites. Afterwards, he asked Tinirau for passage home aboard Tutu-nui, Tinirau's pet whale. Tinirau consented and Kae set out. When he arrived home, instead of allowing the whale to return home, Kae caught and cooked the whale. Tinirau learned of the deception and sent a contingent of women to the island to capture Kae and to return him to Motu-tapu. The women used spells to cause Kae to fall into an enchanted sleep while they carried him back to Tinirau. Once there, Kae was slain. When Kae's people heard of the death of their chief, they gathered a large army, invaded Tinirau's lands, and killed his son Tū-huruhuru in revenge. (Grey 1970:62–76; White 1887b: 127–146.)

In the **Cook Islands** (Mangaia Island), Tinirau is placed high in the pantheon of gods, even before Tāne (Kāne*), Rono (Lono*), and Tangaroa (Kanaloa*). He was born from the side of his mother Vari-ma-te-tahere as the god of the ocean where he resides on the sacred island of Motu-tapu. Here, he amused himself with songs and dances with his pet fish and whales. Meanwhile, Ina (Hina) lived on Nukutere with her wealthy parents. One day, they left, but instructed her to spread their family treasures out in the sun to air. While they were gone, the notorious thief Ngana appeared, gained the heirlooms, and flew away. When Ina's parents returned, they beat her for her neglect, whereupon Ina left and swam to Motu-tapu and to Tinirau. Arriving on Motu-tapu, Ina proceeded to Tinirau's home and found him gone. She beat on a drum and Tinirau returned. Once they met, they fell in love and married. Soon Ina gave birth to two children, a son Koro and a daughter Ature. Meanwhile, Ina's brother Rupe flew to the island as a bird, found Ina, returned home with the news, and thus happily reunited their family once more. When Koro grew up, he became curious as to why his father was absent for days on end. Once, he followed his father to find that he was being entertained by the music and dancing of his pet fish. Koro learned the dance (the *tautiti*) and taught it to his people. He also brought back the pandanus tree used in making leis and planted it for his people. The story ends happily. (Gill 1876:88–104.)

This happy theme is not typical of most versions of the story, especially in Samoa and Tonga. In one **Tongan** story, Sinilau

(Tinirau) coveted the beautiful Hina and plotted the death of her husband. He invited him to go fishing with him and when far out to sea threw him overboard. Hina saw the bloody foam from shore and hastened to her grandmother Hikuleo,* goddess of the underworld,* who returned his spirit to his body so that he could dwell with Hina. (Gifford 1924:183–195.)

Another Tongan legend tells the story of Hina, the beautiful daughter of the Tui Haatakalaua of Tonga. Sinilau, a Samoan chief, heard of her beauty and set sail with his brother to find her. Upon arriving in Tonga, Sinilau found Hina protected with a hundred guards and eight tapu fences (enclosures). Sinilau disguised himself as a guard, entered the enclosures, and found Hina.

At first Hina rejected him and kicked him out of the window, but when she saw how handsome he really was, she changed her mind. It was too late. Sinilau had returned to Tonga. Hina was not to be disappointed. She swam the great distance to Tonga and washed upon the beach. She was found by Sinilau's mother who secretly hid her in her home. When Sinilau found out, he killed his mother, and went to live with his concubines. Hina starved herself until Sinilau found her and returned her to his home.

Meanwhile a contingent from Tonga arrived looking for Hina. The couple was taken back to Tonga where Hina re-entered her tapu house and Sinilau was not allowed to enter. Sinilau starved himself until finally the chiefs agreed to allow the wedding to take place. (Gifford 1924:183–195.)

One short Tongan story, however, proclaims that Sinilau was a god who visited earth and carried off the mortal Samoan woman Mulikivaito. They had twelve sons whom they sent to earth to become the kings of the various Polynesian islands, Tonga, Samoa, Uea (Wallis Island), Futuna, Niue, Rarotonga, etc. Numerous other Tongan stories are told of Sinilau and Hina. (Collocott 1928:20–38; Gifford 1924:194.)

The **Samoan** stories are less detailed. Tigilau was the handsome chief of the island of Vavau (Tonga). Sina (Hina) heard of his beauty and swam across the water separating the island groups. Along the way she encountered an evil, cannibalistic witch. After arriving in Tonga and after a period of indecision and doubt, Tigilau took Sina to wife and reared a family. Another story emphasizes the married life of the two and begins the day after they are married. Tigilau has other wives, one of whom is demonic. She jealously tries to get rid of Sina by accusing her of eating nine baskets of fish belonging to the villagers. Sina flees into the forest in exile. There she gives birth to Tigilau's son and sends to Tigilau for mats and oil. The other wives, however, intercept the news.

Meanwhile, Sina's brother Rupe (Lupe*) hears of her plight, and in the form of a bird arrives and showers family gifts upon her. Tigilau hears of the visit and rushes into the forest to be reunited with his wife and son. Rupe snatches Sina up and transports her back to Samoa where her hand in marriage is sought by the other Samoan chiefs. Eventually, Tigilau's son travels to Samoa, meets his mother, and returns her to Tigilau. (Krämer 1902:127–131; Luomala 1955:108–110.)

In **Hawai'i,** Kinilau is a god of fishermen (Beckwith 1948:90), and he is known also in the famous chant of Kū-ali'i, a royal pedigree of the ancient chiefs of O'ahu, as Kinilau-a-mano, son of Maluapo and Lawekeao. (Fornander 1878:181, 184.)

KINI-MAKA, known also as Walewale-o-kū, the many-eyed Hawaiian goddess who had the habit of eating human eyeballs until the god Kāne* weaned her from it. The appellation, Kini-maka-o-ka-lā, in the Hi'iaka* and Pele* legend most likely refers to the numerous rays or eyes of the sun (Lā) rather than the eye-eating goddess. (Emerson 1915:195.)

KIO, an ancient Tuamotuan god associated with the turtle

purification rites. (Stimson 1964:227.)

KIORE, a Tuamotuan name for a lizard (mo'o*) demon. (Stimson 1964:227.)

KIO-TAETAE-HO, one of two Tuamotuan gods of the night world (underworld*) who receive the souls of the dead. (Stimson 1964:227.) See also **Tama-tū-hau.**

KIRIKIRI-WAWA, or Kirikiri-awa, name of a famous battle fought in Hawaiki* by the ancient Māori chief Manaia.* (Grey 1970:181–182; Tregear 1891:150.)

KIRKIRSASA, a woman from Rotuma whose two maid servants enraged a monstrous giant (mam'asa) who threatened their lives. Kirkirsasa saved them, however, by entertaining the giant with her dancing and gyrations. When the giant observed her intricate tattoo marks in her armpits, he desired the same. Kirkirsasa told him that he had to do exactly as she commanded. She had his four limbs tied to strong stakes while members of the community brought hot coals and tattooed his arms and then the other parts of his body. The bound giant could not defend himself against such torture, and thus in agony he died. (Churchward 1938:222–225.)

KIU, the bird messenger sent down to earth by the Tongan gods during the creation* to see if dry land had appeared on the earth. (Reiter 1907:438–445.) Also, the name of the bird Tuli in the Samoan story of the creation.*

KOAU, one of the three first mortal men brought forth by the Tongan gods of creation. He and his companions Kohai* and Momo* were given wives by Māui* and his brothers, and they populated the islands. (Reiter 1907:438–445.)

KO'E-ULA, superhuman mud worms who had power over humans' lives in the legend of Hi'iaka* and Pele.* (Emerson 1915:117.)

KOHAI, the first mortal woman according to one Tongan legend. She and her male counterpart, Momo, were created from maggots or worms. (Gifford 1924:13.) According to another tradition, Kohai was the first man, the first Tui Tonga* (king of Tonga). (Gifford 1924:25.) According to another legend, Kohai was one of the three first mortal men brought forth by the Tongan gods of creation. He and his companions, Koau* and Momo,* were given wives by Māui* and his brothers, and they populated the islands. (Reiter 1907:438–445.) See also **Creation; Koau; Momo.**

KOHETANGA, a Tuamotuan demon or demigod. (Stimson 1964:235.)

KOHIKOHI, Māori name for the aborigines of New Zealand before the arrival of the Polynesians. (Tregear 1891:155.) See also **Hiti; Kahuitoka; Kahuitupua; Kupe; Moriori.**

KOILASA or KUILASA, a goddess of Loma, Nsangalau, Lau Islands (Polynesian outliers in Fiji), who likes men and who punishes those who displease her with rashes. (Hocart 1929:198.) See also **Raluve.**

KOKE, or ROHE,* wife of the demigod Māui* in Māori legends. (Tregear 1891:421.)

KOKIOHO, a Marquesan god, the son of Papa-Uka and Papa-Ao in the creation, principally worshipped at Uauka; also a legendary land of stone cutters. (Christian 1895:187–202.)

KŌKIRI, Tuamotuan name of one of the two Magellanic Clouds located 25⁰ off the south celestial pole. It is believed to have been the fish eaten by the Milky Way, Te Mango-roa. (Stimson 1964:239.)

KŌKOHU-I-MATANGI, Tuamotuan word for the upper jaw of the god Ātea (Wākea*), the upper half of the universe. (Stimson 1964:241.) See also **Tupere-kauaha-roa.**

KŌLEA-MOKU, the same as the Hawaiian god **Kumu-kahi.***

KO-MAI-NAISOPIU, a terrifying snake god of the Mualevu clan, Lau Islands (Polynesian outliers in Fiji). (Hocart 1929: 196.)

KOMOAWA, a Hawaiian priest (*kahuna*) and advisor to Wākea* (progenitor of the Hawaiian people) who aided him in his love affair with the lovely Ho'ohoku-ka-lani.* (Beckwith 1948:296–297; Malo 1903:314–315; Fornander 1920:319.)

KOMOHANA-O-KA-LĀ, Hawaiian god invoked to cure sickness. (Beckwith 1948:12.)

KŌPŪWAI, a giant who once lived in the southern part of New Zealand. He swallowed the Mataau (Molyneux) River in order to capture a woman named Kaiamio. He was later turned into the mountain Kopuwai in central Otago, and the nearby lake is called Hapua-o-Kaiamio. (Beattie 1918:152.) See also **Giants.**

KŌRAU, the Māori god of edible ferns. (Tregear 1891:167; White 1887a: App.)

KORE, the nothingness or void out of which all creation was made according to Māori tradition. Genealogies differ as to the exact sequence of creation.

One says that Te Kore was first (Shortland 1882:12), another that Te Pō* (the night) was first and that he began Te Ao* (light) who begat Kore* (White 1887a:18). Another says he is the son of Rangi* (sky father) and Papa* (earth mother), brother to Pō (night) and Ao (light), and bears the likeness of a man (Grey 1970:11; Tregear 1891: 168.) See also **Creation; Heavens.**

KOROIMBO, a sea god of the island of Munia, Lau Islands (Polynesian outliers in Fiji). (Hocart 1929:196.)

KOROKOIEWE, a Māori god who presides over childbirth. (Tregear 1891:172; White 1887a: App.)

KORONAKI, a Māori lizard god of inferior rank. (Tregear 1891:172; White 1887a: App.)

KORORŪPŌ, Tuamotuan name for a mythical land in the underworld,* home of the goblin Mokorea* who became the mistress to Kui,* grandfather of the famous hero Rata (Laka*), and who gave birth to two children—a son, Rima-roa,* and a daughter, Rima-poto. (Stimson 1964:253.)

KOROTANGI, an ancient stone carving of a bird, venerated by the Māori in ancient song. It was brought to New Zealand from Hawaiki,* and cast copies are housed in several New Zealand museums. (Tregear 1891:173.)

KOU, second wife of the popular Hawaiian chief Ka-welo.* (Pukui 1971:389; Elbert 1959:64–65.)

KŪ (TŪ), one of the most powerful and widely-worshipped gods in all of Polynesia, the god of creation (procreative powers) as well as the god of war. In **Hawai'i**, one tradition maintains that Kū is one of the trinity of Kāne,* Kū, and Lono,* who created the heavens, the earth, and all living organisms. (Fornander 1920:267, 268, 273–276.) He is more properly identified as the male generative power who, with his female counterpart Hina,* are the great ancestral deities of heaven and earth. Kū is worshipped to produce good crops, good fishing, long life, and prosperity. Numerous epithets reveal his character as a god of growth, a god of rain, a god of forests—Kū-pulupulu, Kū-olonā-wao, Kū-mauna, Kū-holoholo-pali, to mention only a few. At the time of Captain James Cook's arrival in Hawai'i (1778), the Hawaiians were worshipping Kū as a great war god under the name Kū-ka'ili-moku,* and human sacrifices were made to him at their temples (*heiau*). (Beckwith 1948:12–30.)
Similar to the Hawaiians, the **Maoris** of New Zealand and the Chatham Islanders worshipped Tū as one of the primary gods of creation as well as a powerful war god. In the early phase of the creation, Tū suggested that their parents, Rangi* (heaven) and Papa* (earth), be destroyed in order to separate them. After the separation, it was only Tū that could withstand the bitter reaction of Tāwhiri-matea,* the god of tempests, and afterwards he turned in vengeance upon Tangaroa, Rongo, Tāne, and all those who had deserted him. Subsequently, he assumed many epithets—Tū-kariri, Tū-kanguha, etc. (Grey 1855:1–11; Shand 1894:89–92.)
In the **Tahitian** cosmology, Tū was the chief artisan of Ta'aroa (Kanaloa*) in the creation. It is only in more modern times that his dominant position was usurped by a new god called 'Oro* who owes this new position to the Arioi Society* and to his connection with the sacred island of Ra'iātea. (Henry 1928:342.)
In **Samoa**, Tū or Alii Tū is a superior god, a war god, who resides in the heavens and who may be represented on earth as the bird called the rail; red is his sacred color. (Krämer 1902:179, 337; Turner 1884:61.)
In **Mangareva** (French Polynesia), Tū is the god of peace and breadfruit. (Caillot 1914: 153–154.)

KUA, a powerful shark god of Ka'ū, Hawai'i, who attempted to prevent the marriage between the volcano goddess Pele* (his relative) and the mortal chief Lohi'au* from Kaua'i. (Pukui 1971:389; Emerson 1915:160–162.) See also **Kahole-a-kāne; Sharks.**

KUAHA, one of the four ancient Easter Island gods brought to the island by the voyager Hotu-Matua.* (Alpers 1970:237–241; Métraux 1940:58–69.) See also **Kuihi; Opapako; Tongau.**

KŪ'AI-HE-LANI, a mythical cloud land adjoining the earth and the land most commonly named in visits to heaven in Hawaiian legends. The volcano goddess Pele* was born there as well as the children of Kū* and Hina.* It was visited by Kila,* Kū-waha-ilo,* and other mythical characters. It lies to the west, perhaps forty days travel. It is the divine home land, the wonderful land of the setting sun going down into the deep blue sea, the land just below Nu'u-mealani.* (Beckwith 1948:78–79; Emerson 1915:xxv.)

KŪ-'ĀLANA-WAO, a Hawaiian forest god and patron god of canoe makers. He was banished from Hawai'i by the volcano goddess Pele* for protecting her lover Lohi'au from being consumed by her fire. (Beckwith 1948:176–177; Emerson 1915:201.)

KŪ-ALI'I, a famous Hawaiian chief of O'ahu, who subjugated the whole island group to his authority. According to the famous genealogical chant, he is acknowledged as a god, a messenger from heaven, one of supernatural power, a soldier, and a runner of extraordinary swiftness. According to his chronicler he lived to be 175 years old. (Beckwith 1940:394–400; Fornander 1916:364–434, 394–395; Fornander 1878:195–196; 2:278–288; Pukui 1971:389.)

KUALU-NUI-KINIAKUA, chief of the Mū* people who anciently live in Kahiki (Tahiti ?) according to Hawaiian legends. His son Kualu-nui-paukū-mokumoku ruled with him. (Beckwith 1948:325; Green 1936:34, 39–41; Rice 1923:44–46.)

KŪ-A-PĀKA'A, see **Paka'a.**

KUEO, born to the Māori god Rangi* (sky father) after Rangi was wounded by the god Tangaroa (Kanaloa*). (Tregear 1891:180.)

KŪ-HAI-MOANA, a monstrous, man-eating, Hawaiian shark god, brother to the volcano goddess Pele,* said to be thirty fathoms long, and husband to the shark goddess Ka-'ahu-pāhau.* (Beckwith 1948:129.) See also **Sharks.**

KŪ-HELE-I-PŌ, father of the Hawaiian goddess Māpunai'a-'a'ala (daughter of the goddess Haumea*). (Beckwith 1948:278.)

KUHI, grandmother of the hero Tahaki (Kaha'i*) and his half-brother Karihi in the Tuamotuan story. On their journeys, they came to where Kuhi lived. She was blind but caught them stealing her food. Tahaki threw coconuts and hit her in her eyes, and she regained her sight. She recognized her two grandchildren and gave them magical powers to avenge their father's disgrace. She also gave them her magical net which Tahaki later used to catch the goblins of Matuauru in which he clubbed them to death. (Stimson 1964: 259.) See also **Kui.**

KŪ-HOLOHOLO-PALI, a Hawaiian god of the forest and of canoe construction. He steadies the canoe as it slides down the slope toward the ocean. (Beckwith 1948:15–16.)

KŪ-HO'ONE'E-NU'U, a war god worshipped on the island of O'ahu (Hawai'i) whose carved image was used by king Kamehameha I (d. 1819). (Beckwith 1948:284; Westervelt 1915b:47–51.)

KUI, the wife of Tupu-tupu-whenua in Māori legend. They live below the ground, and when a new house on earth is completed, a bunch of grass is sacrificed to them as an offering. Kui is also named as the father of Vahi-vero* and the grandfather of Rata (Laka*) in the Tuamotuan stories. (Tregear 1891:180; White 1885:107.) See also **Kuhi.**

KU'I-A-LUA, patron god of Hawaiian warriors being trained in *lua* fighting (breaking bones). (Beckwith 1948:50.)

KUIHI, one of the four ancient Easter Island gods brought to the island by the voyager Hotu-Matua.* (Alpers 1970:237–241; Métraux 1940:58–69.) See also **Kuaha; Opapako; Tongau.**

KŪ-'ILI-KAUA, a Hawaiian war god who sent aid to the goddess Hi'iaka* in her fight against the monster Pana-'ewa.* (Emerson 1915:41.)

KŪ-'ĪLIO-LOA, a Hawaiian dog-man with supernatural powers, who came to Hawai'i from Kahiki (Tahiti ?) with the god Lono-ka-'eho.* He met Kama-pua'a* (hog man) in battle and was slain. A *heiau* (temple) was erected to him at Kāne-'ilio light house. (Beckwith 1948:347–349.) He is also reported to have been slain by the great voyager Ka-ulu.* (Beckwith 1948:436–437.)

KUIWAI, wife to the ancient Māori chief Manaia* in Hawaiki.* (Grey 1970:128, 134–

135; Tregear 1891:181.) See also **Haungaroa.**

KŪ-KĀ'IE'IE, Hawaiian god of the forests. (Beckwith 1948:15.)

KŪ-KĀ'ILI-MOKU, the most famous Hawaiian war god whose image was once owned by king Kamehameha I. After the king's death in 1819, the keeper of the image placed it on a canoe with food and tapa cloth to go back to Kahiki (Tahiti ?) from whence the god had first come. It was never seen again. (Beckwith 1948:28–29.)

KŪ-KALANI-'EHU, father of Papa* (ancestress of the Hawaiian people) according to the Kumu-honua* genealogy. His wife was Ka-haka-ua-koko. (Beckwith 1948:307; Fornander 1878:188–209.) Also name of a god smashed by the hero Kawelo* when the god did not respond to his prayers regarding his proposed military expedition to Kaua'i. (Beckwith 1948: 28; Fornander 1917:28–31.)

KŪKALI, son of the Hawaiian priest Kū who taught him his magical secrets and gave to him a magical banana skin always full of fruit. Through this miraculous feat, Kūkali was able to undertake great ocean voyages to distant lands of Kahiki (Tahiti). He once stopped on a mysterious island presided over by the great bird called Halulu. Kūkali was captured and thrown into a pit with others. Through his incantations, prayers, and stone armaments, they were able to hack the bird to death. Halulu's sister, Nā-maka-'eha (four eyes), decided on revenge, and when Kūkali ventured down into her bottomless pit, he found Nā-maka-'eha, passed her numerous tests of strength, married her, and returned with her to his home in Hawai'i. (Beckwith 1948:493; Westervelt 1915a:66–73.) See also **'Au-kele-nui-a-iku.**

KŪ-KA-ŌHI'A-LAKA, a Hawaiian rain god, a patron god of the hula, a patron god of canoe builders who use the *'ōhi'a* (ironwood) tree in their construction, brother to the rain goddess Ka-ua-ku'āhiwa, both of whom came from Kahiki to Hawai'i to live. When his sister died, he searched for her spirit. He transformed himself into the sacred *'ōhi'a lehua* tree from whose branch, when broken, flows blood. (Beckwith 1948:16–17; Green and Pukui 1936:146–149.) Another legend refers to him as the husband to Hina-ulu-'ōhi'a,* goddess of the *'ōhi'a* forest and the mother of the voyagers Ka-ulu.* (Beckwith 1948:17.)

KŪ-KA-'Ō'Ō, a Hawaiian farmer's god. Also known as Kū-ke-olowalu.* (Pukui 1971: 390.)

KŪ-KA-UA-KAHI, a Hawaiian owl god who brings souls back to life or who acts as a protector during battle or danger. (Beckwith 1948:42, 123-124.)

KŪ-KE-OLO'EWA, a Hawaiian war god worshipped by the chiefs on Maui and Moloka'i. His image was carved from a trunk of a tree that mysteriously washed up on the shores of One-awa (O'ahu). He is also associated with healing and rain. (Beckwith 1948:110, 113, 284; Pukui 1971:390; Westervelt 1915b:47–51.)

KŪ-KE-OLOWALU, see **Kū-ka-'ō'ō**.

KŪKŪ'ENA, elder sister to the Hawaiian volcano goddess Pele* who acts as a guide to travelers and presides over the kava ceremony. (Beckwith 1948: 192; Emerson 1915:94–95, 221; Green and Pukui 1936:166–167.)

KŪ-KŪLIA, Hawaiian god of husbandry. (Beckwith 1948:15.)

KULA, an ancestral god worshipped on Futuna. (Burrows 1936:105–108.)

KŪ-LEO-NUI, an ancient god worshipped by the Menehune* (little people) of Hawai'i. (Beckwith 1948:328.)

KULI, a dog god of Futuna. (Burrows 1936:105–108.)

KŪ-LILI-'AI-KAUA, a war god who accompanied Pele,* the Hawaiian volcano goddess, from her original home in Tahiti to Hawai'i. (Beckwith 1948:174; Emerson 1915:43.)

KULI-PE'E-NUI, a Hawaiian god of lava flow. (Emerson 1915:205.)

KULU, the principal god on the island of Vaitapu, Tuvalu. (Turner 1884:287–288.)

KŪ-MAUNA, a Hawaiian forest god banished by the volcano goddess Pele* for refusing to destroy her lover, Lohi'au,* whom she suspected was having an affair with her sister, Hi'iaka.* A large lava boulder above Hi'ilea, Ka'ū district of Hawai'i, is said to be Kū-mauna whom Pele overwhelmed with a stream of lava. It is reported that the sacred stone cures disease and brings rain in times of drought. (Beckwith 1948:15–18, 177; Emerson 1915:211–212; 1919:33–35.)

KŪ-MEA-TE-A-PŌ, (KŪ-MEA-TE-PŌ), one of the powers of darkness that fell upon the earth during the birth of the god Tangaroa (Kanaloa*) in Māori legends. (Grey 1855:129; Tregear 1891:182–183.) See also **Unumia-te-kore; Tutakahinahina**.

KUMI-TONGA, a Tuamotuan goddess of feasting mats.

(Stimson 1964:262.) See also **Fakahotu; Tahunui**.

KU-MOANA, the Marquesan god of the ocean. (Christian 1895:194.)

KŪ-MOKU-HĀLI'I, a Hawaiian god of forests and canoe makers, husband to Lea,* banished from Hawai'i by the volcano goddess Pele.* (Beckwith 1948:26, 177.)

KUMU-HEA, a Hawaiian god of worms (caterpillars), originally the son of the god Kū.* He married a mortal and remained with her only at night since during the day he resumed his identify as a worm. One day, his wife followed him and discovered his true identity. He was angry and attacked and destroyed her family's crops. The parents appealed to the god Kāne* who cut Kumu-hea into small pieces that grew into the cutworms (pe'elua) seen in Hawai'i today. (Beckwith 1948: 135; Green 1928:43.)

KUMU-HONUA, a mythical ancestor of the Hawaiian people, the first man created by the gods Kū,* Lono,* and Kāne.* Also the name of a Hawaiian genealogy that traces the nobility from Kumu-honua through Laka* to Nu'u and then to Hawai'i-loa.* (Beckwith 1948: 42–46, 307–308; Fornander 1878:181–185.)

KUMU-KAHI, a Hawaiian demigod who came to Hawai'i from Kahiki (Tahiti ?) with Pele* (the volcano goddess) and her entourage. He and his two wives settled on the eastern most point of Hawai'i that bears his name. The point is called Ladder of the Sun and Source of the Sun, and from here his two wives (in the form of stone) push the sun back and forth between the two solstices. Kumu-kahi may take the form of a bird (Pacific golden plover) or may enter a medium and perform miraculous deeds. (Beckwith 1948:119–120.) Also the name of the younger brother of Mo'i-keha,* the ancient hero of the migrations to Hawai'i from Kahiki. (Beckwith 1948: 353; Fornander 1916:18–21.)

KŪ-NUI-ĀKEA, the head of all the Hawaiian Kū* gods, a national god whose heiau (temple) was constructed at Waolani (O'ahu). He resides in the highest heaven, but is represented in the heiau by a freshly cut block of 'ōhi'a (ironwood). Strict prayers and human sacrifices are made when the tree is felled. (Beckwith 1948:15, 26.) Also the name of Hawai'i-loa's* son from whom descend the high chiefs of Hawai'i. (Beckwith 1948:363–365.)

KUO, the Māori god of night and darkness. (Tregear 1891: 184; White 1887d:129.)

KŪ-'ŌHI'A-LAKA, the father of Hiku-i-ka-nahele* (the Hawaiian hero who rescues his sister's spirit from the underworld).* (Beckwith 1948:147–148.)

KŪ-OLONO-WAO, a Hawaiian forest god. (Beckwith 1948: 15–16.)

KŪPĀ-'AI-KE'E, a Hawaiian forest god, inventor of the adze and thus patron god of canoe makers, a god in the Laka* legend who helps construct his magical canoe. Also a god banished by the volcano goddess Pele* for protecting Lohi'au* (her lover and a chief from Kaua'i) from her fire. (Beckwith 1948:15–16, 176–177.)

KUPE, a famous Māori chief in Hawaiki,* the first Polynesian to discover New Zealand. Once Kupe went fishing with his cousin, Hoturapa, only to leave him to drown far out to sea. Kupe returned to land, kidnapped Hoturapa's wife, Kuramaro-tini, and fled with her in her great canoe *Matahōrua*. They circled the islands of New Zealand and encountered numerous sea demons and monsters. After finding no inhabitants in the new land, Kupe and Kura returned to Hawaiki to tell of their adventures to their family and friends. His stories convinced others to migrate to the new lands. (Best 1927:260–282; Grey 1970:161–171; Tregear 1891:184; White 1887b:179.)

See also **Canoes, Māori Migration; Manaia; Turi.**

KŪ-PEPEIAO-LOA, Hawaiian god of the forests and canoe construction. (Beckwith 1948: 15.)

KUPUKUPU, a Hawaiian god of healing and vegetation. (Emerson 1915:144.)

KŪPŪLANAKĒ HAU, wife to Wākea* (ancestor of all the Hawaiian nobility); or also mentioned as the wife to Kahiko-lua-mea* according to the Kumu-uli genealogy. (Beckwith 1948:294–295, 309; Fornander 1878:187.)

KŪ-PULUPULU, a Hawaiian forest god, a patron god of canoe makers, called the chip maker, invoked when felling the sacred '*ōhi'a* trees to be used in the temples (*heiau*), banished by the volcano goddess Pele* for protecting Lohi'au* (her lover and a chief from Kaua'i) from her fire. (Beckwith 1948:15, 26, 176; Emerson 1915:144, 204.) Also identified as the god La'a-mai-kahiki.* (Beckwith 1948: 359; Fornander 1916:152–155) and as the hero Laka.* (Beckwith 1948:321, 323.) Also son of Lua-nu'u,* father of the Menehune* (little people of Hawai'i). (Beckwith 1948:321; Fornander 1878:97–99.)

KURA, mother of the famous Polynesian hero Rata (Laka*),

wife to Wahieroa (Wahieloa*). Also name of the red wreaths worn by the Māori chiefs in the great migration from Hawaiki* to New Zealand. (Grey 1970:84; Tregear 1891:185.) See also **Canoes, Māori Migration.**

KURA-E-HĀ, Tuamotuan word meaning a god, an exalted person, the moon, or a venerated bird. (Stimson 1964:264.)

KURA-HAU-PŌ, one of the Māori canoes in the great migration to New Zealand, commanded by Ruatea. (Tregear 1891:185; White 1887b:177, 182.) See also **Canoes, Māori Migration.**

KŪ-RAKI, the god of the Māori *kahika* (white pine) tree. (Tregear 1891:185; White 1887a:27.)

KURAMANU, a Tuamotuan creature having the body of a man but the wings of a bird. (Stimson 1964:265.)

KURA-MARO-TINI, daughter of the Māori chief Toto* in Hawaiki* and wife of Hoturapa* in the legend of Kupe* and Turi.* The famous canoe *Aotea** was given to her by her father. Kupe kidnapped Kura-maro-tini and her canoe and set sail for New Zealand. (Grey 1970:161–162; Tregear 1891:185.) See also **Canoes, Māori Migration.**

KŪRĀNGAITUKU, an ogress in the Māori legend of Hatupatu* who has wings and who can spear birds with her lips. (Grey 1970:146, 148; Tregear 1891:185–186.)

KURA-ORA, name of the supernatural beings that dwelt in the lashing holes of Rata's (Laka's*) canoe in Tuamotuan legends. (Stimson 1964:264.)

KURAWAKA, the name of the locale where the first man was created by the god Tāne (Kāne*) in Māori legends. (Shortland 1882:21; Tregear 1891:188.)

KURU-AU-PŌ, one of the Māori canoes in the great migration to New Zealand. Also known as *Kurua-te-pō* or *Kura-hau-pō*. (White 1887b:180, 182.) See also **Canoes, Māori Migration.**

KURU-MEHAMEHA, the Tuamotuan god of fire. (Stimson 1964:266.) See also **Fire, Origin of.**

KŪ-'ULA-KAI, a Hawaiian god of fisherman, husband to Hina-puku-i'a* (goddess of fish and vegetable food). As a mortal, he lived on east Maui where he built the first fish pond, and when he died, he gave his magical implements to his son 'Ai-'ai* and instructed him in the building of stone images and temples (*heiau*). The color red is sacred and taboo to Kū-'ula-kai.

He is also regarded as a fish god on the island of O'ahu where once a stone figure near Waimea was the center of his worship. (Beckwith 1948:19–22, 24; Emerson 1915:98; Fornander 1920:172–175; Thrum 1907:215–249.)

KŪ-WAHA-ILO, a Hawaiian sorcery god, husband of the goddess Haumea* and father to the volcano goddess Pele,* a cannibal, responsible for the introduction of human sacrifices. He appears in several Hawaiian legends ('Au-kele-nui-a-iku,* Kā'ana-e-like,* and Ha-'ina-kolo,* for example) as a god who descends from heaven proceeded by thunder, lightning, and heavy winds. He may appear in various forms and laps up his victims with his thrusting tongue. (Beckwith 1948:29–30; Ellis 1824:272; Fornander 1916:76–85, 1920:279–280.)

KŪWATAWATA, a Māori god, guardian of the gates to the underworld.* (Tregear 1891:188.) See also **Mataora**.

–L–

LĀ, the sun god in Samoan tradition, also known as Tagaloa (Kanaloa*) whose union with the maiden Ui* gave birth to the ruling family of Samoa, the Tui Manu'a. (Krämer 1902:8.)

LA'A-HĀNA, Hawaiian patron goddess of tapa makers, daughter of Maikohā from whose body grew the *wauke* plant (*Broussonetia papyrifera*) used as a beater in making tapa cloth. (Beckwith 1948:99–100; Fornander 1917: 270–271; Malo 1903:82.)

LA'A-KAPU, one of the four Hawaiian brothers (Kī, Kanaloa,* Hawai'i-loa,* and La'a-kapu), sons of Aniani-ka-lani, who first settled the Hawaiian islands from the south according to the Kumu-honua* genealogy and legend. (Beckwith 1948:362.)

LA'A-LA'A, a village god of Savai'i, Samoa, who cares for plantations and guards them with the help of the god of thunder and lightning; also a patron god of wrestlers on 'Upolu, Samoa; a god who presides in war, sickness, and family events. (Turner 1884:33–34.)

LA'A-MAI-KAHIKI, a Hawaiian magician (sorcerer) in the tale of the goddesses Hi'iaka* and Pele.* When Hi'iaka's beloved Lohi'au was consumed in flames by Pele, his spirit languished in Kahiki (Tahiti) until La'a helped restore him to life to be united with his beloved Hi'iaka once again. (Beckwith 1948:177; Emerson 1915:236–237.)

Another La'a-mai-kahiki figures in the Hawaiian legends of Mo'i-keha* and his son Kila* who settled in Hawai'i from Kahiki. As Mo'i-keha became aged, he desired that his bones be returned to Kahiki for burial. He sent his son Kila to escort the high ranking La'a to Hawai'i to supervise the return. Once in the islands, La'a settled down with three wives on Kaua'i, O'ahu, and the Big Island. From them, he had three sons who became progenitors of the ruling families of Hawai'i. (Beckwith 1948:355-359; Fornander 1916: 128–153; 160–173.) La'a was responsible for the introduction of image worship, the *kā'eke* (bamboo) drum, and hula dancing in Hawai'i. (Fornander 1916:152–155.)

LA'AMA'OMA'O, Hawaiian wind god or goddess who acted as a companion to the voyager Mo'i-keha* in his migration from Kahiki (Tahiti) to Hawai'i. (Beckwith 1948:86, 449; Fornander 1880: 53; Malo 1903: 114.) La'a-ma'oma'o is also a Samoan god of war, particularly identified with the rainbow. The center of his worship is on the islet of Manono, off 'Upolu. (Krämer 1902:160; Stair 1897:56; Turner 1884:35.)

LAENIHI, a Hawaiian sorceress, daughter of Wahiawa and Kū-kaniloko, and sister to Hale-mano.* She aided her brother Hale-mano in courting and keeping his beautiful wife, Kama-lālā-walu. Twice she restored him to life after he had died of love sickness. In doing so, she changed into a fish and swam to Puna accompanied by rain, lightning, thunder, and earthquakes. Once she even took the form of a chicken. (Beckwith 1948:523–524; Fornander 1917:228–263.)

LAGATEA, the Rotuman god of creation, the father of Tagaroa (Kanaloa*), husband to Papatea (earth). (Gardiner 1898:466-467.)

LAGE-IKI, one of the five principal gods on the island of Niue that inhabits the western part of the island. His evil actions cause death to come into the world. He has numerous progeny. (Smith 1902:195–218, 1903:1–31; Loeb 1926:157–164.) See also **Fāo; Faka-hoko; Huanaki; Lagi-atea; Luatupua; Maka-poe-lagi.**

LAGEIKIUA, a god of Niue Island. (Loeb 1926:161.)

LAGI, the word for heaven on Rotuma. In the creation, Lagi and Otfiti (earth) were joined together until Tagaroa (Kanaloa*), son of Lagatea (from heaven) and Papatea (from earth) pushed them apart. (Gardiner 1898:466–467.)

LAGI-ATEA, one of the five principal gods of Niue. Like Lage-iki,* he caused death to come into the world and had numerous progeny. (Smith 1903:1–31; Loeb 1926:157–159, 163–164.) See also **Fāo; Fakahoko; Huanaki.**

LAGIHALULU, a god of Niue Island who brings bad luck. (Loeb 1926:161.)

LAGIHULUGIA, a god of Niue Island. (Loeb 1926:161.)

LAGILOA, a god of Niue Island. (Loeb 1926:161.)

LAGIOFA, a god of Niue Island invoked to aid during time of war. (Loeb 1926:161.)

LAGITAITAIA, a fish god of Niue Island with a striped body who makes the seas calm after a storm. (Loeb 1926:161.)

LĀ'IE-I-KA-WAI, heroine of the popular Hawaiian romance by the same name. Lā'ie-i-ka-wai and her twin sister, Lā'ie-loh-eloke, were born to chief Kahauokapaka and his wife, Māla'ekahana, at Lā'ie on the island of O'ahu. The sisters were hidden from their disappointed father who wanted a son. Lā'ie was finally taken to Puna where she was watched after by Waka, her *mo'o* guardian, until a suitable suitor appeared to make her his wife. Several young chiefs were unsuccessful in their attempts until finally a marriage was arranged between Lā'ie and Kekalukalu-o-ke-wa, chief of Kaua'i.

Just before the formal marriage ceremony, a young rascal from Puna named Hala-aniani carried her off and lived with her as his wife. Not to be out done, her patron goddesses (the Maile* sisters) arranged for their eldest brother, who lives in the highest heavens, to marry their mistress. Ka-'ōnohi-o-ka-lā descended to the earth, stripped Lā'ie's enemies of their power, and took Lā'ie upon a rainbow to live with him in Kaha-kaekaea (land of the gods in heaven). All went well until Ka-onohi-o-ka-lā returned to earth and took up with Lā'ie's twin sister. As punishment for this act, his parents banished him to be a wandering ghost in Hawai'i (the first of his kind), and Lā'ie returned to earth to live as the goddess Ka-wahine-o-ka-li'ūla. (Beckwith 1919; Beckwith 1948:526–537.) See also **Ghosts.**

LĀ'IE-LOHELOHE, sister to Lā'ie-i-ka-wai.*

LAKA (AKA, LASA, LATA, RATA), considered one of the most popular and one of the most daring heroes of Polynesia. Lengthy legends of his exploits extend throughout the islands, and the kings of Tahiti and Hawai'i claim him in their royal genealogies.

The fullest account of Rata is found in the **Tuamotus** where it takes several evenings to narrate the entire legend. It begins with Rata's grandfather Kui, a demigod of great magical powers, who takes to wife Princess Puehuehu and sires a son Vahivero. The young child is snatched away by two wild ducks who carry him away to a distant island called Hiva-ro-tahi where the two witches Nua and Mere-hau keep him imprisoned. For over a year, Kui seeks his son. He finally sets out for Hiva-ro-tahi on the back of a flying fish. When the witches see him coming, they send seven huge waves against him. Kui succeeds in swimming through each and arrives on the beach where the witches argue with him and then throw him far out to sea. Kui's magical powers save him from drowning. He then returns to land, rescues his son, ensnares the witches, and kills the two large ducks that were responsible for the abduction.

Years pass and Vahi-vero becomes a man under the tutelage of his father. One day, Vahi-vero goes inland to bathe, spies a water nymph, Tahiti-tokerau, and becomes enraptured by her beauty. Actually, Tahiti-tokerau is Vahi-vero's first cousin, granddaughter of Kui through his liaison with the goblin woman Rima-horo. Her son Rima-roa marries a water nymph, and they become the parents of Tahiti-tokerau. Vahi-vero succeeds in persuading Tahiti-tokerau to become his wife. Before she does, however, she is abducted by king Puna* of the underworld. Following his father's orders, Vahi-vero dives down into the pool until he reaches the nether world (Kororupo) where Tahiti-tokerau is being held. She is rescued while king Puna is away, and they then return home.

Shortly thereafter, Tahiti-tokerau becomes pregnant and bears a son, the mighty Rata. Meanwhile, not long after the birth of Rata, king Puna returns home and is informed of Vahi-vero's abduction of Tahiti-tokerau. One night, Vahi-vero and Tahiti-tokerau go crabbing to get food for their young son. Puna summons the shark Matuku-tagotago, which swallows the couple and takes them back to Kororupo where Tahiti-tokerau is buried head down in the sand.

Now orphaned, Rata is reared by his grandfather. When he later learns of his parents' fate, he decides to build a large seagoing canoe to find them. Taking his grandfather's magical adze, he enters the forest and fells a tree. He returns the next day to begin its construction only to find that the tree is upright again! He learns that goblins have restored the tree, whereupon he ambushes them and forces them to complete the construction of the canoe during the night. Sure enough, the next morning, the wonderful canoe is ready for the long journey.

On his way, Rata encounters the champion warrior Manu-kura and his wife, princess Pupura-to-te-tai (daughter of king Puna). Rata desires the princess, and the two heroes contest for possession of her. Rata wins and returns the maiden to his grandfather while he sets out again to seek his parents. Accompanied by the elves from the forest, Rata nears the land of Puna where the demon monsters of the sea guard its entrance. They attempt to thwart Rata's ship, but each is unsuccessful. When the shark Matuku tries, Rata slices him open and retrieves his father's body. The last ditch effort to stop Rata is the onslaught of the seven waves by Puna. Using his father's magical adze, Rata successfully cuts through them and arrives on shore. He and Puna meet and agree to a contest. It ends in a stalemate. Rata's servant Taraka, however, ambushes Puna and drags him back to the ship where Rata axes him to death. Rata finds his mother, pulls her out of the sand, and restores her to health. Joyfully, they return home where Rata dwells with his

family until his death. (Stimson 1937:96–147).

In the **Tahitian** legend, Rata becomes king of Tahiti when his uncle, king Tumu-nui, and his father, Vahieroa (son of Tafa'i* and Hina*), are swallowed by a great tridacna clam while on their way to Pitcairn Island to visit the king's daughter, Hau-vana'a, now the wife of king Tui-i-hiti of Pitcairn. In Tahiti, Rata's mother Maemae-a-rohi is made regent while he is a minor child. When Rata reaches manhood, his mother, the queen regent, sets out with a chosen crew to visit her daughter on Pitcairn. She arrives safely and is reunited with her daughter's family.

Meanwhile, Rata decides to avenge his father and uncle and makes detailed plans for the perilous journey. Similar to the Tuamotuan story, the tree chosen by Rata is protected by the forest elves, but after being captured by Rata, they agree to build the canoe for him. The next morning the ship is completed and after dedication to the god Ta'aroa (Kanaloa*), the crew sets out toward Pitcairn. Meanwhile, the queen regent and her crew leave Pitcairn for Tahiti, but in route they encounter the great clam and are swallowed up. Shortly thereafter, Rata and crew are sucked down into the same clam, but the warriors use their spears and cut the monster open. Rata's mother and crew are saved, and the skeletal remains of Rata's father and uncle are found and brought back to Tahiti for proper burial.

After recuperating from their journey, Rata and his warriors set out again and encounter other perilous experiences on the open sea, including a visit to the kingdom of Puna to save one of his relative's wives. (Beckwith 1948:263–275; Henry 1928: 468–515.)

In **Samoa**, Lata is a great canoe builder who originally came from Fiji. He builds a huge double outrigger canoe at Tafagataga on the island of Ta'ū (Manu'a group) and sails to Savai'i where a district and a mountain chain are named after him. From Savai'i, Lata sails to Tonga where he teaches them the techniques of canoe building. (Krämer 1902:455–457; Turner 1984:264.)

The **Tongans** tell of Lasa who has the same supernatural experiences with the forest elves as found in the Tuamotuan story. Lasa catches the chief elf Haelefeke who helps to build and to pilot the great canoe on their way to Fiji. In route, they successfully encounter demons who place tests in their paths. (Collocott 1928: 15–16.)

In **New Zealand**, Rata is the son of Wahieroa who is killed by Matuku-Tahōtahō. When he becomes a man, Rata learns the story from his mother, Kura, and then sets out to avenge his father. He builds his magical canoe with the help of the little

people of Roro-tini. Having encountered several monsters on his way, he finally arrives and ensnares Matuku whose bones are then made into spear points for spearing birds. (Grey 1970: 84–90).

In **Hawai'i**, Laka is not only a daring voyager, but a god as well. As an ancestor to the Hawaiian people (son of Wahieloa* and Hina-hāwa'e), Laka plans a voyage to the island of Hawai'i to revenge his father's murder. His canoe building is interrupted each evening by the little gods of the forest, but through his offerings to the great gods, they reward him with two outriggers which he straps together for his long voyage. He and his four skillful companions reach the cave of the old woman Kai-kapu,* trick her into opening the door of the cave, and make off with the bones of Laka's father. (Beckwith 1948:263–275; Thrum 1907: 111–114.)

As the Hawaiian god or goddess, Laka is identified with the hula and the red lehua blossom and may take the form of the deity of fertility and reproduction. In the story of Hi'iaka,* Laka is one of Pele's* sisters (Hi'iaka, Kapo, and Laka), guardians of the woodland. (Beckwith 1948:16–17, 41, 185– 186, 522, 532, 544; Emerson 1915: 142, 151.)

On **Mangaia**, Raka is the father of all the winds, the fifth deity, named "Trouble," brought forth in the creation by the god dess Vari-ma-te-takere.* His progeny of winds and storms is numerous. (Gill 1876:5.) See also the Marquesan **Aka.**

LALATÄVÄKE, a young Rotuman maiden, who, with her younger sister Lilitäväke, married to Tinirau (Kinilau*), were turned into tropical birds rather than being eaten by Tinirau's father, the king. (Churchward 1938:337–339.)

LALO-HĀNA, or sometimes Lalo-honua, wife of the first man, Kumu-honua,* created by the Hawaiian god Kāne. (Beckwith 1948:42–44; Fornander 1920:335, 273–276.) Also the mother of Laka* (Hawaiian god of the wildwood). (Beckwith 1948:41.) See also **Creation.**

LANI-KĀULA, an ancient Hawaiian prophet on Moloka'i, whose arch enemy, the *kahuna* Ka-welo,* stole and burned some of his excrements, thus causing the prophet's death. His bones were covered with stones and buried in a deep pit so that they could never be discovered. (Beckwith 1948: 110–111, 134; Fornander 1917: 674.)

LANI-LOA, a Hawaiian lizard goddess (mo'o) who once lived near the village of Lā'ie, O'ahu, until she was killed and cut into pieces that became five small islets off the coast nearby. (Beckwith 1948:127; Rice 1923:

LANI-WAHINE, is a Hawaiian lizard goddess who lives in Okoa pond, Waialua, O'ahu, and when she appears in human form it foretells some disaster. (Beckwith 1948:126.)

LATA, a benevolent and wise god of Niue Island. (Loeb 1926: 164.) See also **Laka.**

LAU-KA-'IE'IE, a Hawaiian forest goddess, sister to Makani-ke-oe* (Hawaiian god of love) and to Lau-kiele-'ula.* The beautiful Lau-ka-'ie'ie was born as a child of the cliffs and adopted by her aunt Pō-kahi and her husband Kau-kini. When grown, she dreamed of the handsome Kaua'i chief Kawelona as a husband. She sent her brother, Makani-ke-oe, to escort him back to her. The marriage festivities took place at Waipi'o Valley. Upon her death, Lau-ka-'ie'ie turned into the beautiful *'ie-'ie* vine (*Freycinetia arborea*) that graces the forest life in the Hawaiian Islands. (Beckwith 1948:93, 522–523; Westervelt 1915a:36–48.)

LAU-KAPALILI, the sacred gourd in heaven that reveals what is happening on earth in the legend of Lā'ie-i-ka-wai.* (Beckwith 1919; Fornander 1917:406–417.) Also another name for Makani-ke-oe,* the

Hawaiian god of winds and love. (Pukui 1971:392.)

LAU-KIA-MANU-I-KAHIKI, a beautiful Hawaiian maiden, illegitimate daughter of Mākī-i-oeoe (a visiting chief from Kaua'i) and Hina,* who fell in love with her half-brother, and, not being able to consummate her love, she burned down their house and killed all in it except her half-brother, whom she deserted, and returned home. (Beckwith 1948:513–514; Fornander 1916:596–609.)

LAU-KIELE-'ULA, a Hawaiian sweet-scented goddess, sister to the love god Makani-ke-oe and to Lau-ka-'ie'ie.* She is also the wife of Moanaliha-i-ka-wao-kele, father of the Maile* sisters, in the romance of Lā'ie-i-ka-wai.* (Beckwith 1948:93.)

LAUKITI, one of the principal gods on Nanumea, Tuvalu. (Turner 1884:291.)

LA'ULU, a Samoan fisherman entrusted with the magical fishhook that originally belonged to 'Alo'alo.* When 'Alo'alo died, the Tuifiti (king of Fiji) entrusted the fishhook to La-ulu and his wife, Fau-mea.* La'ulu jealously guarded the possession of the fishhook and refused to return it to the Tuifiti. When he and his family set out fishing, their canoes sank and became reefs off the coast of Savai'i. Their daughter Sina-te'e-alofa became the wife of

chief Lavania and gave birth to a daughter named Imoa'sala-ta'i. The daughter once became lost in the forest and married a forest spirit called Afi'a. Their son, Tau-tunu, eventually inherited the magical fishhook of his mother's uncles. Tau-tunu settled on Manu'a and had the power of renewing his youth and assuming a handsome form. (The story breaks off at this point.) (Fraser 1892:243–249; Krämer 1902:77.)

LAUTHALA, god of the Mbaumbunia clan in Yandrana, Lau Islands (Polynesian outliers in Fiji). (Hocart 1929:197.)

LAUTĪ, a young, Samoan girl who served at the household of Sina (Hina*) and who caused Sina's death by catching her soul and giving it to her parents, Gagaluē and Gaguluō. Sina's brother, Matilaalofau, discovered the deed, returned his sister's spirit to the land of the living, and killed Lautī. (Krämer 1902:136–139.)

LAVAKIMATA, a god of Niue Island, whose earthly representation is that of a hat worn in war and fishing to bring good luck. (Loeb 1926:161.)

LAVASII, title of the chief ruler at Lefanga, district of Aana, on the island of 'Upolu, Samoa. The title translates "cloth-lifted-up" and comes from a war in heaven between the followers of the god Tangaloa (Kanaloa*) and several mortals who visited the heavens and competed with the gods. One of their party, Mosofaofulu, used his feathers to cover them from the torrential rain, Fulufuluitolo saved them from the rapids in the river, and lastly, Tuimulifanua beat the Tangloans in hand combat and was presented with a fine mat to wear about his waist. Because it was so long, it trailed on the ground, and Tuimulifanua had to raise it up. Its inconvenience caused him to present it to another follower, Tuimuaiava, who returned to earth with it and the title remained in the family down through the nineteenth century. (Turner 1884: 249–251.)

LEA, Hawaiian goddess of canoe makers, wife to the forest god Kū-moku-hāli'i* and sister to the goddess of fish and vegetables, Hina-puku-i'a* (Hina-puku-'ai*). (Beckwith 1948:15, 69; Malo 1903:82, 133; Pukui 1971:392.) Also, the name of an ancient Samoan, who made an inexhaustible supply of kava* and breadfruit poi for the demons of Salailua, Samoa, and thus saved the village from destruction by the demon king, Moso.* (Krämer 1902:70–71.)

LEATUALOA, an inferior household god of Samoa, seen in the form of a centipede. (Turner 1884:69.)

LE-FALE-I-LE-LANGI, a Samoan goddess who gave birth to the various districts on the islands of Ofu and Ta'ū (eastern Samoa). She and her parents, Fa'a-gata-nu'u and Fa-a-ma-lie-nu'u, swam from the mythical island of Atafu (Tafu*) and reached Vai-tele on the island of Ta'ū. She fell in love with Faia, son of the octopus Fe'e, and had several children from whom the island districts took their name and from whom the great chiefs descended. They were Ta'ū (gentle rain), Aua-pō (reaching into night), Fa'a-lea'sao or Tausao (hardly able to get down), and Nga-nga-nga'e (panting or gasping). The last child Lua-nu'u (two lands) was born on Ofu. When Le-Fale-i-le-langi and Faia neared death, they gathered their sons around them and divided the lands and work between them. (Fraser 1890:200–202; Krämer 1902: 367–368.)

LEFANOGA, a Samoan war god who can take the form of an owl, son of the supreme god Tagaloa (Kanaloa*) and his wife Sināsa'umani (daughter of Sa'umani). Once Tagaloa and his eldest son went to attend a council in heaven. Secretly Lefanoga followed, and the gods caught and forced him to dig kava* for them to drink. He did as was instructed, but he stole the plants and brought them to earth, the first of their kind among mortals. He also fought in the war in heaven with Losi.* Also a brother to the demon Matu'u, a heron, from Manu'a who were beaten by their father for burning his dinner. (Krämer 1902:23, 214, 392, 416–421, 436.) Also a Samoan giant who accompanied Losi* to heaven to fight against the Tagaloa gods. (Fraser 1893: 265–293.) See also **Nafanua; Pava.**

LEKA, the god of Lomanikoro, Nukunuku, Lau Islands (Polynesian outliers in Fiji), embodied in the form of an owl. (Hocart 1929:197.)

LE-LE'A-SAPAI, a Samoan hero who retrieved yams stolen from his grandfather, Tui-Samata, by a winged people called Alele.* Tui-Samata lived at Le-futu on the island of Tutuila with his daughter, Amete, and her son, Le-le'a-sapai. One day the Alele swooped down and stole a crop of yams from them. Le-le'a-sapai set out to retrieve their loss. He approached the land of spirits where he was met by its two chiefs, Salevao (or Saolevao) and Tulia. They suggested he wait until morning to begin his journey, but he argued that he should continue when the moon rose. Since there was no moon that night, Sa-le-vao took pity on him, retired inland to the highest hill, and his bright presence made it appear that the moon had arisen. The two chiefs offered him a war club to use when he met his enemies.

The next morning, Le-le'a-sapai met the Alele as they came down to the water to bathe. They fought over the war club Le-le'a-sapai had placed in the water, and many of them were slain. Finally chief Alele appeared and Le-le'a-sapai forced him to give up the remaining yams and to swear that he would never invade Samoa again. (Fraser 1890:203–206; Krämer 1902:115–116.)

LELEGOATUA, a sacred spot in Mutalau, Niue Island, where the gods supposedly gathered. (Loeb 1926:161.)

LEOMATAGI, a god of Niue Island, invoked for good weather, who captured the winds and put them in a cave. (Loeb 1926:161.)

LEOSIA, name of a coconut tree (watcher) at the entrance of the Samoan underworld.* If a spirit strikes it, it returns to his earthly body. (Turner 1884:258.) See also **Luao.**

LEPE-A-MOA, a Hawaiian demigoddess, daughter of chief Keāhua of Kaua'i and his wife, Kauhao, born in the form of an egg because of the curse of the sea god Akua-peha-'ale. She was reared by her grandparents on O'ahu where she gained the power to take the form of a bird or a beautiful girl. Meanwhile, she had a brother born on Kaua'i by the name of Kauilani who also was gifted with supernatural powers. He set out and found his sister on O'ahu. There he fell in love with the daughter of Kākuhihewa, but he had to help Kākuhihewa win a cock fight in order to obtain her hand in marriage. He secretly concealed his bird-sister, Lepe-a-moa, in his garment, and they won the fight and the hand of the chief's daughter. (Beckwith 1948:428–429; Thrum 1907:164–184; Westervelt 1915b:204–245.)

LESĀ, the Samoan god of agriculture who sends rain and an abundance of food. His earthly representation is the owl. In other parts of Samoa, Lesa is a war god whose earthly appearance in the form of a lizard foretells the outcome of battles. (Krämer 1902:418–419; Turner 1884:46–48.)

LEWA-LANI, name given to the Hawaiian region of the air which lies next to the heavens of the gods. Lewa-nu'u, on the other hand, lies below just above the tree tops. (Beckwith 1948:80.) See also **Creation; Heavens.**

LEWANDRANU, the goddess of the clan of Nakambuta in Nasangalau, Lau Islands (Polynesian outliers in Fiji), sister or mother to Tokairambe.* Her spirit can enter into dogs and when angry make children ill. (Hocart 1929:198.)

LEWA-NU'U, name given to the Hawaiian region of the air which lies just above the tree tops and just below Lewa-lani,* which lies next to the heavens of the gods. See also **Creation.**

LIAVAHA, a fish god of Niue Island who makes the seas calm after a storm. (Loeb 1926:161.)

LĪHAU-'ULA, the progenitor of the Hawaiian *kahuna* (priestly class), son of Kahiko-lua-mea and his wife Kūpūlanakēhau. Līhau-'ula's brother Wākea became the ancestor of all the chiefs (*ali'i*) while his half brother, Maku'u, became the ancestor of the commoners (*maka'āinana*). (Beckwith 1948: 294–295; Fornander 1878:112.)

LIKI, mortal who holds up the heavens in legends from Tamana, a Polynesian outlier in Kiribati. (Turner 1884: 293.)

LIKUTHAVA, a goddess of Valelailai, Lau Islands (Polynesian outliers in Fiji), a sister to the god Tokairambe,* invoked to prevent hurricanes. (Hocart 1929:190.)

LILI, a Samoan god, patron of the subdistrict of Falealili (house of Lili), island of 'Upolu, Samoa. Offerings are made to him during the month of June. (Krämer 1902:287–288; Stübel 1896:74.)

LILINOE, Hawaiian goddess of mists, goddess of the snow-covered mountains, younger sister to Poli-'ahu,* and a rival to the goddesses Pele* and Hina.* (Beckwith 1948:87, 222; Pukui 1971:392.)

LĪLOA, a chief of ancient Hawai'i, favorite and younger son of the hero 'Umi.* (Beckwith 1948:330, 389; Fornander 1916: 178–185.)

LIMA-LOA, Hawaiian god of mirages and guardian of the sea from the island of Kaua'i. Appearing in human form in the Kama-pua'a* (hog man) legend, he gained Kama-pua'a's help in courting the beautiful daughters of Kāne-iki, a chief of Kaua'i. Ironically, Kama-pua'a ended up with both of the sisters as wives. (Beckwith 1948:204–205; Emerson 1915:134; Fornander 1917: 342–363.)

LIMARI, the place where mortal souls go after death according to Rotuman legends, a land under the sea off Losa, full of coconuts, pigs, and all that humans could wish for and where all the ghosts of mortals dwell. (Gardiner 1898:469.)

LIMU, the primeval Tongan god of creation named seaweed, which united with the goddess Kele* (receptacle) in the beginning to create the goddess Touiafutuna* (a metallic stone, from whom all creation descends). (Reiter 1907: 230–240.) See also Creation.

LIMULIMUTA, a benevolent household god of Samoa. Seaweed (limu) is sacred to him. (Turner 1884:71.)

LIPI-OLA, a vindictive Samoan spirit (god) who can enter his priest's body and bring calamity upon his enemies. He can also enter into the bodies of animals or take human form. (Stair 1896:37.)

LITA, an ancestral god worshipped on Futuna. (Burrows 1936:105–108.)

LO'AU, legendary king of Ha-'amea (Tonga) of mysterious origin. During the reign of Momo (tenth Tu'i Tonga), Lo'au appeared in Tonga, first discovered kava* and originated the intricate kava ceremony. Eventually he sailed with his men to the far distant horizon of the ocean and who was sucked down into the vast whirlpool at the end of the sky. Two followers, Kae* and Longopoa* escaped and had their own adventures. Lo'au's wife Ha'amea remained in Tonga and gave birth to a daughter, Nua, who married Momo and had a son Tui'itatu, a famous Tu'i Tonga. (Gifford 1924:139–152; Rutherford 1977:31–33.)

LOHI, a Tongan god who once visited the underworld* (Pulotu*) with three other gods (Haelefeke, Fakafuumaka, and Haveatoke) and goddess (Faimalie*) and collectively defeated the forces of the underworld in drinking, eating, and sporting games. Lohi secretly brought back the taro plant to the upper world for food. (Gifford 1924: 155–170.)

LOHI'AU, a handsome Hawaiian chief from the island of Kaua'i with whom the goddess Pele* fell in love. Pele's younger sister, Hi'iaka,* escorted Lohi'au to the big island of Hawai'i where Pele lived, but during their journey home, Pele suspected the worst between them and consumed Lohi'au with fire. Hi'iaka found his spirit, restored him to life, and they lived together on Kaua'i. (Beckwith 1948:173–177; Emerson 1915.)

LŌ-LUPE, a sorcery god, sometimes called Ololupe, from the island of Maui. He is invoked by priests in the rite of deification of the dead (usually for ruling chiefs) or the restoration of the dead to life. He takes the form of a kite (*lupe*) in the shape of a sting ray. Warrior chiefs greatly fear him. He punishes the souls of those who speak ill of the *ali'i* (nobility). (Beckwith 1948:109; Fornander 1880:239–240; Malo 1903:141, 143.) See also **Pahulu.**

LOMALOMA, god of the Nambutha clan at Yandrana, Lau Islands (Polynesian outliers in Fiji). (Hocart 1929:197.)

LONGABOA, the Samoan equivalent of Longapoa.*

LONGAPOA, accompanied king Loau of Ha'amea, Tonga, on his perilous ocean voyage to the edge of the horizon. When the canoe and crew headed for the monstrous whirlpool, Longapoa and his friend Kae* jumped for safety. Longapoa swam to a deserted island where a magical *puko* tree provided him with food—pigs, fowls, yams, and taro—and with instructions on how to return to his native Tonga. Once home, he failed to plant the branch of the *puko* as instructed, and consequently, it never produced any food. (Gifford 1924:139–152.) A Samoan story tells of Longoboa who has a similar experience as the Tongan story above. (Brown 1917:96–99.)

LONGOLONGOVAVAU, young daughter of the Tongan goddess Hina* and her husband Sinilau (Kinilau*), whom Hikuleo* (god of the underworld*) made queen of his abode. When she became of marriageable age, her uncle, Ofamaikiatama, returned to the upper world to seek a husband for her. He finally chose the handsome Lolomatokelau and tricked Hikuleo in allowing Longolongovavau to return to earth. The couple was married, but the men of Tonga became jealous of Lolomatokelau's good fortune and killed him. His spirit went to

Pulotu* (underworld) where Ofamaikiatama discovered it, returned to his body, and restored him to life and to his distraught wife. (Collocott 1928: 17–20.)

LONGO-NOA, a messenger for the Samoan creator god Tagaloa (Kanaloa*). (Fraser 1893: 265.) See also **Tuli**.

LONO (LOGO, ONO, RONGO, RO'O), is widely worshipped throughout Polynesia. **Hawaiians** regard him as one of their three major gods—Kāne,* Kū,* and Lono*—uncreated and self existing. He aided in the creation of humans. He is identified with heavenly manifestations such as clouds, storms, thunder, lightning, and most important the rainbow. Religious prayers to Lono are sure to bring needed rain. During the rainy months (October to February), ancient Hawaiians celebrate a unique festival dedicated to Lono called the Makahiki that includes singing, celebrations, and games.

According to ancient tradition, the god Lono descended from heaven on a rainbow to marry the mortal woman Kaiki-lani from the Big Island. Because of her great beauty, he became jealous, suspected her of infidelity, and in a rage beat her to death. Repenting of his actions, he instituted the Makahiki games in her honor during which time he went about the land challenging every man he met in a wrestling match. His symbol was an upright pole with a cross piece from which hung feathers and tapa streamers.

Eventually, he constructed a huge canoe, heaped it with food supplies, and sailed off. He promised, however, that he would return one day on a fabulous island abundant with trees, coconuts, chickens, and pigs. When Captain James Cook first sailed into Hawaiian waters during the Makahiki festival (January 1778), the islanders thoroughly believed that Lono had returned. (Beckwith 1948: 31–41; Malo 1903:186–210).

The **New Zealand** Māoris regard Rongo as one of the children of Rangi* (heaven) and Papa* (earth) who proposed that they separate their entwined parents to allow daylight to fall upon their creations. Rongo became identified with cultivated foods and especially with the *kumura* (sweet potato) which he brought in his waist band from Hawaiki* for the Māori people. Rongo was the god of the left side of humans while Rehua* and Tū (Kū) were gods of the right side. In heaven, Rongo-marae-roa and Tū led the rebellious spirits against the god Tāne (Kāne*) who drove both Rongo and Tū to a place called Kaihewa. From here they survived as the gods of evil and sorrow. (Grey 1970: 2–10; White a:31, c:97–108.)

In **Tahiti**, the god Ro'o (shortened from Ro'o-te-ro'oro'o) was the first god to break through the sky into the day and thus became a messenger for the god Tāne. He was a god of many attributes. An invocation to Ro'o was made to cast out diseases and to be cured by him. The neighboring **Marquesas** islanders identify Ono as the god of light. (Henry 1928: 369).

On **Mangaia** in the Cook Islands, Rongo is the oldest son of Ātea (Wākea*) and Papa and, therefore, the principal deity and the national war god of that island. He is represented by a triton shell trumpet in the god house in the island *marae* (temple) and by two stone images on the shore temple. (Buck 1934:162–163.) On Timatara (Austral Group), human sacrifices were offered to him.

LONO-I-KA-MAKAHIKI, Hawaiian god of the annual harvest *makahiki*,* a period of time when taxes are collected (October to February). His symbol is a cross piece mast from which hang feather wreaths and white tapa cloth streamers topped by a carved figure of a bird. (Beckwith 1948:33–37.) See also **Lono.**

LONO-I-KA-'OU-ALI'I, an image god anciently brought to Hawai'i from Ra'iātea (Society Islands) by La'a-mai-kahiki,* a high ranking chief who first in troduced image worship into Hawai'i. (Beckwith 1948:497.)

LONO-I-KE-AWEAWE-ALO-HA, a Hawaiian god of love-making and of mercy, uncle to the volcano goddess Pele.* (Elbert 1959:222–223, 238–239; Pukui 1971:393.)

LONO-KA-'EHO, an eight-headed chief from Kahiki (Tahiti ?) who was killed in battle by Kama-pua'a* (hog man). (Beckwith 1948:205; Fornander 1917: 326–333.)

LONO-MAKA-IHE, a Hawaiian patron god of spear throwers. (Pukui 1971:393.)

LONO-MAKUA, an uncle (or brother) to the Hawaiian volcano goddess Pele,* who keeps the goddess' sacred fire under his armpit. The *makahiki* image also bears his name. (Beckwith 1948:167; Emerson 1915:141; Pukui 1971:393; Westervelt 1915a:69–71.) See also **Loni-i-ka-makahiki.**

LONO-NUI-ĀKEA, the ancient name for the island of Hawai'i. (Beckwith 1940:305.)

LONO-PŪHĀ, a Hawaiian god of healing who was taught the properties of medicinal herbs by the god Tāne.* (Beckwith 1948: 116–118; Pukui 1971:393.)

LOSI, a giant Samoan who fished for the gods in heaven,

caused a war there because of his trickish ways, and returned to earth with the first taro plants. The god Tagaloa (Kanaloa*) instructed Losi to bring them fish. Losi obeyed, but wanting to have fun, laid a fish at the door of each of the gods. The next morning when the gods left their house, they slipped and fell, much to Losi's amusement. Losi snatched a shoot of taro plant to take back to earth with him and hid it in his loin cloth. Tagaloa suspected the thievery, and searched Losi so diligently that Losi was insulted. Losi returned to earth, planted the shoot, and gathered an army of giants and returned to heaven for a friendly visit. After a series of attempted tricks, the gods pitched a battle against the giants, however, Lefanoga* (destruction) conquered and destroyed them and returned to earth with all the food that heaven possessed. (Fraser 1893:264–293; Krämer 1902:393, 398; Stair 1896:36; Stübel 1896: 142; Turner 1884: 105.)

LU, the Samoan Noah, grandson of the god Tagaloa (Kanaloa*). (Krämer 1902:8.) In Tokelau, Lu (son of Ikiiki and Talanga) was responsible for separating the earth and sky and for the introduction of fire to humans. (Macgregor 1937: 17.)

LUA, a war god of Avatele, Niue Island. (Loeb 1926:160.)

LUAFAKAKANA, one of the gods of Niue Island, invoked in order to drive all other gods to the bottom of the sea. (Loeb 1926:161.) See also **Luatotolo; Luatupua.**

LUAFINE, god of Tokelau Islands. (Macgregor 1937:61.)

LUA-NU'U, an ancient Hawaiian with many epithets, ancestor of the Hawaiian Mu* people (a wild people living on bananas in the forest) and the Menehune* (the little people, the original inhabitants of Hawai'i before the Polynesians). Originally from the island of Kahiki-ku (Tahiti ?), Lua-nu'u and his sons sailed to O'ahu (Hawai'i) where they established their home. (Beckwith 1948:307, 321–322; Fornander 1878:97–99.) Another Lua-nu'u is the son of Laka* in the Hawaiian legend. (Fornander 1878:191; Malo 1903:323.)

LUAO, name of the entrance to the Samoan underworld.* It is a hallow pit through which spirits descend to Pulotu.* When they reach the bottom of the pit, a river carries them to a bathing placed called Vaiola (water-of-life). (Turner 1884: 258–259.) See also **Saveasi'uleo.**

LUATOTOLO, a god of Niue Island. Like Luafakakana* and Luatupua,* he can drive all other gods to the bottom of the sea. (Loeb 1926:161.)

LUATUPUA, one of the five principal gods on the island of Niue that inhabit the southern part of the island. Like Luafakakana* and Luatotolo,* he can also drive all other gods to the bottom of the sea. (Loeb 1926:161; Smith 1902:195–218.) See also **Fāo, Fakahoko; Huanaki; Lage-iki; Lagi-atea; Makapoe-lagi.**

LUPE, a Tongan god, a pigeon or dove, son of the goddess Touiafutuna (metallic stone) and twin to Tukuhali. The twins were the progenitors of all the land and water animals on the earth. (Reiter 1907:230–240.) See also **Creation.**

LUPE PANGOPANGO, a female pigeon in Samoan legends who bore a beautiful daughter by the name of Hina-lei-haamoa (Hina*). Lupe gathered numerous possessions for her daughter's dowry, but the creator god Tangaloa (Kanaloa*) looked down from the sky and sent a torrential rain that destroyed nearly all of her possessions. Distraught, Hina walked the beach until a turtle came and offered her a ride to Samoa. Once there, she met and married the handsome Sinilau (Kinilau*). His two other wives became jealous and sent Hina away. She found refuge in the home of friends, and there she gave birth to her son. Mean-while, Lupe sought for her daughter high and low. Finally she found her and her grandson and promised that she would return with the prized possessions of Hina's dowry. Hina was reconciled with Sinilau, and they returned to Lupe's country where they became rulers of the land. (Collocott 1928:20–23.)

–M–

MĀ, epithet of the supreme god in the Tuamotus. (Stimson 1964: 268.)

MĀ-'A'A, a Hawaiian goddess of the wilderness who strings leis for the more powerful deities. (Emerson 1915:138.) See also **Mai-'u'u.**

MAAFU, an ancient Tongan chief whose two sons, Maafu Toka and Maafu Lele, were born to a lizard mother. Because of their mischievous nature, their father sent them on dangerous missions, hoping that they would never return. When they learned of their father's real intent, they decided to go as far away from their father as possible. They chose the sky in which to live, and today they can still be seen by navigators who steer their canoes by the stars Maafu Toka and Maafu Lele, the two Magellanic Clouds in the southern hemisphere 25° off the south celestial pole. (Gifford 1924: 103–110.) See also **Kōkiri.**

MA'ATA'ANOA, father of the first mortal man (Tupufua*) in one Samoan legend. (Krämer 1902:168.) See also **Tiki.**

MA'A-TAHI, a Tahitian sea god. (Henry 1928:359.)

MA'AU, a Tahitian god of unsightliness in the creation myth.

When the god Tāne (Kāne*) put an end to unsightliness, all became beautiful. (Henry 1928: 415.)

MA'AVA, a Samoan demon who once lived on Manu'a and who caught unsuspecting visitors to his cave. His hair and beard were nearly two fathoms long, and his body was covered with feathers. He was finally caught and slain by the warriors of chief Tau. (Krämer 1902:454.)

MAEMAE-A-ROHI, mother of the Tahitian hero Rata (Laka*). (Henry 1928:493.)

MAEWAHO, name of the goblins or fairies in the Māori legend of Tāwhaki (Kaha'i*). (Tregear 1891:190; White 1887a: 80.) See also **Ponaturi.**

MAFAFA, a demon who once lived on top of Mafafa, 'Upolu, Samoa, and who attacked travelers. (Krämer 1902:148.)

MAFOLA, a sea god of Fakaofu, Tokelau Islands. (Macgregor 1937:61.)

MAFUI'E, the Samoan fire god or earthquake god from whom Ti'eti'e-i-talaga (sometimes Ti'iti'i-a-talanga) wrestled the secret of making fire. Mafui'e lived in the underworld,* called Fu'e-aloa, where he shook the earth from time to time in order to obtain food from mortals. His sister Ululepapa fled to the upper world where she married the god Tagaloa (Kanaloa*) and had a son Ti'eti'e-i-talaga. When grown, the young boy followed his father below where Mafui'e tended his ovens. He wrestled Mafui'e for a piece of his wood and then returned to the upper world where he introduced fire and cooking to mortals. (Krämer 1902:393; Fraser 1892:77–86, 1897:107–111; Stair 1896:56–57.) See also Āo-āo-mā-ra'i-ā; Mafuike; Mahuika; Māui.

MAFUIKE, an earthquake god on the island of Futuna, also known as Mafuise Foulou. He sleeps under the island, and once a year he turns over causing tremors and earthquakes. (Burrows 1936:106.) See also **Mafui'e.**

MAGEAFAIGĀ, a ferocious Samoan cannibal who once lived near the village of Nu'u-uli, Tutuila, Samoa. He was cured of his cannibalistic ways by the young boy Malauli whom Mageafaigā thought was a demon. (Krämer 1902:349.)

MĀHANGA, an ancient Māori chief, son of the water god Tū-heita and known for his way-ward disposition. (Tregear 1891:191; White 1887d:59.)

MĀHANG-A-TUA-MATUA, name of one of the Māori ca-noes that legends say brought the first Polynesians to New Zealand. It was sacred because it was manned only by priests. (Tregear 1891:20, 191; White 1887d:23.) See also **Canoes, Māori Migration.**

MAHARA, the eighth age of the existence of the universe according to Māori legends. (Tregear 1891:191; White 1887a: App.) See also **Creation; Heavens; Kore.**

MĀHINA, the Māori chief aboard the *Arawa** canoe who retrieved and kept the red wreath thrown overboard by his colleague Tauninihi when they first spied the beautiful *pōhutukawa* blossoms in New Zealand. Once he discovered the delicate nature of the new flowers, however, Tuaninihi wished his wreath back. Mā-hina refused, hence the Māori proverb, "I will not give it up, 'tis the red head ornament which Māhina found." (English equivalent, "Losers, weepers, finders keepers.") (Grey 1970: 114; Tregear 1891:193; White 1887c:35.)

Mahina is also the name of a legendary canoe in the **Tu-amotus** (islet of Hao) that comes and retrieves the souls of humans who have just died. It is captained by the demigod Ta-horotakarari, who can also cure sickness. Legends say that Ta-horotakarari was the son of a mortal woman, Takua, but before his birth, two spirits from the ocean depths (Panihau and

Takorotakarari) seized him from his mother's womb, reared him to manhood, and constructed the remarkable canoe *Mahina* on which he travels throughout the islands seeking all the departed spirits. (Caillot 1914:61–65.)

MAHINA-I-TE-ONE, a stretch of beach in the Tuamotuan legend of Tahaki (Kaha'i*), owned by the goblins of Matuauru, where no human beings dared to go else they would surely be slain by the goblins. (Stimson 1937:68.) See also **Mupere.**

MAHINATUMAI, a peaceful god of Hikutavaki, Niue Island, associated with the rising moon. (Loeb 1926:160.)

MAHIRUA, a messenger sent by the Māori chief Ue-nuku* to obtain an oracle from the priest Pawa. He was struck dead and then brought back to life. (Tregear 1891:193; White 1887c:7.)

MAHORA-NUI-ATEA, Māori nature goddess, wife of Mākū and mother of Rangi* (sky father) and the four props of heaven (Tokomua, Toko-roto, Toko-pā, and Rangi-pōtiki). (Shortland 1882:12, 56; Tregear 1891:193; White 1887a:18.) See also **Toko.**

MAHU, a glutton, a hoarder of food in the Tuamotuan story of Tahaki (Kaha'i*). Tahaki challenged Mahu to prove his capabilities of eating food,

whereupon Mahu ate everything including the bowls. When he could not relieve himself, he died. (Stimson 1937:93–95.)

MĀHU-ARIKI, a Tuamotuan god, a personification of the god Kio.* (Stimson 1964:274.)

MAHUHU, one of the Māori canoes that legends say brought the first Polynesians to New Zealand, commanded by Rongomai, who lost his life on the way. (Tregear 1891:20, 194.) See also **Canoes, Māori Migration.**

MAHUIE, grandmother of the hero Māui* in Hawaiian legend. (Beckwith 1948:227.)

MAHUIKA, the Māori fire goddess from whom Māui* obtained the secret of making fire. (Grey 1970:34–38; Tregear 1891:194.) In the Tuamotus and the Marquesas, Mahu-ika (Mahuie) is the fire god in the underworld* as well as the grandfather of Māui. Māui wrestled the secret of making fire from him. (Handy 1930:13–18; Stimson 1934:17–23.) See also **Āo-āo-mā-ra'i-ā; Mafui'e; Mafuike; Māhuike.**

MĀHUIKE, Tuamotuan fire god. (Stimson 1964:274.) See also **Āo-āo-mā-ra'i-ā; Mafuie; Mahuika; Māui.**

MĀHU-TŪ-TĀRANGA, a Tuamotuan god who resides in the

underworld.* (Stimson 1964: 274.)

MAIHUNA, father of the Hawaiian hero Ka-welo.* (Beckwith 1948:405, 406, 410.)

MAIKOA (or MAIKOHĀ), an ancient Hawaiian, son of Konikonia, died at Kau-pō on Maui and from whose grave sprang the *wauke* (paper mulberry) plant used in making tapa cloth. He was deified, and he his daughter Lauhuki also became patron deities of tapa beaters. (Beckwith 1948:99–100, 215–215; Fornander 1917:270–271; Wickman 1985:165.)

MAIKUKU-MAKAKA, mentioned as the wife of Tāwhaki (Kaha'i*) and mother of Wahieroa (Wahieloa*) in some Māori legends. (Tregear 1891: 196; White 1887a:129.) See also **Hapai**.

MAILE, four popular, sweet-scented Hawaiian sisters (Maile-ha'i-wale, Maile-kaluhea, Maile-lau-li'i, and Maile-pā-haka) who are represented as four varieties of the myrtle vine (*Alyxia myrtillifolia*). Their fragrances are associated with goddesses, and supposedly their scent still clings to the ancient Hawaiian *heiau* (temples). They appear in numerous romances (Lā'ie-i-ka-wai*, Ha'ina-kolo,* Pā-liuli,* Laka,* for example) and have an especial affinity with the hula dance. (Beckwith 1948:507, 509, 517–518, 530–531; Fornander 1917: 614–619.)

MAIMOA'ALOGONA, Tongan goddess of the creation, daughter to the goddess Touiafutuna, twin to Atugaki, and mother to the goddess Valelahi* (mother of the sky god Tagaloa*). (Reiter 1907: 230–240.) See also **Creation; Heavens.**

MA'I-OLA, a Hawaiian god of healing, who resides in trees that provided a toxin against the poisonous *kālai-pāhoa* wood. (Pukui 1971:393.)

MAIRANGI, mother of the Māori reptile gods (*moko*), wife of Tū-te-wanawana. (Tregear 1891:196; White 1887a: App.) See also **Moko; Mo'o; Tutangatakino.**

MAIRIHAU-O-RONGO, a benevolent Tuamotuan god who resides in the underworld.* (Stimson 1964:275.)

MĀITU, a Tuamotuan night god; a familiar spirit invoked by a priest (*tāura*); a carved, stone idol or image that housed a powerful spirit or demon; a deified ancestor. (Stimson 1964: 275–276.)

MAITUPAVA, a Tuamotuan demigod. (Stimson 1964:276.)

MAI-'U'U, a Hawaiian goddess of the wilderness who strings leis for the more powerful deities. (Emerson 1915:138.) See also **Mā-'a'a.**

MAIWAHO, a Māori god who taught Tāwhaki (Kaha'i*) the required sacred chants to help him continue his heavenly journey. (Tregear 1891:197; White 1887a:51.) Prayers and offerings were made to him by the sick and leprous. (White 1887a:126.)

MAKAHOPOKIA, patron god of the game by the same name (jumping-stones-on-water) on Niue Island. (Loeb 1926:161.)

MAKAIATUAHAEHAE, one of the two original wives of Tini-rau (Kinilau*) slain by his new wife Hina* in the Māori legend. (Grey 1970:62–76; Tregear 1891: 197; White 1887b:127–146.) See also **Makaiatuauriuri.**

MAKAIATUAURIURI, one of the two original wives of Tini-rau (Kinilau*) slain by his new wife Hina* in the Māori legend. (Tregear 1891:197.) See also **Makaiatuahaehae.**

MAKA-KŪ-KOA'E, a Hawaiian god invoked by sorcerers to cause their victims to become insane and palsy. (Malo 1903: 103; Pukui 1971:393.) See also **Uli-la'a.**

MAKALI'I, (MAKALIKI, MA-TALIKI, MATARIKI, LI'I), chief navigator for the Hawaiian explorer Hawai'i-loa* in the migration from Kahiki to Ha-wai'i and progenitor of the commoners (*welo kanaka*). He became a chief of Kaua'i, famous as an agriculturalist, and a month on the Hawaiian calendar bears his name (December/January). During the *makahiki** festival, plants were symbolically dropped from his net. The Pleiades are called the cluster of Makali'i or the nets of Makali'i, and one legend claims him as the father of the demi-god Māui* and a rival to Kama-pua'a* (pig man). (Beckwith 1948:231–232.) He also appears as a lizard (*mo'o*) god in the form of a rain cloud. His wife is Ma-ū, sister to the goddess Haumea* and thus aunt to the goddesses Pele* and Hi'iaka.* (Emerson 1915:92, 94.)

In **Samoa**, (Maka) Li'i was descended from Lu,* the wanderer. Li'i was swallowed by a fish and deified as the Pleiades. His brothers and sister (Lua-aui) settled the island of Manu'a, and Lua-aui's son Tagaloa* became its first chief. (Krämer 1902:8; Stair 1895:116.)

Mataliki also refers to the Pleiades in **Tongan** mythology. In **New Zealand**, Matariki, was the son of Rangi* (sky father) and Papa* (earth mother). (Tregear 1891:226–227.)

Mataliki, the god of male affairs, was the supreme god of the island of **Pukapuka**, and men on Pukapuka referred to themselves as the birds of Mataliki (*te manu o Mataliki*).

Legends claim that Mataliki and the other gods were born from a rock fished up from the bottom of the sea by the Tongan god Tamagei. It was Mataliki that caused light to appear, and as a result, the other gods vanished. Mataliki married Te Vaopupu, the daughter of the god Vaelua, and they gave birth to two children, a son, Tumulivaka, and a daughter, Te Matakiate. As time passed, Tumulivaka became concerned that his father might cede the island to some other god, so in anger, he stamped on the island, split it in two, and lived on the eastern half of the island where he and his sister became the progenitors of the humans, while his parents lived on the western part of the island. (Beaglehole 1938:309, 375–377.)

MAKANI-KE-OE, a Hawaiian wind god, a god of love, who took the form of a plant or tree a branch of which could be used as an amulet or love charm; also, an uncle to the Maile* sisters in the romance of Lā'ie-i-ka-wai.* (Beckwith 1948:93; Green 1926:34–42.) See also **Lau-ka-'ie'ie; Lau-kiele-'ula.**

MAKAPOE-LAGI, one of the five principal gods on the island of Niue, that inhabit the eastern part of the island. (Smith 1902: 195–218.) See also **Fāo; Hunanaki; Luatupua; Lage-iki.**

MAKAPOELAGI, a sky god of Niue Island. (Loeb 1926:161.)

MAKARA, a Māori god who controls the tides. (Tregear 1891:197; White 1887c:49.)

MAKA'U-KIU, a Hawaiian shark god killed by the goddess Hi'iaka* during her trip to Kaua'i. (Emerson 1915:48–49.)

MAKEATUTARA, father of the demigod Māui* in Tuamotuan legends (Grey 1855: 6, 20), sometimes called Tarahunga (White 1887b:64) or Teraka (White 1887b:81).

MAKEMAKE, the supreme god of creation on Easter Island, he first manifested himself in the form of a skull, and the wide-eyed petroglyphs at the village of Orongo are said to be a representation of him. Makemake created humans by copulating with stones and clay; his first offspring were Tive, Rorai, Hova, and Arangi-kote-kote. Legends say that Makemake and the god Haua brought the first birds to Easter Island and introduced the rites of worship concerning them. The birds eventually made their way to the islets of Motu-nui and Motu-iti, and each year in the nesting season, the inhabitants of Easter Island perform a ritual regarding the finding of the first egg and of choosing of a Bird Man for the coming year. The Bird Man in Easter Island art represents the god Make-make. (Barrow 1967:194–199; Métraux 1940:125–127, 311–315; Routledge 1917:254–268.)

MAKIKI, monstrous Hawaiian lizards or dragons (*mo'o*) who could leap and spring like a grasshopper and who were killed by the goddess Hi'iaka.* Their leader was named Mo'o-lau. (Emerson 1915:49–55.)

MĀKINOKINO, the fishhook used by the demigod Māui* in fishing up the Pacific islands according to Tuamotuan legend. (Stimson 1964:277.)

MAKŌRU, Tuamotuan name given to mortals who allegedly can walk on water. (Stimson 1964:278.)

MĀKŪ, or Mangu, a great Māori primeval force, son of Kore* Matua (nothingness or void), husband to Mahora-nui-atea (clear expanse), and father to Rangi* (sky father). (Tregear 1891:200; White 1887a:18) See also **Creation; Heavens**.

MAKUA-'AIHUE , patron god of thieves in Hawai'i. (Malo 1903:82.)

MAKUA-KAU-MANA, Hawaiian prophet in the legend of Pa'ao,* who accompanied him on his journey to Tahiti. (Beckwith 1948:371–372.) Also a Hawaiian farmer who anciently lived on O'ahu with his son.

They were visited by the gods Kāne* and Kanaloa* who observed his piety and kindness and rewarded him with a digging stick, taught him how to pray and offer sacrifices, and to keep the tapus of the god Kāne-huli-honua (giver of land), the god Kāne-pua'a (god of rich crops), the goddess Hina-puku-'ai (goddess of vegetable food), and the goddess Hina-puku-i'a (goddess of abundant fishing).

The gods visited him once again and test his steadfastness in similar manner as Job of the Old Testament. They carried him away to paradise (Kāne-honua-moku*). From paradise, however, he looked up to earth and observed his son being swallowed by a giant shark. Makua-kau-mana could not restrain his tears, and in sympathy, the two gods let him return to the upper world of mortality where he spent the remainder of his days. (Beckwith 1948:69; Rice 1923:116–132.)

MAKUPUTU, the god of the souls of deceased mortals on Mangareva (French Polynesia). (Caillot 1914:154.)

MĀKUTU, Māori goddess of witchcraft who dwells with the wicked goddess Miru (Milu*) in the underworld.* (Tregear 1891:200.)

MALAE-H'A-KOA, a lame chief of Kaua'i with seer power who befriended the goddess Hi'iaka in her attempts to find chief Lohi'au for her sister, the volcano goddess Pele.* His wife was Wailua-nui-a-haone. (Emerson 1915:109–131.)

MALAE TOTOA, name of the tenth Samoan heaven, a place of rest. (Turner 1884:13.) See also **Heavens.**

MALAFU, an ancestral god worshipped on Futuna. (Burrows 1936:105–108.)

MĀLEI, Hawaiian goddess of fisherman, guardian of parrot fish (*uhu*). (Pukui 1971:394.)

MALEKULAULUA, a Tongan god, father of the demigod Māui* and his sister Hina* by his goddess wife Heimoana.* (Gifford 1924:19.)

MALELOA, a god of peace of Lakepa, Niue Island. (Loeb 1926:160.)

MALIETOA, a high-ranking Samoan title. For its origin, see **Atiogie.**

MALIU, sister sorceress to the Hawaiian gods Kāne,* Kanaloa,* and Kau'akāhi. Also said to be the name of a deified Hawaiian chief. (Beckwith 1948: 123, 309.)

MALULAUFA'I, an ancient chief of Manono, Samoa, whose servant Topolei caught a fish which had swallowed a pigeon egg. When Malulaufa'i ate the fish, he took the egg and allowed it to hatch. The emerging pigeon had nine heads. When a descendant of Pili* slew the bird, Topolei (also called Late) killed him. The pigeon and slayer were both turned into stone where they still stand in Aopo, 'Upolu. (Krämer 1902:63–64, 306–308; Stübel 1896:149.)

MAMAIA, a religious sect founded by a prophet named Teau on the island of Tahiti. Combining both Christian beliefs and ancient Polynesian traditions, it flourished in the 1820s and 1830s primarily because of support from Queen Pomare IV. Once she adopted orthodox Protestantism, the cult slowly died out. (Moerenhout 1837:502–505.)

MAMARI, name of one of the Māori canoes that brought the first Polynesians to New Zealand, commanded by Nukutāwhiti. (Tregear 1891:202.) See also **Canoes, Māori Migration.**

MAMI, a shark god of the Lau Islands who can take human form. (Hocart 1929:211–212.) See also **Sharks.**

MANA, sacred power or authority, an embodiment of all energies within the universe which may manifest itself in certain humans either by inheritance or by extraordinary knowledge and power gained through experience or magic. It provides legitimacy to political rulers and respect and divinity to great heros. It is a positive power manifested by great leaders and much admired by Polynesians. (Goldman 1970: 10–13.)

MANAHOE, an evil spirit in the Tuamotus. (Smith 1903:231.)

MANAIA, an ancient Māori chief of Hawaiki* who cursed his wife's brother, Ngātoro, who had already emigrated to New Zealand. Manaia's wife, Kuiwai, sent her daughter, Haunga-roa, and four other female companions to New Zealand to warn Ngātoro of the curse. Finally arriving in New Zealand, Haunga-roa warned her uncle, and in return Ngātoro cursed Manaia and performed the proper religious rites to ward off Manaia's curse. Afterwards he gathered a formidable force of 140 strong warriors who sailed to Hawaiki to avenge Kuiwai's humiliation.

Meanwhile, Manaia's priests had optimistically prepared large ovens in which they believed their gods would bring to them the bodies of Ngātoro's warriors. Ngātoro heard of the situation and schemed a plan of attack. They cut and bloodied themselves and feigned being dead in the pits when Manaia's priests came to the sacred grounds. On the arranged signal, Ngātoro's warriors rose up, killed the priests, and met Manaia's forces in battle. All were slain except Manaia who escaped.

Ngātoro and his crew returned to their home in New Zealand. Shortly thereafter, Manaia gathered another army, set sail for New Zealand, and anchored off the coast of Tauranga (Bay of Plenty). During the evening, Ngātoro and his wife performed enchantments and incantations. About midnight, Tāwhiri-matea, the god of wind and storms, answered their prayers by sending a tumultuous storm that sank the ships and cast Manaia and his crew dead upon the shore. Manaia's curse was thus avenged. (Grey 1970:128–142; Tregear 1891:203–204.)

MANAKO, the tenth age of the existence of the universe according to Māori traditions. (Tregear 1891:204; White 1887a: App.) See also **Creation; Heavens; Kore.**

MANA-MANA-I'A-KALU-EA, a Hawaiian maiden brought back to life by the goddess Hi'iaka.* (Emerson 1915:70–81.)

MANATAFETAU, a war god of Niue Island. (Loeb 1926:161.)

MANATU, a Tuamotuan god. (Stimson 1964:281.) Also a Marquesan god mentioned in the story of Ta'a-pō* and her journey to the underworld.* (Handy 1930:85.)

MĀNAWA-TĀNE, name of the large house occupied by the Ponaturi* goblins in the Māori legend of Tāwhaki (Kaha'i*). (Grey 1970:47–48; Tregear 1891: 206.)

MĀNAWATINA, wife of the Māori demigod Paikea.* (Tregear 1891:206.)

MANGĀ-IA-KI-TE-RANGI, the name of Māui's* fishhook in the Tuamotuan legend. (Stimson 1964:269.)

MANGAMANGA-I-ATUA, the mother of Harataunga* and Horotata,* who were wives of the great Māori hero Tinirau (Kinilau*). (Tregear 1891:210; Grey 1970:63.)

MANGARARA, one of the Māori canoes that brought the first Polynesians to New Zealand, commanded by chiefs Wheketoro, Te-wai-o-Pōtango, and others. It carried aboard various animals needed in their new islands—insects, lizards, birds, dogs, etc. (Tregear 1891: 21, 219; White 1887b:189.) See also **Canoes, Māori Migration**.

MANGO, the original male ancestor according to Futuna legends. His sons were Matangitonga, Fakavelikele (the most powerful), Songia, Fitu, Mala-fu, and Kula. His daughter, Finelasi, is believed to be a demon. (Burrows 1936:106.)

MANGU, see Maku.

MANILOA, a cannibal god who lived at Solosolo, 'Upolu, Samoa, and who was slain by a young Samoan called Polu-leu-ligana. (Turner 1884:238; Krämer 1902:275–276.)

MANINI-HOLO-KUĀUA, noted as the head fisherman of the Menehune* (the little people of Hawai'i) and as a notorious thief on the island of Moloka'i. He lived with his lizard grandmother in a cave which opened and shut on command. Once he stole the canoe of Ke-li'i-mālolo, a swift runner from O'ahu, and set out for the cave. Ke-li'i-mālolo set out in pursuit and with the aid of two supernatural sons of Halulu, Kama-aka-mikioi and Kama-aka-'ulu-'ōhi'a, ordered the cave shut and crushed Manini-holo-kuāua to death. They then entered and divided the spoils of the cave between themselves. (Beckwith 1948:339; Fornander 1917:164–167.) See also **Kao-hele**.

MANO-KA-LANI-PŌ, Hawaiian chief on Kaua'i, husband to Naekapulani, ancestor of the hero Ka-welo,* and deified as a shark god upon his death. (Beckwith 1948:141, 366;

Fornander 1880:93; Westervelt 1915b:173.)

MANŌ-NIHO-KAHI, a Hawaiian shark-man, who once lived at Māla'e-kahana between Lā'ie and Kahu-kū on O'ahu. He warned swimmers about other sharks, but then came and killed them himself. He was discovered and slain by the chief and his men of the district. (Beckwith 1948:142; Rice 1923:111.) See also **Kama-i-ka-'āhui; Ka-welo; Nanaue; Nenewe; Pau-walu; Sharks.**

MANU, Māori bird gods. (Tregear 1891:208; White 1887c: 130.) See also **Birds**.

MANUFILI, a heavenly carpenter who assisted the Samoan god Tagaloa (Kanaloa*) and his son Lu* in constructing the first outrigger canoe. It was brought down to earth at Laueleele before water was formed. (Turner 1884:11–12.)

MANU-I-TE-A'A, a legendary Tahitian bird that can uproot the strongest of trees. It is said that it overturned the hill Ma-'ātea in Vaira'o, Tai'arapu, south Tahiti, which has remained inverted to this day. (Henry 1928:384.)

MANU-I-TE-RA, a Māori god who dwells on Mount Hiku-rangi, New Zealand. (Taylor 1870:283; Tregear 1891:209.)

MANUKU, a Tuamotuan word meaning an ancestral or legendary land. (Stimson 1964: 283.)

MANU-KURA, a famous Tuamotuan warrior in the Rata (Laka*) cycle, whose home was in the ocean and who married Te Pupura-o-te-tai, the daughter of the king of Puna. On his way home, Rata met Manu-kura, and they had a contest of magical girdles. Rata won the hand of the princess and took her to his homeland where she stayed while he continued his voyages to avenge his father. (Stimson 1937:126–128.)

MANUMEA, name of an obscure Tuamotuan god. (Stimson 1964:283.)

MAO, an ancient Samoan chief of the island of Manu'a who cured a demon of his mischievous ways. He rubbed his body with rancid coconut oil and pretended to be another demon. He found the demon's house, burned it down, and then returned to his home. (Krämer 1902:447.) Also a Samoan god of Atua, son of (Le) Folasa. (Fraser 1897:34; Krämer 1902:382.)

MAO-MA-ULI, a Samoan war god worshipped in the form of two teeth from a sperm whale which were said to have come from Fiji. (Turner 1884:35.)

MA'O-PUROTU, the pet shark of the Tahitian god Tāne* (Kāne*). (Henry 1928:389.)

MĀPU, a Hawaiian war god in the legend of Hi'iaka* and Pele.* (Emerson 1915:43.)

MĀPUNAIERE, the sacred axe of the Māori hero Rata (Laka*). (Tregear 1891:212; White 1887a: 73.)

MARAE, ancient religious edifices (outdoor temples) common throughout eastern Polynesia. (In Hawai'i, they are called *heiau*.*) In Tahiti, the *marae* are rectangular stone platforms; at one end stands a rectangular stone wall enclosure. The importance of these *marae* cannot be over emphasized. Their study fills pages of the early Christian writers to the islands. The most sacred and important (but not the oldest) of all the *marae* was Taputapuātea on the island of Ra'iātea, dedicated to the god 'Oro. Sources tell us that up until about A. D. 1350, remote Polynesian islanders as far away as New Zealand customarily sent offerings to this *marae* in great double canoes. Taputapuātea literally means sacrifices from abroad.

Other *marae* for an island or a district were not nearly as large or elaborate as that for the whole island group. Families might have their own small ancestral *marae* (called *marae tupuna*) close by their huts. Wooden images of the gods were carefully guarded by the priests who supervised *marae* activities. These images were generally made of crudely-carved ironwood (*'aito*), wrapped in tapa cloth, and decorated with feathers of sennit. Long and complex prayers were given by the priests who frequently had visual aids (various length of sticks, colored leaves, etc.) to aid them. The priests usually sat crossed legged in the *marae* against large stones set up four to five feet high for that purpose. The priests addressed their gods either by looking upon the wrapped images or towards the sky in a loud, shrilling chant, understood by very few of the gathered multitude.

Sacrifices* were frequent, especially at birth, marriage, death, or victory in battle. Offerings to the gods usually consisted of food such as fish, bananas, coconuts, etc. After the gods had extracted the spiritual substance from them during the ceremonies, the foods were generally eaten by the people. Human sacrifices were offered only on important occasions. They consisted usually of the undesirable people—old men, or prisoners of war, and very seldom women. The bodies of brave warriors or high chiefs who had died would also be exhibited in great honor from the branches of the ironwood trees surrounding the *marae*. These bodies were later secretly buried by their relatives. The noxious smell around the *marae* was frequently reported as being overwhelming. (Emory 1934.)

The *marae* in New Zealand and the *malae* in Samoa designate merely a gathering place in each village and did not necessarily have a religious connotation. (The dwellings for the gods in Samoa were called the *fale-aitu* or the *malumalu-o-le-aitu*, spirit houses.) The *marae-a-hine*, located at Mohoaonui on the Upper Waikato River in New Zealand, was a sacred place, a place of refuge where individuals could flee for protection by the patron deities. Similar cites existed in Hawai'i called *puhonua*. The most famous today is the restored complex on the Big Island at Hōnaunau on the west coast. Samoans also had their designated villages called *Tapua'iga* that gave shelter to defeated warriors.

MARAKI-HAU, a male Tuamotuan mermaid. (Stimson 1964:286.)

MARAMA, son of the Tahitian god Hiro (Hilo*) and his wife Vai-tū-mārie. After Hiro killed his wife, it was Marama who buried her in her sacred *marae** (temple) and who mourned her death. His sister Pī-hō brought about the reconciliation of father and son. (Henry 1928:543–545.) The Tuamotuan story is similar. (Stimson 1957.)

In **New Zealand**, Marama is the moon goddess, daughter of Tongotongo* and Haronga* and sister to Rā, the sun god. Toward the middle of the lunar month, Marama becomes ill and wanes with the disease until she bathes in the living waters of Tāne (Kāne*) and is healed. (Tregear 1891:213; White 1887a:141.) (*Malama* in Hawai'i means light or month.)

MARAMA-KIKO-HURA, one of the wives of the ancient Māori chief Hotu-roa* (commander of the famous *Tainui** canoe in the migration to New Zealand) whose enchantments (or adultery) at one point slowed down the canoe in crossing the Tamakai isthmus. (Grey 1970:116; White 1887d:32.)

MARAMA-TOA-IHENUA-KURA, a pseudonym used by the Tuamotuan figure Hiro (Hilo*) to disguise his identity when he reached upper Hawaiki.* (Stimson 1957.)

MARAU-KURA, the Tuamotuan god of the night world (Stimson 1964:287.)

MAREIKURA, Tuamotuan goddess of the night world and a follower of Kiho.* Her chief duties consist of, among others, plaiting mats, weaving baskets and clothing, and midwifery. (Stimson 1964:287.)

MARERE, an ancient navigator and warrior venerated on in the island of Fakahina in the Tuamotus. His matrimonial conflicts caused him to sail to neighboring islands to establish several separate family connections. (Audran 1919:234–235.)

MĀRERE-O-TONGA, a Māori god, son of Rangi-pōtiki* (one of the props of heaven) and Papa-tū-a-nuku* (earth mother), twin to Takataka-pūtea, and brother to the gods Tū (Kū*), Rongo (Lono*), and Tangaroa (Kanaloa*). (Shortland 1882:18; Tregear 1891:216.)

MĀRIKORIKO, wife of Tiki,* the first man, according to one Māori tradition, formed by the god Ārohirohi (mirage) from the warmth of the sun and Paoro (echo). (Tregear 1891:216; White 1887a:151.)

MARITĪPĀ, a Tuamotuan demon having the body of a fish. (Stimson 1964:288.)

MĀRONGORONGO, a Māori lizard god. (Tregear 1891:218; White 1887a: App.) See also **Lizards; Mo'o.**

MARRIAGE. Throughout ancient Polynesia, marriage ceremonies varied from common-law occurrences to very elaborate social and religious rites. Polynesian societies' approval of sexual liaisons for the unmarried created no biological urge to drive one to early marriage, but most Polynesians married or carried on some sort of heterosexual union throughout their lives.

Most commoners simply began living together, and with the birth of their first child, they were assumed to be married. In some island groups (Samoa, for example), the families of the couple hosted a huge feast where gifts were exchanged on the village green. Marriage by capture was sometimes practiced between enemy tribes. In Tahiti, elaborate public ceremonies were held, and then religious prayers were said over the couple by a priest in the *marae** (temple). The most complex rites were observed in the Marquesas Islands where formal alliances were made between families and tribes, and children were often betrothed even before they were born.

Elaborate ceremonies were common in the chiefly class throughout Polynesia. One in Tahiti was witnessed by the Reverend William Ellis sometime between 1817–1823. On the day of the ceremony, the Arioi Society* performed dramatic dances and pantomime before the assembled crowd of well-wishers. The next morning, the bride's family assembled their ancestral skulls and bones, placed them upon their home altar, and then covered them with white tapa cloth. Gifts of white tapa cloth were also given to the bride by her parents and relatives who attended.

From here, the party moved to the *marae* for the religious ceremonies dedicated to the god 'Oro* or to Tāne (Kāne*). After dressing in sacred clothing, the bride and groom entered the *marae* and took their positions approximately six yards apart. The priest asked each, "Will you not cast away your spouse?" After negative answers from each, he addressed them, "Happy will it be, if thus with ye two." Prayers to the gods were offered in behalf of the happiness of the new couple. Relatives then brought out a large piece of white tapa and spread it out on the pavement of the *marae*.

The couple took their position upon the cloth and clasped hands. The ancestral skulls and bones were often brought in at this point by the family. The bride's relatives then took a piece of sugar cane wrapped in a sacred branch of the *miro* tree (*Thespesia populinea*), touched the head of the groom, and then laid it down between them. The groom's relatives then performed the same ceremony towards the bride. This act symbolized equality between the two families, and thereafter, they were always regarded as one family.

Another large cloth was brought out and thrown over the bride and groom. It is not recorded whether or not they had a sexual union at this time, but it is possible that they did. Afterwards, the parties returned to their home where sumptuous feasting awaited them. The duration of such festivities was according to the rank or means of the families. (Ellis 1825b:568–571; Handy 1927:231).

MARU, a Māori war god, particularly well known in the South Island of New Zealand where he usurped the position of the more common war god Tū (Kū*); also the son of Rangihore (god of rocks and stones) and the grandson of the famous demigod Māui*; his image was brought to New Zealand by Haunga-roa.* (Grey 1970:129–130, 167; Tregear 1891:219; White 1887a: App., 106.) Also a war god on the Chatham Islands, a healer of wounds. His earthly representation is made of plaited ropes. (Shand 1894:89.)

MARUAKE, an ancient navigator and warrior venerated on in the island of Fakahina (Tuamotus). (Audran 1919:236.)

MĀRUKI-AO, a Tuamotuan god of the underworld,* responsible for keeping the light of the sun from penetrating into the world of night. (Stimson 1964:290.)

MARU-TE-WHARE-AITU, the first victim killed by the Māori demigod Māui* in his many exploits. Māui kidnapped the daughter of Maru-te-whare-aitu and killed his crops by having it snow on them. (The Māoris of New Zealand and the Hawaiians are the only Polynesians to experience snow.) Maru retaliated by sending destructive caterpillars to eat Māui's crops, whereupon Māui killed Maru. Both Tuna* and Koiro* (eel gods) were descendants of Maru. (Grey 1970:23; Shortland 1882:57; Tregear 1891:220; White 1887b: 72.)

MASAKI'UNGU, a family god who guards the important graves on Bellona Island by giving trespassers headaches. (Monberg 1966:82.)

MATAEREPŌ, grandmother of the Māori heroes Tāwhaki (Kaha'i*) and Karihi, also known as Whaitiri,* called darken eyes because of her blindness. When Tāwhaki and Karihi visited her, they stole her ten sweet potatoes, one by one. In the subsequent struggle, Tāwhaki touched her eyes, thereby, restored her sight. Reconciled with her two grandsons, she advised them in their journey to the heavens to find Tāwhaki's wife and daughter. (Grey 1970: 53–55; White 1887a:57.)

MATĀHO, a Tuamotuan god worshipped at the *marae**

(temples) at Faite and Ana'a. (Stimson 1964:292.)

MATAHŌRA, one of the celebrated canoes of the Māori migration to New Zealand, commanded by the hero Kupe.* Also called *Ma Tāwhaorua*. (Grey 1970:108, 161–163; Tregear 1891:223; White 1887b:179–180.) See also **Canoes, Māori Migration**.

MATAHŌR U A, one of the Māori canoes that brought the first Polynesians to New Zealand, commanded by chief Reti, a twin to the *Aotea* canoe. It was the first to come to New Zealand. (Tregear 1891:223; White 1887b:179–180.) See also **Canoes, Māori Migration**.

MATA'I-FE'ETIETIE, cooling wind, a Tahitian wind god. (Henry 1928:394.)

MATA'I-I-TE-'URA-RE'A, grandfather of the Tahitian god Tāne (Kāne*). (Henry 1928:349–350.)

MĀTA'ITA'I, one of the chief artisans for the Tahitian god Ta'ere,* patron god of knowledge and canoe building, and dwells in the center of the earth. (Henry 1928:374, 406.)

MATAITIU, a young Rotuman, and his sister Mataikura were children of sky parents. They fled from their home because they had disobeyed their angry parents. In route, they encountered a two-headed giant (*mam'asa*) who tried to capture and eat them. Mataitiu tricked the giant into believing that he could walk on water. When Mataitiu tied rocks around the giant's legs, the giant quickly sank and drowned. Mataitiu and Mataikura returned to shore and gained possession of the giant's property. (Churchward 1938:217–224.)

MATAĪTŪ, the name of the stick used by the great Māori chief Tura* in creating the first fire by friction. (Tregear 1891: 223; White 1887b: 13.)

MATA-MATA-AHO, the demon in the Tuamotuan story of Hiro (Hilo*) who captured princess Tiaki-tau, Hiro's fiancée, and carried her to the bottom of the ocean. (Stimson 1957:137–190.)

MATAMATA-'ARAHU, the Tahitian god who first introduced the art of tattooing. He is also an artisan for Ta'ere* (the god of knowledge and skill). Tahitians invoke Matamata-'arahu's aid when tattooing others. (Henry 1928:287, 374, 406.) See also **Mataora.**

MATA-MATA-VARA-VARA-AHU-RAAI, benevolent Easter Island demon. (Métraux 1940: 317.)

MATAOA, a Marquesan god of the creation, son of Papa-Uka and Papa-Ao. (Christian 1895: 188–189.)

MATAORA, the first Māori to be tattooed. According to legend, Mataora descended to the underworld* to seek the spirit of his deceased wife Niwareke. There, he met his father-in-law, Uetonga, who tattooed him by puncturing. Recovering from the ordeal, Mataora and his wife left the underworld, but because they failed to leave one of his wife's garments with Kūwatawata, the guardian of the door of death, no mortal has ever been allowed to return from the land of the dead. (Grey 1855:38; Tregear 1891:225; White 1887b: 4.) See also **Mata-mata-'arahu.**

MATAORUA, the name of the legendary canoe of the Māori chief Kupe* who first discovered New Zealand. (Grey 1970:161–171; Tregear 1891: 225.) See also **Canoes, Māori Migration**.

MATARAU, another name for Tonga-iti, a black and white spotted lizard god, worshiped in the Cook Islands, the third son of Vatea (Wākea*) with eight heads, eight tails, and two hundred eyes. (Gill 1876:291.)

MATARI'I, name of the Pleiades in Tahitian legend. Once, Matari'i and Pīpīrima were two children whose parents neglected them. In revenge, the children fled to the heavens and became the constellation. (Caillot 1914:115–116; Henry 1928:362.) A different story of Matariki is told in Mangaia. Originally the stars were all one large, brilliant star, but the god Tāne became jealous and splintered it into six fragments named Matariki. (Gill 1876:43–44.)

MATARUA, a Māori sea monster. (Tregear 1891:227.)

MATATA, first human to be created by Te-Tumu (foundation) and Te-Papa (stratum rock) according to the Tuamotuan creation chant. Being ill formed, however, he died. A second man, Aitu, also died. Finally the third man, Hoa-tea (or Haotu) was perfectly formed. He married his sister Hoatu, and from them sprang the human race. (Henry 1928:347.) See also **Creation**.

MATA-TAHI, a Tahitian god with one eye who sees very straight. (Henry 1928:375.)

MATA-TANUMI, a god worshipped by the great voyager Iro (Hilo*) from the island of Aitutaki, Cook Islands. (Large 1903:133–144.)

MATAOA, a Marquesan god, principally worshipped at Nukuhiva. (Christian 1895:187–202.)

MATA-TINA, the patron god of Tahitian fishermen. (Henry 1928:378.)

MATATŪA, name of one of the Māori canoes that brought the first Polynesians to New Zealand, commanded by chief Ruaauru who brought the taro plants with him. (Tregear 1891:21, 227; White 1887b:181.) See also **Canoes, Māori Migration**.

MATAU, Tahitian god of strength and vigor.

MATA'U, a god who, with his grandson 'Isoso, guards the forests on Bellona Island. (Monberg 1966:82.)

MATĀUHETI, one of the dwelling regions of man in the Tuamotuan concept of the universe. (Stimson 1964:294; see diagram of universe in Henry 1928:348.) See also **Creation; Heavens; Rangi-Pō**.

MATA'ULUFOTU, a Samoan youth, whose decapitated head spoke to his parents in their quest to bring back to life the daughter of the king of Fiji. The couple Fine and Sau first gave birth to a sea-eel who ate their second and third sons. When Mata'ulufotu, their fourth, was born to them, they fled inland for safety, but Sau nevertheless killed and ate her son. When he father returned home, the decapitated head of Mata'ulufotu told him to put his head in a basket on the back of his wife. In their travels, they met a traveling party from Fiji which had come to seek a doctor to aid Sina, the ailing daughter of the king. Mata'ulufotu's head instructed his parents to convince the party to take them to Fiji.

Once there, Mata'ulufotu's spirit traveled to the ninth heaven to the woman Fulu'ulaalematato, who devoured men, to ask for the girl's spirit. Fulu'ulaalematato was not there, but her son showed Mata'ulufotu the basket that contained the spirit of the king's daughter. Mata'ulufotu seized the basket and returned to earth. In recognition of his great deed, the king of Fiji rewarded Mata'ulufotu with a leaping (flying) fish that returned to Samoa with them. (Krämer 1902:121–124; Stübel 1896:147.)

MATA-VARA-VARA, an Easter Island god, whose name means rain with heavy drops. (Métraux 1940:316.)

MATAWHAORUA, one of the celebrated canoes of the Māori migration to New Zealand, commanded by the hero Kupe.* Also called *Matahorua*. (Grey 1970:108, 161–163; Tregear 1891:228; White 1887b:179–180.) See also **Canoes, Māori Migration**.

MATI, the father of One-kura,* mother of Tiki* in Tuamotuan legends who lives in Havaiki-te-araro. One-rua visited her homeland and returned with a wife for Tiki. (Stimson 1937:3–6.) See also **Hina**.

MATILA FOAFOA, a god of Niue Island invoked when making or throwing the spear. (Loeb 1926:164.)

MATIPOU, a Māori lizard god (*mo'o*). (Tregear 1891:230; White 1887a: App.)

MATIROHE, a demon in the Taumotuan underworld* who possesses the body of an eel. (Stimson 1964:295.)

MATITI, son of the Māori god Rongo-ma-tāne* and guardian of the door where sweet potatoes (*kumara*) were kept. (Tregear 1891:230; White 1887a: App.)

MATOETOEĀ, a mortal hero who was the first mortal to suffer a violent death. When Tukaitaua,* a malevolent god of the underworld,* heard of Matoetoeā's famous exploits, he became jealous, came to Mangaia, and felled the mighty warrior. The act was revenged, however, when Tutavake killed the invisible Tukaitaua. (Gill 1876:282–283.) See also **Ve'e-tina**.

MĀ-TOHI-FĀNAU-'EVA, son of the Tahitian god Ātea (Wākea*) and Papa-tu'oi, artisan for the sky god Ra'i-tupua-nui, known also as Mā-tohi. (Henry 1928:356, 414.)

MATOKA-RAU-TĀWHIRI, wife of Wahieroa (Wahieloa*) and mother of the Māori hero Rata (Laka*). Wahieroa, son of Tāwhaki (Kaha'i*), met his death in searching for the *koko* birds his wife longed for. (Tregear 1891:230; Wohlers 1874:45.) See also **Matuku**.

MATUA, Tahitian god of strength and vigor.

MĀTUA-PAPA, Tuamotuan name for the rock foundation of the underworld.* (Stimson 1964:296.)

MATUAURU, Goblins of. See **Mupere**.

MATUKU, a Māori fire god, an evil being, son of the god Tarangata. He wanted to become the ruler of the world, and a great battle ensued between him and a great wave of water. Matuku fled to the rocks and trees where two humans, Toitipu and Manatu, discovered him in the trees, and, in gratitude, he taught them how to make fire. (Hare Hongi 1894:155–158.) Also Matuku was an ancient Māori chief who treacherously killed Wahieroa (Wahieloa*), son of Tāwhaki (Kaha'i*) and father to Rata (Laka*). Rata avenged his father's murder by entrapping and slaying Matuku at his favorite washing place. Matuku's bones were then made into spear points for spearing birds. (Grey 1970:84–86; Tregear 1891: 232.)

MĀTUKU-TAGOTAGO, a shark belonging to king Puna of the underworld* in the Tuamotuan story of Rata (Laka*). Mātuku swallowed Rata's father, whereupon Rata killed the shark. (Stimson 1937:115–117; Stimson 1964:296.)

MATUTU-TAOTAO, a demon bird that carried off the family of Rata* (Laka*) in the Tahitian and Tuamotuan epics and was eventually slain by the great hero. (Henry 1928:494–509.)

MATU'U, a Samoan war god worshipped at Manono islet off the northwestern coast of 'Upolu. (Stair 1896:56; Turner 1884:35.)

MĀUI, sometimes called Māui-of-a-thousand-tricks, is the most widely known mythological character in all of Polynesia. He fished up the islands of the Pacific, stole fire for humans, slowed down the sun, and unsuccessfully sought immortality for mortals. The most complete narrative of Māui's life is found in New Zealand. Here he was miraculously born to Taranga, wife of Makeatutara. Being delivered prematurely, he was thrown into the sea by his mother, but his divine ancestor Tama-nui-te-rangi nourished him until adolescence. He then returned to his mother, to his jealous brothers (all named with the prefix Māui), and to his sister Hina.* One day he followed his mother to her underground abode where he first met his father and received his divine blessing. The blessing, however, was faulted, and, as a result, immortality was thus denied to the young Māui. (Analogy to the story of the Greek hero Achilles.)

After obtaining a magical jawbone from his ancestress Muri-ranga-whenua, Māui's first great exploit was to snare the sun to slow it down and to lengthen the daylight hours so that humans could complete their work. He and his brother set out on their journey. Arriving at the appropriate spot, they built a noose from plaited ropes and laid their trap. When the sun rose, Māui pulled the snare, captured the sun, and beat him with his enchanted jawbone until the sun agreed to travel slower across the sky so people could carry out their daily chores.

Being chided by his family for not going fishing with his brothers each day, Māui decided to flaunt his extraordinary powers. He formed a great fishhook from the jawbone of Muri-ranga-whenua and then stowed away in his brothers' canoe. When they were far out to sea, he emerged from his hiding place. Although his brothers complained, Māui persuaded them to sail further out. Then Māui lowered his enchanted fishhook to the bottom of the ocean and snared a great piece of land in the form of a fish. Anchoring it to shore, M āui sought a priest to perform befitting prayers and ceremonies for the occasion. While gone, his hungry brothers cut up the fish, and, as a result, the land was broken up into smaller islands that were slashed with mountains and valleys. The island chain of New Zealand was thus formed.

Until the time of Māui, fire had to be kept burning continuously in the villages because no one knew the secret of making it anew. Māui determined to find a sure way of making fire from his ancestress, the powerful fire goddess Mahu-ika.* He visited her, and his tricks aroused her wrath. She used her last sparks to set the earth on fire, but M āui invoked the rain gods who came to his rescue. The last sparks jumped into a few trees; and since then, people rubbed the sticks together whenever they want fire.

M āui's jealousy of his brother-in-law's successfully fishing accomplishments caused M āui to turn him into a dog, the first of its kind. When Māui's sister Hina saw what had happened to her husband (Irawaru), she became distraught and threw herself into the sea, but was rescued by her brothers.

Māui's last feat was to try to obtain immortality for humans. Although discouraged by his parents, he was determined to accomplish this formidable task. He set out with his feathered friends, the birds, to seek the night goddess Hina-nui-te-pō (Great-lady-of-the-night). To gain immortality, Māui had to enter her between her thighs and exit out of her mouth before she awoke. Māui warned the birds to remain absolutely quiet while his task was being performed. Unfortunately, just as he thought that he was successful, the little Tiwakawaka bird, unable to hide its laughter any longer, broke out in song. The powerful goddess awoke, saw what was happening, and crushed the hero to death. (Best 1929:1–26.)

In **Tonga**, Māui-atalanga (son of Vele and her husband, Tonga-fusifonua) appeared during the creation as he fished up the Tongan Islands which later become his home. Many Tongan topographical sites are said to be the results of his deeds. Each day at dawn, it is Māui-atalanga who goes to his underground garden, and once his son Māui-kijikiji followed him. Here, he played many tricks on his father, one of which was stealing fire from the fire god and then making the sparks dwell in a certain kind of wood. Afterwards, he and his father decided to rid the world of dangerous creatures, and they went monster slaying. They killed a cannibalistic rat, a great *moa* bird, a carnivorous tree, and an enormous dog. In this last exploit, Māui-atalanga was slain, and Māui-kijikiji wasted away for love of his father. Meanwhile, Māui-atalanga's wife Sina (Hina*) set out to find her family. As she stepped over the bones of her husband, she became pregnant, and her resultant son, Tui Mahuliki (Motuliki), became the ancestor of the ruling family of Tonga, the Tui Talau. (Collocott 1921:45–58; Reiter 1907: 445–448; Caillot 1914:260–305.)

In **Samoa**, Māui is known as Ti'iti'i, son of Talaga and Vea. It was through a wrestling match with the earthquake goddess Mafui'e* (Mahuika*) that he gained a knowledge of making fire. He also stole food plants from the gods who were unwilling to share them with humans.

In **Tahiti**, Māui (with-the-eight-heads) was born prematurely to Uahea and her husband Hita-Rā (the sun god). It was Māui who drew up the sky in the creation, who helped build the first *marae** (temple), and who was the first priest to the great god Ta'aroa (Kanaloa*). Because there was not enough day left to properly cook food and to complete the building of the *marae* at Fa'ana, Māui snared the sun with a rope made from Hina's hair. He beat the sun until he swore to slow his course. Māui also prophesied that one day people would arrive on their shores in canoes without the aid of outriggers. (Henry 1928:408–433).

The **Tuamotuan** legends of Māui are erotic, symbolic, and lengthy. The story begins with the seduction of Huahega by Ataraga, who become Māui's parents. After having lived together for a while, Huahega decided to return to the underworld with her younger son Māui. Afterwards, Ataraga married Hina-hava who reared Māui's four other brothers. One day Huahega tole Māui of his birth and of his father. Immediately, Māui desired to visit him. Māui arrived at his father's home and was recognized by him, and a great feast was planned in Māui's honor. Returning again to his mother's family, Māui tricked his grandfather Māhuike into giving him his magical powers and the secret of making fire. Then, using four strands from his mother's hair, he snared the sun and held it fast.

Once, Māui and his brothers went fishing. As he pulled up the great lands from beneath the sea, his brothers interfered and the line snapped. He again fished. This time, he pulled up the legendary land of Havaiki,*

the ancestral homeland of all Polynesians.

The origin of the coconut is also found in the Tuamotuan legend of Māui. In the land of Tāne-nui, Māui took Hina as a mistress, although she was already the mistress of Tuna, the eel god. Jealousy results, and Tuna and Māui battle. Māui won and cut Tuna into pieces. He gave Tuna's phallus to Hina, and the head he gave to his mother Huahega. Huahega planted it, and it grew into a towering coconut tree, the first seen by humans. Māui sang a song of triumph and how the coconut was acquired as food for earth.

When Māui sought immortality, he attempted to exchange stomachs with the sea slug Rori-tau. His brothers' reproach for such a revolting act prevented him from succeeding. As a result, humans never gained triumph over death. Meanwhile, Hina took another lover by the name of Ri. When Māui found out about it, he turned him into a dog.

One of Māui's brothers sought to find out how Māui was able to tie down the sun. When he finally reached the place at dawn, the sun rose and one of its rays pierced his body, and his blood flowed out. Since then the evening and morning skies are tinged with his blood. None of the Tuamotuan legends tells of Māui's death. (Stimson 1937:11–60).

In **Hawai'i**, similar stories are told. Akalana (Taranga) was his father. His great fish-hook was called Manaikalani and was baited with a wing from Hina's pet bird, the *alae*. The hook brought up the Hawaiian islands, although his attempt to unite them into one larger island failed because of the interferences again of his brothers. He snared the sun at Hale-a-ka-lā on the island of Maui so that his mother Hina could have more daylight hours to dry her tapa. (Beckwith 1948: 226-227; Westervelt 1910.)

Many variations of these stories of Māui exist between island groups as well as between islands within those groups. The best single work on the legends of Māui is Katharine Luomala's *Maui-of-a-Thousand-Tricks*. See also **Fire, Origin of; Coconut, Origin of.**

MĀUI-OLA or **MAULI-OLA**, a Hawaiian god of health, the breath of life. (Emerson 1915: 94–95, 119, 135; Malo 1903:109; Pukui 1971:394.)

MAUMAU, one of the principal gods on Nanumea, Tuvalu. (Turner 1884:291.)

MAUNGATAPU, see **Hiku-rangi.**

MAUNU-TE-A'A, a Tahitian god who destroys plants. (Henry 1928:377.)

MAURI, the spiritual essence, consciousness, spirit or soul of gods as well as humans as recorded in Tuamotuan mythology. (Stimson 1964:299.)

MAU'U, a great Tahitian god whose presence is announced by a loud sound resembling a cannon shot. (Henry 1928:376.)

MA'U'U, tooth grinder, an important Tahitian god who presides over the royal *marae* * (temple). (Henry 1928:128.)

MBATINGASAU, the god of Ndreketi, Nsangalau, Lau Islands (Polynesian outliers in Fiji), embodied in the form of a hawk. (Hocart 1929:198.)

MBATININGGAKA, crab's claw, is an ancestor god of Narothake, Lau Islands (Polynesian outliers in Fiji), given to planting, and who is embodied in the form of a crab or a hawk. (Hocart 1929:197.)

MBEREWALAKI, ancestor god of Kambara, Lau Islands (Polynesian outliers in Fiji) responsible for the introduction of mosquitoes on the island of Oneata. (Hocart 1929:199.) See also **Wakulikuli.**

MBULAKAMBIRI, the god of Vandravua, Vakano, Lau Islands (Polynesian outliers in Fiji), embodied in the form of a rat with white stripes, and all of the children on Vakano are called rats. (Hocart 1929:197.)

MBUROTU, a mythical land of spirit women that lies below the ocean and that rises and disappears again as reported in legends from the Lau Islands (Polynesian outliers in Fiji). (Hocart 1929:195.)

ME-HA'I-KANA, the Hawaiian goddess of breadfruit, also identified as the goddess Papa.* (Emerson 1915:79.)

MEHARA, a chiefess of Ra-'iātea (French Polynesian), who was courted by Pōfatu from the island of Mo'orea, although she fell in love with Fago, a young chief from her own island. Pōfatu had Fago cut into pieces and thrown into the sea. Through her gods and magic, Fago's sister restored him to life, whereupon he married the beautiful Mehara and ruled with her. (Beckwith 1948:154; Stimson Ms.) See also **Pamano**.

MEHAU, daughter of the famous Tuamotuan hero Tahaki (Kaha'i*) and his mistress Horahora. To avenge the disgrace of his father, Tahaki went to the land of Horahora where he seduced her, and she became the mother of Mehau. (Stimson 1934:62.)

MELE, the benevolent goddess of weaving of Niue Island. (Loeb 1926:164.)

MENEHUNE, see **Elves and Fairies**.

MERE-HAU, one of the two witches who turned into wild ducks, abducted Vahi-vero, the father of Rata (Laka*) in the Tuamotuan story, and carried him off to their home in Hivaro-tahi. (Stimson 1937:96–147.)

MEREURU, a Tuamotuan god. (Stimson 1964:301.)

METIKITIKI, Tikopian name for the Polynesian demigod Māui.*

METO, the lowest extremity of the Māori underworld* (pō) where human souls are annihilated. (Tregear 1891:240; White 1887a: App.) See also **Ameto**.

MIHIMIHITEA, a Māori god whose aid is sought during time of epidemics. (Tregear 1891:241; White 1887a:40.)

MIHI-TOKA, a Marquesan god of the creation, the son of Papa-Uka and Papa-Ao. (Christian 1895:188–189.)

MILIMILI, a Marquesan who died, and his spirit went to the underworld* (pō). His wife's grief prompted the god Tangata-no-te-Moana to attempt its rescue. At first the gods of the underworld refused his request, but when he beat their wooden gong so loudly, they threw the soul of Milimili out of the underworld, and Tangata-no-te-Moana restored it to life. (Beaglehole 1938; Beckwith 1948:150.) **Hiku-i-ka-nahele; Hutu; Kanikani-a-'ula; Kena; Pare.**

MILU (MIRO, MIRU), deity of the underworld* in many Polynesian mythologies. In Hawai'i, Milu was a ruling chief in Waipi'o (on the island of Hawai'i) who was swept down into the underworld to the uttermost depths of night because of his disobedience to the gods. He became the ruler of the land of the dead, replacing the old god Manua. Milu's underworld lay in the west, sometimes referred to as under the ocean. (Beckwith 1948:114, 118, 155, 159.)

In **New Zealand**, Mery or Miru is the goddess of the lowest three underworlds. Her abode is called Tatau-o-te-pō (door-of-the-night) at the foot of Cape Reinga, the leaping off place of the spirits of the departed. Several songs describe her snatching and dragging off such souls in her net. (Cowan 1925:52, 54; Reed 1957:91, 95.)

In **Mangaian** myth, Miru-kura is an ugly old woman, a confirmed cannibal who devours all the spirits of the dead which enter her underworld. Akaanga assists her by catching the souls in a large net, feeding them on worms and black beetles, drugging them on kava,* and then throwing them into an oven. She has one son, Tautiki (patron god of dancing), and four lovely daughters— Kumutonga-i-te-pō, Karaia-i-te-ata, Te-rau-ara, and Te-poro. (Tregear 1891:243.)

On **Rarotonga**, Muru is a male god who catches his spirits in a net on the west coast of the island between the villages of Avarua and Arorangi. He and Akaanga dash out the brains of their victims and take them to be eaten to the underworld. (Buck 1934:204.)

On **Mangareva** (French Polynesia), Miru is the god of the night world. (Caillot 1914: 153–154.) See also the Samoan god of the underworld, **Elo.**

MIMIAHI, son of the Māori god Rangi* (sky father). (Shortland 1882:19; Tregear 1891:241.)

MIRU, name of sorcerers on Easter Island who brings about an increase in food supplies by making chickens lay eggs. (Routledge 1917:240–241.)

MOAKURA, the Māori goddess who drank up the waters of the deluge* thus saving the few mortals who had fled to Hikurangi.* (Tregear 1891:245; White 1887c:49.) See also **Ruatapu.**

MOANA-NUI-KA-LEHUA, Hawaiian goddess or mermaid who accompanied the volcano goddess Pele* from Kahiki to

Hawai'i. She lived in the ocean between Kaua'i and O'ahu. When Māui* tried to fish up the islands, she and others snagged his hook on a rock. Māui finally caught Moana's fish body and laid it upon a shrine. Her spirit briefly visited Kahiki, and then it returned to Hawai'i where it took the form of a *lehua* tree. (Emerson 1915:160–161; Pukui 1971:394.)

MO'E, a Tahitian god invoked during the launching of the great canoe of Hiro (Hilo*) just before his journey from Tahiti. (Henry 1928:551.)

MOEAMOTU'A, along with his brothers, Moealagoni and Moeatikitiki, became the three stars in Orion's belt. According to a lengthy Rotuman legend, they were the sons of Mafi and Lū, and their exploits are similar to those of Māui* (Māui-tikitiki) and his brothers. (Churchward 1937:489–497.)

MOEAVA, the greatest ancient hero known in the Tuamotu Islands, a navigator of extraordinary abilities, a warrior beyond compare. He was born at Takaroa Island, the son of Kanaparua and Puritau (or Puna-keu-ariki). Upon the death of his brother Tangaroa-Tiraora, Moeava adopted his several children. After some time Moeava set out adventuring, settled on Napuka Island for a while where he married Huarei, and they had a son Kehauri. Moeava, Huarei, and Kehauri returned to Takaroa, but dissention between the two groups of children led Moeava to return back to Napuka.

After his departure, he engaged in a vengeful contest against a giant warrior named Patira who had kidnapped his wife, Huarei. Moeava put on his magical belt, his Manava-apoapo, and with his large sling, killed the mighty warrior. The stone lies in the harbor of Makemo to this day. Shortly thereafter, a large contingent of Patira's family and allies descended upon Takaroa and massacred all of Moeava's adopted children except Reipu and his sister Kakaia who had hid themselves from the warriors high in a tree. Eventually Moeava heard of the dastardly news and returned and savagely avenged the slaughter of his children. He brought all of the islands under his control and lived out the rest of his life on Takaroa. (Audran 1918:26–35, 1919:31–38.)

MOE-HAKAAVA, the Marquesan god of fishermen. (Christian 1895:190.)

MO'E-HAU, a Tahitian household god. (Henry 1928:377.)

MO'E-HAU-I-TE-RA'I, the beloved daughter of the Tahitian creator god Ta'aroa (Kanaloa*) and his wife Papa-raharaha. (Henry 1928:407.)

MOEKILAIPUKA, one of the four gods who rules the earth according to legends from Vaitupu, Tuvalu. (Turner 1884: 283). See also **Tapufatu; Terupe; Moumousia.**

MŌEMŌENENEVA, the Tuamotuan name for Rata's (Laka's*) spear and canoe hull. (Stimson 1964:307.)

MO'E-RURU'A, an old Tahitian goddess named in the creation chant who guards the world. (Henry 1928:416.)

MOFUTA-AE-TA'U, a Tongan god worshipped by chief Tamale of Niutoua in east Tongatapu, associated with the god of the underworld.* His temple was burned when Christianity was introduced. (Collocott 1921:227–228.)

MO'I-KEHA, a chief from the ancient land of Kahiki (Tahiti) who became incensed after being rejected by his brother's wife, and thus set out to settle the Hawaiian Islands. He first beached on the island of Kaua'i and then made his home on Hawai'i. Before his death, he sent his son Kila* back to Kahiki to escort the high priest La'a* to Hawai'i to insure the proper disposal of his body. (Beckwith 1948:353–355; Johnson 1979:57–67.)

MOKE-HAE, a chief Marquesan lizard god who causes sickness in humans; also a god of house building and carpentry. (Christian 1895:190.)

MOKO, an evil Tuamotuan lizard god. (Stimson 1964:309.) See also **Mo'o.**

MOKOAKA, an evil Tuamotuan god who appears in the form of a skeleton. (Stimson 1964:309.)

MOKOIRO, one of the three principal gods of Mangaia, progenitors of the Mangaian tribes through his wife Angarua. (Buck 1934:167; Gill 1876:15–18.) See also **Rangi; Akatauria.**

MOKOMOKO, a Māori lizard god, son of Tū-te-wanawana* and his wife, Tupari. (Tregear 1891:249–250; White 1887a: App.)

MOKONGĀRARA, a Tuamotuan lizard god. (Stimson 1964:309.)

MOKONUI, an attendant to Korokoiewe, the Māori god of childbirth. (Tregear 1891:250; White 1887a: App.)

MOKOREA, a Tuamotuan demon of gigantic proportions with long blond hair and skewerlike nails that gains the affection of humans who then sacrifice their spouses to save their own lives. (Stimson 1964:310.) Also a female goblin who stole food from Kui,* a demigod and grandfather of Rata (Laka*). Kui captured and married her, and they became the parents of a son Rimo-roa and a daughter Rima-poto. (Stimson 1937:96.)

MOKOROA, an immense Māori lizard god who anciently crossed the sea from Hawaiki* to New Zealand. (Tregear 1891: 250.) Also mentioned in Cook Island legends (Aitutaki) as having been a monster encountered by Te Erui and his brother Matarea in their first visit to that island. (Gill 1911:150.) See also **Katotiae; Uika.**

MOKOTITI, a Māori lizard god who causes lung diseases. (Tregear 1891:250; White 1885: 114.)

MOKU-HINIA, a Hawaiian lizard goddess from the island of Maui who was reported seen by thousands of spectators at a funeral of a chief in 1838. (Beckwith 1948:126.)

MOLOTI, a principal god on the island of Nukulaelae, Tuvalu, represented by a stone. (Turner 1884:280–281.)

MOMO, the first mortal man according to Tongan legends. He and his female counterpart, Kohai,* were created from maggots or worms. (Gifford 1924:13.) According to another legend, Momo was one of the three first mortal men brought forth by the Tongan gods of creation. He and his companions Koau* and Kohai* were given wives by Māui* and his brothers, and they populated the islands. (Reiter 1907:438–445.) See also **Creation.**

MOMO-ITOOI, an ancient hero of Bellona Island who killed 'Angokutume'a, the last cannibal on the island. (Monberg 1966:89.)

MONA, a god of Nukunono, Tokelau Islands. (Macgregor 1937:61.)

MONGI-HERE, a beautiful princess of great magical powers in the Tuamotuan Hiro (Hilo*) cycle. Mongi-here decided to prevent Hiro from coming to her island. She first halted the wind, and then she brought a great gale. Nothing could stop the famous hero, and he landed on her island. He played an erotic trick on her, and she fled in anger. At last, Hiro finally caught up with her at the very gates of Hawaiki* and expressed his love to her. Her angry and fury vanished, and they returned to Hiro's home where she became his mistress. (Stimson 1957:137–190.)

MONO'I-HERE, a handsome Tahitian who became the secret lover of the goddess Hina.* When Hina's cannibalistic mother, Nō-na, learned of the affair, she ambushed and killed him in a cave at Tahara'a. Hina sought asylum at 'Uporu (Point Venus) where chief Noa (sweet odor) avenged Mono'i-here's death by killing the detested Nō-na. Noa and Hina then became the parents of Hema, father of the famous hero Tafa'i (Kaha'i*). (Henry 1928:552–554.)

MONOMONOTAGATU, a god of Niue Island. (Loeb 1926:161.)

MO'O, lizards or sacred gods of the royal 'Oro-pa'a family on the island of Tahiti; also another name for the god Tipa, the Tahitian healing god. (Henry 1928:383.) See also **Moko**.

MO'O-I-NANEA, the ancestress and matriarch of all Hawaiian *mo'o* (lizard) gods and goddesses and the first born of Kāne-hūnā-moku.* She brought all her progeny from Ke-'alohi-lani (a mythical land) to O'ahu. She appeared as the man-eating ancestress of the hero 'Aukele-nui-a-iku* to whom she gave instructions and guidance in his many journeys. In the romance of Ha'ina-kolo,* she stretched her body into a bridge across which Ha'ina-kolo walked to her husband in Kū-'ai-helani. She is also named as the great grandmother of the heroine Ke-ao-melemele. (Beckwith 1948:71, 78, 127, 264, 491, 492, 507, 519, 531.)

MOO-TII, the patron god of the *eva* tree in the Marquesas that produces poisonous fruit often used in committing suicide. (Christian 1895:190.)

MO'O-'URI, a Tahitian god invoked to prevent sailors from hitting low islands or atolls. (Henry 1928:377.)

MŌRIANUKU, the Māori name for Hades, the land of death and shadows. (Tregear 1891:253.) See also **Pō**; **Underworld**.

MŌRIORI, name of the aborigines of the Chatham Islands before the arrival of the first Polynesians, sometimes called Hiti.* (Shand 1894:76–92; Tregear 1891:568; White 1887c:188–189.) See also **Tutu-mai-ao**.

MOSO, a Tongan sea god of the island of Mo'unga'one; also the Samoan god who unsuccessfully attempted to steal Tanoa, one of the Tongan islands, and to carry it away to Samoa. The Tongan gods Tafakula* and Haelefeke* discovered the plot, whereupon Moso dropped Tanoa so that instead of being flat, the island stands on edge. (Gifford 1924: 87.) A vindictive, Samoan war god. (Stair 1896:37; Turner 1884:36–38.)

MOSO'OI, an inferior household god of Samoa, worshipped in the form of a yellow-flowering tree, the *Conanga odorata*. (Turner 1884:71.)

MÖSTŌTŌ, an ancient Rotuman whose seafaring exploits aroused the jealous of his cannibalistic king. After having eaten Möstōtō's parents and sister, the king sent the young boy on several adventures reminiscent of the Sinbad-the-sailor stories. On his last adventure with his sisters, Puakleva and Puaknifo, Möstōtō became enraged at the king and slew him. (Churchward 1938: 462–469.)

MOTIKTIKI, the Anutan equivalent of the demigod Māui* who fished Anuta and subsequently all of the Pacific islands up from the ocean floor. (Feinberg 1988:11.)

MOTORO, a deified ancestor of the Mangaians, son of the god Rangi,* who first set sail with his brothers, Ruanuku, Kereteki, and Utākea, to discover the island of Mangaia. Only Kereteki and Utākea survived to settle the island. Motoro, called the living god, became one of the supreme deities of the island. His priests were called Amama (open-mouthed). Kereteki and Utākea were also worshipped as gods. (Buck 1934: 21–22, 166; Gill 1876:26–28.)

MOTUA-ANUA, a god mentioned in the Easter Island creation chant. (Métraux 1940: 321–322.) See also **Anua-motua.**

MOTU-HAIKI, a Marquesan god of house building and carpentry. (Christian 1895:190; Steinen 1933:43.)) See also **Hope-kou-toki.**

MOTUMOTUAHI, one of the Māori canoes of the first migration to New Zealand, commanded by chief Puatautahi. (Tregear 1891:21, 255; White 1887b:182–183.) See also **Canoes, Māori Migration.**

MOTU-TAPU, sacred or forbidden island, popular Polynesian name for a legendary island and, as such, almost every archipelago has a Motu-tapu. In Tahiti, it lies in Pape'ete harbor; in New Zealand, it is the island of Mokoia; in Tonga, it lies northeast of the island of Tongatapu; just off the western coast of Bora-Bora; east of Ra'iātea; Rarotonga, and the list goes on. The most famous Motu-tapu is the residence of Tinirau (Kinilau*) and Hina.* (Grey 1970:63, 65; Tregear 1891: 256.)

MOUARIKI, a Tuamotuan god. (Stimson 1964:314.)

MOUMOUSIA, one of the four gods who ruled the earth according to legends from Vaitupu, Tuvalu. His duty is to watch and kill thieves. (Turner 1884:283). See also **Tapufatu; Terupe; Moekilaipuka.**

MŪ, a legendary island that once sank beneath the sea in Tuamotuan legends. (Stimson 1964:314.) Also an ancestor of the Māori demigod Māui.* When Māui's mother threw him into the sea, Mū and Weka (sea gods) nursed him to life. (White 1887f:63, 71, 81.) See also **Tama-nui-te-rangi**.

Mū is also the name of an ancient **Samoan** who lived near Palauli, Savai'i, who captured a demon by trickery, and thereby rid the island of his mischievous acts. Mū rubbed himself with remains of a rotted fish, met the demon who commented on his delicious smell, and then suggested they travel to the village where the rest of the meal awaited them. When they neared the village, Mū threw the demon in a fire, and the rest of the villagers, who were waiting for them, beat him to death. (Stair 1896:52–53.)

MŪ PEOPLE, banana-eating people of primeval Hawai'i. Like the Menehune,* they represent the original inhabitants of the islands. The Mū originally lived on the mythical island of Kāne-huna-moku* but migrated to Hawai'i to aid the Hawaiian chief Ola* in his construction projects on Kaua'i. They were dwarf in size, banana eaters, and hairy with round stomachs as distinguished from the Menehune who had smooth skin and distended stomachs. Their common ancestor was Lua-mu'u.

Once their work was completed, most of the Mū returned to their native homeland. Some remained, however, and their descendants are suppose to inhabit the isolated valleys in the islands. (Beckwith 1948:321–326, 330–332; Green 1928:34, 39–41; Wickman 1985:166.) See also **Elves and Fairies.**

MUA, a Māori god worshipped in the temple at Wharekura. (White 1887a:9.)

MUA-TA'AROA, the Tahitian night god. (Henry 1928:331.) See also **Kanaloa.**

MU-E-O, guardian of the gates of Havaiki (Hawaiki*), probably the underworld* in the Tuamotuan Māui* chant. Māui forced Mu-e-o to allow him to pass to the underworld to find Mahu-ika,* the keeper of fire, from whom mortals received the first fire. (Stimson 1934:17–18.)

MUITAUTINI, a god of Niue Island responsible for transmission of the arts. (Loeb 1926:164.)

MUIU'ULEAPAI, grand daughter of the Samoan sun god Tagaloa (Kanaloa*) through his son Tagaloaui* and his wife Sināsa'umani.* Muiu-'uleapai married Tuifiti, the king of Fiji, and went there to live. She was accused of causing a famine in Fiji, was badly treated, and was sent into exile. Her elder brother Taeotaloga heard of her plight and gained the assistance of two sailors, Gaiuli and Gaisina, to transport him to Fiji. After enduring many hardships, they finally arrived in Fiji and found Muiu-'uleapai and her son Leataa-ofiti. Taeotaloga planted huge breadfruit tree plantations, ended the famine, and reunited his sisters with her husband's family. (Krämer 1902:419–427.)

MŪKĪ-KERI-VAE, a Tuamo-tuan chant wherein the sorcerer performs incantations over a footprint, or earth from such a footprint, to cast evil spells. (Stimson 1964:316.)

MULI-'ELE-ALI'I, father fo the Hawaiian voyagers Mo'i-ke-ha.* (Beckwith 1948:352–353.)

MUMUTEAWHĀ, Māori god of whales. (Tregear 1891:258; White 1887a: App.) See also **Kae**.

MUNANUI, a legendary king of Hao Atoll in the Tuamotus, whose exploits have been matched by no other human. He defeated all of his rivals who wished to dethrone him, he single-handedly captured the huge fish of the ocean, and he brought peace of mind to his subjects. When he died, he was interred into a great grotto on the island, was mourned deeply by his followers, and after his death, no one became king of the island. (Caillot 1914:31–42.)

MUNI-MATAMAHAE, regarded as the Hercules of Tongan mythology, son of the brave Motukuveevalu and his wife Kae. The legends relate that once there lived in Tongatapu a wicked chief called Pungaloto-hoa who killed and ate his people. Fearful of their lives, Motukuveevalu fled into the bush and persuaded his pregnant wife to take refuge with her parents on the island of Ha-'apai. In route, Kae was killed and eaten by the crew, and the unborn child thrown overboard. An old couple of Lofanga found the child on the beach, named him Muni, and reared him as their own.

He grew into a naughty, mischievous young man whom the villagers disliked and wished to have destroyed. The elders decided to present his family with several impossible tasks, and the failure to perform them would mean their execution. First they had to weave half of an enormous fishing net, while the rest of the villagers wove the other half. The chiefs were surprised when Muni presented before them his completed net. They then required him to complete half of a fence around a huge enclosure by the next day, then to build a single outrigger canoe and construct a boat house for it. Having failed to daunt the young man, the elders decided to trick him into watching aboard the boat by night, and then they cut the lines so that it drifted out to sea without any provisions. When Muni woke up, he found the boat sinking. With only a food bowl, he was able to bail out all the water, and with a torn plank from the side of the vessel, he paddled back to shore. Once there, his adopted parents told him of their finding him as a small child and of his real father Motokuveevalu and of his plight in Tonga.

Muni set sail and found his father who told him about the wicked chief Pungalotahoa. Muni grew angry and set out to revenge his people. Arriving at Pungalotahoa's dwelling, he tore down the gate, raped his concubines, and pulled up his prized kava plant in the yard. The angry Pungalotahoa challenged Muni to a throwing contest and then a boxing match. In the battle, Pungalotahoa's body was completely crushed, but he revived and awarded Muni all the lands, titles, and possessions. Muni brought his father to live in his new, comfortable house, and then united the people together under his benevolent rule. (Gifford 1924:120–138; Brown 1916: 426–432.)

MUPERE, a Tuamotuan sea demon who became king over the goblins of Matuauru. Once Mupere went walking along the beach and met Tauiti, a cannibal as well as king of the goblins. They boasted of their prowess, and a fight ensued. Mupere won, and as a result became king over the goblins at Matuauru. They especially liked the beach called Mahina-i-te-one (moonlight on the sands), off limits to all humans. Mupere and his goblins played a major role in the Tahaki (Kaha'i*) epic story. (Stimson 1937:68–71.)

MŪ-RARO-HENŪA, a Tuamotuan god created by Tāpeka (the supreme creator god). (Stimson 1964:317.)

MURI-RANGA-WHENUA, goddess and ancestress of the Māori demigod Māui* whose enchanted jawbone Māui used to beat the sun to make him travel slower across the heavens. Māui also used it as a fishhook to fish up the Pacific islands. (Grey 1970:24–29, 34; White 1887c:69.) Another Māori version states that Muri-ranga-whenua was Māui's grandfather, and Māui killed him in order to obtain the enchanted jaw bone. (Tregear 1891:259; Wohlers 1875:38.)

MURIWHAKAROTO, the Māori goddess of small fish. (Tregear 1891:259; White 1887a: App.)

MUTAI, an ancestral god worshipped on Futuna. (Burrows 1936:105–108.)

MUTU, an evil Māori god dwelling with Miru (Milu*) in the underworld.* (Tregear 1891:260.)

–N–

NĀEA, a Tuamotuan god; also refers to the dual personality of the supreme deity. (Stimson 1964:319.)

NAFANUA, the Samoan war goddess, daughter of Saveasi'uleo* or Leosia* (god of the underworld* and his wife Tilafaigā (or her sister Taemā). She was born as a clot and thrown away by her mother, but her father retrieved her and gave her birth. Prayers for success in battle were made to her, and coconut fonds were tied about the waist in her honor. Her husband was Falealupo whom she freed from his enemies. She was attributed with having marked out the administrative districts on the islands of 'Upolu and Savai'i. A coral reef was also named after her. (Abercromby 1891:459–463; Fraser 1893:171–183; Krämer 1902:39, 45, 72, 80–81, 107, 199, 342; Stübel 1896:155.) See also **Lefanoga; Pava; Taemama.**

The **Tongan** Nafanua is a rain goddess, daughter of Tokilagafanua* and his sister Hina-tuafuaga,* twin sister to Topukulu,* mother to the goddess Tafakula. (Reiter 1907: 743–754.)

NAHERANGI, the highest or tenth heaven in the Māori cosmos, the heaven of Rehua,* the god of kindness and health, also called Tūwarea. (Tregear 1891:

261; White 1885:117; White 1887a: App.) See also **Creation; Heavens.**

NĀIA, name of Māui's* adze in the Tuamotuan epic. (Stimson 1964:320.)

NAITERANGI, the highest or tenth heaven in the Māori cosmos, the heaven of Rehua* (the god of kindness and health). Also called Tūwārea. (White 1885:117; White 1887a: App.) See also **Creation; Heavens.**

NĀ-KEO-LANI, a Hawaiian goddess of healing. (Emerson 1915:146.)

NĀ-KOLO-I-LANI, a hunchbacked Hawaiian god, leader of all the forces that cause thunderstorms. (Beckwith 1948:48.)

NĀ-MAKA-O-KAHA'I, an older sister of the Hawaiian volcano goddess Pele,* born from the breasts of her mother Haumea.* Her husband, 'Aukele-nui-a-iku,* left her for her sister Pele,* and it was because of this conflict that Pele migrated to Hawai'i. Nā-maka-o-kaha'i became the chiefess of the Mū* and Menehune* people and had three supernatural bodies, a fire, a cliff, and a sea as well as the supernatural powers of flying, resurrecting her body after being cut into pieces, and reducing others to ashes by turning up her skirt

at them. (Beckwith 1948:170–171, 330, 490–491, 495–496; Emerson 1915:xxv, xxx, 112.)

NĀ-MAKA-O-KA-PĀO'O, superhuman son of the Hawaiian god Kū*-'ula-o-kaha'i and Po-ka'i, a woman of O'ahu. As a young child he infuriated his step-father Puali'i and slew him. Chief Amau of O'ahu was also slain, and Nā-maka-o-ka-pāo'o set his mother up as chiefess of the island. After visiting the island of Hawai'i, he set out to find his real father. (Beckwith 1948:480–481; Fornander 1917:274–283.) See similar tales of **Ahoeitu; Tū-hu-ruhuru; Te-hina-tū-o-kae**.

NAMUEFI, a war god of Fatiau, Niue Island. (Loeb 1926:160.)

NANA, an artisan for the Tahitian god Ta'aroa (Kanaloa*). (Henry 1928:356, 365.)

NĀNĀ-HOA, an ancient Hawaiian who abused his wife and as punishment was turned into a phallic rock on Moloka'i. (Pukui 1971:395.)

NANAUE, a Hawaiian sharkman, who once lived on the Big Island and then Moloka'i, the son of Ka-moho-ali'i and Kalei. He was eventually discovered, and the demigod Unauna struggled with him to the death. See also **Kamaika'ahui; Ka-**

welo; Nenewe; Mano-niho-ka-hi; Pau-walu.

NANDURUVESI RAISOROVI, also called Weleilakemba, the god of Wathiwathi, Lau Islands (Polynesian outliers in Fiji), who is invoked in preparation for war or a long voyage. (Hocart 1929:198.)

NĀ-PŌ-TATĀ and N Ā-PŌ-TĪTĪ, these two demons were created by the Tahitian god Ta'aroa (Kanaloa*) for Ti'i (Tiki*), the first man. (Henry 1928:402.)

NAREAU, creation god of Tarawa, Gilbert Islands. He made the heavens and earth while he lived in Samoa with his daughter Kobine of the underworld.* He lived in Tarawa for twenty-seven generations, changed his name to Tautebū, and returned to Samoa in an outrigger canoe, the first of its type ever seen in Samoa. (Newell 1895:231–235.)

NĀ-TUPŪA, Tuamotuan word for the first two primordial gods Tupūa and Tahito. (Stimson 1964:325.)

NAU ARIKI, one of the major gods of the island of Anuta. (Feinberg 1981: 151.) See also Nau Pangatau.

NAU PANGATAU, one of the major gods of the island of Anuta. (Feinberg 1981:151.) See also Nau Ariki.

NAVE, patron god of the village of Amanave (stone-of-Nave), Tutuila, Samoa. (Turner 1884: 40.)

NAVENAVE, a messenger for the Tahitian war god 'Oro.* (Henry 1928:375.)

NAWA, the god of Longaniu, Lau Islands (Polynesian outliers in Fiji). (Hocart 1929:199.)

NDAUTHINA, a god of war at Ndalithoni, Lau Islands (Polynesian outliers in Fiji). (Hocart 1929:196.)

NDIMAILANGI, the goddess of war on Uruone, Lau Islands (Polynesian outliers in Fiji) who can take the form of a monitor. (Hocart 1929:196.)

NDROKA, the god of Tandravula, Lau Islands (Polynesian outliers in Fiji), possibly of Melanesian origin. His name "raw" refers to his uncooked food often found in the ovens. (Hocart 1929:191.)

NENEWE, a Hawaiian shark-man, who once lived on the Big Island. He warned men going fishing that some of them would be killed before they return. Several Hawaiians captured and killed him. See also Ka-maika'ahui; Ka-welo; Nanaue;

Mano-niho-kahi; Pau-walu; Sharks.

NEVANEVA, a messenger or herald for the other Tahitian gods, especially appointed to communicate with the god Ta'ere* at the center of the earth. (Henry 1928:163, 164, 357, 374, 407.)

NGĀ-ARIKI, joint name of the two supreme gods of the Tuamotuan underworld.* (Stimson 1964:86.)

NGĀ-ATUA, name of the sixth Māori heaven ruled over by Tāwhaki (Kaha'i*). (Tregear 1891:273; White 1887a: App.) See Also **Creation; Heavens**.

NGAE, see **Kae**.

NGAHUE, the Māori chief of Hawaiki* who first discovered New Zealand. Forced to leave his homeland, Ngahue set sail with his precious jade stone (Pautini) and landed on the shores of New Zealand (Ao-tearoa). He eventually returned to Hawaiki, shaped his Pautini into two adzes, and with these, he constructed the great canoes of the migration (*Arawa*,* *Tainui*,* etc.) (Grey 1970:106–108; Tregear 1891:275; White 1887a:73.) See also **Canoes, Māori Migration**.

NGANA, a Māori god of the air, son of Hau-ngangana (blustering wind), and ancestor of Tiki,* the first man. (Shortland 1882:13; Tregear 1891:276.) According to another myth, Ngana was the Māori sun god, the second son of Rangi* (sky father) and Papa* (earth mother). (Hare Hongi 1907: 109–119.)

NGANA'EIKE, eldest son of the twentieth Tu'i Tonga* (ruler of Tonga), who visited Samoa to court the beautiful Hina.* He was accompanied by his handsome brother, Nganatatafu, with whom Hina fell in love. She made love to Nganatatafu, but married Ngana'eike and returned to Tonga. During the passage, the deception was made known, and Nganatatafu was thrown overboard. He reached shore at 'Uiha where he became the progenitor of the high-ranking chiefly title Tu'i Ha'angana. When Hina reached Tonga, she gave birth to a son, Malupo, who became the first Malupo, a title of nobility in Tonga. The paternity of the child, however, was never questioned. (Rutherford 1977: 34–35.)

NGANAHAU, name of the supernatural beings of the Tuamotuan Rangi-pō, underworld,* especially the leader of the spirits of the god Kiho.* (Stimson 1964:89.) See also **Io**.

NGANAHEKE, a Tuamotuan demon of the ocean appearing

either in the form of an eel or an octopus. (Stimson 1964:89.)

NGANA-TU-A-RAU, name of one of the two ships commanded by the famous Tuamotuan hero Rata (Laka*). (Stimson 1964:90.) See also Moemoeneneva.

NGANGANA, name of a Tuamotuan octopus god. (Stimson 1964:87.)

NGĀRARA-HUARAU, a Māori enchantress, part human, part lizard, who was burned to death in the legend of Rūrūteina.* (Tregear 1891:278; White 1887b:29; Wohlers 1876: 117.)

NGĀRARANUI, elder brother of the Māori chief Tūtānekai in the romance of Hine-moa.* (Grey 1970:183–191.)

NGAROARIKI, the beautiful wife of Ngata, an ancient king of Rarotonga, who was frequently saved from harm by the great god Tangaroa (Kanaloa*). (Gill 1876:130–135.)

NGAROTŌ, name of the third heaven of Rangi* in the Māori cosmos, ruled over by the god Maru.* (Tregear 1891:279; White 1887a: App.)

NGARU, an ancient hero of Mangaia, a Hercules, who lived in Avaiki (Hawaiki*) with his mother Vaiare and his grandfather Moko (the great lizard). His beautiful wife, Tongatea, was the envy of everyone around. Ngarau decided to prove his prowess. He conquered the monsters of the deep, descended and returned successfully from the underworld,* and defeated the sky fairies and the sky demon Amaite-rangi. (Gill 1876:225–250.)

NGATA-ARIKI, a Cook Islander from Rarotonga who once rescued the souls of his wife, Ngaro-ariki-te-tara, and his father-in-law, Kuiono, from the underworld* through the intervention of divine messengers from the god Tangaroa.* (Te Ariki-tara-are 1918:178–198.)

NGĀTI-NAU, name of a group of demons residing in the underworld* in the legends from Fangatau, Tuamotus. (Stimson 1964:93.)

NGĀTI-RŪ, refers to the heaven builders in Tuamotuan creation chants, usually identified as the children of Āteanuku-mau-atūa* (Wākea*) and Fakahotu.* They consisted of Rū-hiti, Rū-takoto, Rūtuanohu, Rū-farara, Rū-poto, Rūroa, Rū-pingao, Rū-tope, Rū-'ea, Rū-kana, Rū-titi, Rū-kaho, and Rū-ngaohe. On the island of Ana'a, however, they appear as different personifications of the earthquake god Rū. (Stimson 1964:93.)

NGĀTORO-I-RANGI, name of the Māori priest in the migration legends who was at first denied command of the great *Tainui** canoe by Tama-te-ra-pua. Ngātoro and his wife, Kēaroa, were enticed on board the *Arawa** canoe and were then insulted by Tama-te-ra-pua. Ngātoro caused the canoe to head into a great whirlpool (Te Parata) until the cries of the women and children caused him to release the spell. When they arrived in New Zealand, Ngātoro caused springs of water to appear where he stamped his foot and caused volcanos to belch forth fire, and in general, left his mark wherever he went. (Grey 1970:109–127; Tregear 1891:280–281.) See also **Manaia**.

NGAUMATAKI'ONE, a goddess on Bellona Island, brought anciently from their traditional homeland called 'Ubea. She had a daughter, Tungi'one, and granddaughter, Ngaumataki-'one, all of whom were malevolent and drove people mad. (Monberg 1966:75–76.)

NGAVEVE, malevolent spirits of Tokelau who spent their entire existence playing tricks on mortals, especially capturing their souls and running off with them. Also known as Kaufiola. (Macgregor 1937:62.)

NGE'OBIONGO, a patron goddess of ovens on Bellona Island who harms those violating the local taboos surrounding the ovens; she also protects homes from attack. (Monberg 1966:77.)

NGEIPAU, a district goddess of the Kaitu'u clan on Bellona Island, daughter of the goddess Ekeitehua.* (Monberg 1966:67.)

NGĒ UKU, a Māori god invoked to secure a victory in battle. (Tregear 1891:283.)

NGINGONGINGO, Māori demons who haunt ruins and who attack and kill mortals. (Tregear 1891:283; Wohlers 1875:112.)

NGIO, name of a god from Raroia Island in the Tuamotus. (Stimson 1964:96.)

NGIRENGIRE, an evil, Tuamotuan demon. (Stimson 1964:96.)

NG TONGALELEVA, patron god of the *kanava* tree who punish all those who cut them without the permission of the priests. (Macgregor 1937:61.)

NGUAKABANGEA, one of the many district gods of the Kaitu'u clan on Bellona Island, the son of the principal god Tehu'aingabenga.* (Monberg 1966:67.)

NGUATINIHENUA, one of the many district gods of the Kaitu'u clan on Bellona Island, married Ngeipau, daughter of the god Ekeitehua. (Monberg 1966:65–66.)

NGUATINIHENUA, one of the many district gods of the Kaitu'u clan on Bellona Island, sometimes called Nguatunihenua, the son of the principal god Tehu'aingabenga.* (Monberg 1966:67.)

NGUATUPU'A, an important sky goddess of Bellona Island especially to the Tanga clan. She married her brother, Tepoutu'uingangi,* and both are represented as sacred stones worshipped by the islanders. Their mother was Sinakibi (blind Sina) and a story is related how Sinakibi prevented her two children from stealing the life spirit (the *ma'ungi*) from the mortal man Moesabengubengu because his wife had restored Sinakibi's eyesight. Nguatupu'a and her brother husband were extremely sacred, and humans had pray to other gods to intercede for them. (Monberg 1958: 46–49.)

NĪʻAUEPOʻO, a young Hawaiian, born to his mother Hina* on the Big Island. His father, Kū-alaka'i, returned to Kahiki (Tahiti ?) before his birth but gave him tokens of his identity, a loincloth, a red canoe, and a feather cape and helmet.

The young boy eventually wished to visit his father and did so by the services of his ancestor Niu-ola-hiki (or Niu-loa-hiki), a stretching tree which catapulted him from Hawai'i to Kahiki. Not knowing who he was, his father's family drowned him in the sea, but his ancestor restored him to life whereupon he produced his tokens and was accepted by his father. Hina, however had heard of the incident, and in a rage set out to Kahiki where she turned her husband into an *alaka'i* fish. Upon her return to Hawai'i, she resided at Ka-ū (south Hawai'i) and gave birth to a daughter Maniania. (Beckwith 1948:479; Green and Pukui 1971:179–185.) See also **Kalanimanuia; Niu-ola-hiki.**

NIFO, a god of Niue Island. (Loeb 1926:163.)

NIFOLOA, a mischievous Samoan war god who resides at Falelima and whose bite with his long tooth brings death. Also known by the name Gaugatolo. (Krämer 1902:23; Stair 1896:37; Stübel 1896:81; Turner 1884:41–42.)

NĪHEU, a Hawaiian trickster god, son of Hina and younger brother to the stretching god Kana,* also nicknamed the mischievous (*kolohe*). (Beckwith 1948:207, 396; Pukui 1971: 395; Emerson 1915:114.)

NIHONIHO-TEITEI, or **NI-HONIHO-TETEI**, one of the old goddesses who are guardians of the world according to Tahitian legend. Nihoniho-teitei is a fierce man killer. The other guardians are 'Aiāru, Fa'aipu, Fa'aīpō, 'Ōrerorero, Tahu'a, and Tamaumau-'ōrere. (Henry 1928:417.)

NIHOOLEKI, a Hawaiian demigod, born on Hawai'i, but lived mainly on O'ahu at Waianae where he became the ruling chief. He was famed as a mighty fisherman through the powers of his pearl fishhook (pāhuhu) and his huge double canoe. After his death, his spirit returned incognito to his wife on Kaua'i where he performed several superhuman fishing feats and then returned to his tomb and disappeared. (Beckwith 1948:420–421 Fornander 1916:488–497.)

NINI-A-RANGI, a god of the Chatham Islands. (Shand 1894:90.)

NIOLOPUA, Hawaiian god of sleep. (Pukui 1971:395.)

NIU, an ancient Tuamotuan word for sacred (*tapu*). (Stimson 1964:332.)

NIU-KURA, first cousin to Tahaki (Kaha'i*), the famous Tuamotuan hero. Niu-kura's mother, Arimata, was sister to Huauri, the mother of Tahaki.

Niu-kura became jealous, killed Tahaki, and cut him into pieces. Huauri, however, gathered the pieces together and restored her son to life. In revenge, she invoked her sea gods who swallowed Niu-kura and his brothers, and they turned into porpoises. (Stimson 1934:50.)

NIU-LOA-HIKI, a mythical land in Hawaiian tradition where spirits of deceased mortals go who have kept the tapus; an ancestor of Nīauepo'o* (who sought his father overseas) who took the form of a stretching tree to carry the young child back home. (Beckwith 1948:67–68, 478–479, 484–487; Pukui 1971:395.)

NIU-LOLO-HIKI, a surviving brother to the demigod Māui in Hawai'i, who took the form of a coconut tree; *lolo* or "stupid" describes his behavior. (Wickman 1985:169.)

NIUTAKOUHUA, the foundation or base of the underworld* according to Tuamotuan legends. (Stimson 1964:332.)

NIWAREKA, wife of Mataora* (the first Māori to be tattooed). Being mistreated by her husband, Niwareka returned to the underworld* (*pō*) to her father, Uetonga* (grandson of Rū, the earthquake god). Mataora followed her and brought her back to the world of day. (White 1887b:5.) Also the name of the canoe belonging to the great Māori hero Rata (Laka*). (Tregear 1891:268; White 1887a: 71.)

NIWARŪ, the name of Rata's (Laka*) canoe which was made by the fairies in the Māori legend. (Tregear 1891:268; Wohlers 1875:7.) See also Niwareka; Riwaru.

NO'AITENGENGA, one of the many district gods of the Kaitu'u clan on Bellona Island, the son of the principal god Tehu'aingabenga.* (Monberg 1966:67.)

NOHO-A-MO'O, one of two malevolent sorcerer gods who were toll keepers on a bridge near the town of Hilo, Hawai'i, and who were killed by the goddess Hi'iaka.* (Emerson 1915:56–47.) See also Pili-a-mo'o.

NOHO-ARI'I, king of Ra'iātea in the Tahitian legend of the creation of the breadfruit.* (Henry 1928:423–426.)

NOMA-MAKAI-TANGATA, a Tuamotuan god of the night world. (Stimson 1964:336.)

NONA, the wicked ogress in the Tuamotuan epic of Hiro (Hilo*) whose sweet scented oil Hiro had to obtain in order to marry the king's daughter, Tiaki-tau. (Stimson 1957:137–190.) In Tahiti, No-nā was a cannibalistic high chiefess of the district of Mahina (Northern Tahiti), the wife of chief Tahiti-To'erau who had forsaken her. No-nā's beautiful daughter Hina hid her lover (Mono'i-here) in a cave at Tahara'a, but No-nā found and devoured him. Hina fled from her mother to the protection of chief No'a-huruhuru who killed No-nā and married Hina. Their sons were Pû-a'a-ri'i-tahi and Hema,* father of the famous hero Tafa'i (Kaha'i*). (Henry 1928:552–555; Leverd 1912:1–12.)

NONIA, a village god in Samoa who cures illness. Prayers and sacrifices in the form of cockles are especially effective during the month of May. (Turner 1884:40–41.)

NUA, one of the two witches, who turned themselves into wild ducks and abducted Vahivero, the son of Kui and the father of Rata (Laka*) in the Tuamotuan epic. Nua and Merehau lived in a land called Hivaro-tahi. (Stimson 1937:96–147.)

NU'A-KEA, Hawaiian goddess of lactation and nursing mothers, lived on earth as the wife of Ke-olo-'ewa (a chief on Moloka'i). (Beckwith 1948:32, 207, 464.)

NUJKA'U, a Rotuman woman, and her sister, Nujmaga, ate a young girl by the name of Kau-'utufia. From her head grew a giant tree that reached up to the heavens. The two sisters climbed the tree in fear of the revenge of Kau'utufia's grandmother. In heaven, the two sisters played a trick on a pair of blind Siamese twins they found there, but eventually they cured the twins of their blindness and separated them. They lived happily ever after. (Churchward 1938:326–331.)

NUKU, the Māori god of the rainbow. (Tregear 1891:271.) See also **Koroti; Ue-nuku**. A Tuamotuan word for the vast expanse of space. (Stimson 1964:338.) See also **Wākea**.

NUKU-MAI-TORE, Māori elves* or fairies found by the great voyager Whiro (Hilo*) and his brother Tura.* These small creatures had short arms which they waved from their favorite resting places among the foliage and fruit of the *kiekie (Freycinetia banksii)*. Tura's wife was one of them. Their children were always born by cesarian section. (Tregear 1891:272; White 1887b:32.) See also **Ponaturi**.

NUKU-MAU-ATŪA, a Tuamotuan word that collectively refers to the gods as a group. (Stimson 1964:337–338.) See also **Nuku-mau-tangata**.

NUKU-MAU-TANGATA, a Tuamotuan word that collectively refers to the human race as a group as opposed to the gods or immortals (Nuhu-mau-atua). (Stimson 1964:337–338.)

NUKUMERA, son of the Māori god Rangi-pōtiki* (prop of heaven) and Papa* (earth mother), brother to the gods Tū (Kū*), Tangaroa (Kanaloa*), Rongo (Lono*), and Rongo-marae-roa.* (Shortland 1882:18; Tregear 1891:272.) See also **Heavens**.

NUKUPOURI, chief of the fairies in Māori legends. (Shortland 1882:50; Tregear 1891:272.) See also **Elves; Ponaturi**.

NUKUROA, a heavenly being once visited by the Māori god Tāne (Kāne*). (Tregear 1891:272; White 1887a:135.)

NUKUTAIMEMEHA, name of Māui's* canoe in Māori legends. (Tregear 1891:272; White 1887b:70.)

NUKU-TE-RĀ-TAI, one of the Tuamotuan demons of the underworld* (pō*), god of the ocean. (Stimson 1964:338.) See also **Nuku-te-rā-uta**.

NUKU-TE-RĀ-UTA, one of the Tuamotuan demons of the underworld* (pō*), god of the ocean. (Stimson 1964:338.) See also **Nuku-te-rā-tahi**.

NUKUTERE, name of the Māori canoe used by Whiro

(Hilo*) in his voyage to New Zealand. It supposedly arrived eight months before the great flood (deluge*). (Tregear 1891: 21, 272.) See also **Canoes, Maori Migration**.

NU'U, an ancient Hawaiian priest who survived the great deluge* by making appropriate sacrifices to the gods. (Beckwith 1948:314–315; Fornander 1920: 269–270, 335; Fornander 1878: 91–95.)

NU'UMEALANI, Hawaiian goddess of the clouds. (Beckwith 1948:80; Emerson 1892:15.) Also the name of the sacred land of the Hawaiian gods, located above Kū'ai-he-lani, home of the goddess Haumea.* (Beckwith 1948:79–80, 279.)

–O–

'OĀ, the Tahitian mud god who can assume the appearance of a man. (Henry 1928:84, 548.)

'OĀ-HĪ-VARI, the Tahitian god of quagmire also known as Hae-i-te-'oa* and Hae-nō-vaiurua.* Mottled and resembling a man, he is the great spirit that guards the *marae** (temple) Tahu-'e'a on the island of Ra'iātea. His earthly manifestation is in the form of a black-and-white speckled rail or mud hen (*'oā*). (Henry 1928:376, 385, 452, 454.)

ŌĀTEA, Tuamotuan name for the god Ātea (Wākea*). (Stimson 1964:341.)

OEOE, the Marquesan god of the pandanus tree and its fruit. (Christian 1895:190.)

OHOPĀ, a Māori water monster who once inhabited the Hokianga River in New Zealand, the son of Āraiteuru.* (Tregear 1891:289.)

OHOTARETARE, a Māori god who descended to earth and married a mortal woman Kurae-moana. (Tregear 1891:280; White 1887d:25.)

'OHU-TŪ-MOUA, Tahitian goddess responsible for the greening of the earth, daughter of Tefatu* and Fa'ahotu.* (Henry 1928:373.)

OI'O, see **Huaka'i-pō.**

OKEHU, the celestial sphere from which the Māori god Tāne (Kāne*) obtained stars and other ornaments to decorate Rangi,* his sky father. (Wohlers 1875:3; Tregear 1891:290.)

OKOMĀKURA, a Tuamotuan word used to designate the procreative powers of the gods. (Stimson 1964:344.) See also **Toura.**

OLA, chief of the Menehune,* the original inhabitants of the Hawaiian Islands. Born on the island of Kaua'i to chief Kūalu-nui-paukū-moku-moku from Waimea and his wife Kahapu-ola, he supervised the construction of numerous projects: building the *heiau* (temple) at Hauola, planting fields of taro, constructing huge ovens near Waimea, laying a road of sticks through the swamps, to mention only a few tremendous feats ascribed to these little people. (Beckwith 1948:325–331; Thrum 1923:94–97; Thrum 1907110–111; Westervelt 1915b: 44–46.)

'OLOPANA, a Hawaiian chief, uncle (and stepfather) to the demigod Kama-pua'a* (pig man). When Kama-pua'a stole 'Olopana's chickens, 'Olopana attempted to slay him, but he was always rescued through the efforts of his grandmother. Once captured, Kama-pua'a broke out of his bindings and killed 'Olopana and all of his men. (Beckwith 1948:202–204; Fornander 1880:43–44, 1917: 314–327.)

'Olopana, a high chief on the island of O'ahu, figures in the migration story from Kahiki (Tahiti ?) to Hawai'i. His grandfather Māweke came with his three sons (eleventh or twelfth century), Muli-'ele-ali'i (father of 'Olopana), Keaunui, and Kalehenui, and became the ruling chiefs of the island. The famous Mo'i-keha* was 'Olopana's brother. (Beckwith 1948: 352–353; Fornander 1878:166, 197–198, 2:47–59; Fornander 1916:18–21.)

'OLU-WALE-I-MALO, one of Pele's* sons in the Hawaiian legend of Hi'iaka* and Pele who aided Hi'iaka in her journey to Kaua'i to obtain chief Lohi'au for Pele. (Emerson 1915: 41–46.) See also **Kilioe-i-ka-pua.**

ONE-KURA, wife of the first man, Tiki,* according to Tuamotuan legends. She lived with her father, Mati, in the land called Havaiki-te-araro. Tiki's mother, One-rua, came to Havaiki-te-araro and brought One-kura back as Tiki's bride. Having been married for some and time and being without child, she called upon the gods, and, as a result, she was blessed with the birth of a daughter, the famous Hina.* (Stimson 1937: 3–6.)

ONE-RUA, demigoddess and mother of the famous hero Tiki* in Tuamotuan legend. She and her husband, Ahu-roa, lived in the land of Havaiki-nui-a. (Stimson 1937:3–6.) See also One-kura.

ONO, a Marquesan god, prematurely born in the form of an egg to a mortal couple, Kua-iana-nei and his wife, Tana-oa-kau-hue. He was saved and nurtured on air by his grandfathers, Ii-po and Ii-ao, to maturity. Many fabulous tales are told of Ono. He killed his brothers for not acknowledging the proper taboos regarding sacrifices for the gods, and then he brought them back to life. His fishing exploits astonished everyone. He took to wife Peau-Tona, the daughter of chief Tū-Fiti, and then in anger killed his brother-in-law. In a rage, he hit a mountain and caused an earth slide to overwhelm a group of entertainers (hoki) which had vexed him. He fell large trees single handedly. Soon, his enemies gained the upper hand and beheaded him, but he was brought back to life through his sister's efforts.

Not long after that, he stretched himself to the skies and then became small again. He blew himself to pieces and then resurrected himself. He visited the island of Mohotani where he cunningly gained sovereignty from chief Mata-oa, and there he dwelt ever after. (Handy 1930:104–107.)

Ono was also an ancient hero and voyager in Mangaian legends. He alone could fell the famous iron wood tree protected by the demon Vaotere, and from his chips sprang all the iron wood trees on the island. (Gill 1876:77–87.) See also Ho-no'ura.

'Ō'ŌIA, or 'Ō'Ō'A, a learned artisan, nicknamed swiftness, created for the Tahitian god Tāne (Kāne*). (Henry 1928:370.)

OPAPAKO, one of the four ancient Easter Island gods brought to the island by the voyager Hotu-Matua. (Alpers 1970:237–241; Métraux 1940:58–69.) See also Kuaha; Kuihi; Tongau.

'ŌPELU-NUI-KAU-HA'ALILO, a Hawaiian god of thieves and medical practitioners, son of the volcano goddess Pele* by Kama-pua'a* (pig man). (Beckwith 1948:206–207).

ORAMATUA, a personal god of the ruling Pomare family of Tahiti, a drawing of which appears on the frontispiece of the book South Sea Islander in 1820. (South Sea Islander, frontispiece.)

OREOOREO, the Easter Island god represented in human form with conventionalized big eyes, painted on a slab at Orongo. (Métraux 1940:316.)

'ŌRERORERO, the Tahitian god of consultation (Henry 1928: 357); also a daughter of the sun god Ra'a and recognized as one of the guardians of the world. The other guardians are 'Aiāru, Fa'aipu, Fa'aīpō, Nihoniho-tetei, Tahu'a, and Tamaumau-'ōrere. (Henry 1928:416.)

ORI, a Tuamotuan god. (Stimson 1964:347.)

ORIRĀ, a Māori water monster, son of Āraiteuru.* (Tregear 1891:294.)

'ORO (KORO), the most powerful god in the Tahitian pantheon, was born to the supreme god Ta'aroa (Kanaloa*) and Hina-tū-a-uta (Hina*) at Opoa on the island of Ra'iātea where Tapu-tapu-ātea, the most sacred *marae** (temple) in all of Polynesia, was constructed. Originally, this *marae* had been dedicated to the creator god Ta'aroa, but sometime later, perhaps in the thirteenth or fourteenth century, this unique position was usurped by his powerful son 'Oro, and Ta'aroa thus slipped into the background. At first, 'Oro was the god of peace, but his new dominant position in the pantheon made him the supreme god of war, and his three daughters (To'i-mata, 'Ai-tūpuai, and Mahu-fatu-rau) were always known to accompany him into battle. From Ra'iātea, the 'Oro cult spread throughout the Pacific. It was even claimed that distant islands such as New Zealand, Rotuma, and others sent sacrifices to 'Oro at Taputapu-ātea.

One day in anger, 'Oro pushed his wife Tū-fe'ufe'u-mai-i-te-ra'i to earth where she became a heap of sand. His daughters decided to go to earth to find him another wife. Finding the women on the islands of Tahiti, Hu'ahine, and Ra'iātea too plain for their father, the sisters made their way to Bora-Bora where they met the beautiful Princess Vai-rau-mati. A marriage pact was signed, and 'Oro descended to meet his new bride on a rainbow. He was embarrassed with all the gifts presented to him by his new bride, and, as a result, he turned his two sons, 'Uru-te-tefa and 'Oro-te-tefa, into sacred pigs which were never to be killed. He presented them to his father-in-law, king Tamatoa I, and they became the patron gods of the Arioi Society*. 'Oro's earthly image, constructed by Tahitian, was a shapeless, two or three foot long, sennit-covered club embellished with red and yellow feathers. It was publicly exhibited only on very sacred occasions. (Henry 1928:123–126, 230–234, 374–375).

In other Polynesian mythologies, 'Oro (Koro) plays only a minor role. In New Zealand, Koro is the daughter of the goddess Hina and Tinirau*, the god of fishes. Koro sometimes has been identified with the Hawaiian god Lono*, but the hypothesis lacks sufficient evidence to prove the connection. (Beckwith 1948:37–41). See also **Lono; Sacrifices, Human.**

OROI, a cannibalistic god of Rotuma who devours human spirits. (Russell 1942:249.) Oroi was also one of the first immigrants to Easter Island who set sail from the island of Maraerenga. Because of a conflict with his rival Hotu-Matua,* Oroi hid in Hotu-Matua's canoe. Having landed, he found shelter in the caves near the beach and as time passed, Oroi began the old conflict again by slaying Hotu-Matua's five sons. Oroi was finally caught and slain. (Alpers 1970:237–241; Routledge 1917:277–289.)

'OROI-TA, the name of the Rotuman "unseen region" (underworld*) where mortal spirits (*'atua*) go upon death. They remain there for four days, and then on the fifth, they return to earth to see if their bodies are actually dead. They then return to the unseen world for good. (Churchward 1938:472.)

'ORO-I-TE-MARO-TEA, 'Oro-of-the-yellow-girdle, the earthly manifestation of the Tahitian god 'Oro, usually in the form of a light-yellow thrush. (Henry 1928:384.)

'ORO-I-TE-MARO-'URA, 'Oro-of-the-red-girdle, the earthly manifestation of the Tahitian god 'Oro, usually in the form of a red and green *a'a* bird. (Henry 1928:385.)

'ORO-'ORO-I-PU'A, grandson of the Tahitian goddess Hina* in the Tafa'i (Kaha'i*) legend, killed in Havai'i when attempting to uproot a tree possessed by a demon. (Henry 1928:555, 562.)

'ORO-PA'A, lord of the ocean in the Tahitian creation chant, a great spirit ever pervading the depths who has a roaring voice. He lies with his head upwards; the white foaming breakers are his jaws; he swallows everyone despite their station in life. The whale and the man-of-war-bird (the *'ōtaha*) are his messengers. (Henry 1928:165, 344, 358, 388, 494.) See also **'Olopana.**

'ORO-PUA'A-MAHUI, when a pig becomes possessed in Tahitian legends, he is known as *'Oro-pua'a-mahui*, 'Oro-the-pig-revealing-secrets. When such an event occurs, the pig can devour a human. (Henry 1928:383.)

'ORO-RAHI-TO'O-TOA, when priests from Ra'iātea built the first *marae** (temple) to their god 'Oro* at Tautira, south Tahiti, they held a ceremony during which time their great god 'Oro entered the idol they had constructed. The idol was then called 'Oro-rahi-to'o-toa, great-'Oro-of-the-toa-image. (Henry 1928:130.)

'ORO-TAUA, Tahitian war god, son of the creator Ta'aroa (Kanaloa*). (Henry 1928:375, 376.)

'ORO-TE-TEFA, son of the Tahitian god 'Oro* and the beautiful Bora-Bora maiden Vai-rau-mati. 'Oro-te-tefa and his brother 'Uru-te-tefa (Hoa-tapu*) were turned into sacred pigs and worshipped by the Ar-ioi Society* in the islands. They are both called 'Oro-i-te-pua'a-mahui. (Henry 1928:232, 238.)

OROVARU, Tuamotuan name for the underworld,* the world of night or darkness. (Stimson 1964:349.)

'ORO-VEHI-'URA, a Tahitian god associated with the red feathered duck (*mo'orā'ura*) which lived on the lake at the top of mount 'Orohena, the tallest summit on Tahiti. (Henry 1928:384.)

OTFITI, the word for earth on Rotuma. In the creation, Lagi (heaven) and Otfiti were joined together until Tagaroa (Kana-loa*), son of Lagatea (from heaven) and Papatea (from earth) pushed them apart. (Gardiner 1898:466–467.)

OVIRI-MO'E-AIHERE, Tahitian god of mourning. (Henry 1928:293, 378.)

OUENUKU, a god of the Chatham Islands. (Shand 1894: 90.)

–P–

PA'AO, an ancient priest from Tahiti who migrated to Puna, Hawai'i, and brought with him specific religious rituals that he introduced into Hawaiian culture: human sacrifice in the *heiau* (temples), the red feathered girdle as a symbol of nobility, the prostrating tapu, the feathered war god Kā'ili,* image worship, and sacred plants. Pa'ao also returned to Tahiti to bring back a royal chieftain of pure blood to establish a ruling family in Hawai'i. (Beckwith 1948:370–375; Emerson 1893:5–13; Fornander 1917: 656; *Hawaiian Almanac and Annual* 1932:109; Malo 1903:25–26.)

PA'A-O-WALI-NU'U, a Hawaiian goddess. (Henry 1928: 571.)

PAE, a benevolent spirit god who lives in Nu'uanu Valley, O'ahu, Hawai'i. (Beckwith 1948:137; Green 1928:48–49, 1936:178.)

PAEA, daughter and the last born child of the Māori god Rangi* (sky father). (Shortland 1882:19; Tregear 1891:298.) See also **Paia**.

PAE-ATUNA, divine or sacred stones placed in front of a chief's house on the island of Futuna, dedicated to the supreme god Fakavelikele. (Burrows 1936.)

PAEPAE-A-TARI-VERA, benevolent Easter Island god who saved a famous warrior whose soul had been kidnapped by another spirit. (Métraux 1940: 317.)

PAERAU, synonym for the Māori underworld.* (Tregear 1891: 299.) See also **Reinga**.

PAE-TAHI, messenger of the Tahitian god Pūnua-moe-vai, a coastal land breeze. (Henry 1928:377, 393.)

PĀHAKA, Māori god who supervises the harvesting of crops, the son of Rongo-matāne.* (Tregear 1891:299; White 1887a: App.)

PAHI, a Marquesan god of the creation, son of Papa-Uka and Papa-Ao. (Christian 1895:188–189.)

PĀHIKO, son of the Māori god of forests, Tāne-mahuta;* tutelary god of the *kaka* parrot. (Tregear 1891:300; White 1885: 115; White 1887a: App.)

PĀHUA-NUI-'APĪ-TA'A-I-TE-RA'I, a great demon of the sky in Tahitian legend that resembles the great tridacna at the bottom of the ocean. (Henry 1928:470, 495.) See also **Pahūa-tūtahi**.

PAHŪA-TŪTAHI, Tuamotuan demon that resembles a giant tridacna. (Stimson 1964:356.) See also Pahua-nui-'apī-ta'a-i-te-ra'i.

PAHULU, Hawaiian patron goddess of sorcery possessed of great *mana** who came to Hawai'i and ruled Moloka'i and part of Maui from her home on Lāna'i. Her family of spirits on Lāna'i was killed off by the Moloka'i prophet Lani-kāula.* Some survived and made their way to the other islands. (Beckwith 1948:107–109, 430; Fornander 1917:428.) See also Lō-lupe.

PAI, ancient hero of the island of Tahiti, son of chief Rehia and his wife, Huauri. Once a canoe laden with food for the royal family in Tautira happened to stop at Rehia's home at Ata'aroa. While the entourage was there, Rehia traded feather cloaks and mats for the food, and then he and his neighbors prepared a great feast. Some of Rehia's neighbors in the interior of the island heard rumors that Rehia had stolen the food, and in revenge, they visited Rehia and Huauri and arranged to adopt their new baby daughter, Hina-ari'i, and take her to the king. In route, they bashed out her brains and then buried her in a nearby *marae** (temple).

When Rehia and Huauri heard what had happened, they were heart stricken. Some time later, Huauri became pregnant again, and Rehia decided to go hunting to obtain some of her favorite yams. While searching, two witches appeared and told him where he could find the most delectable yams. They directed him to the *marae* where the remains of his daughter had secretly been buried. Sure enough, he found the huge yam vines described by the witches. To get the tubers, however, he had to dig far down into the ground. While gathering the plants in the pit, the two old witches rushed in and buried him alive.

Some time later, Huauri prematurely delivered a stillborn son whom she called Pai after the memory of her husband. She carefully laid him in a basket near the *marae* and prayed to the gods to take pity on the boy and nourish him to life. The gods carried Pai down into the underworld* where he was adopted by the god Ta'aroa (Kanaloa*) himself. Some time later, the gods placed the young boy in a newly-constructed home in a fertile valley and warned him never to eat the sacred food of the gods he found growing there. Becoming exceedingly hungry, Pai disobeyed their warnings and ate a banana, nothing happened; then he began to eat everything in sight.

When the gods returned, they sent the disobedient Pai back to his own earthly home. Having been nourished on the gods' sacred food, he had become a handsome and Herculean young man. When the jealous warriors of king Ta'ihia heard that he had returned, they challenged him to a duel. Pai accepted and faced the nine challengers with bows and arrows he had especially made out of the limbs of the sturdy ironwood tree. Each one of the nine warriors unsuccessfully attempted to kill him. In the end, Pai won, and in compassion, he forgave them for their offenses. Afterwards, Pai sought out the two wicked witches in the mountains, killed them, and used their bones to tip his magical war spear.

Pai's greatest feat was the rescue of Mount Rofui (the peninsula between Cook's Bay and Opunohu Bay on the island of Mo'orea located slightly northwest of the island of Tahiti) from Hiro and his fellow thieves from Ra'iātea. The thieves had planned to tie slings around the mountain and to drag it off to Ra'iātea from whence it had originally come. Hearing what was happening, Pai threw his magic spear from Tahiti to Mo'orea and woke up the roosters who began to crow. Believing dawn was approaching, the thieves headed home with only a small portion of the mountain they had ensnared. They took the cone-shaped hill to Opoa, Ra'iātea, by the seaside where islanders claim it still stands with the same unique trees that grow only on Mount Rofui (Mo'orea). (Henry 1928:578–589.)

On Niutao, **Tuvalu**, legend states that two women, Pai and Vau, came from the Gilbert Islands with a basketful of earth. Wherever they sprinkled it, islands sprang up. Their principal god was Kulu.* (Turner 1884: 287–288.)

PĀIA, daughter of the Māori god Rangi* (sky father) and goddess Papa* (earth mother), wife to the god Tāne,* and the mother of the human race. (Tregear 1891:302; White 1887a: 39.) See also **Paea**.

PA'I-ALO, a Hawaiian goddess who slaps the chest as one does in the hula. (Emerson 1915:139.) See also **Pa'i-kua.**

PĀIAO, son of the Māori god Rangi* (sky father) and goddess Papa* (earth mother), the first of their children to attempt to separate them. (Tregear 1891: 302.)

PA'I-KAUHALE, a Hawaiian goddess who arouses the villagers. (Emerson 1915:139.)

PAIKEA, an ancient Māori chief regarded as a demigod, known originally in Hawaiki* as Kahutiaterangi. He and 140 other important chiefs were invited aboard the fatal canoe of Ruatapu that set sail to New

Zealand. The canoe sank, and Kahutiaterangi survived by being carried to New Zealand on the back of a *paikea* (sea monster or a whale). He became the progenitor of the Māori people. When he died, he was met in heaven by Tāwhaki (Kaha'i*), and Paikea's wife Hine-nui-o-te-kawa became Tāwhaki's wife.

Paikea is also the name of a sea monster (Ponaturi*) responsible for killing Hema,* father of the heroes Tāwhaki and Kariki. (Tregear 1891:303; White 1887a:22, 3:31, 40, 52, 59.)

PA'I-KUA, a Hawaiian goddess who slaps the back as one does in the hula. (Emerson 1915:139.) See also **Pa'i-alo**.

PAIMAHUTANGA, granddaughter of the Māori hero Rata (Laka*) through her father Poumatangatanga. She was abducted by chief Ue-nuku* who married her. (Tregear 1891:303; White 1887c:8.)

PA'IPA'I-A-HONU, known as the turtle boy in eastern Polynesian legends. He was born to a mortal couple, Po'ura and his wife Tumarae, and grew up in a stream of water. When he reached maturity, he revealed himself to his parents as their son, and each evening he would come and sleep at home, but in the day he would return to the stream of water.

One day, the king's daughter heard of the turtle boy and wished to take him home with her. Pa'ipa'i-a-honu refused unless she married him. At first she refused, but then upon the advice of her father, a huge marriage ceremony was conducted, the stream decorated, and a huge pavilion built for the occasion. After the ceremony, the dancing, and the festivities, the king's daughter went home. Pa'ipa'i-a-honu left the pool in the form of a man, went to his wife's door and knocked upon it. She had never seen a more handsome figure. He spent the night, and the next morning returned to his pool as before.

After some time, he was finally persuaded to stay out of his shell and to remain with his human family. The king proclaimed the young man king over them all, and from this marriage descended the royal family. (Stimson 1957:124–130.)

PAKA, son of the Māori chief Hotunui of the *Tainui* canoe and his second wife, the sister of Te Whatu.* Paka married the eldest daughter of Te Whatu and had a celebrated daughter called Kāhu-rere-moa. Paka's brother-in-law was Maru-tū-ahu.* (Tregear 1891:304.)

PĀKA'A, son of an ancient chief on Kaua'i who entrusted him with the secrets of controlling the winds. When banished to Moloka'i by his enemies, he taught his son Kū-a-pāka'a his secrets, and Kū-a-pāka'a used the powers to avenge his father. (Beckwith 1948:86–87; Fornander 1917: 72–135; Rice 1923:69–89.)

PAKAUNEKU, a god from Nui, Tuvalu, whose right eye was used to form the sun. (Turner 1884:300.) See also **Aulialia.**

PAKAWAI, Māori name for the magical canoe of Rata (Laka*). (Tregear 1891:305.)

PAKIRAHO-NUI, Tuamotuan demons who line the path to the underworld,* Havaiki-tumu, to hinder the souls of the dead with temptations of carnal pleasure. (Stimson 1964:360.)

PAKOTI, ancestress as well as wife to the Māori god Tāne (Kāne*). He left her because she only brought forth flax. (Shortland 1882:21; Tregear 1891:308.)

PĀLĀMOA, a Hawaiian god of fowls whose grand child Lepe-a-moa* was born in the shape of an egg. (Beckwith 1948:120; *AA* 28 (1926): 187–190; Westervelt 1915b:204.)

PALAPU, a Samoan woman who once lived between Loto-faga and Falefā, 'Upolu, Samoa. One day she happened upon some demons of the forest dancing, and she joined them. When they touched her, she fled into a stone for protection. The demons attempted to scratch through the stone, but without success. (The stone still stands with numerous cracks in it.) After this episode, Palapu then fled to Falelatai where she herself turned into a stone. (Krämer 1902:286–287.)

PALILA, a Hawaiian demigod, born as a cord, thrown away, and then rescued by his grandmother Hina.* When grown he saved his father from his enemies by felling a whole forest of trees in one swoop, and his club formed a huge hole in the ground at Waihohonu, Kaua'i. He vaulted over to O'ahu using his club and killed the giant Olomana (now a mountain peak on O'ahu). Traveling on to Hilo, Hawai'i, he aided chief Kulukulua and then became the ruling chief upon his death. (Beckwith 1948:414–415; Fornander 1917:136–153, 372–375.)

PĀ-LIULI, the Hawaiian counterpart of paradise, the earthly home of the gods where the first two human beings were made and where they first dwelt, sometimes pictured as floating above the clouds or resting upon the earth at the will of its keeper, ever fruitful where sugar cane and bananas grow until they fall over, where the hogs grow until their tusks are long, where the chickens and dogs grow until delicate and savory. (Beckwith 1948:72–73; Fornander 1878:77–78.) See also **Fale-ula; Havaiki; Kāne-huna-moku; Tanranga-i-hau-ola.**

PĀMANO, a Hawaiian from island of Maui, proficient in the art of the hula and chanting, who was killed by his jealous friends because of his love for the beautiful Keaka. Pāmano's sisters found his spirit and restored him to life. At a dance, he revealed himself to Keaka through chants that are only known to the two of them. His enemies were slain, and he and Keaka were married. (Beckwith 1932:12; Beckwith 1948:153; Fornander 1917:302–313.) See also **Mehara.**

PANA-'EWA, a Hawaiian demon monster slain by the goddess Hi'iaka and her forces in her trip to Kaua'i to obtain chief Lohi'au for the goddess Pele.* (Emerson 1915:30–46.)

PANAKOTEAO, name of a constellation affixed to the heavens (Rangi*) by the Māori god Tāne (Kāne*). (Tregear 1891:310; Wohlers 1875:33.)

PĀNEKENEKE, name given to the dwarf aborigines of New Zealand by the arriving Polynesians. (Tregear 1891:311.) See also **Elves and Fairies; Hiti; Turehu; Upokotoea.**

PANGATORU, one of the Māori canoes that legends say brought the first Polynesians to New Zealand, commanded by chief Rakewānangaora. It was forced to return to Hawaiki* because of attacks by aborigines. (Tregear 1891:21; White 1887b:181.)

PANI, Māori god or goddess of the *kumara* (sweet potato), one of the staple foods of the Polynesians. Māoris offer the first fruits of the crop to Pani. (Tregear 1891:311; White 1887a: App.; White 1885:115; White 1887c:114.) See also **Rongo-ma-tāne.**

PĀ'OA, best friend to the Hawaiian chief Lohi'au* in the story of Pele* and Hi'iaka.* When Pā'oa learned of Lohi-'au's death, he vowed vengeance on Pele. Once he found the goddess, however, he became her lover for three days until Pele gave him to her bereaved sister, Hi'iaka. Once Hi'iaka and Pā'oa returned to Kaua'i, Lohi'au returned from the spirit world, restored his body, and claimed Hi'iaka. In shame, Pā'oa then cast himself into the sea. Pele named her famous digging stick *pā'oa* in his honor. (Beckwith 1948:177, 184–185; Emerson 1915:8–9; Fornander 1920:343–344; Westervelt 1916: 72–138.)

PAOO, a Marquesan god who once captured the spirit of the mortal woman Taa-pō and took it to the underworld.* (Handy

1930:81–85.) See also **Te-haa-nau.**

PAORO, echo and the sun's warmth were molded together by the hands of Ārohirohi* (mirage) to form Kau-ata-ata,* the first Māori woman. (Tregear 1891:313; White 1887a:151)

PAORU, a Māori reptile god. (Tregear 1891:313; White 1887a: App.) See also **Mo'o; Moko-moko.**

PAOWA, a Māori chief who killed the great sorceress Ru-ahine-kai-piha* by throwing hot stones down her throat. (Tregear 1891:313; White 1887b: 55)

PAPA, earth mother, wife of the Māori god Rangi* (sky father) with whom she lay embraced until their children, the powerful gods Rongo, Tū, and Tangaroa, rent them apart. Papa, as the lowest earthly world, consisted of ten division from the earth's surface down into the inner darkness of death and the *pō*.* The first four are ruled by Hine-nui-te-pō,* the next three by Rohe,* and the lowest three by Miru (Milu*). (Grey 1970:1, 2, 3, 7, 11; Tregear 1891:315; White 1887a:211.)

In **Hawai'i,** Papa appears on the chart of the chiefly Ulu and Nana-Ulu genealogies beginning with Wākea and Papa. When Wākea committed adultery with Hina,* Papa went to live with Lua and gave birth to the island of O'ahu. Frequently Papa is identified with the goddess Haumea,* as the mother of all the Hawaiian people. (Beckwith 1948:293–306; Fornander 1878:161, 171, 172, 185–188, 205.) See also **Creation; Heavens; Papa-raharaha.**

A story from **Samoa,** tells of Papa, flat rock, (daughter of a woman named Fanga) who was born without a vagina. Her husband Olomataua devised a plan to rectify the error. He took a shark's tooth and carved her private parts upon the stone after which she became pregnant and bore a son, Ulufanu-ase'ese'e. (See the entry Saveasi'uleo for a similar story.) Ulufanuase'ese'e took to wife Sinalalofutu and gave birth to twins, Taemā* and Tilafaigā,* who were responsible for the introduction of tattooing* among the Samoans and who eventually were turned into goddesses. Taemā (or Tilafaigā) married Saveasi'uleo, god of the underworld,* and became the mother of Nafanua,* the Samoan war goddess. (Abercromby 1891:455–463; Krämer 1902:45.) See also **Heavens.**

PAPAARIARI, Māori name of the axe given to the hero Rata (Laka*) by Ngahue* in Hawaiki.* (Tregear 1891:316; White 1887a:73.)

PAPA-IEA, the Marquesan god who presides over feasts and kava drinking. (Christian 1895: 190.)

PAPANUKU, Tuamotuan name for the earth. (Stimson 1964: 366.)

PAPA-RAHARAHA, stratum rock, the mother of all living, and the mother of all islands in the Tahitian creation chant. The great god Ta'aroa (Kanaloa*) created husband Tumu-nui* (great foundation) as well as Papa-raharaha. To them was born a son, Te-fatu,* the lord of hosts and of the skies. (Henry 1928:338, 342, 356, 358, 374.) See also **Creation; Heavens; Papa**.

PAPA-RA'I, sky rock, the Tahitian god of harvest. (Henry 1928:376.) See also **Papa**.

PAPAROA, Tuamotuan name for the earth. (Stimson 1964: 367.)

PAPAROA-I-TE-ITANGA, a Cook Island goddess in the creation chant, the wife of Ātea (Wākea*). They were the parents of Te Tumu, foundation rock, who married Paparoa-i-te-opunga (Paparoa-at-the-sunset). (Gill 1911:136.) See also **Uke**.

PAPATEA, the earth goddess in Rotuman legends and wife to the heavenly god, Lagatea.* Their son, Tagaroa (Kanaloa*) forced the heavens and earth apart in the creation. (Gardiner 1898:466-467.)

PAPA-TU'OI, consort to the goddess Ātea (Wakea*) in the Tahitian creation chant; both were parents of the legendary god Tāne (Kāne*). (Henry 1928:356, 364.)

PAPE-HAU, one of the Tahitian gods who took pity on the mortal child Pai* and persuaded Ta'aroa (Kanaloa*) to give him a name and a loin cloth to cover his nudity. (Henry 1928:581.)

PAPERURUA, see **Pape-hau**.

PĀ-PŪLEHU, a companion traveler to the goddess Hi'iaka* in her trip to Kaua'i to fetch chief Lohi'au for the volcano goddess Pele.* Because she was not of divine origin and because she did not acknowledge the correct eating tabus, she was not given extraordinary powers accorded to the others. (Emerson 1915:27–29.)

PARATA, a Māori water monster who creates tides by swallowing and belching forth the sea (Grey 1855: 29, 74; White 1887b:28; Tregear 1891:320); also one of the Māori chiefs who built the famous *Arawa** canoe used in the Polynesian migration to New Zealand. (Grey 1970:107.)

PARA-WHENUA-MEA, son of the Māori god Tāne (Kāne*) and his wife Tū-pari-maunga, the Māori Noah. According to one legend, Para-whenua-mea and his friend Tupu-nui-a-uta unsuccessfully attempted to teach humans the story of the separation of Rangi* (sky father) and Papa* (earth mother). They built a raft, and through their incantations brought on the great deluge.* The raft floated for seven months until it landed on Hawaiki* where they offered sacrifices and prayers. The survivors became the progenitors of the human race. (White 1887a:163, 172–180.) Also the name of the wife of Paikea* (the Māori sea god). See also **Tuputupuwhenua.**

PARE, a high ranking Māori woman who killed herself because her amorous advances were rejected by Hutu,* a stranger of lower birth. He was seized by Pare's relatives and threatened with death. He persuaded them to allow him to live and to journey to the underworld* to recover her spirit. He was guided on his way by Hine-nui-te-pō,* goddess of the underworld, but when he reached Pare's spirit, it refused to go with him. Eventually he persuaded her to get on his back, and they then catapulted themselves back home where he performed the necessary rites to restore her to life, and then he married her. (Beckwith 1948:

148; White 1887b:163–167.) **Hiku-i-ka-nahele; Hutu; Kani-kani-a-'ula; Kena; Milimili.**

PAREKŌRITAWA, a daughter born to the great Māori goddess Hine-nui-te-pō* after she fled to the underworld.* Parekōritawa eventually married the great hero Tāwhaki (Kaha'i*) and went to live with him in the heavens where they had two children, Ue-nuku* (rainbow) and Whatiritiri (thunder). (Shortland 1882:23.) Another source identifies Tāwhaki's wife as Tongotongo.* (Grey 1970:52–61; Tregear 1891: 322.)

PARETAO, a fern which the Māori god Tāne (Kāne*) mixed with clay when he formed Tiki,* the first man. (Tregear 1891: 323; White 1887a:154.)

PAROROTEA, a Māori god of the air, son of Tū-āwhio-rangi, and father to Hau-tuia. (Shortland 1882:13; Tregear 1891:324.)

PASIKOLE, a Samoan who once lived in Tonga and was beloved by two goddesses, Sisi and Faingaa, because of his fair hair. According to the Tongan story, Pasikole loved his wife and not the two goddesses. He decided to get rid of the two by deceiving them. First he asked them to climb into two baskets that he planned to carry into the mountains, but he told them that they were to lie back and observe only the sky and the clouds until they arrived at their destination. Pasikole carried the baskets only a short way and then placed them between two trees.

For several months, the goddess observed the sky and the moving clouds until the baskets rotted and they fell to the ground. Pasikole then took them fishing and tricked them into diving into his net which he then weighed down with rocks. The two goddesses struggled for some time, and at length were only rescued through the efforts of the god Tangaloa (Kanaloa*). (Brown 1916:430–432; Gifford 1924:197–199.)

PĀTITO, an ancient Māori warrior whose spirit returned from the underworld* to challenge his son's expertise with the spear. The old man won, and as a result, humans never won over the consequences of death. Pātito's niece attempted to follow him to the underworld, but she was transformed into a rock when he turned around and glanced at her. (Tregear 1891:327; White 1885:105.)

PAU, a spirit in the Tuamotus who once was swallowed by a shark and cast up on a foreign land. A beautiful maiden became his mistress, and for a long time he lived with her family (another sister and a mother) until he became home-sick for his own lands. The girls offered the services of two whales, their brothers, over the objections of their mother who knew that Pau's relatives ate whales. Despite her objections, the whales were so enlisted and transported Pau back to his island.

Sure enough, when the eldest whale neared the shore, the inhabitants captured him and hacked him to pieces for food. Some of the food was thrown back into the sea where the younger brother gathered them up and restored him to life, but only half his original size. When the two whale brothers returned home, their family was distraught and planned revenge. The two sisters returned to Pau's island on the backs of their brothers where they found Pau and invited him to a rock-throwing contest. Pau's rocks failed to reach his opponent, but the young sister's rocks solidly reached Pau and knocked him dead. The sisters wrapped Pau's body in coconut fonds, and after a vengeful walk across the island cutting it into numerous islets, they finally returned home where they cooked and ate the remains of Pau. (Caillot 1914:69–92.) See also **Kae**.

PA'U, a Tahitian god who dwells in the heavens with the god Tāne (Kāne*). (Henry 1928:371.)

PAUIRIRĀIRA, one of the Māori canoes that legends say brought the first Polynesians to New Zealand, commanded by chief Rakataura. (Tregear 1891: 21; White 1887b:188.) See also **Canoes, Māori Migration.**

PĀ'ULA, a beautiful Hawaiian girl from the Ka-ū district of Hawai'i who was turned into stone because she was caught playing jack-stones with the lover of the goddess Pele.* The two can still be seen at the point called Ka-lae-o-kimo where Pele found them playing. (Beckwith 1948:191; Green 1936:55.)

PAUMAKUA, chief of ancient Hawai'i who became famous for his many ocean-going voyages. Chants mention his circumnavigation of all the islands outside of Hawai'i and how he returned from Kahiki (Tahiti ?) with three tall foreigners with light-colored skin who became priests on the island of O'ahu. It is said he also introduced the practice of circumcision among his people. (Beckwith 1948:328, 352, 378, 385; Fornander 1880: 24–26.)

PA'Ū-O-PALA'Ā, moist fern, a nurse and trusted messenger to the goddess Hi'iaka* in the legend of Hi'iaka and Pele,* who traveled with Hi'iaka to the island of Kaua'i to obtain chief Lohi'au* for Pele. (Emerson 1915:10–25.)

PAU-TERE-FENUA, a Tahitian god responsible for creating part of the land, especially charcoal. (Henry 1928:341.)

PĀ'ŪTU-ROA, a Tahitian god of mourning. (Henry 1928:293, 378.)

PAU-WALU, a Hawaiian shark-man, who once lived at Wailua, Maui. He warned men going fishing that some of they would be killed before they returned. Several Hawaiians (Akeake, Pakolea, and Ohia) captured him and threw him into their fire. See also **Kamaika'ahui; Ka-welo; Nanaue; Nenewe; Mano-niho-kahi.**

PAVA, a Samoan war god, the son of Faga and Fue, who settled at Falealili, 'Upolu, after being driven out of Manu'a by the god Tagaloaui (Kanaloa*). Warriors wear taro or banana leaves around their heads in his honor. His two sons were Telemū and Maifa'i and were responsible for the introduction of kava* into Samoa. (Krämer 1902:23, 287, 329, 371, 393, 405, 410–411; Turner 1884:42–43.) Another legend maintains that Pava was a mortal who stole the secret of kava making from the gods. After his death, he became the war god of the district of Falealili, 'Upolu. (Fraser 1892:96–140.) See also **Lefanoga; Nafanua; Tagaloaui.**

PAWA, an ancient Māori priest in Hawaiki* responsible for preserving oracles. When a servant of chief Ue-nuku* approached him, he was struck dead but was later brought back to life. (Tregear 1891:329; White 1887c:7.)

PĒAHA, Tuamotuan name of one of the regions in the sky (Rangi-pō*). (Stimson 1964: 376.)

PEAITENUKU, one of the many district gods of the Kaitu'u clan on Bellona Island, the son of the principal god Tehu'ainga-benga.* (Monberg 1966:67.)

PEAMASAHU, one of the many district gods of the Kaitu'u clan on Bellona Island, the son of the principal god Tehu'ainga-benga.* (Monberg 1966:67.)

PEHŪ, a Tuamotuan high priest, supervisor of all sacred customs, chants, and genealogies. (Stimson 1964:377.)

PEKA, name of the Tuamotuan chants dedicated to the gods Tāne (Kāne*) and Māui* and which include long lists of sacred marae * (temples). (Stimson 1964:377.) Also the name of the land through which Hina* traveled in search of a new lover after her affair with Tuna. She became the mistress to the demigod Māui,* but was then carried off by the Peka clan, and was raped by their leader, Peka.

Māui followed in the form of a bird and killed Peka while he was asleep. (Stimson 1934:28–33.)

PEKEHAUĀ, a Māori water monster who dwelt at Te Awa-hou and who was slain by Pī-taka and the men of Rotorua. (Tregear 1891:332.)

PEKEPEKE (BEKEBEKE), a Tongan god worshipped in the form of a flying fox by a minor chief in Ahau, west Tongatapu. (Collocott 1921:227.)

PELE (PERE), the volcano goddess, is scarcely known outside of Hawai'i. Reference to her as Pere in Tahitian myth is slight and may have come about after European contact (Henry 1928: 144, 359, 417). Traditionally, Pele, the Hawaiian goddess, was born to Haumea* and her husband Moemoe in the land south of Hawai'i called Kahiki (Tahiti ?). Her family consisted of eight sisters and five brothers.

The myth tells of the migration northward from Kahiki in her great canoe Honua-i'a-kea and of her effort to dig a pit with her pā'oa rod deep enough in the earth to house her family members who were traveling with her. Their arrival at the Hawaiian chain is marked by lightning and eruptions. Pele is forced to travel from island to island seeking a place to live. Each time as she digs deeply, the sea rushes in and drives her away. On O'ahu, for example, she digs Diamond Head, Koko Crater, and Makapu'u and then moves to Maui where she digs the famed Hale-a-ka-lā crater. She finally reaches the big island of Hawai'i where she establishes her home in the Kī-lau-ea crater on Mauna Loa.

One day while Pele and her retinue go on an excursion to the ocean, they catch sight of Hōpoe and Hā'ena, two friends of her sister Hi'iaka,* indulging in a dance. At its conclusion, Pele asks her sisters to perform in return. They all are unable to do so except the youngest, Hi'iaka, who decorates them all first with her favorite *lehua* blossoms. Hi'iaka performs what is considered the first hula. As a result, Hi'iaka becomes the supreme patroness of the hula, and all prayer chants (*mele pule*) for the hula are named after her or her sister Pele.

Shortly thereafter, Pele falls into a deep sleep, and her spirit travels to Kaua'i where she becomes enraptured with chief Lohi'au. Upon awakening, Pele proposes that one of her sisters returns to Kaua'i to accompany Lohi'au back to Hawai'i. None except Hi'iaka will accept the challenge. After receiving supernatural powers and instructions from Pele (she must return within forty days, and she must not touch or embrace Lohi'au), Hi'iaka leaves Hōpoe in the care of Pele, and then she sets out. The legend of Hi'iaka tells of the dangers and challenges the young sister encounters on her way to and from Kaua'i.

On their return trip, the faithful Hi'iaka and Lohi'au are delayed by spirits who oppose the proposed liaison between a goddess and a mere mortal. The delay has enraged Pele who believes her sister has betrayed her. She belches forth fire and lava in which Hōpoe and her *lehua* blossoms are killed. Meanwhile, Hi'iaka suspects the worst, and she and Lohi'au swear their love to each other. It is not until Hi'iaka returns home and learns of the death of her beloved Hōpoe on the very brink of Kī-lau-ea crater that she finally decides to deceive her sister. Hi'iaka and Lohi'au embrace amidst the fire and smoke Pele jealously sends forth on them. Lohi'au is consumed, but Hi'iaka's magical powers save her. Hi'iaka succeeds in rescuing Lohi'au's spirit and in restoring him to life, and they are reunited to each other.

There are many stories and legends about Pele's vengeance on those who offend her. More popularly, however, is the love story between Pele and Kamapua'a* (the pig man). Kamapua'a comes to woo Pele at Halema'uma'u crater disguised as a handsome mortal. She recognizes him, however, and refuses his advances by sending flames toward him. He retorts with deluges of water. Pele finally concedes, and the two divide the island of Hawai'i between them. Pele receives Puna, Ka-ū, and Kona (the volcanic, lava lands), and Kama-pua'a receives Kohala, Kamakua, and Hilo (the wet, windward districts). Pele eventually falls in love with him, however, and they have a son, 'Ōpelu-nui-kau-ha'alilo, who becomes an ancestor of the chiefs of Hawai'i. (Beckwith 1948:167–213; Emerson 1915; Henry 1928:576–597.)

PELE-'ULA, a Hawaiian prophetess on the island of O'ahu who competed for the possession of chief Lohi'au, lover to Hi'iaka* and husband-to-be to the volcano goddess Pele.* When Hi'iaka escorted Lohi'au from his home on Kaua'i to the Big Island for Pele, they stopped off at Honolulu where they visited Pele-'ula in Nu'u-anu valley. Hi'iaka and Pele-ula competed in a game of *kilu* for Lohi'au's favors. (*Kilu* is similar to spin-the-milk-bottle, but the rewards are a little more erotic.) After a night of playing *kilu*, of matching wits, and dance, Hi'iaka wins, and the two set off again for their destination where Pele waits for them on the Big Island of Hawai'i. (Beckwith 1948:176–182; Emerson 1915:170–185.)

PEPERU, an artisan for the Tahitian god Ta'ere* who

dwells in the center of the earth. (Henry 1928:374, 406.)

PERE, the Tahitian fire goddess, a counterpart to Pele* in Hawaiian legends. She travels through the bowels of the earth with numerous retinue, including deceased members of the Tahitian royal family. Pere's hair is light auburn resembling the fine, glossy threads of lava blown out of the volcanos by the wind. (Henry 1928:576–579.)

PERO, son of the Māori god Irawaru,* the god of dogs, and Ihiihi.* (Tregear 1891:334; White 1887a: App.)

PETIPETI, a Māori sea god, ancestor of Paikea* who killed Hema,* father of the heros Tāwhaki (Kaha'i*) and Kariki. (White 1887c:11; Tregear 1891:334.)

PĪ, Māori god of growing food plants. (Tregear 1891:334.)

PĪHANGA, daughter of the Māori hero Tāwhaki (Kaha'i*) and Hāpai. (Tregear 1891:335; White 1887a:114.)

PIHO, daughter of Hiro (Hilo*), the mighty warrior in Tuamotuan legend. (Stimson 1964:385.)

PI'I-KA-LALAU, a Hawaiian lizard goddess (mo'o) from Kaua'i who takes the form of a giant, pigmy, or lizard to fight its battles. (Beckwith 1948:127.)

PI'I-KEA, a Hawaiian god of roaches. (Emerson 1915:205.)

PI'I-LANI, an ancient chief who ruled on Maui, Hawai'i, and later parts of Moloka'i, Lāna'i, and Kaho'olawe, the father of Lono-pi'ilani, Kiha-pi'ilani, and Pi'ikea (wife to chief 'Umi*). (Beckwith 1948:385–387; Elbert 1959:154–159; Pukui 1971:396.)

PIKI, a Tongan god of the creation, son of Touiafutuna, twin brother to his sister, Kele, with whom he mated and gave birth to twins, Tau-fuli-fonua (the ancient one) and Havea-lolo-fonua (parents of the god Hikuleo*). (Reiter 1907:230–240.) See also **Creation.**

PIKIAWHEA, Māori name for the canoe of Māui.* (Tregear 1891:337.)

PIKIRAWEA, Māori name for the famous fishhook of Māui.* (Tregear 1891:337; White 1887b: 91.)

PIKOI-A-KA-'ALALĀ, a Hawaiian demigod, a rat-man, born on Kaua'i to 'Alalā (crow) and 'Ōpe'ape'a (bat). As a young boy he was pushed into the rapids by his playmates and was carried to Kou (Honolulu), O'ahu, where he was taken to his sisters' home. He competed in a rat-shooting contest with his bow and arrow and then in a riddle contest, both of which he won. He competed once more in ridding the island of some unwanted *'elepaio* birds (fly catchers) and became a wealthy man. They say he could stand on Kauiki (Maui) and shoot a rat lying asleep in Kohala across the channel. (Beckwith 1948: 425–427; Fornander 1916: 450–463; Green 69.)

PILI, a Samoan demigod or lizard who came to earth and became the progenitor of the ruling families of Samoa, called the Malietoa.* Variants in parentage appear in the numerous legends. According to one, he was the son of the god Tagaloa (Kanaloa*), came to earth in the form of an eel (lizard), and ravished Sinaleana (Hina*), daughter of the high chief. His four sons Tua, Ana, Saga, and Tolufalo (the last two were twins) became the ancestors of the ruling families of Samoa.

Another account has him the son of Loa and Sina of Fagaloa. His sister, also named Sina, was wed to the Tuifiti (king of Fiji) and took Pili along with her to her new country. Famine stalked the country, and the Tuifiti planned to devour Sina. Pili, however, warned her and miraculously provided her with the necessary food. His demon qualities made Sina throw him into the sea where he was rescued by his two brothers,

Fuialaiō and Maomao. Pili visited Fiji once more, provided food for the starving people, moved on to Aopio where he did the same for the people there. He married the daughter of the Tui A'ana, and they became the parents of the four sons mentioned above. After many years, the sons separated. Tua founded Atua, Ana went west and founded A'ana, Saga remained and founded Tuamasaga, and Tolufalo founded Savai'i. Not long after that, a disagreement broke out between them that resulted in what is known in Samoan history as the War of the Brothers, a rivalry that continued into historic times. (Bülow 1898:80–82; Fraser 1892:254–261; Krämer 1902:24, 26–27, 46, 63, 190, 140, 393, 438–443; Stübel 1896: 68; Turner 1884:44, 232–234.) See also **Fitiaumua.**

PILI-A-MO'O, one of two malevolent sorcerer gods who were toll keepers on a bridge near the town of Hilo, Hawai'i, and who were killed by the goddess Hi'iaka.* (Emerson 1915:56–47.) See also **Noho-a-mo'o.**

PĪMOE, a Hawaiian demigod in the form of a fish, snared by the hero Māui* in his attempt to fish up the islands of the sea. When the cord broke, Pīmoe slipped away. (Beckwith 1948: 228, 230; Pukui 1971:396.)

PINEKI, a nineteenth-century mortal deified and worshipped after his death by the inhabitants of Niue Island. His prowess supposedly came because he had two lungs and two hearts. (Loeb 1926:165–166.)

PINGAO, a god worshipped by the Ngāti-rū tribe in New Zealand. (Stimson 1964:384.)

PIPI, the first mortal to settle the island of Fakaofu, Tokelau Islands, with his wife Hekei, although other traditions give the names of Te Ilo and his two sons, Kava and Singano, or the couple Kava and Pi'o who came from Samoa. (Macgregor 1937: 17–19.)

PIPIRAU, Māori word for part of the underworld* (*pō*). (Tregear 1891:339.)

PIPITA, a Tuamotuan word used to designate the spirit or ghost of a person recently deceased. (Stimson 1964:388.)

PĪTAKA, an ancient Māori hero celebrated for slaying water monsters, especially Pekehauā.* (Tregear 1891:341; Grey 1855: 151.)

PITARAHAU, a Tuamotuan ghost or spirit of a deceased mortal that returns to earth in the form of a skeleton and that relives the past with singing, dancing, and playing the nose flute. (Stimson 1964:392.)

PITI-'IRI, in one Tahitian legend of the origin of the coconut tree, Piti-'iri was the father whose three children (two sons, Pā-rapu, Taerau-roa, and a daughter Hā-muri) died from famine. From the graves of the three children grew the beginnings of all the various types of coconut trees. (Henry 1928:422.) See also **Coconut, origin of**.

PŌ, the underworld,* the world of spirits, the world of night, as well as the world of gods in Polynesian mythology; antithesis of *Ao*,* the world of light and humans, but not to be identified as the Christian hell or the classical Hades. *Pō* is a region to which the spirits of the dead pass on as a matter of course. (Buck 1934:200–204.) See also **Creation; Heavens; Kore; Milu**.

PŌHĀ-KŪ, grandfather to the Hawaiian volcano goddess Pele,* a rock originally formed by the great demigod Māui* supposedly located on the island of O'ahu near Ka'ena point. (Emerson 1915:3–4, 105)

POHU, an ancient Marquesan voyager from Hiva Oa, the youngest of thirteen children all of whom had neither arms or legs except Pohu. Pohu, however, did not have *mana*,* life-giving power. Pohu's brothers and sisters accompanied him on his many voyages and providing the needed power to attain his goals. He won numerous contests, including the slaying of a monstrous caterpillar and the capturing of a wife (Hua-nai-vaa) for him. The original story is fragmented and incomplete. (Handy 1930:115–117.)

POHŪ-HŪIA, a beautiful young maiden of Maunga-whau, New Zealand, who eloped with a young chief, Te Ponga, from the rival tribe of Āwhitu. Eventually through his courage and constancy, Ponga won over their relatives to their side. (White 1887d:116, 140; Grey 1970:232–238.)

POKI, a dog-like creature who guards certain areas around Honolulu, Hawai'i, frequently appearing in the form of a cloud hovering over Moana-lua valley and accompanied by the wailing of a dog. (Beckwith 1948:21, 346; Westervelt 1915a:1–13.)

POKI-RUNA, sister to Rī whom the Tuamotuan hero Māui* turned into a dog. Poki-runa lamented and returned home where she told Rī's comrade, Togi-o, what had happened. Togi-o set out to avenge his friend, but Māui also turned him into a dog, but not before Togi-o seduced Māui's mistress Hina.* (Stimson 1934:37–46.)

POKOHARUA-TE-PŌ, first wife to Rangi* (the Māori sky

father), sister to the creator god Tangaroa (Kanaloa*), mother of Tāwhiri-matea (lord of tempest), and daughter of Temoreta. (Tregear 1891:349; White 1887a:17, 24.)

POLI-'AHU, the beautiful Hawaiian goddess of the snow-covered mountain Mauna Kea on Hawai'i, a rival to the volcano goddess Pele* on mount Mauna Loa on the south side of the island who pours her fiery lava over the landscape. Once she unsuccessfully contended against the beautiful maiden Hina-i-ka-malama for the love of 'Ai-wohi-kupua.* In anger, she enveloped the lovers in alternate waves of heat and cold until they were forced to separate, and then she retired to her home on Hawai'i. (Beckwith 1948:221–223.)

POLU, grandson of the god Tagaloa-lagi (Kanaloa*) through his daughter Timu-ateatea who married a Samoan chief. When Polu was old enough, he visited his grandfather in the heavens who asked him the island's name from which he came. Polu could not answer, for the island was not named. Thereupon,Tagaloalagi named the island 'U-polu, the-crowded-Polu. (Krämer 1902: 147; Turner 230–231.)

POLU-LEULIGANA, a young Samoan chief responsible for killing Maniloa,* the dreaded cannibal god. (Turner 1884:238–240.)

PONATURI, wicked goblins in the Māori stories of Tāwhaki (Kaha'i*) and Rata (Laka*). Tāwhaki and his brother Karihi set out to avenge the murder of their father and the capture of their mother by the Ponaturi. They learn that the goblins are vulnerable to daylight, and thus they seal all the holes in their sleeping place. The next morning, the Ponaturi oversleep, and when they open the doors, the bright rays of the sun pour in, and the Ponaturi perish. (Grey 1970:47–51.)

Tāwhaki's grandson Rata also encountered the Ponaturi. In avenging the murder of this father, Wahieroa (Wahieloa*), Rata came upon the Ponaturi who were offering prayers to their gods by using Wahieroa's bones. Rata first listened carefully and memorized the incantation (the *Tikikura*) and then sprang forth, killed the priests, and seized his father's bones. The Ponaturi chased him back to his own fortress where Rata's men met them in battle. Rata used the magical spell to restore his slain men, and together they killed the thousand Ponaturi who had rushed after them. His father's death was thus avenged. (Grey 1970:88–90; Tregear 1891:350.) See also **Elves and Fairies**.

PONGA, the Māori god of hard tree ferns, the son of Haumia-tiketike* (god of food growing). (Tregear 1891:351; White 1887a: App.)

PŌ-NUI-A-HINE, a Māori maiden turned into a grasshopper and then into a rock in the ocean because she had not received the protection against the incantations of her priestly father, Kai-awa. (White 1887b: 193.)

PŌPŌ-'ALAEA, a high chiefess on Maui, Hawai'i, whose husband, Ka'ahe'a (Make'a), became jealous and killed her in the cave called Wai-ana-panapā. It is said that on certain days of the month, the pool from the cave runs red as a sign of her innocence. (Beckwith 1948:381.)

PORAPORA, a Māori god who assisted Tāne (Kāne*) in decorating his father, Rangi* (sky). (Tregear 1891:354.)

PORAPORA-I-RAU-'ATA, first-born-of-varied-laughter, a Tahitian god who dwells with Tāne (Kāne*) in the heavens. (Henry 1928:371.)

PORO-A-TAI, proclaimer-sea-ward, a Tahitian god who dwells with Tāne (Kāne*) in the heavens. (Henry 1928:371.)

PORO-ATUA, proclaimer-in-land, a Tahitian god who dwells with Tāne (Kāne*) in the heavens. (Henry 1928:371.)

PŌRUA, a Māori chief from Hawaiki* who commanded the ill-fated *Ririno* canoe in the migration to New Zealand. Pōrua and crew accompanied the *Aotea** canoe until the *Ririno* hit the reef of Taputapuātea and sank. (Grey 1855: 134; Tregear 1891:357.) See also **Canoes, Māori Migration.**

PŌTAKA-TĀWHITI, a dog once owned in Hawaiki* by the ancient Māori chief Haumai-Tāwhiti, but killed and eaten by chiefs Ue-nuku* and Toi-te-Huatahi. The dispute over the dog's death lead to the war in Hawaiki and the migration of the first Polynesians to New Zealand. (Grey 1970:99–100; Tregear 1891:357.)

PŌ-TANGOTANGO, a Māori god of night and the underworld.* (Tregear 1891:357.) See also **Kore.**

PŌTI'I-TĀ-RIRE, the Tahitian goddess of sorcery. (Henry 1928:379.)

PŌTIKI, father of the twin stars in the heavens (Gemini ?) by his wife Tarakorekore according to Mangaian legends. (Gill 1876: 40–43.)

PŌTIKI-ROROA, a young Māori boy in Hawaiki* who was slain by high priest Ue-nuku.* Pōtiki-roroa's relative Turi* avenged his death by slaying the son of Ue-nuku, but in return he had to flee Hawaiki. He lead the first migration of the Polynesians to New Zealand aboard the *Aotea* canoe (Grey 1970:158–159; Tregear 1891:358.)

PO-TIRI-AO, a spiritual messenger of the Tuamotuan god Kiho.* (Stimson 1964:403.)

POTORŪ, a Māori chief who captained the fatal *Te Ririno* canoe in the Māori migrations to New Zealand. It was because of the obstinacy of Potorū that his canoe was dashed to pieces on the reef and was lost at sea, hence the Māori saying "You are as obstinate as Potorū." Also known as Porua. (Grey 1970:167–169; Tregear 1891:358.)

PŌTUKEHA, a chief of the *Tainui** canoe in the Māori migrations to New Zealand. (Tregear 1891:359.) See also **Canoes, Māori Migration.**

POU, a god of fish on Chatham Island. (Shand 1894:89–92.) According to Māori tradition, Pou was the ancient chief who traveled to Hawaiki* on the back of his pet whale, Pua-nuku, to procure the sweet potato from the god Tāne-nui-a-rangi. (Locke 1921:40–47.)

POUA, a mythical bird, now extinct, said to have inhabited the Chatham Islands. (Tregear 1891:359.)

PŌUAHAOKAI, an ogre who helped kill the Māori hero Tāwhaki (Kaha'i*). He himself was slain by hot stones being thrown down his throat. (White 1887c:2; Tregear 1891:359.)

POUAKI or **POUAKAI** a mythical bird which inhabited the South Island of New Zealand, a source of terror to humans and fairies alike until the Māori hero Pungarehu smashed its beak and killed it. (White 1887b:33; Tregear 1891:359; Beattie 1918:152.)

PŌUATEHURI, a Māori reptile (*mo'o*) god. (Tregear 1891:359; White 1887a: App.)

POUHENI, a group of seventy men in the Māori migration stories who set out from Hawaiki* without food or fire. They were found dead by the main body when they reached New Zealand, but they were then miraculously restored to life. (Tregear 1891:360.)

POUNAMU, a Māori fish god, son of Tangaroa (Kanaloa*) and Te-anu-mātao, born inside a shark. (Shortland 1882:18; Tregear 1891:360.)

PŌU-NUI, the Tuamotuan name of the central pillar of the netherworld (Rangi-pō), which holds up the Rangi-ao and the Rangi-reva, erected by the supreme god, Kio. (Stimson 1964:405.)

POURANGAHUA, a Māori chief who journeyed to Hawaiki* on the backs of two birds to obtain starts of the sweet potato (*kumara*) plant. (White 1887c:117; Tregear 1891: 360.)

POUTINI, a mythical green stone (jade) used by the Māori hero Ngahue* in forming axes and ornaments. (Grey 1970: 106–108.)

POUTURI, the seventh descending division of the Māori underworld.* (Tregear 1891: 361; White 1887a: App.) See also **Kore; Po; Reinga.**

PŌWHAWHA, one of the Māori gods of night. (Tregear 1891: 361.) See also **Pō; Kore.**

PUA, a Hawaiian sorcery goddess on the island of Moloka'i who takes both human and mud-hen forms and who causes the swelling of abdomens. (Beckwith 1948:112–114; Malo 1903:155, 156, 158.)

PU'A, an inferior household god of Samoa who supposedly lives in the *pu'a* tree (*Hernandia peltata*). (Turner 1884:72.)

PUA'A-LOA, a Hawaiian pig god, one of the followers of Pana-'ewa* who attempted to thwart Hi'iaka's* trip to Kaua'i to get chief Lohi'au* for her sister, the volcano goddess Pele.* (Emerson 1915:45.)

PU-A'A-RI'I-TAHI, son of the Tahitian goddess Hina* and chief No'a* of 'Uporu (Point Venus), uncle, therefore, to the legendary hero Tafa'i (Kaha'i*), (Henry 1928:555, 561.)

PU-'ĀHIUHIU, whirlwind and brother to the Hawaiian volcano goddess, Pele.* (Beckwith 1948:169; Rice 1923:7–10.)

PUA-INA-NOA, a woman in Marquesan legends who was thrown into the sea by her daughters-in-law and who then gave birth to various fish. (Handy 1930:110–113.) Also the wife of the Marquesan god Tāne (Kane*), mother of Papa-Uka, and ancestress of queen Vaekehu of the islands. (Christian 1895:193.)

PUA-KAI-MAHUKI, a Tuamotuan demon of the underworld.* (Stimson 1964:408.)

PUAKO-MOPELE, a Tongan goddess with a pig head and woman's body, who rules the gods of Ha'apai; the gecko is sacred to her. (Beckwith 1948: 178; Gifford 1929:294–295.)

PŪ-ARANGA, an ancient Tu-amotuan god. (Stimson 1964: 408.)

PUARATA, a Māori magician who, with his magical talisman (a wooden head), killed all who came near his home on sacred mountain. Puarata and his tal-isman were destroyed by the legendary sorcerer Hakawau.* (Grey 1970:216–220; Tregear 1891:365.)

PUARĀTENŌNŌ, Tuamotuan name for the canoe of Tāne (Kāne*). (Stimson 1964:408.)

PUARŪTŌRŌ, house of the Tuamotuan god Tāne (Kāne*). Stimson 1964:408.

PUATAUTAHI, a Māori chief who captained the *Motumotu-ahi* canoe in the migrations to New Zealand. (White 1887c:181; Tregear 1891:366.) See also **Ca-noes, Māori Migration.**

PU'A-TŪ-TAHI, one of the demons of the deep in the Tahi-tian legend of Rata (Laka*) (Henry 1928:469–495.)

PUEFOU, a god of drought on Niue Island. (Loeb 1926:161.)

PUE-NUI-ĀKEA, a Hawaiian owl god who brings wandering souls back to life. (Beckwith 1948:124.)

PUEO-KAHI, a Hawaiian owl god from Hāna, Maui, who married Pele's* older sister, Kapo-'ula-kīna'u. (Pukui 1971: 397.)

PUHAORANGI, a celestial be-ing in Māori legend who beheld the beautiful Kura-i-moana, wife of Toi-te-huataki* of Hawaiki,* and who descended to earth in the form of a pigeon. They had four sons from whom descended the Māori leaders of the great migration to New Zealand. (White 1887d:25; Co-wan 1925:21; Tregear 1891:367.)

PUHAVAO-ATUA, a goddess of Easter Island who produces green leaves, the wife of Atua Metua.* (Métraux 1940:322.)

PUHI-NALO, once an eel lover of a Hawaiian girl from Wa-ianae, O'ahu, Hawai'i. When her brothers discovered he was an eel, they threw him against a cliff where he can still be seen today. (Beckwith 1948:136; Mc-Alister 1933:117–119.)

PUI-O-HIRO, a principal Tu-amotuan god. (Stimson 1964: 411.)

PUKEĀTEA-WAI-NUI, one of the Māori canoes that brought the first Polynesians to New Zealand, commanded by chief Ruaeo.* (Grey 1970:117; Tre-gear 1891:369.) See also **Ca-noes, Māori Migration.**

PUKEHĀPOPO, the mountain on which Māori legends say

humans took refuge to flee the great deluge.* (Tregear 1891: 370; White 1887c:53.) See also **Hikurangi**.

PUKUTŪARO, a Māori monster who anciently lived at the headwaters of the Rakaia River in New Zealand. (Beattie 1918: 152–153.)

PULELE'I'ITE, an ancient Samoan of Savai'i who was responsible for chief Malietoa* giving up cannibalism. Pulele'i'ite was the son of the fishing woman Sasa'umani.* When she gave birth to him on the beach, she placed him under several rocks in the water. When she returned, to her astonishment, he was standing fishing. She took her son fishing with the villagers, and he aided in their catch of a huge fish and turtle.

Once, the Malietoa of 'Upolu demanded his daily meal of human flesh from the villagers on Savai'i. Pulele'i'ite hid himself in the canoe, and when they reached 'Upolu, he presented himself before the chief. Because he was able to answer correctly the riddles and tasks assigned to him, the Malietoa swore that he would give up cannibalism. The Malietoa, on the other hand, was unable to interpret Pulele'i'ite's metaphor regarding his wish for a wife. (Krämer 1902:108–112.)

PULOTU, name of the Tongan underworld,* presided over by the god or goddess Hikuleo,* located northwest of the island chain, the home of Pukolea, the speaking tree, and Vaiola, the water of life. Other accounts refer to Pulotu as a jumping-off place of spirits making their way to the underworld, a belief held by other Polynesian islanders. Numerous Tongan legends tell of visits to and from Pulotu (Uluvalu* and Haelefeke,* for example). (Collocott 1928:12–20.)

Also Pulotu (Bulotu) is the name of the Samoan underworld presided over by the god Saveasi'uleo* or Elo.* See also **Nafanua**.

PŪ-MAI'A, a Hawaiian who was slain by his chief, Kū-ali'i,* but who returned to life through the prayers of his wife and daughter. (Beckwith 1948:123; Fornander 1916:470–477.)

PUNA, king of the Tuamotuan land called Matuauru, whose daughters (star maidens) took the eyes of Hema* and used them for light. Tahaki (Kaha'i*) avenged his father, Hema, by recovering his eyes from them. In the Rata (Laka*) cycle, king Puna abducted Tahiti-tokerau, Rata's mother, who was subsequently rescued by Rata. (Stimson 1937:60–147.)

PUNA-'AI-KOA'E, chief of the island of O'ahu and lover of the Hawaiian goddess Ka-lama-i-nu'u.* He has supernatural powers and takes the form of a tropic bird and hovers over the cliffs of Kī-lau-ea on Hawai'i. He became the husband of the goddess Haumea,* was killed, but was then rescued by his wife. He later became Pele's* lover. (Beckwith 1948: 194–195, 282; Westervelt 1915a:152–162; 1915b:23–29.) See also **Kiha-wahine**.

PUNA-HOA, according to one Hawaiian account, mother of the goddess Hi'iaka* by her husband Kai-pala-o'a. (Emerson 1915:55.) See also **Haumea; Pele**.

PUNA-PAE-VAI, see **Puna-moe-vai**.

PUNGA, Māori god of sea creatures and the son of Tangaroa (Kanaloa,* the lord of oceans). (Tregear 1891:374.) Others say Punga is the son of Rangi-pōtiki* (sky father) and Papa-tū-a-nuku (earth mother) and a twin brother to Here. (Shortland 1882:17, 18.) He is also named as the brother to Karihi (Alihi*) and Hema* in the epic of Tāwhaki (Kaha'i*). (White 1887a:95, 125.) See also **Puna**.

PUNGAHEKO, an ancestor of the Māori god Tāne (Kāne*) who supplied materials for the creation of Tiki,* the first human man. (Shortland 1882:22; Tregear 1891:374.)

PUNGAREHU, a Māori who was driven out to sea and who landed in a country inhabited by fairies, the Nuku-mai-tore. While there, he taught them to make fire by friction and to cook their raw meat. He then killed a giant man-eating bird that had been annoying them before leaving for home. (Tregear 1891:374–375; White 1887b:33.)

PUNGAWERE, the Māori god of winds mentioned in the stories of Tāwhaki (Kaha'i*) and in the curse of Manaia.* (Grey 1970:129, 135; Tregear 1891: 375.)

PUNGUTIAITENGENGA, one of the many district gods of the Kaitu'u clan on Bellona Island, the son of the principal god Tehu'aingabenga.* (Monberg 1966:67.)

PUNIA, a trickster son of Hina* from the island of Hawai'i. He tricked a group of sharks to attack each other while he escaped with their lobsters. The king shark swallowed him, but Punia survived ten days in his stomach by scraping meat from his insides and cooking it. The shark finally made his way to shore where Punia's friends cut him out. (Beckwith 1948:443; Fornander 1917: 294–301.)

PUNIAVA, a Tuamotuan god. (Stimson 1964:414.)

PŪNUA-MO'E-VAI, a Tahitian god who causes heavy rain to pour upon religious ceremonies if they are not conducted according to strict protocol. His messenger is Pae-tahi, land breeze. He was the patron god of king Mo'e in Tai'arapu, south Tahiti. (Henry 1928:128, 163, 164, 377.)

PŪONOONO, persistence, one of the old Tahitian goddesses who is responsible for guarding the world. (Henry 1928:416.)

PŪPŪALENALENA, a Hawaiian demigod (*kupua*) who can take the shape of a yellow dog and who is also a clever thief. His greatest feat was stealing the famous conch shell, Kihapū, from the spirits who originally stole it from its resting place in a *heiau* (temple) on O'ahu. Supposedly, the conch shell is preserved in the Bernice P. Bishop Museum in Honolulu. (Beckwith 1948:349–351; Fornander 1880:72.) See also **Pikoi-a-ka-alala.**

PUPU'E, a Marquesan god mentioned in the story of Ta'apō* in her journey to the underworld.* (Handy 1930:85.)

PŪPŪ-HULU'ENA, a Hawaiian priest (*kahuna*) who cleverly tricked the spirits of Ka-ū into returning the food plants that once grew in Kohala. (Beckwith 1948:430–431; Fornander 1916: 570–573.)

PUPUI-TOTO, a vindictive Samoan spirit (god) who can enter his priest's body and bring calamity upon his enemies. He can also enter into the bodies of animals or take human form. (Stair 1896:37.)

PUPU-MA-TE-AREAREA, one of the two divine grandfathers of Tāne (Kāne*) in the Tuamotuan legend. (Henry 1928:349.)

PUSI, a Samoan demon, a sea eel, which lives off the coast of Apolima (an islet off 'Upolu, Samoa) and sinks boats that come near. (Krämer 1902:161.)

PUTA, an ancient Māori prophet who lived in Hawaiki* and whose prayer to Rangi* to upset the earth brought about the great deluge.* (Tregear 1891:380; White 1887a:168, 181.)

PUTAHI-NUI-O-REHUA, the highest of the ten Māori heavens, the domain of the god Rehua.* (Grey 1970:63, 671; Tregear 1891:381.)

PŪTAKE, a son of the Tuamotuan creation god Ātea-rangi and his consort Pakahotu. (Stimson 1964:419.)

PU TAURARO, one of the major gods of the island of Anuta. (Feinberg 1988.)

PU TEPUKO, one of the major gods of the island of Anuta, a deified ancestor, inferior to the supreme god Tearakura.* (Feinberg 1981:151.)

PUTIO, a Marquesan giant (seven fathoms tall) who warred against the giant Taua-haai (forty-eight feet tall) from Puamau. Putio won and returned to his home in Hivaoa. Some time later, his daughter was slain by Puaa-kai-epo, a warrior from Taaoa. He set out to revenge his daughter's death. By disguising himself as an old man, Putio was able to enter his enemy's house and slay them. (Handy 1930:126–127.) See also **Giants.**

PU'UHELE, a less-known sister to the Hawaiian volcano goddess Pele.* When she was born to Ka-hina-li'i prematurely, she was thrown across the 'Ale-nuihāhā Channel where she landed at Nu'u, east Maui, in the form of a beautiful woman. She toured the island and then vowed to remain at Wānana-lua. Upon her death, she became the hill Ka'uiki by the sea. (Beckwith 1948:188–189, 379; Fornander 1917:544–549.)

PU'UPEHE, son of Kapō-'ili'ili'i from the island of Lāna'i, Hawai'i, who performed supernatural feats while still in his mother's womb. (Beckwith 1948:230–231; Fornander 1917: 554–561.)

PU-WHAKARERE-I-WAHO, the Māori god of unjust death, the destroyer, an evil being, ancestor of Rehua* and Rangi-taiapo. (Hare Hongi 1907:109–119.)

–R–

RĀ (LĀ, LAA, RA'A), generally recognized and worshipped throughout Polynesia as the sun god. His name implies sacredness, holiness, greatness, and glory. In New Zealand, Rā is the sun of Haronga* and his wife Tongotongo* and the brother to Marama,* the moon goddess. It is Rā whom the great demigod Māui* snared to slow his path through the heavens. (Tregear 1891:383–384.) Another Māori legend names him as the son of Tangaroa-akiukiu. His two wives live in the ocean—Hine-takurua (winter) in the north and Raumati (summer) in the south. Rā alternates his annual visits to them, north to one and south to the other. (Best 1899:93–121.)

In **Samoa,** Lā is the sun god, but of minor importance. Once his rays impregnated a mortal woman name Magamagaifatua whose son, 'Alo'alo* (child of the sun), visited his father and received a dowry for his bride consisting of blessings tied up in a bundle. Lā is also the name of the son of the great Samoan hero Tafa'i (Kaha'i*) by his wife, Sinataeoilagi (Hina*). (Krämer 1902:412–416, 455.)

In **Tahiti,** the god Ra'a bestows sacredness upon all solemn assemblies and ceremonies for both gods and humans. His wife is Tū-papa, and 'Iri-nau is his chief messenger. When angered, he sends a destructive westerly wind from his residence on Bora-Bora. The woodpecker (*ruro*) is sacred to him. (Henry 1928:394, 520.) The Tongan sun god is Laa. See also **La'a-la'a.**

RA'A-MAU-RIRI, the Tahitian god who causes eclipses. When angered, he swallows the sun or moon. The priests and people then flee to the *marae** (temple) to pray and make offerings for him to eject the luminary again. This god also inhabits the halo that encircles the sun by day and the moon by night. The shadow or earthly representation of this god is the woodpecker. Ra'a-mau-riri is also the father of the famous god Hiro (Hilo*), the trickster and the god of thieves, by his second wife Fai-mano-ari'i. (Henry 1928:227, 306, 377, 385.) See also **Te-hei-'ura.**

RAHO, the first mortal to settle the island of Rotuma. According to tradition, he and his granddaughter brought soil from the island of Savai'i, Samoa, and created the island. (Churchward 1937:112–116; Russell 1942:229–255.) Another legend maintains that the first settler, Titofo, was sent down from the heavens by the great king Tüfeua. Titofo found the place suitable, returned to the heavens, and gave his report. Tüfeua sent another contingent to earth including his daughter Päreagsau who became pregnant by her brother Fagatriroa.

Her third child, Tu'iterotuma, named by Raho himself, became the first ruler of Rotuma. (Churchward 1937:251–255.) See also **Hanitemau; Rahou.**

RAHOU, the legendary chief of Rotuma who fished the islands up from under the sea, possibly the same as Raho.* According to the story, Rahou originally was from Samoa and lived under the rule of king Gofu. Their two daughters played together, but eventually the two had a violent quarrel over their catch of fish. As a result, Rahou was told by two sister goddesses (Hauliparua) to pack up and leave with his extended family. Rahou took two baskets of sand from Samoa on board, and at a given signal from the birds who lead them, he cast them overboard, and the Rotuman islands were pushed up from under the sea. After numerous other topographical creations, Rahou finally settled down in Hatana where he died. Several sites of his grave can still be seen. (Gardiner 1898:503–506.)

RA'I-PU'A-TĀTĀ, one of the props of heaven according to Tahitian mythology. (Henry 1928:413.) See also **Creation; Heavens; Rangi.**

RA'I-TUPUA-NUI-TE-FĀNAU-'EVE, son of the Tahitian god Ātea (Wākea,* vast expanse) and Papa-tū-'oi, who caused the evolution and development of the earth. (Henry 1928:356.)

RAKA, the god of winds on Mangaia, Cook Islands, the son of the great goddess Vari-ma-te-tahere,* from whom he received his great basket of winds. He and his wife, Takatipa, had two sons, Tū-matangi-rua and Mama-tuitui-rora, and a daughter, Takanga. (Buck 1934: 11, 23.) See also **Laka.**

RAKAIHAITU, the Māori god responsible for forming the great lakes of the South Island by using an enormous digging tool with a sharpened end. (Cowan 1925:42.)

RAKA-MAU-RIRI, Tuamotuan name for the Tahitian god Ra'a-mau-riri.* Also the name of a legendary, Tuamotuan hero. (Henry 1928:227, 306, 377, 385; Stimson 1964:427.)

RAKATAUĀ, a Māori chief whose son, Kōwhiti-nui, was slain by the hero Rata (Laka*). When the Polynesian sailed from Hawaiki* to New Zealand, Rakatauā was left behind, but he followed, however, on the back of a water monster. (Shortland 1882:6; Tregear 1891:387.)

RAKATAURA, Māori goddess of the air and of music, daughter of the god Tāne (Kāne*), and mother of the air goddess Wheke* (White 1887a: App.;

White 1885:172); according to another Māori tradition, Rakataura is the legendary discoverer of New Zealand. He left his ancient homeland of Hawaiki,* sailed around the North Island of New Zealand, returned home, and told his friend Kupe* of his find. (Tregear 1891:387; White 1885:172; White 1887b:188.)

RĀKEI-ORA, a Māori god whose image was brought to New Zealand from Hawaiki* by Manaia* and his crew aboard the *Tokomaru* canoe. (Grey 1970:181; Tregear 1891:388; White 1887b:181.) Also mentioned as a god of the Chatham Islands. (Shand 1894:90.)

RAKEIPA, a god of the Chatham Islands. (Shand 1894: 90.)

RAKEORA, son of the Māori chief Ruatapu* (responsible for causing the great deluge*). (Shortland 1882:14; Tregear 1891:388.) See also **Tupu-tupu-whenua**.

RAKI, Māori god of the north. (White 1885:114; Tregear 1891: 388.)

RAKIORA, the Māori god of harvest and successful crops, patron god of the sweet potato,* the son of Rongo (Lono*). (Tregear 1891:388.)

RAKURŪ, the first mortal thief in Māori legend. He lived in Hawaiki* where he stole a supernatural fishhook. Upon being discovered, he committed suicide. (Tregear 1891:389; White 1887a:170.)

RALUVE, goddess of Loma, Nsangalau, Lau Islands (Polynesian outliers in Fiji), who likes men and who punishes those who displease her with rashes. (Hocart 1929:198.) See also **Koilasa**.

RA MARAMA, goddess of the Sau clan in Yandrana, Lau Islands (Polynesian outliers in Fiji), feared by the men of that island. (Hocart 1929:196.) See also **Iloilokula**.

RANGAHORE, ancestress and wife to the Māori god Tāne (Kāne*). After she brought forth only stones in the creation, Tāne left her. (Shortland 1882:21; Tregear 1891:391.)

RANGI, the oldest of the Māori gods, known as sky-father, and progenitor of myriads of other gods and goddesses by his several wives, the most popular being Papa (earth-mother). Originally the two clung together in a close embrace, so intertwined that there was little room left for their progeny. After much discussion, the gods Tū (Kū*), Tāne (Kāne*), Tangaroa* (Kanaloa*), and Rongo (Lono*) decided to rend them apart. Only Tāwhiri-matea,* the god of winds and storms, opposed their action, but he was unsuccessful.

From that time forth, light appeared, and all creatures multiplied upon the face of the earth. Sky father and earth mother were separated, yet they still love each other. Papa's sweet sighs rise upwards in the form of mists and dew, and Rangi's rain drops are mournful tears that fall to his lover's bosom.

Rangi's domain of heaven and Papa's domain on earth are both divided into ten regions. The heavens are in ascending order called (1) Kiko-rangi, (2) Waka-maru, the heaven of rain and sunshine, (3) Ngā-Roto, heaven of lakes, (4) Hau-ora, the living water of Tāne, from whence comes the spirits of new-born children, (5) Ngā-Tauira, abode of those who attend the inferior gods, (6) Ngā-Atua, home of the inferior gods as well as the hero Tāwhaki,* (7) Autōia, where mortal souls are created, (8) Aukumea, where time is allowed for souls to live, (9) Wairua, home of attendant gods who serve the higher gods, (10) Naherangi, Tūwarea, or Rangi-whaka-no-hinohi, residence of the supreme gods. Heavens* one through three are ruled over by Maru,* four through six by Tāwhaki (Kaha'i*), and seven through ten by Rehua.* (Grey 1970:1–11; Tregear 1891:391–392; White 1887a:17–35, App.) Rangi is also a major god of **Mangaia** whose wife Tepotatango was the first settler of Mangaia from Savai'i, Samoa. (Gill 1876:15–18, 24.)

RANGI-ATEA, a sacred Māori temple in ancient Hawaiki* from which Kuiwai (wife of chief Manaia*) stole the five god images to transport to the new land of New Zealand. (White 1885:125; Tregear 1891:394.)

RANGI-HIKI-WAHO, a shark god of the Chatham Islands. (Shand 1894:90.)

RANGI-HORE, the Māori god of rocks and stone, son of Māui* and Rohe,* and the father of the war god Maru.* (Tregear 1891:394; White 1887a: App.)

RANGIKAPITI, Māori name for a sacred temple located in the legendary land of Rarotonga.* (Tregear 1891:394; White 1887c: 20, 39.) See also **Whena**.

RANGI-MANA, a god of the Chatham Islands. (Shand 1894: 90.)

RANGIMAOMAŌ, a god of the Chatham Islands who gave birth to all the winds and months of the year. (Shand 1894:122.) See also **Tāwhiri-mangatē**.

RANGIMEHOE, a god of the Chatham Islands. (Shand 1894: 90.)

RANGI-PŌTIKI, one of the props of heaven according to Māori tradition. (Tregear 1891: 394.) See also **Creation; Heavens; Rangi; Toko.**

RANGIPOURI, the chief of the Māori fairies. (Shortland 1882: 50; Tregear 1891:394.) See also **Elves and Fairies**.

RANGITITI, a Tuamotuan god. (Stimson 1964:425.)

RANGITOKANO, the Māori god who separated sky father (Rangi*) and earth mother (Papa*) according to Chatham Islands' mythology. (Tregear 1891:394.)

RANGIUAMUTU, one of the legendary canoes used by the first Māoris in settling New Zealand, commanded by Tamatea-rō-kai. (Tregear 1891:21, 394; White 1887b:183.) See also **Canoes, Māori Migration.**

RANGI-URU, mother of the ancient Māori chief Tūtānekai, wife to chief Whakauekaipapa (ancestor of the Ngāti-Whakaue tribe). (Grey 1970:183.)

RANGI-VARU, the legendary land of Princess Mongi-here in the Tuamotuan legend of Hiro (Hilo*). (Stimson 1957.)

RANGI-WHAKA-NOHINOHI, one of the names given to the highest heaven according to Māori mythology. (Tregear 1891:394.) See also **Creation; Heavens.**

RANGIWHENUA, the Māori god of thunder. (Tregear 1891: 394.)

RANGO, the Māori god of revenge. (Tregear 1891:394.)

RANGOMAI-TAHA-NUI, a Māori god of whales who saved chief Paikea* (ancestor of the Māori people). (Tregear 1891:426; White 1887c:11.)

RANGOMA-WHITI, another name of the Māori god Rongo-mai.* (Tregear 1891:426.)

RANU, Tuamotuan god of floods. (Stimson 1964:430.) See also **Vai-puna-anki.**

RAPAHANGO, a minor Easter Island god associated with the family by the same name. (Métraux 1940:317.)

RAPARAPA-TE-UIRA, name of the heavenly home of Whaititiri,* grandmother of the Māori hero Tāwhaki (Kaha'i.*) (Tregear 1891:396; White 1887a:87.)

RĀ-PĀTIA, a destructive, westerly wind sent from the island of Bora-Bora by the Tahitian god Ra'a* (sacredness). (Henry 1928:394.)

RAPAWHENUA, an evil Māori god who dwells with Miru (Milu*) in the underworld.* (Tregear 1891:396.)

RAPUWAI, name of an ancient people who inhabited the South Island of New Zealand before the coming of the Māoris. (White 1887c:124, 126.) Also the Māori name given to the progenitor of the Europeans as Hine-tītama is given as the progenitor of the Māori (Polynesian) race. (Smith 1911:12–14; White 1887c:123.)

RARAKU, an Easter Islander known for slaughtering thirty mischievous and murderous demons. (Métraux 1940:317.)

RARO-NUKU, the land of Tāne (Kāne*) in Tuamotuan legends through which Hina* fled from her lover Tuna* (eel) in an attempt to find another lover. (Stimson 1934:28–33.)

RAROTONGA, the legendary home of Hine-nui-te-pō,* the Māori goddess of the underworld* (Locke 1883:459); also the father of Kohu, the god of mists (White 1887a:38; Tregear 1891:399). The famous *Arawa* canoe of the Māori migrations is said to have been built in Rarotonga located on the other side of Hawaiki.* (Grey 1970: 107.)

RATA, the Tuamotuan Noah who survived the great deluge*

with his wife Pupuraitetai and his three sons, Ataruru, Atamea, and Ataia, who repopulated the earth. (Caillot 1914:10–11, 23.) For the great hero, see **Laka.**

RĀ-TĀ-'IRI, Tahitian god of winds whose wife is Te-muri (Henry 1928:374); also the name of the father of the first three coconuts. (Henry 1928:421.) See also **Coconut, origin of the**.

RĀ-TŪ-NUI, the Tuamotuan sun god. (Stimson 1964:422.) See also **Rā**.

RAUAIKA NUI, the ocean god in Mangaian legends. (Gill 1876:18.)

RAU-'ATA-'URA, one of the several daughters of the great Tahitian creator god Ta'aroa (Kanaloa*) and his wife Paparahraha* who proclaim upon the mountains for Ta'aroa. (Henry 1928:374.)

RAU-HAU-A-TANGAROA, one of several women sent by the Māori hero Tinirau (Kinilau*) to capture the magician Kae* who had killed Tinirau's pet whale. (Grey 1855: 57, 1970:72–74; Tregear 1891:402.) The others were **Rau-kata-mea; Rau-kata-uri; Rekareka.**

RAU-KATA-MEA, one of several women sent by the Māori hero Tinirau (Kinilau*) to capture the magician Kae* who had killed Tinirau's pet whale . (Grey 1855: 57; Grey 1970:72–74; Tregear 1891:403.) The others were **Rau-hau-a-tangaroa; Rau-kata-uri; Rekareka;**

RAU-KATA-URA, Māori goddess of music whose name is invoked in the expiation of cursing; also, the mother of Wheke.* (Tregear 1891:403; White 1887a: App.)

RAU-KATA-URI, sister to the Māori heroes Rupe* and Māui* (Tregear 1891:403; White 1887a:85); also the name of one of several women sent by the Māori hero Tinirau (Kinilau*) to capture the magician Kae* who had killed Tinirau's pet whale. (Grey 1855: 57; Grey 1970:72–74.) The others were **Rau-hau-a-tangaroa; Rau-kata-mea; Rekareka.**

RAU-MAHORA, a beautiful Māori maiden whose beauty stopped a famous intertribal battle at Taranaki. She and her father, Rangi-rā-runga, were dying of thirst because of the siege. An enemy chief by the name of Takarangi took pity on her and brought the war between the two adversaries to an end forever. The two were married, and their descendants became the rulers in and around the modern city of Wellington. (Grey 1970:228–230.)

RAUMATI, the Māori personification of summer, son of Anukukawewera and a descendant of the supreme god Io.* (Tregear 1891:403.) Mentioned as the wife of the sun god Rā (La*) who bore a son Tāne-rore (heat waves). (Best 1899:93–121.) Also the name of an ancient Māori chief in the *Tainui*￼ canoe of the Polynesian migration to New Zealand. (Grey 1970:125–156.) See also **Canoes, Māori Migration.**

RAUTI, an artisan for Ta'aroa (Kanaloa*), the Tahitian god of creation whose work was primarily in the ocean. (Henry 1928:356.)

RAWEA, the fifteenth age of the universe according to Māori tradition. (Tregear 1891:405.) See also **Creation; Heavens; Kore.**

RE'ARE'A, Tahitian goddess of joy, daughter of the sun god Ra'a* and his wife Tū-papa. (Henry 1928:357.)

REHU, one of the offsprings of the Māori gods Rangi* (Sky father) and Papa-tū-a-nuku. (Shortland 1882:56; Tregear 1891:406.)

REHUA, the omnipotent Māori god of kindness who dwells with his immense host in the tenth, or highest heaven, the son of Rangi-pōtiki* and Papa-tū-a-nuku. Once, he was visited by the hero Rupe* in his search for his sister Hina.* (Grey 1970:63–67.) Rehua can cure the sick, blind, and diseased and raise the dead. He was the first to make fire. (White 1887a:5; White 1885:114; Tregear 1891: 407.) Another Rehua is a minor reptile (*mo'o*) god. (White 1887a: App.)

REHUA-I-TE-RA'I, a Tahitian god worshipped by the demigod Māui*as he fished up the Pacific islands. (Henry 1928:410.)

REINGA, the Māori world of departed spirits, the *pō*, or underworld,* the third lowest division ruled over by the goddess Hine-nui-te-pō.* (Tregear 1891:407–408.)

REI-TŪ, a divine messenger for the Tahitian gods Tū (Kū*) and Te-mehara* (goddess of wisdom). (Henry 1928:163, 164, 357.)

REKAREKA, one of several women sent by the Māori hero Tinirau (Kinilau*) to capture the magician Kae* who had killed Tinirau's pet whale. (Grey 1855: 57; Grey 1970:72–74; Tregear 1891:409.) The others were **Rau-hau-a-tangaroa; Rau-kata-mea; Rau-kata-uri.**

REKAUTU, a god of the Chatham Islands. (Shand 1894: 90.)

REKEREKE, the god of pleasure on Mangareva (French Polynesia). (Caillot 1914:154.)

REPO, the mother of Hina* and the wife to Māui* in Māori legends. (Tregear 1891:411.)

REREAKALOU, god of the Mbaumbunia clan in Yandrana, Lau Islands (Polynesian outliers in Fiji) whose earthly form is the dog. (Hocart 1929:196.)

REREKIEKIE, a Tuamotuan demon having the body of an eel. (Stimson 1964:449.)

RETI, the legendary Māori explorer and navigator of the *Matahorua** canoe which was subsequently seized by Kupe* (the first discoverer of New Zealand). (Grey 1970:161; Tregear 1891:412.)

RĪ, a handsome young man who seduced Hina,* wife of the demigod Māui,* in Tuamotuan legends. When Māui learned of the deception, he turned him into a dog. (Stimson 1934:11–60; Stimson 1964:450.) See also **Irawaru**.

RIKORIKO, the Māori word identifying those malevolent spirits who haunt deserted houses and villages. (Tregear 1891:415; Wohlers 1876:112.)

RIMA-HORO, the goblin mistress of Kui,* grandfather of the Tuamotuan hero Rata (Laka*).

She lived in Kororupo, the underworld* and had two children by Kui—a son, Rima-roa, and a daughter, Rima-poto. (Stimson 1937:96–147.)

RIMA-ROA, father of Tahiti-tokerau,* the wife to Rata (Laka*), the great Tuamotuan hero. (Stimson 1937:96–98.) Also the Tahitian god of war and an artisan for the god Tāne (Kāne*). (Henry 1928:356, 365.)

RINO-O-TAKARIU, name of a coconut leaf used by a Tuamotuan high priest during a funeral ceremony. It is placed upright near a corpse to lend *mana* to his prayers and incantations. (Stimson 1964:457.) See also **Riu**.

RIO, patron god of Tahitian fishermen, the son of the great creator god Ta'aroa (Kanaloa*) and his wife, Papa-raharaha.* (Henry 1928:361–374.)

RIRINO, a Māori canoe in the great migration to New Zealand, commanded by chief Pōrua. It accompanied the more famous *Aotea* canoe, but it and all aboard were lost on the reef of Taputapuātea. (Grey 1970: 167, 169; Tregear 1891:21, 418..) See also **Canoes, Māori Migration**.

RIRI-TUNA-RAI, an Easter Island goddess who, with Atua-metua,* conceived the coconut. Métraux 1940:322.)

RĪU, a name of a coconut leaf used by a Tuamotuan high priest during a funeral ceremony. It is placed upright near a corpse to lend *mana* to his prayers and incantations. (Stimson 1964:457.) See also **Rino-o-takariu**.

RIUKARAKA, a Māori canoe on the great Polynesian migration from Hawaiki* to New Zealand. (Tregear 1891:420.) See also **Canoes, Māori Migration**.

RĪWARU, the Māori name for the canoe built for Rata (Laka*) by the wood fairies. (Grey 1970:88; Tregear 1891:420.)

RŌATA, a Tuamotuan god. (Stimson 1964:457–458.) See also **Rōiti**.

RO-FERO, one of the ancestors of the hero Māui* in the Tahitian legend of his miraculous birth. (Henry 1928:408–409.)

RŌ-FERO-RO'O-ATA, one of the twin sons of Ta'aroa (Kanaloa*), the Tahitian god of creation, and his wife, Papa-raharaha.* (Henry 1928:407.) See also **Rō-'ura-ro'o-iti**.

ROGO, a rain god of Mangareva (French Polynesia). (Caillot 1914:154.)

ROGO-MAI-HITI, the Tuamotuan prince in the Hiro (Hilo*) cycle whom Hina met and with whom she fell in love. They lived together without her brother Hiro's consent and had a son called Tāne-manu (Tāne, the bird god). (Stimson 1957.)

ROGO-TAU-HIA, a Tuamotuan hero, born in the form of an egg to Taiva and Gaitua on the island of Ana'a, also known as Rogo-rupe. (Beckwith 1948: 429; Stimson, ms.) See also **Ulukihe-lupe.**

ROHE, wife of the demigod Māui* in Māori legends who, because of Māui's jealousy of her beauty, visited the underworld* where she became the goddess of the *pō.** By Māui, she had a son Rangihore, the god of rocks and stones. Also she is known as Koke.* (Tregear 1891:421; White 1887a: App.)

ROHUTU, the Tuamotuan paradise, a beautiful land of the underworld.* (Stimson 1964: 460.)

RŌIATA, one of the Tuamotuan gods of the underworld.* (Stimson 1964:461.) See also **Rōi-iti.**

RŌI-ITI, one of the Tuamotuan gods of the underworld.* (Stimson 1964:461.) See also **Rōiata.**

ROIROIWHENUA, son of the Māori god Tū-taka-hinahina,* sometimes said to be the god Tangaroa (Kanaloa*). (Tregear 1891:422; White 1887b:48–57.)

RŌITI, the Tuamotuan god who created the first mortal pair. (Stimson 1964:461.) See also **Rōata.**

ROI-VAHA-NUI, a sea monster in the Tuamotuan legend of Rata (Laka*). (Stimson 1964: 461.)

ROLI, a god of Niue Island, who serenades fishermen. (Loeb 1926:162.)

ROMA-TĀNE, a Tahitian god who guards the gates of paradise (Rohutu-noanoa); he only allows those spirits to enter who have red (*'ura*) feathers as peace offerings; he frequently is worshipped as the patron god of the Arioi Society.* (Henry 1928:201, 238.)

RONA, a woman in several Māori legends who cursed the moon for going behind a cloud and thus causing her to stumble. Offended by her oaths, the moon seized Rona and her calabash and carried her home where she can be seen on a clear night reclining against the rocks. (Tregear 1891:423; White 1887b: 20–26.)

RONGO, see **Lono.**

RONGO, the god of fish in the Chatham Islands. (Shand 1894: 89.)

RONGO-KAKO, a Māori chief of the *Taki-tumu* canoe that brought the first Polynesians to New Zealand. (Tregear 1891:425; White 1887b:193, c:77.) See also **Canoes, Māori Migration.**

RONGOMAI, one of the Māori gods brought to New Zealand by Haungaroa* and her female companions in the story of Manaia.* He is the son of the god Tangaroa (Kanaloa*), the father of Kāhukura,* a war god, and ancestor of some of the Māori tribes. Once Rongomai and his friends, Ihenga and a party of seventy, visited the goddess Miru (Milu*) in the underworld* where they learned magical charms, songs, dances, and witchcraft, but two of them, Ngo and Kewa, were caught and sacrificed by Miru for payment of the sacred lore.

On another occasion, Rongomai took the form of a whale and almost lost his life when a group of Māoris took him for dead and nearly cooked him. In historical times, the Ngāti-hau tribe invoked the assistance of Rongomai in their war against the Ngāti-awa tribe. Immediately Rongomai streaked across the heavens in the form of a shooting star or meteor, landed on the *marae** (court yard) with a loud noise, and created a huge hole in the ground. The Ngāti-hau tribes successfully defeated their enemy. (Grey 1970:128–130; Kararehe 1898:59–60; Tregear 1891:425; White 1887a:108–109.) See also **Ave-aitu; Faka-konaatua.**

RONGO-MAI-AWAITI, a god of the Chatham Islands. (Shand 1894:90.)

RONGO-MAI-TAUIRA, a god of lightning and eels in the Chatham Islands. (Shand 1894:90.)

RONGO-MA-RUANUKU, the Tuamotuan god of the sea and patron god of ships. His canoe is called *Te Piu*. (Stimson 1964:459–460.)

RONGO-MA-TĀNE, the Māori god of the sweet potato (*kumara*), the staple food among the Polynesians, sometimes known as Rongo-marae-roa, Rongo-ma-tāne, Rongo-i-tua, or Rongo-i-amo, all perhaps epithets of the god Rongo (Lono*). According to the legend, Rongo went to heaven to obtain the *kumara* from his brother Whānui. He concealed several tubers in his loin cloth, returned to earth in the form of a rainbow, and impregnated his wife Pani. She gave birth to the *kumura* in a stream of water. Afterwards she became angry at her sons and fled to the underworld* where she continues to cultivate her *kumara*. It is Rongo-i-amo who first brought the *kumara* from Hawaiki* to New Zealand for the Māori people. (Tregear 1891:424–425; White 1887c: 98–117.)

RONGO-RONGO, wife to the Māori chief Turi* of the famous *Aotea** canoe, which had been given to her by her father, Toto. (Grey 1970:160, 162, 172; Tregear 1891:426.) See also **Canoes, Māori Migration.**

RONGO-TAKAWIU, a Māori sea god who formed Whaka-tau* (Rata's* grandson) from his mother's apron which she had thrown into the sea. (Grey 1970:91–92; Tregear 1891:426.)

RONGO-TIKI, wife to the ancient Māori chief Manaia* of Hawaiki.* Because of assaults upon her by Manaia's workmen, a war ensued and forced Manaia to emigrate to New Zealand. (Grey 1970:173–176; Tregear 1891:426.)

RONGO-TUMU-HERE, a Tuamotuan demon octopus. (Stimson 1964:460.)

RONGO-TUPŪA, a Tuamotuan spirit of the night world. (Stimson 1964:460.)

RONGO-UA-ROA, or also **RONGO-UE-ROA,** youngest child of the ancient Māori chief Ue-nuku* (deified ancestor of the Māori people), who survived a massacre to crawl away and inform Ue-nuku who then avenged the death of his children. (Grey 1970:230; Tregear 1891:426; White 1887c:5.)

RO'O, messenger of the Tahitian god Tāne (Kāne*) and the son of the creator god Ta'aroa (Kanaloa*), frequently confused with the gods Lono* or Rongo. (Henry 1928:369–372.)

RO'O-MA-TĀNE, see **Roma-tāne.**

RO'O-NUI, husband to the Tahitian goddess Haumea* who left her to visit the underworld* (*pō*). Haumea was angry and became a cannibal. Their son, Tuture-i-te-a'u-tama, swam away from Tahiti, but Haumea followed, whereupon Tuture-i-te-a'u-tama killed her by pouring hot stones down her throat. Her body floated to shore, however, and was restored to life as Nōna-niho-niho-roa (Nōna-of-the-long-teeth). (Beckwith 1948: 196–197; Henry 1928:554; Leverd 1912:1–3.)

RO'O-TE-RO'ORO'O, the Tahitian god invoked by sacred (*tapu*) men weeding and cleaning the *marae** (temple) to make it attractive to Ro'o-te-ro'oro'o; also a god who defies magicians and evil spirits; the firstborn son of Ātea (Wākea*) and Fa'ahotu. (Henry 1928:159, 160, 162, 164, 209–210.)

RORI-I-TAU, the firstborn child (son) of the demigod Māui* and

Hina* according to Tuamotuan legends. (Stimson 1934:46–49.)

RORI-MATA-POPOKO, a sea slug at the bottom of the ocean in Tuamotuan legends whom Māui* visited in his journey to find eternal life. Māui's mother had told him that the sea slug's stomach could give him eternal life. Māui forced the sea slug to give up his stomach after which Māui began swallowing it so it would become his own. When his brothers laughed at his unusual behavior, he became embarrassed, disgorged the stomach, and thus was never able to gain his goal of eternal life. (Stimson 1934:46–49.)

RORO'O, a Tahitian god, son of the god Ātea (Wākea*) and Hotu,*who inspires chanting priests in the *marae** (temple). His shadow or earthly representation is the *miro* tree (*Thespesia populinea*) always planted around the *marae.* (Henry 1928:382.)

RŌ-'URA-RO'O-ITI, one of the twin sons of the Tahitian god Ta'aroa (Kanaloa*) and Paparaharaha in the creation chant; also an ancestor of the demigod Māui.* (Henry 1928:407–408.) See also **Rō-fero-ro'o-ata.**

RŌVARU, Tuamotuan name of a region of the underworld.* (Stimson 1964:466.)

RŪ, the god of earthquakes in **New Zealand** and the **Tuamotus,** the son of Rangi* (sky father) and Papa* (earth mother), but he remained unborn in the womb of his mother. (Tregear 1891:429–430; White 1887a: 21, 1:App.)

In **Tahiti,** Rū is the famous brother of Hina,* and the two make long distant voyages from their home in New Zealand to discover the Society Islands (Tahiti, Mo'orea, Bora-Bora). (Henry 1928:459–462.)

The **Cook Islands** have a similar story of Rū who settled their island of Araura with about two hundred immigrants. (Henry 1928:464–465.) Also the name of the first man who founded Aitutaki in the Cook Islands. He supposedly came from Havaiki (Hawaiki*) in a outrigger canoe with a group of settlers. (Low 1934:17–24; Pakoti 1895:65–70.) See also **Kū.**

RUA, the god of the abyss in the Tahitian creation chant. (Henry 1928:344.) See also **Creation.**

RUA-AI-MOKO, a Māori god of earthquakes and volcanic eruptions who struggles to free himself from his mother's womb. (Hare Hongi 1907:109–119.)

RUA-ATU, a supernatural being (god ?) of Mangaia, Cook Islands, to whom offerings are made for successful fishing. (Buck 1934:167.)

RUAEO, an ancient Māori chief of Hawaiki,* eleven feet tall, who arrived in New Zealand aboard the *Pukā-tea-wai-nui* canoe. He and his men declared war on his rival, Tama-te-ka-pua, for abducting Ruaeo's wife. Ruaeo won and then they left to settle in some other dwelling place. (Grey 1970:110–120; Tregear 1891:431.)

RŪ-'ĀFA'I-RA'I, one of the names of the Tahitian god Rū (Kū*) who divided the earth in east, west, south, and north. (Henry 1928:407.)

RUA-HATU, god of fishermen and of the ocean who figures prominently in the Tahitian deluge* story. (Henry 1928:148, 164, 448–454.) Also an important god on the island of Napuka in the Tuamotus. (Audran 1918:134.) See also **Rua-hatu-tini-rau**.

RUA-HATU-TINI-RAU, chief Tahitian god of fishermen, Neptune of the sea, half man, half fish. Fishing *marae* (temples) are dedicated to him. (Henry 1928:148, 358, 448–450.)

RUA-HAU-A-TANGAROA, one of several Māori women responsible for the rescue of a pet whale belonging to Tinirau (Kinilau*). (Grey 1970:72.)

RUA-HAUPARĒA, a Tuamotuan god. (Stimson 1964:468.)

RUAHINE, patron god of eels in Māori legend, son of Tū-te-wanawana and Whatitiri.* (White 1887a: App.; Tregear 1891:431.) In the Tuamotus, Ruahine is a witch or sorceress who possesses great magical powers. (Stimson 1964:468.)

RUAHINE-KAI-PIHA or RU-AHINE-MATA-MORARI, a Māori ogress or witch destroyed by chief Paowa* who threw hot stones down her throat. (Tregear 1891:431; White 1887b: 55–59.)

RUAHINE-MATA-MORARI, a supernatural being, a fairy, mother to Turaki-hau and thus mother-in-law to the ancient Māori chief Tura.* (Tregear 1891:431; White 1887b: 18–19.) See also **Ruahine-kai-piha.**

RUA-HINE-METUA, one of several old Tahitian goddesses who guard the world, called old-mother, she bestows happiness and contentment upon mortals. (Henry 1928:416.) See also **Rua-hine-nihoniho-roroa**.

RUAHINE-NIHONIHO-RO-ROA, one of several old Tahitian goddesses who guard the world, called old-woman-with-long-teeth, she also brings strife and cruelty. (Henry 1928:417.) See also **Rua-hine-metua.**

RUA-I-FA'A-TOA, Tahitian god of strength and bravery who

enjoys a good cockfight. He normally takes the earthly form of a rooster, and his voice crying from a valley is an ominous sign to warriors. (Henry 1928: 278, 376.)

RŪAIMOKOROA, Māori god of earthquakes. (Tregear 1891: 431.) See also **Ru.**

RUA-I-TE-PAPA, a Tuamotuan god. (Stimson 1964:468.)

RUAMANO, an ocean monster in the Māori legend of Paikea.* (Tregear 1891:431; White 1887c: 52.)

RUĀNGE, wife to Akatauria* (one of the three principal gods of Mangaia), progenitor of the Mangaian tribes. (Gill 1876:15–18.) See also **Mokoiro; Rangi.**

RUANOKU, the god of the heavens on Mangareva, French Polynesia. (Caillot 1914:153.)

RUANUKU, an Easter Island god. (Métraux 1940:315.)

RUA-NU'U, Tahitian god of armies, son of the god Ra'a* (sacredness) and and his wife Tū-papa.* The reef egret is sacred to Rua-nu'u, and when anyone offends him, he twists their neck so that their face looks behind. (Henry 1928:322, 349, 357, 385, 412.)

RUA-O-TE-RĀ, the Māori name of the opening of the heavenly cave through which the morning rays of the sun penetrate. (Tregear 1891:431.)

RUA-PAPA, wife of the Tahitian god Rū* who divided the earth into north, south, east, and west; also grandmother of the demigod Māui.* (Henry 1928: 408.)

RUA-PUNA, Tahitian god of the ocean who has no nostrils so that he does not pant for breath. (Henry 1928:377.)

RUA-PUPUKE, an ancient Māori chief whose son was captured by the sea god Tangaroa (Kanaloa*) and dragged to his house beneath the sea where he was lashed to a pole over the doorway (as a *tekoteko* carving). Rua-pupuke learned of the tragedy, dived beneath the sea, found his son, and destroyed the fairies (Ponaturi*) by shutting them up in their house until daybreak and then by allowing the sun light to kill them. Rua-pupuke returned with his son and portions of the house carvings, and thus he was responsible for initiating the practice of the unique house carvings among the Māoris. (Tregear 1891:431–432; White 1887b: 162–163.)

RUARANGI, a Māori whose wife was kidnapped by the Patupaiarehe fairies and then restored to life through the incantations of a learned *tahunga* (priest). (Shortland 1882:48; Tregear 1891:432.)

RŪA-TA'ATA, a Tahitian who sacrificed his own life to bring forth the first breadfruit to save his family from starvation. (Henry 1928:423–424.) See also **Breadfruit**.

RUA-TAMAINE, a supernatural being (goddess ?) of Mangaia, Cook Islands, to whom offerings are made for successful fishing. (Buck 1934:167.)

RUA-TAPU, an ancient Māori chief responsible for bringing about the great flood (deluge*). Rua-tapu was a younger son of the great chief Ue-nuku.* When he was caught using the sacred comb of his elder brother, Kahutia-te-rangi, he was severely chastised by his father. In revenge, Pua-tapu enticed the elder sons of the noble families into his canoe, sailed out into the ocean, and then "pulled the plug." All perished except Paikea* who carried the tragic news ashore.

　　Meanwhile Rua-tapu prevailed upon his gods, who ruled the tides, to destroy the surrounding land and all of it inhabitants. When the sea rose, Paikea and his family fled to mount Hiku-rangi,* and just before the flood engulfed the mountain top, they were saved through the intervention of the goddess Moa-kura-manu, who drank up the water of Rua-

tapu. One legend claims that Rua-tapu perished in the flood, and from his bowels were formed the first jellyfish. Another states he sailed away never to be seen again. (Tregear 1891:432; White 1887c:48–56.)

RUA-TEA, Māori chief of the *Kura-hau-pō* canoe in the Polynesian migration to New Zealand. (Tregear 1891:432; White 1887b: 183.) See also **Canoes, Māori Migration**.

RUA-TE-PUPUKE, an ancient Māori chief who learned the art of wood carving from the god Tangaroa (Kanaloa*), and ever since, wood carving is known as the art of Rua. (Best 1928:257–259.)

RUATIKI, a Tuamotuan demon who enters the stomachs of his victims and causes them to swell up in great pain and to die. (Stimson 1964:469.)

RUATIPUA, one of the props of heaven in Māori legends used to separate Rangi* (sky father) from Papa* (earth mother). (Tregear 1891:432; White 1887a: 41.) See also **Heavens; Toko**.

RUA-TUPUA-NUI, the Tahitian god who, during the creation, destroyed the great octopus Tumu-ra'i-fenua,* who held the shells of earth and heaven together, and thus allowed further creation. (Henry 1928:

418–420.) See also **Creation; Heavens**.

RUA-TUPUTUPŪA, a powerful Tuamotuan demon who, if not invoked, brings disaster to sea-going vessels. (Stimson 1964: 469.)

RŪ-AUMOKO, Māori god of earthquakes. (Tregear 1891: 432.) See also **Rū**.

RŪ-FAU-TUMU, the Tuamotuan name of the canoe from which the demigod Māui* fished up the Pacific islands. (Stimson 1964:469.)

RUKU-I-HENUA, Tuamotuan name of the fish line used by the demigod Māui* in fishing up the Pacific islands (Stimson 1964:471.)

RUKU-TIA, a Māori woman slain by her husband, Tama-nui-a-Paki, after she had deserted him because of his cold and wrinkled skin. He buried her body, but when he went to exhume the bones, Ruku-tia was found in perfect form sitting on top of her grave. (Tregear 1891:433; White 1887b: 35–37.)

RUMIA, the name of the shell in which the Tahitian god Ta'aroa (Kanaloa*) resided for eons of time before he began the act of creation. (Henry 1928:436–437.) Rumia became the name of the sky when Ta'aroa broke forth from his abode. The god Rū* attempted to raise Rumia above the mountains of Bora-Bora and Ra'iātea, but he failed in his attempts. His work exhausted him and caused him to be hunched back. His small intestines dropped away and became the low clouds which still cover Bora-Bora.

Then the demigod Māui attempted to raise the sky even further. He tried to sever the tentacles of the great octopus (Tumu-ra'i-fenua*) that held the sky and earth together. He took ropes and tied down the land, and with stones, he propped up the sky. He then set out to find workers who could dig away the land from the sky. He flew through the heavens until he reached the highest (tenth) heaven of the god Tāne,* and asked for his aid. Tāne gathered together his sea shells for cutting and began to work.

Sky father (Ātea) was enraged because of the pain, but Tāne went on boring and pushing until Ātea was detached and pushed higher and higher. Ātea was thus freed, and light came into the world. The great octopus that had held land and sky together fell away southward and became land, the island of Tubuai (Austral Islands). The long night of Rumia thus came to an end. (Henry 1928:409–413.)

RŪNUKU, son of the Māori god Rangi* (sky father) and his wife Papa* (earth mother), created before their separation. (Grey 1970:11.)

RUPE, brother to the demigod Māui* and his sister Hina.* When Hina fled her homeland and became the wife of Tinirau (Kinilau*), Rupe ascended to the tenth heaven to consult the god Rehua* (his ancestor) as to her whereabouts. Rehua informed him that Hina lived on Motu-tapu* (sacred island), and swiftly Rupe flew there in the form of a pigeon. He revealed his identity to her, gathered up her and her newborn child, and returned to dwell in heaven. Rupe also taught humans how to form and use the first axe. (Grey 1970:62–68; White 1887a:85–86.)

RURU-ATAMAI, the pet owl of the Māori chief Ue-nuku,* who acts as guardian of his food stores. (Tregear 1891:436; White 1887c:5.)

RURU-MAHARA, a servant (a guardian owl) to the Māori hero Tinirau (Kinilau*) who told him that it was his wife, Hine-te-iwaiwa, who had broken his reflecting water pools. (Tregear 1891:436; White 1887b:134.)

RURU-TEINA, a Māori chief who traveled with his brothers to a distant land to win the hand in marriage of the beautiful Roanga-rāhia. On their return when they stopped to cook their food, Ruru-teina set out to search for fire wood. He happened upon the hut of the sorceress Ngārara-hua-rau who wound her serpent tail around him and tried to retain him. Ruru-teina's brothers surrounded the hut, burned it down, and the witch perished. Afterwards they recommenced their journey and arrived home safely with their prize, the beautiful Roanga-rāhia. (Tregear 1891:436; White 1887b:26–30.)

RŪTANA, a deified Māori chief, descendant of Tiki,* the son of Rauru, and great-great grandfather of Ruatapu.* (Tregear 1891:436.)

RUTERAGI, the god of stars on Mangareva (French Polynesia). (Caillot 1914:154.)

RU-TE-TOKO-RANGI, the god on Aitutaki, Cook Islands, responsible for the raising of the heavens. (Pakoti 1895:65–70.)

RŪ-WHĀRŌ, a Māori chief of the *Takitumu** canoe in the Polynesian migration to New Zealand. Known for his thievish tricks, he brought some sand from his ancient homeland of Hawaiki* to New Zealand and scattered it on the beach called Te Māhia, now a favorite place for spotting whales. (Tregear 1891:432; White 1887c:42–47.)

–S–

SA'AITU, name for a group of ghosts (*'atua*) on Rotuma who frequently help warriors be victorious in battle. The ghosts company consists of only men who have not been circumcised during their lifetime. (Churchward 1938:470–471.)

SAATO, a Samoan rain goddess (or god) from the island of Savai'i. She is the daughter of Foge* and Toafa.* (Krämer 1902:23, 58; Stübel 1896:149–150; Turner 1884:24–25.)

SACRIFICES, HUMAN. Human sacrifice by the ancient Polynesians was widespread, but uncommon. Only certain very sacred ceremonies conducted in religious temples (*marae* or *heiau*) required human sacrifices—success in war, the restoration of health of a very high chief or high priest, the investiture of a new ruler, etc. Without a human sacrifice, there could be no formal possession of position or estate.

Unlike other parts of the world where living human sacrifices were made, the Polynesians offered only those bodies of humans who were already dead. There was no sacrificial slaying of living victims upon the altars to their gods. In general, the common Polynesian had little to fear from this ritual.

When it was determined in council that a human sacrifice was required, messengers were dispatched throughout the districts to locate a proper victim. More often prisoners of war or undesirable members of the society were previously marked for this particular occasion. Women were never considered proper subjects. The victim could not be killed by knife or spear but had to be hit at the back of the neck to prevent any disfiguration to the rest of the body.

The body was then wrapped carefully in plaited palm fronds and then placed on a long pole. It was transported to the temple in a sacred canoe which had been constructed especially for this purpose. Having arrived at the marae or heiau, the sacrifice was placed on the high altar in solemn procession attended by great chiefs and priests. After the proper prayers had been completed, the body would then be buried either in the temple or out at sea. Months later, the body would be exhumed from the ground, the skull cleaned and placed around the altar, and the remainder thrown away.

In Hawai'i, the god Kū*-waha-ilo, the husband of Haumea* and father of the fire goddess Pele,* introduced human sacrifice to humans. In Tahiti, sacrifices were generally made to the god 'Oro* or Tāne.* In Mangaia, they were made to Rongo (Lono*) where legends say Vaioeve was the first human to be sacrificed. See also **Cannibalism.**

SA'ENGEITEKABA, one of the many district gods of the Kaitu'u clan on Bellona Island, the son of the principal god Tehu'aingabenga.* (Monberg 1966:67.)

SA'ENGEITETUHU, one of the many district gods of the Kaitu'u clan on Bellona Island, the son of the principal god Tehu'aingabenga.* (Monberg 1966: 67.)

SA-FULU-SA, a war god of 'Upolu, Samoa, whose earthly representation is the kingfisher bird. (Turner 1884:48.)

SAGATEA, the Samoan goddess of twilight. Also the name of an ancient Samoan chief who married Sinapapālagi whose three brothers, Letava'etoto, Uli, and Ma'o, were demon sons of Folasa and Maia. Sagatea's second wife was Fa'autumanu'a, daughter of the Tui-Manu'a, the highest-ranking chief in Samoa. Because Sagatea beautified his second wife's house more than his first, Sinapapālagi fled to heaven where she burned her lucky wishes that she had received as a dowry. (Fraser 1898:15–21; Krämer 1902:437–438.)

SAKU, a deified mortal, the most powerful god of Tikopia. He has power over all earthly forms and was responsible for the introduction of most of Tikopian culture into the island. He is worshipped by several names—Mapusia, Te Atua-i-kafika, Te Atua, etc. (Firth 1967: 94–108.)

SAKUMANI, an ancestral god worshipped on Futuna. (Burrows 1936:105–108.)

SALEVAO (SAOLEVAO), the Samoan god of rocks, who, in the creation, married earth mother, and Moa, the center of the earth, was born. He is worshipped as a war god in several villages, and his earthly representation is that of a white dog. In other villages, he is a god who cures illness. (Krämer 1902:7; Turner 1884:10, 49–51.) Also, a mischievous and feared ghost of Fakaofu, Tokelau Islands, who resides in the bush at the northern end of the village and who flies about gathering the souls of the villagers (especially pregnant women) with a large net. (Macgregor 1937:61.)

SAMA, a cannibal god of Savai'i, Samoa. (Turner 1884: 48–49.)

SAMANI, an inferior household god of Samoa, worshipped in the form of a turtle, sea eel, octopus, or lizard. (Turner 1884: 72.)

SANGAMA'UNGI, a district god of the Lake district, Rennell Island, the son of the principal god Tehu'aingabenga.* (Monberg 1966:67.)

SA'O'ANGABA, one of the many district gods on Bellona Island. (Monberg 1966:71.)

SAOLEVAO, a Samoan god and son of Taufailematagi and Papatea, the guardian spirit of Samata and Tuamasaga (oldest settlements on the island of Savai'i). (Krämer 1902:8, 23, 75, 79–80, 105, 115.)

SA'OPUNUASEE, a mischievous god of Bellona Island. (Monberg 1966:57.)

SASA'UMANI, a Samoan goddess, daughter of the war god Fe'e.* She married a Samoan chief from Gaga'emalae (west coast of Savai'i) and gave birth to a daughter, Pulelei'ite, ancestor of the hero Pili.* (Krämer 1902:45–46, 108, 160, 392, 409, 412, 420.)

SATIA, an inferior, cannibalistic god of Samoa. (Turner 1884:73.)

SAU-ALII, a Samoan term used to designate ghosts and other spiritual apparitions, an inferior order of spirits. (Stair 1897:34.)

SA'UMANIAFA'ESE, an ancient Samoan whose mother delivered him prematurely and threw him into the sea where he was nurtured by the waves until grown. Once he successfully captured a huge turtle and dragged it to the village of Sagone on the south coast of Savai'i. Pieces of the turtle shell were preserved for many years and were supposed to have wrought miracles in curing the sick. On occasion, the Tuifiti (king of Fiji) traveled to Sagone for pieces of the shell. The last piece was planted in a cave which reflected the sun's rays and formed them into a rainbow, seen over Savai'i every afternoon. (Krämer 1902:108; Stair 1896:134–136.)

SAUMA'EAFE, a minor Samoan god who lives at Saleimoa on the island of 'Upolu, who walks about as a woman, changing form, and who haunts the handsome sons of chiefs. (Krämer 1902:23, 232; Stübel 1896:82.)

SAVEASI'ULEO, a Samoan god, king of the underworld,* half human form and half eel, whose ancestors are rocks. His grandmother is Popto, round rock, the daughter of Papa (rock) and Maluapapa (cavernous rock). Originally, she had no genitals, but still she tried to obtain a husband. She finally met Masa, a rock in Tufutafo'o, who took a shark's tooth and made a vagina.

Their daughter Taufa married Alao and gave birth to Saveasi'uleo and his brothers Salevao and Ulufanuase'ese'e. According to an agreement among the three brothers, Saveasi'uleo went to Pulotu* to become king there, Ulufanuase'ese'e became the chief of Alataua, and Salevao's daughter, Tilafaigā, swam to Tutuila where she married the chief of that island. (Krämer 1902:104–108; Turner 1884:259.)

SEGA, a Samoan parrot (*Coriphilus fringillaceus*) who had its origin in the heavens. Sega was the offspring of O, son of Tagaloapu'u in the first heaven, and Ua (or Lua), daughter of Tagaloalualua in the second heaven. Because it was born as a clot of blood, it was nurtured by members of the Tagaloa (Kanaloa*) family. It eventually was captured by two gods, Olo and Fana, who took it to the king of Fiji (the Tuifiti), who was the husband of the Samoan chiefess, Muiu-'uleapai,* and introduced it into Samoa. (Fraser 1892:369; Krämer 1902:428–431.) Another legend says that it was brought to Samoa by Tangaloaui* who gave it in return for reforms being made by the Malietoa.* (Krämer 1902:431–434.)

SEKETOA, a Tongan nobleman who became a benevolent fish

(shark) god. Seketoa and his older brother Moimoi were grandsons of chief Maatu. Moimoi became jealous of his younger brother because he felt that Maatu favored Seketota. Moimoi thereupon decided to kill him with his club. Seketoa, however, escaped, left the island, and became a fish god to protect his people so that none of them were ever eaten by fishes. (Collocott 1928:56–58; Gifford 1924:83–84.)

According to another legend, Seketoa from Niuatoputapu had a daughter named 'Ilaheva. He sent her south to find a husband. She went from one island to another until she came to Tongatapu where she remained under the name Va'epopua. The god Tagaloa (Kanaloa*) looked down from heaven, became enchanted with the beautiful maiden, and came to earth, and lived with her for a while. She delivered a son, 'Aho'eita, and when mature, he went to visit his father in the sky. His jealous brothers killed and ate him, although Tagaloa resurrected him, sent him to earth, where he became the first Tu'i Tonga* (king of Tonga) and his descendants rule over Tonga with divine power. (Gifford 1924:25–28; Rutherford 1977:27–28.)

SEMO, a god of Yawelevu on Yandrana, Lau Islands (Polynesian outliers in Fiji), who is incarnated as a grasshopper. (Hocart 1929:197.)

SEMOANA, the first naturally-born god of Tikopia. In the Tikopian creation chant, all the gods were born from a woman who had illicit sexual relations with a man. Tafito, the first born, exited from his mother's head. Semoana's placenta was thrown into the ocean and thus sprang the god Atua-i-faea; and from the umbilicus came Tapuariki. After Semoana also came Rakiteua and Sakura. Rakiteua and Tapuariki are the gods of thunder, hurricanes, and high waves. (Firth 1967:28–32, 35.)

SENGI VAVE, an inferior household god of Samoa incarnate as an old man. (Turner 1884:73–74.)

SEPO-MALOSI, a Samoan war god worshipped at Leone and Pago Pago. His earthly representation is that of a large bat or flying fox. (Stair 1896:41; Turner 1884:51.)

SHARKS. In Tahiti, sharks are generally regarded as messengers to the various gods. High chief Moe in southern Tahiti had a pet shark named Vivi-te-rua-ehu which protected his family and prevented canoes from landing in their district. One of chief Moe's servants once requested the shark to bring him his son which he had left several miles away. The shark found the boy playing, decoyed him into the sea, and then carried him unharmed to his father who was waiting in the passage of the reef.

A modern story tells of Tae-hau-moana, an ancestral shark of the Rutia family from the eastern side of the island. When the French navigator Bougain-ville visited the island in 1768, his ship's line broke from its anchor. The islanders insist that it was Tae-hau-moana that ate the line through because it was jealous of foreigners invading his mooring place. (Henry 1928: 389–390, 403–404.) Numerous shark stories are told in Hawai'i as well, most, however, are of more recent origin. (Beckwith 1948:132–135.) See also **Ka-moho-ali'i; Sharks.**

SIANPUAL'ETAFA and **SIAN-PUAL'EKIA'A**, two sisters in Rotuman legends who deserted their dreaded husbands and became two constellations in the heavens, the Pleiades and Orion. (Churchward 1937:364–366.)

SIKINGIMOEMOE, sister and wife to the god Tehainga'atua of Bellona Island, a ferocious goddess who punishes mortals for breaking taboos or for deserting her worship. (Monberg 1966:54–56.) See also **Tehu-'aingabenga.**

SILI VAAI, a Samoan war god whose omens in the form of a bird foretell the outcome of battles. (Turner 1884:48.)

SINA, see **Hina.**

SINA'AI-MATA, Sina-the-eye-eater, an inferior household god of Samoa. Fish eyes are sacred to him and are never eaten. "Do not make such a noise or Sina, the eye-eater, will come and pick out your eyes" is a common expression. (Turner 1884:74.) See also **Hina.**

SINAFAKALAU, a goddess of Tuvalu, the daughter of Alona (a cannibal) and Sina (Hina*). She had as her best friend the goddess Sinafofalangi who lived with her parents, Langi and La, in the heavens. Once Sinafofalangi came to earth to play with Sinafakalau, but she was eaten by Alona. Sina-fakalau was so distraught that her father disgorged the girl, and after three days, she was resurrected and flew away home. (Roberts 1957:371–373.)

SINAKIBI, a goddess of the island of Bellona, mother of the sky goddess Nguatupu'a.* (Monberg 1958: 46–49.)

SINĀSA'UMANI, a Samoan goddess, daughter of the war god Fe'e,* married the god Tagaloaui* (son of the sun god Tagaloa), and had six children. Sister to Sasa'umani.* (Krämer 1902:45–46, 108, 160, 392, 409, 412, 420.)

SINA-SENGI, a Samoan witch who causes shadows of people and their deeds to be printed on the glassy surface of her pool. (Cowan 1945:40–42.)

SINGANO, a goddess of Bellona Island. Also known by the name Ekeitehua.* (Monberg 1966:58–74.) See also **Sikingimoemoe**.

SISI, a Tongan goddess who was in love with Pasikole,* a Samoan who once lived in Tonga. (Gifford 1924:197–199.)

SISIMATAILAA, the son of the sun in Tongan legend. Once the Tui Tonga* (king of Tonga) betrothed his daughter to a young man named Sisimatailaa in a distant village. After the engagement, Sisimatailaa returned to his mother and asked how he might find his father to whom he wished to announce his good fortune. He was informed that the sun was his father and that he might talk to him after seeking advice from an old woman who lived on an island beyond their own. Following her instructions, Sisimatailaa arrived at the designated spot at daybreak and in a loud voice addressed his father and told him of his planned marriage. The sun told him to return to the old woman who had two bundles called Monu (lucky) and Mala (unlucky). He was to have Monu for his wedding present. Unfortunately, the young boy chosen to take both back with him in his outrigger canoe.

In route, he opened Mala, and a great hurricane swept him back to shore. He finally arrived at the home of the Tui Tonga. When the wedding ceremonies commenced, the couple was swamped with presents from the bride's family, but when they awoke the next morning and opened Monu, the whole place became filled with pigs, kava, yams, as well as people, leaving no space for the Tui Tonga's people and his goods. (Gifford 1924:111–114.) One variant story relates that Sisimatailaa's bride could not wait until they reached shore before opening Mala, whereupon the weight of all the presents and gifts sank the boat, and the couple drowned. (Gifford 1924:116.)

SI'U, a Samoan god, patron of the village of Faleasi'u, 'Upolu, Samoa. In one village, the god appears in the form of a skull once a year during the month of May. (Krämer 1902:154; Turner 1884:74, 248.)

SI'ULEO, a Samoan god of fishermen who originally came from Tonga. (Turner 1884:52.)

SOESAI, an inferior household god of Samoa incarnate in domestic fowl, eel, octopus, or turtle, who cures sickness and aids in childbirth. (Turner 1884:74.)

SOLOSOLOMBALAVU, the god of the nobility of Navu-anirewa, Lau Islands (Polynesian outliers in Fiji), who really has no name but is referred to as a child, "Solosolombalavu," and is most likely of Melanesian origin. (Hocart 1929:189.)

SONGIA, an ancestral god worshipped on Futuna. (Burrows 1936:105–108.)

SOURAGPOL, a man of Rotuma who once turned himself to stone while he was building a stairway to heaven. His surviving son, Fuoga, became a strong warrior, killed several rival chiefs, and took the name of Fouma. (Gardiner 1898:517–518.)

STRETCHING GODS, see **Apakura; Hono'ura; Hilo; Kana; Lima-loa; Ono; Toouma.**

SUNGELE, the name of a demon on the island of Futuna who lived at Velema. He forbade any shouting or whistling near his domain. Once a human came by shouting and whistling, and the demon pursued him. The man climbed a coconut tree, and Sungele followed. The tree and the man fell into the sea, and Sungele turned him into a stone which can still be seen jutting out from the sea. (Burrows 1936.)

SUPA, a cunning demon mentioned in the Samoan legend of Tigilau (Kinilau*). (Krämer 1902:130.)

SWEET POTATO, Origin of. See **Rongo-ma-tāne**.

−T−

TAABASIA, one of many family gods who guard the important graves on Bellona Island. (Monberg 1966:81–82.)

TAAFANUA, a Samoan war god whose earthly representation is the rail bird. (Turner 1884:52.) See also **Nafanua.**

TA'AKINA, one of many family gods who guard the important graves on Bellona Island. (Monberg 1966:82.)

TA'A-PŌ, a Marquesan woman, the daughter of chief Tupa* and his wife Tuhoe-vai, whose spirit was taken to the underworld by the gods Paoo and Te-haa-nau.* There she learned sacred chants from the god Ivi-ei-nui and his wife Hou-heana. After committing these to memory, she returned to her body on earth and taught the songs to her relatives. Together as a troupe (*hoki*), they visited all the neighboring islands, entertaining and teaching the people wherever they went. (Handy 1930:81–85.)

TA'AROA, see **Kanaloa.**

TA'AROA-I-MANU-I-TE-A'A, a huge Tahitian bird that could uproot the largest trees, and legends state that it overturned the little hill of Ma'atea in Vaira'o, Tai'arapu (Tahiti), which has remained upside down to this day. (Henry 1928: 384.)

TA'AROA-'ŌFA'I-I-TE-PARI, a patron god of Tahitian fishermen living in the vicinity of Pari, district of Tai'arapu. Anciently, a man from this district went fishing, but no matter which direction he cast his line, he always pulled up the same rock which he always threw back. Finally, he carried it ashore where the priests examined it and discovered it was possessed by the spirit of the god Ta'aroa (Kanaloa*). They placed it in a crevice of the stony bluffs overlooking Pari where it has ever remained, worshipped by the local fishermen. (Henry 1928: 382.)

TAEMĀ, Samoan goddess of war and tattooing, a siamese twin sister to Tilafaigā,* born on the island of Ta'ū in the Manu'a group to Fai-malie and Fai-tama'i. When grown, they decided to swim to the neighboring islands, and in doing so, they were severed in two by a floating log. When they reached the island of Tutuila, they worked wonders including the making of war clubs from huge rocks on the island. From here, they made their way to Fiji where they learned the art of tattooing* from Filelei and Tufou. In a twist of language, Tilafaigā took the name Nafanua* (Na-fanua, "Na's place.") The two goddesses defended Na's family from a waring tribe and brought peace to the land.

They returned to Samoa where they introduced the art of tattooing and became goddesses on Savai'i and Tutuila. In eastern Samoa, the goddesses Taema and Titi are siamese twins, and everything double (double yams, bananas, etc.) are sacred to them. It is an affront to the goddesses for humans to sit back to back. (Fraser 1896:171–183; Turner 1884:55–56.) See also **Taemamā**.

TAEMĀ, founder of the high-ranking chiefly title on Tutuila, Samoa. According to legend, Taemā and her sister Tilafaigā* had originally swam from Fiji aboard a magical outrigger. When they arrived on Tutuila, they became the wives of chief Togiola. After living a while on Tutuila, they decided to continue their journey to Pulotu,* the underworld,* where Taemā delivered a son named Le'iato'oletu'itu'iotoga (shortened to Le'iato) who became the first of the ruling chiefs on Tutuila. Her sister Tilafaigā gave birth to the goddess Nafanua.* (Krämer 1902:331–333; Turner 1884:55.)

TA'ERE, or **TAERE**, a Tahitian god of the creation, the source of all knowledge and skill. His many artisans include Atari-heui,* Fāro, Feu,* Hō-ani,* Māta'ita'i,* Matamata-'arahu,* Ti'iti'ipō,* Tū-tono,* Mātohi-fānau-'eva,* and Tahu'a-amuri.* He is also a patron god of Tahitian canoe builders. (Henry 1928:146–147, 156.) Also the name of the Tahitian underworld.* (Henry 1928:353–354.)

TA'ERE-MAOPO'OPO or **TA-'ERE-MAOPOPO**, a god of-all-skill invoked by the Tahitian hero Rata (Laka*) when he was preparing to fell a tree needed to build his canoe. (Henry 1928:163, 406, 484.)

TAFAKULA, a Tongan god who prevented the Samoan god Moso* from stealing the Tongan island of Tanoa. Variant legends also include the Samoan gods Tuvuvota, Sisi, and Faingaa and the small islands of Kao, Nukunamu, and Lotuma. (Gifford 1924:86, 88–90.) Another Tongan legend relates that the goddess Tafakula was responsible for the origin of the papaya. (Collocott 1928:51.)

Another maintains that she is the daughter of the goddess Nafanua* who was turned into stone because of her incestuous relations with her father Toki-lagafanua.* She brings fruitful harvest and protection from hurricanes. (Collocott 1921:237; Reiter 1907:743–754.) See also **Haelefeke; Heimoana.**

TAFEHEMOANA, a powerful sea god on Niue Island. (Loeb 1926:161.)

TAFOLOA, a whale god of Futuna. (Burrows 1936:105–108.)

TAFU, the Samoan god of good fortune who lives on the mythical island called Atafu. (Fraser 1890:202.) See also **Le-fale-i-le-langi**.

TAGALOA, see **Kanaloa**.

TAGALOA-ATULOGOLOGO, the Tongan messenger god who, with his colleagues, created the Tongan islands. (Caillot 1914:147–252; Reiter 1907:438–445.) See also **Creation; Tagaloa-like; Tama-pouli-ala-mafoa.**

TAGALOA FAFAO, a god of Niue Island invoked to counteract the influence of Tagaloa-motumotu (a malevolent god). (Loeb 1926:162.)

TAGALOA FAKAOLO, the rainbow god of Niue Island. (Loeb 1926:162.)

TAGALOA-FOFOA, a goddess of Niue Island. (Loeb 1926:162.)

TAGALOA-LAHI, a goddess of Niue Island. (Loeb 1926:162.)

TAGALOA-LIKE, the Tongan god of heaven who, with his colleagues, created the Tongan islands. (Reiter 1907:438–445.)

See also **Creation; Tagaloa-at-ulogologo; Tama-pouli-ala-mafoa.**

TAGALOA-MOTUMOTU, a malevolent god of Niue Island. Also the name of a goddess of Niue Island, wife to the god Kalua. (Loeb 1926:162.)

TAGALOA-PUIPUIKIMAKA, a fishing god of Niue Island. (Loeb 1926:162.)

TAGALOA TATAI, younger brother of Tagaloa Fafao* (rainbow god) of Niue Island. Also the name of a goddess of Niue Island who is wife to Kolua. (Loeb 1926:162.)

TAGALOA-TUFUGA, the Tongan artisan god who, with his colleagues, created the Tongan islands. (Reiter 1907:438–445.) See also **Creation; Tagaloa-at-ulogologo; Tagaloa-like; Tama-pouli-ala-mafoa.**

TAGALOAUI, son of the Samoan sun god Tagaloa (Kanaloa*) and his wife Ui* (darkness). After the death of his mother and uncle (Luama'a), Tagaloaui went to find other people living on the islands. He came upon the home of Pava* (a demon and war god of 'Upolu) and his two sons Telemū and Maifa'i. They drank kava* and conversed together for two days. He continued his journey until he reached Lefaga where he lived until he died. He supposedly married the sea princess Sinā-sa'umani* and through their son Ta'e-o-tagaloa gave rise to the high chiefly title Tui Manu'a.* Their other sons were Lefanoga (a war god), Lele, and Asiasiolagi, and their daughters were Muiu'uleapai* (or Moeu'uleapai) and Moatafao (or Sina-tauata).

Tagaloaui constantly visited heaven where he met in council (*fono*) with the other gods, and he brought his sacred home (*Fale'ula*) to earth for the residence of the Tui Manu'a. Ta'e-o-tagaloa took two wives, Laulau-a-le-folasa and Sina, both of whom delivered sons at the same time. It was Sina's son, Fa'a-ea-nu'u (exalter-of-the-people) who was the first mortal to be given the title Tui Manu'a, although he also is attributed with divine powers. (Fraser 1893:293–301; Krämer 1902:403–409.)

TAGALOA-ULUULU, a goddess of Niue Island. (Loeb 1926:162.)

TĀHAE-O-TE-KORAHA, name of the Māori fairy who stole the child of Takaraho. (Taylor 1870:285.)

TAHATUNA, name of one of the sacred Māori canoes that brought the first Polynesians to New Zealand. (Tregear 1891:21, 441; White 1887b:178.) See also **Canoes, Māori Migration.**

TĀHAU-RI, an ancient Māori priest (before the deluge*) who instructed others in all the sacred rites, ceremonies, and incantations. (Tregear 1891:441; White 1887a:170.)

TAHA-'URU, Tahitian god of the seashore. (Henry 1928:378.)

TAHITI-TOKERAU, a water nymph in the Tuamotuan Rata (Laka*) cycle, caught by chief Vahi-vero,* and they became the parents of the famous hero Rata. (Stimson 1937:96–100.)

TAHITO, a Tuamotuan god frequently associated with the god Tupūa.* (Stimson 1964:482.) Also mentioned vaguely in Māori legends as the ancient one, a supernatural creature, or possibly a god. Kahiko-lua-mea (very ancient and sacred) appears in Hawaiian genealogies as the father of Wākea,* the progenitor of all the Hawaiian people. (Beckwith 1948:294–295; Tregear 1891:500.)

TAHITO-HENUA, a Tuamotuan god who presides over a region of the underworld.* (Stimson 1964:482.)

TAHIVI ANUNAHAU, a personal god of the ruling Pomare family of Tahiti, represented as a sacred fan handle, a drawing of which appeared on the frontispiece of the book *South Sea*

Islander. (South Sea Islander, frontispiece.)

TAHU, the first born of the Tahitian god Fa'ahotu* and Ātea (Wākea*) to encompass armies. He is herald for the god Tāne's. From Tahu, mortals learned to kindle magic with the gods and demons. (Henry 1928:372–373.)

TAHU'A, an old Tahitian goddesses, the artificer, who acts as one of the guardians of the world. The other guardians were 'Aiāru, Fa'a'ipu, Fa'aîpō, Nihoniho-tetei, 'Ōrerorero, and Tamaumau-'ōrere. (Henry 1928:416.)

TAHU'A-AMURI, an artisan for the Tahitian god Ta'ere* who resides at the center of the earth. (Henry 1928:374.)

TĀHUHU, the ancient Tuamotuan name of the Society Islands (Tahiti, Mo'orea, Tetiaroa, etc.). (Stimson 1964:483.)

TĀ-HUI, a deified shark in Tahitian myth. (Henry 1928: 192.)

TAHUKUMEA, one of the many children sired by the Māori god Tāne (Kāne*) by his daughter Hine-nui-te-pō.* (Tregear 1891:445; Wohlers 1875:34.)

TAHUKUMEATA, one of the many children sired by the Māori god Tāne (Kāne*) by his daughter Hine-nui-te-pō.* (Tregear 1891:445; Wohlers 1875:34.)

TAHUKUMEATEPOŌ one of the many children sired by the Māori god Tāne (Kāne*) by his daughter Hine-nui-te-pō.* (Tregear 1891:445; Wohlers 1875:34.)

TAHU-NUI, one of the three Tuamotuan goddesses of the feasting mats. (Stimson 1964: 483.) See also **Fakahotu; Kumitonga.**

TAHUOTIATU, one of the children sired by the Māori god Tāne (Kāne*) by his daughter Hine-nui-te-pō.* ((Tregear 1891:445; Wohlers 1875:34.)

TAHURI-MAI-TO'A, Tahitian god of rocks in the ocean. (Henry 1928: 344.)

TAHU-MATA-NUI, the Marquesan god of marriage* and concubinage. (Christian 1895: 190.)

TAHUNUA, a god of the Chatham Islands. (Shand 1894: 90.)

TAHUWHAKAIRO, one of the many children sired by the Māori god Tāne (Kāne*) by his daughter Hine-nui-te-pō.* ((Tregear 1891:445; Wohlers 1875:34.)

TĀIARANGA, a Tuamotuan god. (Stimson 1964:484.)

TA'I-'AU, husband of Hina*-tū-a-uta, and adoptive father of the god of war, 'Oro,* in Tahitian legends. (Henry 1928:81, 375.)

TAIEPA, an inferior Māori god who assists Kōrako-i-ewe (the god of birthing). (Tregear 1891: 446; White 1887a: App.)

TAI-HARURU-TAUARO, one name of the Tuamotuan underworld,* sacred to the god Ātea (Wākea*). (Stimson 1964:485.) See also **Tai-haruru-tautūa; Tai-haruru-te-pō-o-taranga.**

TAI-HARURU-TAUTŪA, one name of the Tuamotuan underworld,* sacred to the god Tāne (Kāne*). (Stimson 1964:485.) See also **Tai-haruru-tauaro; Tai-haruru-te-pō-o-taranga.**

TAI-HARURU-TE-PŌ-O-TA-RANGA, one name of the Tuamotuan underworld,* sacred to the god Tangaroa (Kanaloa*). (Stimson 1964:485.) See also **Tai-haruru-tautūa; Tai-haruru-tauaro.**

TAIKEHU, an ancient Māori chief of the *Arawa** canoe who commanded the landing party upon their arrival in New Zealand. Also the name of a chief aboard the *Tainui* canoe. When they neared Katikati, Taikehu accidentally dropped his jade adze overboard. Through incantations, he caused the ocean floor to rise and to give up his adze. Today that raised land is a shoal called Te-ranga-a-Taikehu. (Grey 1970:115, 120; Tregear 1891: 447.)

TAINDREVE, the god of the Mataivungalei clan in Wathi-wathi, Lau Islands (Polynesian outliers in Fiji), represented as a large stone five feet high surrounded by small stones. (Hocart 1929:198.)

TAINUI, name of one of the sacred Māori canoes that brought the first Polynesians to New Zealand. It was captained by chief Hotu-roa.* (Tregear 1891: 21, 447; White 1887b:177; White 1887d:28, 58.) The name is also popular in the Tuamotus where several similar stories are told of canoes named *Tainui, Tainuia* (captained by Hotu-roa), and *Tainui-atea* (captained by Tahorotakarari) that left the islands and never returned. (Stimson 1964:485.) See also **Canoes, Māori Migration.**

TAIO-AIA, the supreme god of the island of Tubuai. Sacrifices of children used to be offered to him at the *marae** called Too-ura located near the village of Avera. (Aitken 1930:115.)

TAIRI, the god of thunder on Mangareva (French Polynesia). (Caillot 1914:154.)

TAISUMALIE, a Samoan war god or goddess who appeared in the form of an eel (or bat). The ti (*Dracaena terminalis*) leaf is especially sacred to her. Also a Samoan god of healing. (Turner 1884:56–59.)

TAITAI, the Māori god of hunger. (White 1887a: App.)

TAITAI-ARO-HIA, name of the canoe in which Māui* and his brothers sailed when Māui fished up the island of Tahiti in the Tuamotuan epic. (Stimson 1934:23.)

TAI-TAPU, younger sister to the Marquesan war god Tū.* (Handy 1930:110.) See also **Hiihia; Deluge.**

TA'I-TE-ĀRA'ĀRA, a Tahitian god invoked to resanctify desecrated land. (Henry 1928:322.)

TĀ-ITI, one of the Tahitian gods of mourning. "Look at the mourners, and beware of Tā-iti, or there will be a storm." is the mourners' proverb. (Henry 1928:378.)

TAITIMUROA, See **Tutaeporoporo.**

TA'I-TI-TE-ĀRA'ĀRA, a patron god of Tahitian warriors at sea. (Henry 1928:328.)

TAIVA, a messenger for the Tahitian god of creation, Ta'aroa (Kanaloa*). (Henry 1928:356.)

TA'I-VĀRUA, the Tahitian god of peace, a weeper-for-souls. (Henry 1928:375.)

TĀKĀ, wife to the principal god Rongo (Lono*) in Mangaian legends, who bore a daughter, Tavake, who, in turn, gave birth to the gods Rangi,* Mokoiro, and Akatauria, the first inhabitants of Mangaia and progenitors of the three major tribes on the island. (Gill 1876:15–16.)

TAKAKOPŌRI, ancestor of the Māori tribe Ngāti-paoa through his celebrated wife Kahu-rere-moa.* (Grey 1970: 203–210; Tregear 1891:451.)

TAKAPŌTIRI, patron god of the Māori parrots, son of Tānemahuta (lord of the forests). (Tregear 1891: 451; White 1887a: App.)

TAKA-RITA, wife of the ancient Māori chief Ue-nuku.* After she had committed adultery with Tū-mahu-nuku and Tū-mahu-rangi, Ue-nuku killed her and fed her cooked heart to their son Ira. When her brother Tā-wheta heard the news, he gathered his relatives, and they ambushed a number of Ue-nuku's people and killed them. This act began the deadly feud between the two tribes.

(Tregear 1891:452; White 1887c:14–15.)

TAKAROA, another name for the Māori god Tangaroa (Kanaloa*), lord of the oceans. (Tregear 1891:452; White 1887a: 44, 181.)

TAKATAKA-PŪTEA, son of the Māori god Rangi-pōtiki* and his wife Papa-tū-a-nuku,* thus brother to the gods Tū (Kū*), Rongo (Lono*), Tangaroa (Kanaloa*), and others; twin brother to Mārere-o-tonga.* (Shortland 1882:18; Tregear 1891:452.)

TAKERE-AOTEA, an ancient Māori canoe in the Polynesian migrations to New Zealand. (Tregear 1891:453; White 1887b: 188.) See also **Canoes, Māori Migration.**

TAKERETŌ, an ancient Māori chief of the *Takere-aotea** canoe in the Polynesian migrations to New Zealand. (Tregear 1891:453; White 1887b:188.) See also **Canoes, Māori Migration.**

TAKE-TAKE, an ancient Māori priest who built a new type of house and who originated the custom of blessing new houses. (White 1887a:169.) In Marquesan legends, Take-Take (or To-ho) is the progenitor of all the Polynesian people through his twelve famous sons. (Tregear 1891:453.)

TAKI, younger brother to the hero Māui* in Māori legends who assisted him in all of his work. When Taki grew old, Māui chanted incantations that allowed Taki to ascend to heaven. Because of his handsome features, his right eye became Taki-ara, the bright pole star. (Tregear 1891:454; White 1887b:90.)

TAKITUMU, name of one of the canoes that brought the first Polynesians to New Zealand, captained by chief Ruawhārō (name varies with legend). The canoe was turned into stone at Murihiku. (Tregear 1891:21; White 1887b:177, 179, 183, c:42, 72.)

TĀKOHUA, name of the lowest region of the Tuamotuan underworld,* or the exact center of the universe. (Stimson 1964:493.)

TAKURUA, Māori name of the star Sirus who was also mother to the stars Aotahi (Canopus) and Puaka (Orion); the Tahitian name of the planet Venus. (Tregear 1891:456.)

TAKUTAI-O-TE-RANGI, Māori name of one of the battles in heaven between the gods Tū (Kū*) and Rongo (Lono*) against Tāne (Kāne*). (White 1887a:37; Tregear 1891:456.)

TALIAI TUBOU, a Tongan god worshipped by the ruling chiefs, the Tui Kanokupolu, in west Tongatapu. His sacred representation was a black volcanic stone called Tui Ahau (king of Ahau). (Collocott 1921:229–230.)

TALIMAINUKU, a sea god of Niue Island, who gave birth to robbers, the father of Fakatafetau* and Fakalagalaga,* war gods, and the progenitor of the famous hero Puga (Punga*). (Loeb 1926:162.)

TAMA-AHUA, an ancient Māori demigod who had two wives, Hine-kura and Wai-ta-iki. When Wai-ta-iki deserted him, he pursued after her and caused numerous geographical changes in the topography. When they eventually returned to their cave, they were turned into stone. (Hare Hongi 1896: 233–236.)

TAMA-EHU, a Tahitian fire god, brother to the volcano goddess Pere (Pele*). Also the god of salamanders. (Henry 1928:359, 377, 391, 417, 453.) See also **Tama-tea; Tama-Teina.**

TAMA-FAIGĀ, a powerful Samoan war god who reigned tyrannically over all of Samoa until about 1829. (Krämer 1902: 193; Stair 1896:41.)

TAMAHIVA, a god of the Chatham Islands. (Shand 1894: 90.)

TAMA-IHU-ROA, son of the famous Māori chief Ihenga* and Hine-te-kākarau and father of several celebrated monster slayers—Pītaka,* Purahokura, Reretai, Rongohaua, and Rongohape. (Colenso 1879: 87; Tregear 1891:457.)

TAMA-I-KOROPAO, son of the Māori god Rangi-pōtiki* (prop of heaven) and Hine-ahu-papa. (Tregear 1891:457.)

TAMA-I-WAHO, a celestial being or Māori god who dwells in the heavens and from whom the hero Tāwhaki (Kaha'i*) demanded redemption payment (in the form of incantations) for the death of his father Hema.* (Tregear 1891:458; White 1887a: 125.)

TAMALAFAFA, a god of Niue Island. (Loeb 1926:163.)

TAMA-NUI-ARAKI, an ancient Māori chief whose wife (Rukutia*) and daughters left him because of his cold and wrinkled skin. He followed after them in the disguise of a crane, but when he was noosed by some old women, he became mortal again. Then he disguised himself by having his body tattooed so his relatives would not recognize him. Finally, when he caught up with his wife, he hacked her to pieces and buried her remains. Some time afterwards while he was in mourning and chanting his soul's lament, he heard noises coming from his wife's grave site. When he reached it, he found his wife restored to life, sitting on top of her grave, and welcoming him with open arms. (Tregear 1891:457; White 1887b: 35–47.)

TAMA-NUI-A-RANGI, son of the Māori sky god, Rangi,* and his wife Hekeheke-i-papa, the father of Haumia-tiketike* (god of the fern root). (Tregear 1891:458; White 1887a:19–20.)

TAMA-NUI-KI-TE-RANGI, a Māori god who saved the great hero Māui* at birth when he was thrown into the sea by his mother, Taranga.* (Grey 1970: 14, 22; Tregear 1891:458.)

TAMA-NUI-TE-RĀ, both Tahitian and Māori names for the sun (god). (Grey 1970:28, 42; Henry 1928:466; Tregear 1891: 458.)

TAMA-'ŌPŪ-RUA, a Tahitian shark god, ancestor to the female demon Fe'e-matotiti. (Henry 1928: 612.)

TAMA-POULI-ALA-MAFOA, the Tongan god of the heavens who, with the assistants of his Tagaloa (Kanaloa*) colleagues, created the Tongan islands and the first mortal men. (Caillot 1914:247–252; Reiter 1907:438–445.) See also **Creation; Tagaloa-atulogologo; Tagaloa-like; Tagaloa-tufuga.**

TAMARAU-ARIKI, a shark god of the Chatham Islands. (Shand 1894:90.)

TAMARORO, a god of the Chatham Islands. (Shand 1894: 90.)

TAMA-TEA, brother to Tama-ehu* (the Tahitian fire god of heaven and earth) and colleague of the volcano goddess Pere (Pele*). (Henry 1928:359, 377, 391, 417, 453.) See also **Tama-Teina.**

TAMATEA, a Māori fire god of great antiquity, a descendant of Rangi* (sky-father). (Colenso 1880; Tregear 1891:458–459.)

TAMATEA-HUA-TAHI-NU-KUROA, Māori chief of the *Taki-tumu* canoe, the same as Tamatea-pokai-whenua.* (Tregear 1891:459; White 1887b: 181.)

TAMATEA-KAI-ARIKI, a Māori chief of ancient Hawaiki,* from whom several ancient heroes claimed descent—Uenuku,* Toi-te-huatahi, Hou-mai-Tāwhiti, Whaka-turia, Tama-te-kapua,* etc. (Grey 1970:105; Tregear 1891:459.)

TAMATEA-POKAI-WHENUA, a celebrated ancestor of the Māoris who, because of intertribal strife, emigrated from Hawaiki* to New Zealand in the *Taki-tumu* canoe (some say the *Arawa* canoe). They landed at Tauranga where Tamatea and his wife, Iwi-pupu, settled and became ancestors of the Ngāti-kahu-ngunu tribe. Tamatea and his son Kahu-ngunu left their home to investigate their new country. After numerous encounters with other tribes and supernatural beings, father and son went their separate ways. Finally, Tamatea and his thirty companions lost their lives going over the Huka Falls. Their canoe, the *Ua-piko*, was turned into a stone which can be seen there to this day. (Tregear 1891:459; White 1887c: 71–87.)

TAMATEA-RŌ-KAI, an ancient Māori chief of the *Rangi-ua-mutu* canoe in the Polynesian migrations to New Zealand. (Tregear 1891:459.) See also **Canoes, Māori Migration.**

TAMA-TEINA, Tahitian god of surgery, broken bones, and medicine; also the younger brother to Tama-'ehu* (the prominent fire god). (Henry 1928:377, 391.)

TAMA-TE-KAPUA, an ancient Māori hero, the giant son of Houmai-Tāwhiti,* who lived in Hawaiki* before the migration to New Zealand. He and his brother Whakaturi set out to find their father's dog, Pōtaka-Tāwhiti. They discovered that he had been slain and eaten in the village belonging to chiefs Toi-te-huatahi and Ue-nuku.* In revenge, they stole the fruit from Ue-nuku's trees, but in fleeing, Whakaturia was caught and incarcerated in Ue-nuku's house. Tama-te-kapua rescued his brother, and the two made their way home, but war erupted between the two villages. The tribes decided to build canoes and emigrate from Hawaiki. Tama-te-kapua commanded the famous *Arawa** canoe, and he tricked the priest Ngātoro-i-rangi and his wife Kearoa* to come aboard just as they set sail.

Once out to sea, Tama-te-kapua took advantage of Kearoa, and in anger, Ngātoro-i-rangi called forth a giant whirlpool to engulf the ship. The ship and its crew were saved just at the moment of desperation. Afterwards, they sailed on until they reached the North Island of New Zealand only to find the land on which they landed claimed by the people who came in the *Tainui** canoe. They eventually made their way to Tangiaro where Tama-te-kapua died. On his death bed, he ordered his people to settle at Maketu. His two sons, Tū-horo and Kahumata-moemoe, buried him on mount Moe-hau (Cape Colville). (Grey 1970:99–121; Tregear 1891:459.)

TAMA-TE-PŌ, ancient Māori progenitor of the Ngāti-Ron-gou tribe, one of the sons of

Maru-tūahu* and his wife Te-Whatu. (Grey 1970:198.)

TAMA-TE-RĀ, ancient Māori progenitor of the Ngāti-Tamatera tribe, one of the sons of Maru-tūahu* and his wife Te-whatu. (Grey 1970:198.)

TAMATŪ-HAU, a Tuamotuan god of the underworld.* (Stimson 1964:496.)

TAMAUANUU, a Samoan sea god. (Turner 1884:26–27.)

TĀMAUMAU-'ŌRERO, a Tahitian goddess, a tale-bearer, assigned as one of the guardians of the world. The other guardians were 'Aiāru, Fa'aipu, Fa'aîpō, Nihoniho-tetei, 'Ōrerorero, and Tahu'a. (Henry 1928:416.)

TAMA-URI-URI, a supernatural power or god in the Māori version of the Rata (Laka*) epic who helped Rata destroy Matuku-takotako, the goblin who had killed his father Wahieroa (Wahieloa*). (Grey 1970: 84; Tregear 1891:459; White 1887c: 4–5.)

TAMA-WHIRO, an ancient Māori priest of Hawaiki,* who angered the old priests by teaching their sacred lore and knowledge to commoners. They attacked Tama-whiro in battle on numerous occasions, but were unsuccessful in their at-tempts to murder him. (Tregear 1891:460; White 1887b:47–48.)

TĀ-MINAMINA, a water monster allegedly living in a deep water hole at Waipapa, New Zealand. (Tregear 1891: 460.)

TAMI-TA-RA, the sun god of the Chatham Islands. (Shand 1894:89.)

TAMUMU-KI-TE-RANGI, a spirit who was sent to locate the lost Hautupatu by his parents in Māori legend. When Tamumu-ki-te-rangi discovered that Hautupatu had been slain by his brother for stealing their best food supplies, he found his body, and restored him to life. (Grey 1970:145; Tregear 1891: 460.)

TĀMURE, an ancient Māori sorcerer of Kāwhia, New Zealand, who once matched wits with his rival sorcerer Kiki* at Waikato. Tāmure's incantations were more powerful than those of Kiki's, and as a result, Kiki became sick and died. Both sorcerers passed their craft down to their descendants. (Grey 1970:211–214; Tregear 1891:460.)

TĀ-MURI, a Tahitian guardian spirit who follows people and watches over them. (Henry 1928:376.)

TĀNE, see Kāne.

TANE, four of the thirteen principal gods of Mangaia, all having the suffix Tane. Tane Papa-kai (the highest ranking), Tane Ngakiau, Tane-i-te-ata, and Tane Kio, the fifth son born to Vātea (Wakea*) in Avaiki (Hawaiki*). A lengthy Mangaian legend relates how Tane came to earth to obtain himself a beautiful wife, Tekura-i-Tanoa, in competition with his friend Ako. He was unsuccessful, and it is only after the intercession of Kui, his blind grandmother from the underworld,* that Tane was successful in his pursuits of finding a wife; but it was Kui's own daughter, Ina, whom Tane married. (Gill 1876:107–113.)

TĀNE-MAHUTA, a Māori god of trees and birds, son of Rangi* (sky father) and Papa* (earth mother). (Hare Hongi 1907: 109–119.)

TĀNE-MANU, the beautiful red bird killed in the Hiro* (Hilo*) epic by Hiro's friends, but revived by the incantations of Hiro-te-tāne. The bird was eventually banished forever to heaven. (Henry 1928:540–543.) See also **Tāne-ma'o**. Tāne-manu is also the name of the son of Hina* and Te Rogo-mai-hiti in the Tuamotuan Hiro (Hilo*) epic. He battled with his uncle Hiro and sank his ship. (Stimson 1957.)

TĀNE-MA'O, the Tahitian shark god in the Hiro (Hilo*) epic who revenged the murder of Tāne's red bird (Tāne-manu*) by swallowing Hiro's colleagues. (Henry 1928:541.)

TANE-NGAKIAU, a deified ancestor of the Mangaians, famous for his assistance to Rangi* in the first battles on Mangaia against the invading Tongans. His *marae* (temple) was constructed at Maputū and was famous for the numerous human skulls collected there. (Gill 1876:30–31.)

TANE-PAPA-KAI, the fifth and last son born to the great god Vātea (Wākea*) in Mangaian legends. (Gill 1876:11.) See also **Tangiia; Tonga-iti.**

TĀNE-ROROA, daughter of the Māori hero Turi,* born in ancient Hawaiki.* (Grey 1970:160; Tregear 1891:462.)

TĀNE-TE-HOE, one of the Tahitian gods of mourning. (Henry 1928:378.)

TĀNE-TE-VAI-ORA, name of the grandfather of Huahega* who performed the sanctification rites for her when she gave birth to her son, the famous hero Māui,* by her husband, Ataranga, in the Tuamotuan story of Māui. (Stimson 1934:8.)

TĀNE-TE-VAI-ROA, the father of Hapai,* who became the

mistress of Tahaki (Kaha'i*) in the Tuamotuan epic. Tāne-te-vai-roa appears in the last exploits of the epic. Tahaki has to pass the three tests given to him by Tāne-te-vai-roa before he will allow him to become Hapai's husband. (Stimson 1934: 70–77.)

TANGA-KĀKĀRIKI, a dog offered up as a sacrifice to the Māori gods by the crew of the *Te Ririno* canoe during their migration from Hawaiki* to New Zealand. The canoes commanded by Turi* and Potoru* developed leaks, and the crew barely reached a small island in mid-ocean. In gratitude to their gods for protection, they offered Tanga-kākāriki as a sacrifice. (Grey 1970: 167–168; Tregear 1891:463.)

TANGALOA, see **Kanaloa.**

TANGAROA, see **Kanaloa.**

TANGAROA-HURUPAPA, the principle god of Mangareva, French Polynesia. He, along with Atu-Motua and Atu-Moana, created the heavens and earth. (Caillot 1914:153.)

TANGAROA-MATA-VERA, a Tuamotuan god, one of Tāne's warriors in his fight against the god Ātea (Wākea*). (Henry 1928:351.)

TANGAROA-MIHI, an ancient Māori chief who owned a monster named Kataore. (Colenso 1879:95; Tregear 1891: 464.)

TANGATA, an inferior Tuamotuan god. (Stimson 1964: 478.)

TANGIAITEKABA, one of the many district gods of the Kaitu'u clan on Bellona Island, the son of the principal god Tehu'aingabenga.* (Monberg 1966:67.)

TANGIIA, the fourth son born to the great god Vātea (Wākea*) in Mangaian legends. A statue of this god carved from the ironwood tree was sent to the museum of the London Missionary Society. (Gill 1876: 11, 24.) Also a deified ancestor of the Mangaians, brother to Tutapu, who became deadly foes to each other. His sons Motoro, Ruanuku, Utakea, and Kereteki set sail to Mangaia to settle the island. Ruanuku and Motoro were slain along the way, and they became deified ancestors. (Buck 1934:165; Gill 1876:23–27.) See also **Tane-pape-kai; Tonga-iti.**

TANGIIA-KA-RERE, a Mangaian demon from the east, who,when angered, swallows the sun and thus causes solar eclipses. (Gill 1876:47.) See also **Tuanui-ka-rere.**

TANGINGORINGO, the name of the supreme god worshipped

by the Tuamotuan warrior Moeava.* (Audran 1919:38.)

TANGO, a Mangaian god of fishing, the son of the great goddess Vari-ma-te-takere,* and progenitor of a great family of fishing gods. He and his wife, Tumu-te-tangotango, had two sons, Tuoro-pekapeka and Tau, and a daughter Rauei, and six grandsons through Tuoro-pekapekata—Aketoa, Makona, Tutu-mai-tonga, Tutu-mai-to-kerau, Matutu, and Mautake, all great fishermen. (Buck 1934: 12–13.)

TANGOTANGO, the heavenly maiden who visited the Māori hero Tāwhaki (Kaha'i*) in his sleep and who became his wife. When their daughter, Arahuta, was born, the couple quarrelled, and Tangotango seized the child and sprang to heaven. The epic of Tāwhaki tells of his exploits to find his wife and daughter. (Grey 1970:52–61; Tregear 1891:467.)

TANIFA, the hammer-head shark god of Maftau on Rotuma whose benediction cures illness and all minor troubles. Food sacrifices to him are placed in the ocean. (Gardiner 1898:467–468.)

TĀNIWHA, a collective term for Māori monsters or demons. Stories regarding these supernatural beings are numerous and frequently local. The Tipua or Kura are spirits who inhabit stones, trees, fish, and streams. The *tāniwha* Uenuku-tuwhatu possesses the rock in the harbor of Kawhia where childless women come to become fertile. Papakauri is an enchanted tree at Opokura near Okauia on the Waihou River where once it mysteriously floated upstream and possessed great mana* (power). Hina-kura is a red-colored stone near Opotiki that also possesses great mana. Whatu-kura of the Whanau-a-Apanui tribe is greatly venerated, and it once was represented as a phallic symbol carving over their meeting house. Numerous other *tipua* or *kura* exist. (Gudgeon 1906:27–58.)

Other *tāniwha* were monstrous lizards or reptiles and greatly feared by the population. Kaiwhakaruaki, for example, once lived in a stream near Collingwood, South Island, and devoured humans. He was finally trapped and killed by chief Potoru and his tribe. (Te Whetu 1894:18–19.) Ngārara-Huarau slew thousands of Māoris because one woman ate tapu food. The woman was captured and taken to his cave to live with him. Her relatives finally rescued her, and when the monster was slain, his tail flew off and took up abode near Lake Moawhitu (Greville Harbor). The child conceived by the woman was part human and part reptile. (Best 1893:211–219.)

Another story is told of the remarkable swimming feat of Hine-popo who lived in the North Island. She once swam after her husband's canoe from one island to another on the backs of *tāniwhas* and Hapuku (the cod fish god). (Pakauwera 1894:98–104.) Para-hia is a sea monster or *tāniwha* near Otuhira to whom the first fruits of all food, especially taro, and the first birds of the season are sacrificed. (Skinner 1897:156–157.)

Mokonui or Ngārara-Huarau, a famous *tāniwha* that ravaged the countryside in the search of his sister Parikawhiti, was finally slain by the Ngāitara tribe who lured him out of his canoe. All that remains of him is a heap of stones near Tupurupuru. (Gudgeon 1905:184–193; Te Aro 1894:166–167.) See also **Haumia; Ureia.**

TAOFIALIKI, an ancestral god worshipped on Futuna. (Burrows 1936:105–108.)

TAOMAGA, a war god of Niue Island. (Loeb 1926:162.)

TAPAAI, a war god of Tutuila, Samoa, who lives in a trumpet shell. (Turner 1884:54.)

TAPA-HURU-MANU, father of Tiki* who, in Māori legend, was the father of the first man Tiki-te-pou-mua. (Shortland 1882:13; Tregear 1891:470.)

TAPAKAU, Tuamotuan word for the surface of the earth, the mat of the god Tāne. (Stimson 1964:499).

TAPAKAUMATAGI, a god of Niue Island who rules the winds. (Loeb 1926:162.)

TAPATAPAFONA, a witch who lives in Tuvalu with her son, Ume, and who once fought with another witch named Leti, who lived with her three children, Iseloa, Isepuku, and Isopoto in the heavens. (Roberts 1957:369–371.)

TAPATAPA-HUKARERE, name of the war canoe of the Māori demigod Whakatau* in his expedition to burn the Uru-o-mānono temple belonging to his enemies. (Grey 1970:78–79; Tregear 1891:470.)

TAPATU, one of the war gods of Niue Island. (Loeb 1926:162.) See also **Tapatulele; Tapatutau.**

TAPATULELE, one of the war gods of Niue Island. (Loeb 1926:162.) See also **Tapatu; Tapatutau.**

TAPATUTAU, one of the war gods of Niue Island. (Loeb 1926:162.) See also **Tapatu; Tapatulele.**

TAPAURIKI, the principal god of the Gilbert Islanders. (Newell 1895:231–235.)

TĀPEKA, one of the names of the supreme creator, the first god in Tuamotuan mythology. (Stimson 1964:500.)

TA-PEPU, the Marquesan god of lust and prostitution. (Christian 1895:190.)

TAPINGAAMAMA, a cave in Tefisi (Vavau, Tonga) said to have been anciently inhabited by cannibals and demons. (Collocott 1928:12.)

TAPIRINOKO, a young boy from Nanumea, Tuvalu, who cried to visit the sun. It was too hot, so he visited the moon where he can be seen to this day. (Turner 1884:292.) On the island of Vaitupu, the land is known as Terete. (Turner 1884:284.)

TĀPŌ, a member of the crew aboard the *Aotea** canoe, commanded by Turi,* in the Māori migration to New Zealand. Because of his insolence, he was cast overboard, but was immediately saved when the crew believed he was being protected by the war god Maru.* (Grey 1970:167; Tregear 1891:472.)

TAPUAKIU, a benevolent god of Aliutu and Tamahamau, Niue Island, who, along with Tapu-

alagi,* bestows gifts on mortals. (Loeb 1926:160.)

TAPUALAGI, a benevolent god of Aliutu and Tamahamau, Niue Island, who, along with Tapuakiu,* bestows gifts on mortals. (Loeb 1926:160.)

TAPUARIKI, the principal god of Arorae, a Polynesian outlier in Kiribati, who supposedly originated from the sacred island of Manu'a in Samoa. (Newell 1895:234; Turner 1884:294.)

TAPUFATU, one of the four gods who ruled the earth according to legends from Vaitupu, Tuvalu. (Turner 1884:283). See also **Moekilaipuka; Terupe; Moumousia.**

TAPUITEA, daughter of the ancient Samoan chief Tapu and his wife Sina (daughter of Ui and Tea). When she was born, her mouth was on the top of her head. She was thrown into the sea, and she swam to Fiji where she married the Tuifiti (king of Fiji) and had several children whom she devoured. She then fled to heaven to become the evening star Tapuitea. Her one son Toivā escaped and returned to Samoa where he became a ruling chief. (Krämer 1902:100; Stübel 1896:62.)

Another Samoan legend relates that Tapuitea was the daughter of Tapu and his wife Itea and became the wife of the king of Fiji. She developed horns on her head, became a cannibal demon, and returned to Falealupo, Samoa. Her son, Toivā, finally persuaded her to go to heaven where she became the planet Venus. (Turner 1884: 261–262.)

TAPUTAPUĀTEA, name of the most famous *marae** (temple) in all of Polynesia. It is located on the island of Ra'iātea and is dedicated to the god 'Oro. Sources say that up until about A. D. 1350, remote Polynesian islanders as far away as New Zealand customarily sent offerings to this *marae* in great outrigger canoes. Taputapuātea literally means sacrifices-from-abroad. (Henry 1928: 186, 190, 192, 194.)

TARA, a Māori chief who killed the lizard monster Hine-huarau* at Wairarapa, New Zealand. (Colenso 1877:85; Tregear 1891:474.)

TARAKA, mother of the Māori hero Māui.* See **Taranga**.

TARA-KAKAO, a malevolent Māori god who assumes the form of a night bird. Its flight signifies an evil omen. (Tregear 1891:477; White 1887b:17.) See also **Hokīo; Kakao.**

TARAKA-PIRIPIRI, a water monster allegedly living near Pakerau, New Zealand. (Taylor 1870:159; Tregear 1891:477.)

TARAMAINUKU, grandson of the famous Māori hero Tama-te-kapua.* (Shortland 1882:53; Tregear 1891:477.)

TARANGA, the mother of the famous hero Māui* according to one Māori legend (Grey 1970:8; White 1887b: 91), father of Māui according to another (White 1887b: 63, 81.)

TARA-PA'A, a Tahitian god of mourning. (Henry 1928:293, 378.)

TARAURI, or **TAUAURI,** a giant monster who allegedly dwelt at Whanganui, New Zealand. When he fell from a cliff, his decaying corpse killed all the fish in the river. (Tregear 1891:478.) Also son of the Mangaian god Tangaroa (Kanaloa*) and inventor of the game called *kokopu* (catching small fish with thorns made from the pandanus ribs), famous for his competition against the seven dwarf sons of Pinga. (Gill 1876:118–121.)

TARE, a minor Easter Island god. (Métraux 1940:317.)

TARE-TE-HEI-FARE, Tuamotuan name for the house belonging to the god Tāne (Kāne*). (Stimson 1964:506.)

TARI, an ancient Māori chief who first discovered how to carve fishhooks from wood. When his brother-in-law, Rā-kuru, saw the success Tari had, he stole the hook from him and became the first thief in human history. The tribe, however, discovered the whereabouts of the hook, and sent Hine-i-taitai (Tari's sister) to return it. On the way, she married Kumi-kumi-maro and gave birth to a son, Tau-tini,* through whose exploits the famous fishhook of his uncle was eventually recovered. (Tregear 1891:493; White 1887a:170–172.)

TARINGA-HERE, a Māori elf or fairy whose face resembles that of a cat. (Tregear 1891:481.) See also **Elves and Fairies.**

TĀTAKA, a division of the underworld* according to Tuamotuan legends. (Stimson 1964:510.)

TATAU, Māori word for door, and the name given to Urutonga* by the Ponaturi* fairies in the legend of Tāwhaki (Kaha'i*), Urutonga's son. (Grey 1970:48–49; Tregear 1891:483.) See also **Tautu.**

TĀ-TO'A, a messenger created for the Tahitian god Ruatapua-nui (source of great growth.) (Henry 1928:358.)

TATTOO. One highly sophisticated art form from ancient Polynesia that has been widely disseminated and imitated throughout the world is that of body tattoo (from the Tahitian *tatau*). In Samoan mythology, the goddess Taemā* and her twin sister Tilafaigā* visited Fiji and were impressed with the Fijian custom of tattooing of their women. They brought back the custom to Samoa. While on their way, they chanted the details of the custom "Women alone are tattooed, but not the men." When they neared Samoa, the cold and the strain of their long journey caused them to forget the original words of the song, and they began to sing, "Only men are tattooed, but not women." As a result, only Samoan men are highly tattooed. (Abercromby 1891:461–467; Krämer 1902: 120–124; Turner 1884:55.)

Polynesian tattooing was originally achieved by puncturing the skin with sharp, serrated combs (anciently made of bone) that had been dipped into a mixture of candlenut soot mixed with oil. The combs were attached to a six-inch rod which was struck by a longer rod of about twelve to eighteen inches in length. Simple designs for the Samoan women came from geometric patterns, stars, or abstract insects. Young men were ceremoniously tattooed from the waist to the knee with designs reminiscent of ancient Lapita pottery such as rectangles, squares, bars, and triangles.

From Samoa, the custom spread with the Polynesians wherever they went—to the

Marquesas, the Society Islands, New Zealand, and Hawai'i—and the variations of custom and design varied from one island group to another. Of all the Polynesian peoples, the Marquesans tattooed their bodies far more extensively than the others. In some cases, the body was almost totally black from the procedure. For many years, the art form in Polynesian died out due to Western and Christian influences, but today it is experiencing a revival especially in Samoa. (Taylor 1981.) See also **'Ana-muri; Arioi Society; Matamata-'arahu; Mataora; Tohu; Tū-ra'i-pō; Uetonga; Vie Moko.**

TA'Ū, the eastern Samoan island and seat of the high-ranking title Tui Manu'a,* is said to have been the offspring of Lefaleilelagi (daughter of Fa'agatanu'u and Fa'amalienu'u from Atafu) and Faia (son of the Samoan war god Fe'e*). (Krämer 1902:367–368.)

TĀUA-KI-TE-MARANGAI, Māori ancestress of the god Tāne (Kāne*) who aided him in the creation of the first humans. (Tregear 1891:488.)

TAUA-MANAOA, a tribal god of Vaipae, Uauma, in the Marquesas, a deified mortal invoked to enforce a tapu or solemn prohibition. (Christian 1895:190.)

TAUĀURI, a giant monster who allegedly dwelt at Whanganui, New Zealand, but who fell from a cliff, and its decaying corpse killed all the fish in the river. (Tregear 1891:478.) Also known as **Tarauri**.

TAUFA, a Tongan sea god worshipped by chief Tungi of east Tongatapu and later by the royal family of Tonga because George I (ruled 1845–1893) was cured through his intercession. He also protects gardens. (Collocott 1921:228–229.)

TAUFELELEAKI, war god of Niue Island that flies from one side to the other in a long war. (Loeb 1926:162.)

TAU-FUILI-FONUA, the Tongan creator god, the son of Piki* and Kele,* he-who-overturns-the-water, who in the beginning cohabited with his twin sister, Havea-lolo-fonua,* and gave birth to Hikuleo* (god of the underworld*). (Gifford 1924:14; Reiter 1907:230–240.) See also **Creation.**

TAUITI, a demon, the king of the goblins of Matuauru* who live on Mount Tarava-kura in the Tuamotus. He and Mupere* from the land under the ocean happened to meet one day. They argued over their lands, and in a frenzied fight, Tauiti was defeated, and Mupere became ruler over the goblins. (Stimson

1937:68–71.) Also named as the patron god of dancing in the Cook Islands, the son of Miru (Milu,* goddess of the underworld*). (Buck 1934:201.)

TAU-KI-PULOTU, a Tongan god once worshipped in east Tongatapu by a priestess named Teletele. (Collocott 1921:227.)

TAUMANUPEPE, an inferior household god in Samoa, incarnate in butterflies and supposedly has three mouths. (Turner 1884:76.)

TAUNA, a god of the Chatham Islands. (Shand 1894:90.)

TAU-NE'E, one of the many Tahitian gods responsible for the creation of the earth. (Henry 1928:341.) See also **Creation; Heavens**

TAUNGAPIKI, a Māori reptile god. (Tregear 1891:490; White 1887a: App.)

TAUNGERI, a water monster or sea god who, along with his companion, Arai-te-uru, guards the Hokianga Bar in New Zealand. (Tregear 1891:490.)

TAU-NUI-A-TARA, a Māori god who presides over the tides. (Tregear 1891:490; White 1887c: 49.)

TAUPŌTIKI, a Māori god who assisted the god Tāne (Kāne*) in propping up the sky (Rangi*).

(White 1885:98; Tregear 1891: 491.) See also **Heavens**.

TA'URUA-NUI, the Tahitian guiding star of evening (Jupiter), the star that mounts upon the back of early dawn in his season. Ta'urua-nui took to wife Te-'ura-taui-i-pā and begat many constellations, including Mata-ri'i (the Pleiades), Mere (Orion's belt), and Te-'uru-meremere (the rest of Orion). (Henry 1928:362.)

TAUTINI, an ancient Māori chief, the son of Kumi-kumi-maro and Hine-i-taitai, who fashioned a canoe in the shape of a bowl in order to sail away to rescue his own canoe which had been stolen by his friend, Titipa. He traveled through many lands for a number of years, married two women, Tī-mua and Tī-roto, and then returned home. He also recovered a famous fishhook stolen from his uncle Tari.* (Tregear 1891:493; White 1887a:170–172.)

TAUTŌHITO, a Māori wizard who possessed a magical wooden head along with his fellow sorcerer Puarata.* They allowed no humans to come near their sacred mount on the North Island of New Zealand. Hearing of their foul deeds, another very powerful sorcerer, Hākawau,* gathered up all of his incantations and supernatural powers and besieged the mount. All of the evil spirits of Puarata and Tautōhito were slain, and Hakawau departed after having brought security once again to the district. (Grey 1970:215–220; Tregear 1891: 493.)

TAUTU, the favorite son of Hiro (Hilo*) in the Tuamotuan epic. When Tautu went to serve king Puna* and was imprisoned by him, Hiro set out to seek revenge. (Stimson 1957.) See also **Tatau**. Also, the Tahitian god of comedians and of cooking. (Henry 1928:375–376.)

TAUVAKATAI, a major god of the island of Anuta. (Feinberg 1988.)

TAVĀ, an ancient Tuamotuan sorcerer, witch, or magician who could change his appearance at will. (Stimson 1964:517–518.) Also, a race of Tuamotuan giants* who built temples (*marae**) wherever they went. They possessed red skins, and they slept upright with their hands and heads resting on the tops of trees. (Audran 1918:90–92; Stimson 1964:518.)

TĀVAKA, one of the goblins in the Tuamotuan story of Rata (Laka*) who hindered Rata from felling a tree in the sacred valley. Rata captured him and forced him to build his marvelous canoe during the night. Also the name of one of Rata's crew members aboard his ship.

(Stimson 1937:117–126; Stimson 1964:518.)

TAVAKE, mother to the three major gods who settled Mangaia—Rangi,* Mokoiro,* and Akatauria*—by her father, Rongo (Lono*). (Gill 1876:15–16.)

TAWAKE-HEIMOA, elder brother of Tūtānekai* (the celebrated lover and husband of the Māori heroine Hine-moa*). (Grey 1970:183–191; Tregear 1891:495.)

TAWAKI-MOE-TAHANGA, an ancient Māori chief of Rotorua, a grandson of the famous Māori hero Tama-te-kapua* through his son Kahu-mata-moemoe. (Grey 1970:99–121; Tregear 1891:495.)

TĀWHAITIRI, one of the two guardians of the gate to the Māori underworld.* Mortals whose spirits are light fly quickly through; if heavy, they are caught and destroyed. (Tregear 1891:496; Wohlers 1876:111.) See also **Tuapiko**.

TĀWHARE-NIKAU, offspring of the Māori goddess Papa* (earth mother) by her second husband, Whiawhia-te-rangi-ora. (Tregear 1891:498; White 1887a: App.)

TĀWHERE, one of the malevolent Māori gods who dwell with

Miru* (goddess of the under-world*). (Tregear 1891:498.)

TĀWHIRI-MANGATĒ, a god of the Chatham Islands who gave birth to all the winds and months of the year. (Shand 1894:122.) See also **Rangimaomaō**.

TĀWHIRI-MATEA, the Māori god of tempest, son of Rangi* (sky father) and Papa* (earth mother). When his brothers Tū (Kū*), Tāne (Kāne*), Tangoroa (Kanaloa*), Rongo (Lono*), and Haumia* proposed to separate their parents to allow light to enter their vast creation, Tāwhiri-matea violently opposed such a plan. War between them resulted, and despite Tāwhiri-matea's hurricanes, thunderstorms, and threatening clouds, he was unable to prevent his parents' separation. His storm-cloud children, brought forth to punish his brothers, were Aonui, Aoroa, Aopouri, Aopotango, Aowhetuma, Aowhekere, Aokahiwahiwa, Aokanapanapa, Aopakakina, Aopakarea, and Aotakawe. Because of his violent outburst, however, a great part of mother earth was submerged. (Grey 1970:2–11; Tregear 1891:499.)

TĀWHIRIOHO, a child of Puhaorangi* (a heavenly being who came to earth and fathered the Māori race through the mortal woman Kura-i-moana).

(Cowan 1925:21; Tregear 1891:499; White 1887d:25.)

TĀWHITI, one of the descendants of Rangi* (sky father) and Papa* (earth mother) that became stars in the heavens after their separation. (Tregear 1891:500; White 1887a:48.)

TEA, the Tuamotuan name of the world of light versus the underworld.* (Stimson 1964:519.)

TEABAIKATAPU, one of the many district gods on Bellona Island. (Monberg 1966:71.)

TE-AILOILO, a god of the underworld* on the island of Futuna. (Burrows 1936:105–108.)

TE-AGIAGI, the god of war on Mangareva, French Polynesia. (Caillot 1914:154.)

TE-AIO, see **Tiaio**.

TE'AITUAHE, one of the many district gods of the Kaitu'u clan on Bellona Island, the son of the principal god Tehu'aingabenga.* (Monberg 1966:67.)

TE'AITUAHU, one of the many district gods of the Kaitu'u clan on Bellona Island, the son of the principal god Tehu'aingabenga.* (Monberg 1966:67.)

TE'AITUMATAHONGAU, one of the many district gods of the

Kaitu'u clan on Bellona Island, the son of the principal god Tehu'aingabenga.* (Monberg 1966:67.)

TEAILOILO, name of the guardian to the gates of heaven in legends from Futuna. (Burrows 1936:107.)

TE-AIO, see Tiaio.

TE-AKA-IA-ROĒ, the primary being, the root of all existence in Mangaian mythology, represented in the creation as the lower stem of the universe which is shaped in the form of a coconut. (Buck 1934:9, 23; see drawing in Gill 1876:2.)

TE-ANOA, the Tahitian goddess of heat of the earth, born of Ta'aroa (Kanaloa*) and Paparaharaha.* (Henry 1928:377.)

TE-ANU, the Marquesan god of creation, meaning space, cohabited with Tangae (gasping), and produced a progeny of gods as well as the mortal descendants who inhabit Nuku Hiva island. (Christian 1895:196.)

TE-ANU-TI-ANANUA, lord of the ocean in Marquesan legends, also known as Kee-Moana. (Christian 1895:189.)

TEARAKURA, the supreme god of the island of Anuta, source of welfare for the entire island. (Feinberg 1981:151.)

TE-ARI'I-TAPU-TUUA (TŪ-TIA), a sacrificial god in Tahitian mythology. (Henry 1928:357.)

TEATAMAOFA, the principal god of heaven on the island of Vaitupu, Tuvalu. (Turner 1884:283.)

TE-ATA-TUHI, glimmer-of-light, wife of Rangi* (sky father) in one Māori tradition and thus mother of Marama (the moon goddess). (White 1887a: 49–51.)

TE-A'U-MOANA, one of the ghost sharks that inhabit the water around the island of Bora-Bora. (Caillot 1914:131–141.) See also Te-auta; Te-hi-uta.

TE-A'U-ROA, a great Tahitian sea god in the legend of Honoura.* (Henry 1928:528.)

TE-AUTĀ, one of the ghost sharks that inhabit the water around the island of Bora-Bora. (Caillot 1914:131–141.) See also Te-au-moana; Te-hiuta.

TEELE, a war god of Niue Island. (Loeb 1926:162.)

TE EMU, an Easter Island god, the name meaning landslide. (Métraux 1940:316.)

TE-ERUI, an ancient Mangaian god, son of Te-tareva of the underworld.* Te-erui and his brother Matareka set and found the land of light, known to mortals as the island of Aitutaki (Cook Islands). (Gill 1876:139–142.)

TE-FA'ANAUNAU, one of the Tahitian gods of mourning. (Henry 1928:378.)

TE-FAKAHIRA, an ancient navigator and warrior venerated on in the island of Fakahina (Tuamotus), the son of Marere.* (Audran 1919:235.)

TE-FATU, Tahitian lord of hosts, lord of the skies, lord of the ocean, a god invoked in building and launching canoes, the son of Tumu-nui* and Papa-raharaha.* (Henry 1928: 146, 356.)

TE-FATU-TIRI, a powerful Tahitian god of thunder and lightning. (Henry 1928:376, 394.)

TEFOLAA, the first inhabitant of the island of Nanumea, Tuvalu. According to tradition, two women, Pai and Vau, came to Nanumea from Hawaiki.* There they met Tefolaa who had come from Samoa. When the two women quarreled, Tefolaa traveled to Samoa for a wife, and returned with numerous people who settled on the island. (Roberts 1958: 396.)

TE-HAA-NAU, a Marquesan god who captured the spirit of the mortal woman Taa-pō* and took it to the underworld.* (Handy 1930:81–85.) See also **Paoo.**

TEHAINGA'ATUA, the primary sky god on Bellona Island, generally a benevolent god, regarded as the god who gives life, married the goddess Nguatupua. He was originally brought to the island from a distant land called 'Ubea (Hawaiki*) by Kaitu'u. He is considered the owner of things—canoes, paddles, tapa, walking and dancing sticks. Once the malevolent god Tangangoa stole his children, and he and his grandson, Tehu-'aingahenga, used barbed spears to kill him. Tehainga-'auta is not always benevolent and must be appeased. He may send hurricanes, bad crops, or health. Sacrifices of uncooked food are made to him. (Monberg 1966:50–51.)

TEHAU, father of the Tuamotuan god Tāne (Kāne*) by his wife Metua (parent). (Henry 1928:349, 350.) Name of the Māori god of the forests, son of Rangi-pōtiki* and his wife Papa-tua-nuku,* thus brother to the gods Tū (Kū*), Rongo (Lono*), Tangaroa (Kanaloa*), and others. (Shortland 1882:17–18.) Also the name of the son of Tiki* (the first man) and Kau-ata-ata* (the first woman) in Māori legend. (Tregear 1891: 444; White 1887a:App.)

TEHAU, father to the god Tāne (Kāne*) in Tuamotuan cosmology and husband to Metua. His name signifies peace. (Henry 1928:349, 350.)

TE-HEI'URA, red-wreath, the Tahitian god who inhabits the halo around the sun or moon. (Henry 1928:377.) See also **Ra'a-mau-riri.**

TE-HINA-TŪ-O-KAE, son of the Marquesan goddess Hina* and the sorcerer Kae.* As a young boy, he went to visit his father who at first did not recognize him. The boy's destructive play almost had him killed, but at the last minute his identity was made known, and he was saved through his father's intervention. (Beckwith 1948: 482; Handy 56–63; Steinen 1933:347, 349.) See similar tales of **'Aho'eitu; Nā-maka-o-ka-pao'o; Tū-huruhuru.**

TEHITI, a malevolent god of Bellona Island, represented in the form of a stone. (Bradley 1956:333.)

TE-HIUTA, one of the ghost sharks that inhabit the waters around the island of Bora-Bora. (Caillot 1914:131–141.) See also **Sharks; Te-au-moana; Te-auta.**

TEHONO, a mighty warrior, king of Havaiki (Hawaiki*) in the Tuamotuan legend of Hiro (Hilo*). Te-hono challenged Hiro to battle, and when it ended in a draw, Te-hono departed, leaving Hiro his title of king. (Stimson 1957.)

TEHU, an ancient navigator and warrior venerated on in the island of Fakahina (Tuamotus), famous for introducing various staple food plants to Fakahina, especially the coconut, the taro, and the breadfruit. (Audran 1919:235.)

TEHU'AINGABENGA, the principal god of Bellona, who married the mortal woman, Nu'usanga or Hakakamu'eha, and had a son, Tupuimanukatu'u, the second major god of the island and rival to his father. Tehu'aingabenga protects his followers, and in one story, he obtained the life-giving spirit of Teosi, one his worshippers, from the fearsome goddess Sikingimoemore. He and his family live in the eastern skies in a place called Nuku-ahea. (Monberg 1966:58–74.)

TE-IPE, a god of the Teipe sub-tribe, Vaiaua, Mangaia, Cook Islands. (Buck 1934:166.)

TE-KAIARA, a national god house on Mangaia, Cook Islands, where idols of the gods were stored and cared for. It stood in the Keia district between the inland temple of Rongo and the temple of Motoro, destroyed at the advent of Christianity. Not to be confused with the *marae** or temples where tribal gods were publicly worshipped. (Buck 1934:172–173.)

TE-KANAWA, a Māori chief of Waikato, New Zealand, who once became lost with his hunting party on Mount Puke-more when night fell. They soon found themselves surrounded by a troop of curious and friendly fairies.* Te-Kanawa offered them some of his jade and other ornaments, but they took only the "shadows" of the ornaments and departed. The next morning, the hunting party quickly descended the mountain without stopping to hunt. (Grey 1970:225–227.) Also the name of a Māori god invoked when the war party of chief Ue-nuku* attacked Tāwheta and his clan. (White 1887c:20; Tregear 1891:122.)

TE-KARARA-HUARAU, a monster who once lived at Taupo and Waitata, New Zealand, and who captured the women named Ruru. He was finally burned to death by the people who feared him. (Beattie 1918:153.)

TEKAUAE, a mortal in Mangaian legends who died and went to the underworld* ruled over by the goddess Miru (Milu*). Having outwitted the goddess, Tekauae was allowed to return to the world of life. (Gill 1876:172–174.)

TE KOPUTU-AUE, a Marquesan god of the creation, son of Papa-Uka and Papa-Ao. (Christian 1895:188–189.)

TE-KŪ, one of the descendants of Rangi* (sky father) and Papa* (earth mother) who became stars in the heavens after their separation. (White 1887a:48; Tregear 1891:500.)

TEKURAAKI, a god worshipped on Mangaia, introduced into the island from Rarotonga. His statue made from the ironwood tree was destroyed by the Christian missionaries in 1824. (Buck 1934:166; Gill 1876:31.)

TELA, an ancient Samoan carpenter whose noise irritated the god Tagaloa (Kanaloa*) in his visit to Samoa. Tela agreed that he would never again make noise while a chief was passing along the public path, thus the Samoan custom of not working when a chief comes nearby. (Krämer 1902:305.)

TELAHI, one of the principal gods on Nanumea, Tuvalu. (Turner 1884:291.)

TE LAUMUA, a god of Fakaofu, Tokelau Islands, who aids mortals in retrieving the souls of departed relatives from mischievous spirits. (Macgregor 1937:61.)

TE LIO, a god of Fakaofu, Tokelau Islands, who appears as a great mat and who lives near the beach along his domains, the lagoons. (Macgregor 1937:61.)

TEMAHARO, a personal god of the ruling Pomare family of Tahiti, a drawing of which appeared on the frontispiece of the book *South Sea Islander*. (South Sea Islander, frontispiece.)

TE-MANAVA-ROA, a primary being in Mangaian mythology, represented in the creation as a part of the stem of the universe which is shaped in the form of a coconut. He also inhabits the sacred mountain named Rangi-motia. (Buck 1934:9, 23; see drawing in Gill 1876:2.) See also Te-aka-ia-roē; Te-tangaengae.

TEMANGUAHENGA, one of the many district gods of the Kaitu'u clan on Bellona Island, the son of the principal god Tehu'aingabenga.* (Monberg 1966:67.)

TEMANGUTAPU, one of the many district gods of the Kaitu'u clan on Bellona Island, the son of the principal god Tehu'aingabenga.* (Monberg 1966:67.)

TE-MARAHA, one of the many Tahitian gods invoked during religious ceremonies at the famous *marae** (temple) at Taputapuātea* on the island of Ra'iātea. (Henry 1928:163.)

TEMATUKUTAKOTAK, name of a supernatural monster in the Tuamotuan legend of Rata (Laka*). (Stimson 1964:522.)

TE-MAURI, an ancient navigator and warrior venerated on the island of Fakahina in the Tuamotus, the son of Te-Fakahira.* (Audran 1919:235.)

TE-MEHARA, the Tahitian goddess of wisdom who lives in the district of Vaira'o and who emerges on moonlight nights to comb her long hair. Women seek her favor and hold conversations with her at a spring called Vai-ru'ia (darkened-water.) (Henry 1928:85.)

TE-MEHARO, one of the chief Tahitian gods who presides over the royal *marae* * (temple) on Tahiti; also the Tahitian god of strangulation. His earthly manifestation takes the form of a whistling plover (*torea*). (Henry 1928:128, 376.)

TE MOANA, the son and second god in ranking to Tui Tokelau* on the island of Fakaofu, Tokelau Islands, a sea god who takes the form of a water spout. He creates large waves to protect the islanders from invaders. (Macgregor 1937:60.)

TE-MO'O-NIEVE, an ogress in the Marquesan legend of Huuti,* an ancient ancestress of the people living in the Taaoa Valley, island of Hiva Oa. (Handy 1930:21–25.)

TE-MUHUMUHU, son of the Tahitian sun god Ra'a* and his wife Tū-papa. (Henry 1928:357.)

TE-MURI, the mother of all winds in Tahitian mythology. Her husband is Rā-ta'iri. (Henry 1928:364.)

TENGAUTETEA, one of the many district gods of the Kaitu'u clan on Bellona Island, the son of the principal god Tehu'aingabenga.* (Monberg 1966:67.)

TE-OHIU-MĀEVA, a powerful Tahitian god who takes possession of humans, often called the god of fools. His earthly representation is the streaked lizard. (Henry 1928:377, 383.)

TE-'ORE, a Tahitian god of disenchanters. Tahitians seek his aid when a sorcerer has cast a spell upon one of them. (Henry 1928:213.)

TE-PAPA, the Tuamotuan mother of creation. (Henry 1928:347.) See also **Papa.**

TE-PARA-KŪ-WAI, one of the descendants of Rangi* (sky father) and Papa* (earth mother) who became stars in the heav-ens after their separation. (Tregear 1891:500; White 1887a: 48.)

TE-PORA-PORA, one of the descendants of Rangi* (sky father) and Papa* (earth mother) that became stars in the heavens after their separation. (Tregear 1891:500; White 1887a: 48.)

TEPOU, a malevolent god on Bellona Island. (Monberg 1966: 76.)

TEPOUTU'UINGANGI, a sky god from Bellona Island, husband to Nguatupu'a.* (Monberg 1958: 46–49.)

TE PUHI-NUI-O-AUTOO, king of the Marquesan eels. (Christian 1895:190.) See also **Tuna.**

TEPUPURA-O-TE-TAI, daughter of king Puna in the Tuamotuan Rata (Laka*) epic. She was won through contest by Manu-kura, a champion warrior of the deep. She later became the wife of Rata after a battle between the two warriors. (Stimson 1937:129–134.)

TE PUSI, an eel god of Atafu, Tokelau Islands whose bite can bring about death. (Macgregor 1937:63.)

TERAKA, name of a parent of Māui* in Māori legends, same as Taranga.* (White 1887b:71.)

TERE-HĒ, a young Tahitian maiden responsible for the ancient division of the island of Tahiti from its original creation. Anciently, it was believed that all of the islands in the chain were all one, connected together, called Havai'i (Hawaiki*), the home of the gods, now called Ra'iātea. Once the gods called a sacred meeting at Opoa and proclaimed that no humans should venture from their home while the sacred ceremonies were being conducted.

Disregarding the order, Tere-hē secretly stole away to swim in a nearby river. The gods were angry at this disrespect, and they caused her to sink below the surface. As she sank and drowned, a giant eel thrashed about and tore the land in two between Ra'iātea and Hu'ahine. The girl's spirit then entered the loosened land, and like a great fish, it started swimming away. Only the god Tū (Kū*) took notice of the fish. He dashed away from the religious services being held at Opoa and guided the fish safely south and eastward.

As it swam, its dorsal fin stood up and formed Mount Orohena (on Tahiti), and its other one broke off and formed an island to its rear (Mo'orea). Other fragments dropped off and formed the other windward islands of Me'etia, Te Tiaroa, and Mai'ao. All the Society Islands had thus been created. A look at the modern map of these island will show why the ancients believed the island of Tahiti had originally filled the space between Ra'iātea and Hu'ahine. (Henry 1928:438–439.)

TE-REHU-O-TAINUI, a Māori war god of more recent origin, prematurely born to a woman named Rehutu but whose spirit entered into a green lizard, the *moko-kakariki*. A priest named Uhia became the medium for the new god, and his prophecies and oracles regarding the outcome of war became famous. After the death of Uhia, other mediums never acquired his power and prestige, and the reputation of Te-rehu-o-tainui gradually waned. (Best 1897: 41–66.)

TERE-MĀHIAMĀ- H I V A , a shark god, ancestor to the Tahitian hero Tafa'i (Kaha'i*) who accompanied him on his famous sea travels. (Henry 1928:561.)

TERI'I-Ā-PŌ-TŪ-'U R A , another name for the great god 'Oro* of the ruling Pomare family of Tahiti, a drawing of which appeared on the frontispiece of the book *South Sea Islander*. (South Sea Islander, frontispiece.)

TE RIRIKATEA, a deified ancestor of Easter Islanders, supposedly who lived in their ancient homeland called Marae-renga (Hawaiki*).

TERUPE, a secondary god of the night world on Mangareva (French Polynesia). (Caillot 1914:155.) See also **Miru**. Also, one of the four major gods who rule the earth according to legends from Vaitupu, Tuvalu. His duty is to watch and kill thieves. (Turner 1884:283). See also **Moekilaipuka, Tapufatu, and Moumousia.**

TESIKUBAI, a mischievous god of Bellona Island. (Monberg 1966:57.)

TE-TANGAENGAE, or sometimes called Te-vaerua, a primary god of Mangaia, represented in the creation as a part of the stem of the universe shaped in the form of a coconut. (Buck 1934:9, 23; see drawing in Gill 1876:2.) See also **Te-aka-ia-roe, Te-manava-roa.**

TETINOMANU, a god of Bellona Island responsible for causing storms. (Monberg 1966:90.)

TE TOA-O-TE-ARA, a pseudonym used by the Tuamotuan demigod Hiro (Hilo*) when he traveled through upper Havaiki (Hawaiki*). (Stimson 1957.)

TE-TŪ-A-HATU, the Marquesan god who presides over childbirth. (Christian 1895:190.)

TE-TUMU, the Tuamotuan creator god who, with his wife Te-papa (stratum rock), created all living things. He is the god of life and rewards departed spirits according to their merits. (Henry 1928:347, 349, 553.) See also **Creation; Underworld.**

TE-TUPU-'O 'AI'AI, one of the Tahitian gods who aided in the creation of the earth. (Henry 1928:341.)

TEUHIE, one of the parents of Hina's pet eel in the Tongan legend of the origin of the coconut.* (Gifford 1924.) See also **Kaloafu.**

TEUKULATAPU, a god of Niue Island who rules family affairs. (Loeb 1926:162.)

TE-'URI, the goddess of darkness, sister to the Tahitian god of war 'Oro.* Once she descended to earth to obtain a wife for her brother. (Henry 1928:231, 375, 410.)

TEU'UHI, a goddess of Bellona Island, sister to Ekeitehua* and Titikanohimata (brother of Tehahine'angiki*), mother to the goddess Tesikubai, but has no husband. (Monberg 1966:83.) See also **Ekeitehua; Tehainga-'atua.**

TEVAE, one of the two principal gods on the island of Nukufetau, Tuvalu. (Turner 1884:285.) See also **Foilape.**

TE-VAHINE-NUI-TAHU-RA'I, patron goddess of fire walkers on the island of Ra'iātea. She and her friend Hina*-te-'a'ara dress in ti leaf skirts and garlands. The ti plant is, therefore, an essential element in the fire walkers' performance. Sacrifices are also made to her after one recovers from a serious illness. She is benevolent and affords protection to her friends. (Henry 1928: 214, 216, 290, 464.)

TE-VA-HUNUHUNU, son of the Tahitian god Ra'a* and his wife Tū-Papa.* He heals wounds and illness on the battlefield. (Henry 1928:357.)

THURUTANGITANGI, the god of Nauto-nggumu, Nasangalau, Lau Islands (Polynesian outliers in Fiji), embodied in the form of an owl. (Hocart 1929: 198.)

TIA, one of the famous Māori chiefs who anciently arrived in New Zealand aboard the *Arawa** canoe. (Shortland 1882: 51; Tregear 1891: 507.) Also the name of the underworld* or Hades on the island of Nukufetau, Tuvalu, located just under the earth. (Turner 1884: 286.)

TIAFTOTO, a young maiden of Rotuma, who once lived in an oyster shell. Her brother, Miarmiartoto, betrothed her to Tinirau (Kinilau*), the king's son, but the marriage did not work out, and Tiaftoto returned to her shell. (Churchward 1938: 331–335.)

TIAIO, a deified ancestor of the Mangaians, famous for his many superhuman exploits, a food-eating god, and generally associated with the god Motoro.* (Gill 1876:29–30.) The spelling is corrected to Te-aio in Buck 1934:166.

TIAKI-TAU, daughter of the king of upper Havaiki (Hawaiki*) in the Tuamotuan legend of Hiro (Hilo*). Hiro won her hand in marriage through a series of fabulous feats. (Stimson 1957.)

TI'AMĀ-TA'AROA, a Tahitian god who acts as a pillar in supporting the sky (Rumia*). (Henry 1928:343.) See also **Heavens.**

TI'A-O-TEA, a messenger of the gods in Tahitian legend. (Henry 1928:163, 164, 413.)

TI'A-O-'URI, a messenger of the gods in Tahitian legend. (Henry 1928:163, 164, 413.)

TIE-MAOFE, the daughter of king Puna,* who married the Tahitian hero Rata (Laka*). (Henry 1928:506, 512.)

TI'ETI'E, a Samoan responsible for bring fire down from the heavens for mortal use. Ti'eti'e was the son of chief Talaga in 'Upolu, who descended to the underworld* (Pulotu*), and obtained fire and a wife (Si'isi'imane'e) from the fire god Mahui'e.* (Krämer 1902: 400–401.)

TĪFAI-O-TE-PEHO, patron god of Tahitian wood cutters, invoked when building canoes. He prevents wood from splitting. (Henry 1928: 379.)

TIHATALA, a god of Niue Island. (Loeb 1926:163.)

TI'IPĀ, a Tahitian god who causes sterility in women. (Henry 1928:377.) See also **Tipa.**

TI'ITI'IPŌ, an artisan for the Tahitian god Ta'ere* who dwells in the center of the earth. (Henry 1928:374.)

TIKARAU, a god on the island of Fangarere who sprang from his mother's body without having a father. His name means spear-turning-back. Also the name of the magical sword of the hero Tinirau (Kinilau*) which would return by itself after having been thrown. (Firth 1961:37.)

TIKI (KI'I), a god or demigod in many Polynesian islands. In others, he is the first man created on earth. In the **Marquesas**, Tiki is a general name for gods, such as Tiki-vae-tahi, etc., and one legend maintains that

he was the first man, the son of Ātea (Wākea*) and his wife Owa.

In the **Tuamotus**, Tiki is the son of the demigod Ahu-Roa and his wife One-rua who lived in the ancient land of Havaiki-nui-a-na-ea (Hawaiki*). They were commanded by the god Ātea to bring forth man, and they, therefore, produced a son, Tiki. When Tiki became older, his mother sought a wife from him among a family in Havaiki-te-araro. She returned with One-kura, and she and Tiki lived together for a long time without having children. Finally after the proper rituals and incantations, One-kura became pregnant, delivered a daughter they named Hina, * and then shortly thereafter One-kura died.

Hina was reared by her maternal grandparents until she reached puberty. She set out to find her father against her grandparents' warnings. Through trickery, Hina became her father's mistress and bore him three children—Hau-ata, Te-ata-ha-hau, and Tamaru. Upon Hina's deathbed, she taught Tiki the proper incantations to use to restore her to life, and so it was done. When Tiki died, however, Hina refused to use her magic to bring him back to life. Her in-laws were furious, and they quarrelled day after day.

Finally, she was driven away with bitterness and, and she

resolved to sail away to the moon. But first she visited lands belonging to the Kautu clan where she became the mistress of the giant eel Tuna*-te-vai-roa. Afterwards, she became the mistress of the hero and demi-god Māui,* and the tale of Tiki is concluded. (Stimson 1937:1–10.)

In **Tahiti**, the gods Tū (Kū*) and Ta'aroa (Kanaloa*) looked down upon their created world and were pleased. They decided to conjure up the first man whom they named Ti'i (fetcher). Ti'i married Hina, the daughter of the god Te-fatua and his wife Fa'ahotu, and their children mingled with the gods, and they became the high royal families of the world, those privileged to wear the red feathered girdle, the symbol of royalty. Commoners, on the other hand, were simply conjured up by Ti'i and Hina. When the royal families intermarried with the commoners, a middle class was born. (Henry 1928:402–403.)

In **Hawai'i**, Ki'i is regarded as human, and the progenitor of the Hawaiian race, twelfth in descent from Wākea, but of less significance than in the southern Polynesian groups. The first man in Hawaiian mythology is Kumu-honua.* (Beckwith 1948: 276–277, 293–294, 310–31.)

The **Māoris** regard Tiki in one legend as a god, the son of Io* (a supreme creator) (White 1887b:2), but most stories regard him as the first man, the child of Rangi* (sky father) and Papa* (earth mother), made from red clay. His wife was Mā-riko-riko, the first woman, and they lived in a land called Hawaiki.* (White 1887a:151–160.) Other legends maintain, however, that Kau-ata-ata* was the first woman, formed by the god Rā and his wives Rikoriko and Ārohirohi. (Tregear 1891:510–511; White 1887a:App.)

In some **Marquesan** legends, Tiki rules the underworld with his wife Hina-mataone. (Christian 1895:190.) The **Samoan** stories of Ti'iti'i, the son of Pipi, who obtains taro and fire for humans, most likely refers to the demigod Māui-tikitiki. (Lesson 1876:594–597.)

TIKI-AU-AHA, member of the fourth begotten family of the Māori god Rangi* (sky father) and Papa* (earth mother), the progenitor of man. (White 1887a:142.)

TIKIHAOHAO, a Māori god born to Whiro-te-tupua after the separation of Rangi* (sky father) and Papa* (earth mother). (Grey 1970:11; Tregear 1891:511; White 1887a: App.)

TIKIKANOHIMATA, a god of Bellona Island who protects flying foxes, brother to the goddess Tehahine'angiki. (Monberg 1966:82.)

TIKI-KAPAKAPA, the second begotten family of the Māori

god Rangi* (sky father) and Papa* (earth mother), the progenitor of fish. (White 1887a: 142.) See also **Tiki-au-aha.**

TIKI-TE-HATU, the Easter Island equivalent of the god Tiki,* the first man in many Polynesian legends. Tiki-te-hatu copulated with the goddess Hina* and bore Hina-kauhara who is connected with the great god Makemake.* (Métraux 1940: 322–323.)

TIKI-TŌHUA, one of the first born of the Māori god Rangi* (sky father) and Papa* (earth mother), the progenitor of birds. (White 1887a:142.)

TIKI-WHAKA-EAEA, a descendant of the Māori god Rangi* (sky father) and Papa* (earth mother), the progenitor of the sweet potato (*kumara*). (White 1887a:142.)

TIKOKKE-PUTA, the Marquesan god of songs and poetry. (Christian 1895:190.)

TILAFAIGĀ, a Samoan goddess of war and tattooing,* sister to Taemā,* and mother to Nafanua.* (Abercromby 1891: 459–463; Fraser 1896:171–183; Krämer 1902:107.)

TILALOFONUA, a god of Niue Island. (Loeb 1926:163.)

TILI-TILI, a Samoan god of lightning, responsible for caus-

ing quarrels, war, and darkness. (Turner 1884:59–60.)

TIMĀTEKORE, father of the goddess Papa* (foundation) and husband to Tamaiti-ngava-ringavari in Mangaian mythology. (Gill 1876:8–10.)

TIMIRAU, see **Kinilau.**

TINI-O-TE-HAKUTURI, name of the Māori wood fairies, children of the forest god Tāne (Kāne*) in the legend of Rata (Laka*). (Tregear 1891:513.) See **Elves and Fairies.**

TINIRAU, see **Kinilau.**

TINOPAU, a mortal from the island of Bellona who died and went to the underworld.* He composed a song that irritated the god Tehainga'auta* so much that he grabbed his hair and yanked him out of the underworld. (Monberg 1966:53.)

TINO-RUA, the Tahitian lord of the ocean, and sharks are his messengers. (Henry 1928:148, 344, 359, 389, 410, 439.)

TINOTONU, a god of Bellona Island, son of the primary god Tehu'aingabenga,* who battled unsuccessfully with his father over a beautiful mortal woman named Kaukaugogo. (Monberg 1966:63.)

TIPA, the Tahitian god who rules over sickness and who

heals diseases, the patron god of the rulers of northern Tahiti. His earthly representation is the *mo'o 'āreva*, a lizard with a forked tail. (Henry 1928:145, 383, 567.) Also a Tahitian wind god, a personal god of the ruling Pomare family of Tahiti, a drawing of which appeared on the frontispiece of the book *South Sea Islander*. (South Sea Islander, frontispiece.) See also **Ti'ipā**.

TIPŪ-TUPU-NUI-A-UTA, an ancient Māori chief whose prayers to the great god Tāne (Kāne*) brought about the great deluge.* He and his two sons, Paru-whenua-mea and Turi, survived the eight-month flood in a covered canoe. Sometimes referred to as Tupu-nui-a-uta, Tupu-tupu-nui-a-uta, or Tupu-tupu-whenua. (Tregear 1891:516; White 1887a:166, 172, 180.)

TITIHAI, a Māori god who presides over the ankle. (Tregear 1891:518; White 1887a: App.)

TITI-MANU, grandfather to the Tuamotuan hero Tahaki (Kaha'i*), husband to Kuhi, and father to Huauri (mother of Tahaki). Titi-manu instructed his two grandsons in the formulas and chants they need to avenge their father and to rescue him from the goblins of Matuauru.* (Stimson 1937:60–68.)

TĪTĪ-MĀ-TAI-FA'ARO, one of the Tahitian gods who assisted in the creation. (Henry 1928: 355.)

TITI-USI, a Samoan god worshipped during the full moon. The ti leaf girdle is especially sacred to him. (Turner 1884:60.)

TITI-USO, a Samoan god invoked by prophets or sorcerers to locate stolen objects, to bring about revenge, or to heal the sick. (Stair 1896:43.)

TIU, progenitor of the Marquesan tribe by the same name in Taaoa, Hiva Oa. The story states that his mother, Niniano, from Tahauku valley gave birth to an egg that was swept downstream where it hatched into a fishlike character named Tiu. Niniano instructed her daughter, Te-ipo-atu, to find and wash the child with medicinal herbs that would heal the sores on his body. When she had done has she had been instructed, Tiu took human form and set out to seek his grandfather Makemake.* Once there, he succeeded in gaining possession of an image (*tiki*) that gave him great power. He then went to live in Taaoa valley where he had numerous descendants. (Handy 1930:125.)

In **Samoa**, Tiu was an ancient chief noted for his bravery in war. He was given some pigeons by the god Tagaloa (Kanaloa*), and the spot where he constructed a house (*fale*) for them became known as the-house-of-Tiu, which became the village of Faleatiu, 'Upolu, Samoa. (Krämer 1902:155–156.)

TIVE, an Easter Island god mentioned in their creation myth as being created by the supreme god Makemake,* a name not known in other Polynesian islands. (Métraux 1940: 315.)

TOAFA, a Samoan rain god or goddess, also the name of a mountain ridge between Matautu and Safatu, Savai'i. She and and the god Foge* are represented in the form of two oblong, smooth stones and are said to be the parents of the rain goddess Saato. (Krämer 1902: 23, 58; Stübel 1896:149–150; Turner 1884:24–25.)

TO'A-HITI, a Tahitian god of land and sea, who saves people from falling off cliffs. The rustling of wind is his sound. He is a messenger for the more powerful gods. The mighty hero Rata (Laka*) went into To'a-hiti's sacred valley to find a suitable tree to fell to build his marvelous canoe. To'a-hiti has several suffixes to his name to identify his character—for example, To'a-hiti-mata-nui, To'a-hiti-o-te-vao, To'a-hiti-o-te-vave'a, and To'a-hiti-a-to'a. (Henry 1928:163, 164, 379, 498.)

TOA-MIRU, a highly-respected goddess of childbirth on Mangareva, French Polynesia, the eldest daughter of Miru (Milu,* god of the underworld*). When a child is born, the goddess is invoked by repeating her name three times and then the statement, "give life to this child which has just come from Pouaru [the other world]." Her servants are named Matogatoga, Taparaihaha, Teakapekepe, Pupanuiamiru, Tapugaverevere, Pohoko, and Atireo. (Caillot 1914:150, 156.)

TOGA-MAUTUTU, a monster whale in Tuamotuan legend, son of Tini-rau and Puta-rua. He and his brother, Tutu-nui, guard the entrance to the land of king Puna in the Rata (Laka*) cycle. (Stimson 1937:96–146.)

TOGI-O, a comrade of Rī whom Māui* turned into a dog in Tuamotuan legends. Tegi-o heard of his fate through Rī's sister, Poki-runa. Togi-o went to the land of Māui, seduced his wife, Hina, and then Māui turned Togi-o into a dog. (Stimson 1934:37–46.)

TOGO, brother to Huahega* mother of the Tuamotuan hero Māui.* When Huahega was pregnant with Māui, Toga went to find a priest to perform the necessary sanctification rites for the newborn child. (Stimson 1934:8.)

TOGO-HITI, a goblin in the Tuamotuan legend of Rata who hindered Rata from felling a tree in his sacred valley. Rata (Laka*) captured him and forced him to build a voyaging canoe for him during the night. Also the name of one of Rata's sea captains in his voyage to the land of Puna to avenge his father. (Stimson 1937:117–126.)

TOHAEREROA, Māori god of the rainbow, also known as Kahukura.* (Tregear 1891:522; White 1887a: 6.)

TOHE-TIKA, a Marquesan god, born from his mortal mother's ear (or arm pit). He made his home with the other gods. He then appeared to his mother in a dream and instructed her to send food to him by way of his brothers. His brothers tarried along the way, and Tohe-tika, in the form of a huge bird, killed them. The parents set out after them, and when they found their sons' bodies strewn over the mountainside, they fled and hid in a nearby village.

Meanwhile, Tohe-tika married the daughter of Tū-Fiti and angered his father-in-law so much, that he hacked him to pieces. His head was taken to the home of his parents, and his mother conceived and gave birth to various parts of the new body of Tohe-tika. In revenge, Tohe-tika caused a huge flood that killed numerous people, struggled with others in combat, and killed them, including the gods Heouho and Pohoa. (Handy 1930:107–109.)

TOHITIKA, a powerful Tuamotuan god. (Stimson 1964: 546.)

TŌHO'I-MARO, a Tahitian god invoked by the worshippers in the *marae** (temple) when the image of the god is revealed from its resting place among its red and yellow-feathered coverings. (Henry 1928:167.)

TOHO-TIKA, the Marquesan god of war, thunder, and violent rain, a dreaded god of Haapa Valley who requires human sacrifices to placate his anger. (Christian 1895:190, 197.)

TOHU, the patron god of Tahitian tattooers, a sea god who paints the designs upon fish, and sometimes he is regarded as a shark god. (Henry 1928:234, 377, 389.)

TOHUTIKA, a powerful Tuamotuan god. (Stimson 1964: 547.)

TOI, name of a legendary people who supposedly inhabited the islands of New Zealand before the arrival of the first Polynesians, the Māoris, also known as Nuku-tāwhiti. (Grey 1970:8, 29; Tregear 1891:425.) See also **Hiti; Moriori; Mū People.** Toi was also the name of the Māori chief of Hawaiki* who killed and ate the dog belonging to Houmai-tāwhiti. The resultant conflict led to the emigration of the Māoris to New Zealand. (Grey 1970:99–105.)

TOIĒ, a stranger from the eastern islands who, with his wife Toipata, was responsible for the introduction of the mosquitos into Samoa. According to the legend, they came from the east with coconut vessels full of mosquitos and landed at Aunu'u on Tutuila. There, a young girl by the name of Taunu'u asked for water, and the couple gave her one of the coconuts which she opened and let the mosquitos out. The couple traveled on to 'Upolu and Savai'i where they opened their other coconuts. The Samoas on Savai'i were furious with their affliction and threatened to kill Toiē and Toipata. The couple fled to Aunu'u where they were turned into stone near Fagalele. (Krämer 1902:357.)

TOIKIA, a minor but strong god of Fakaofu, Tokelau Islands, famous for winning a wrestling match with the god Vevea. (Macgregor 1937:60.)

TOIMAU, the Māori god who presides over that portion of heaven nearest the earth, husband to Monoa (daughter of the god Whiro*), and a descendant of Tama-a-rangi. (Tregear

1891:525; White 1887a: App.) See also **Creation; Heavens.**

TOIRAGONI, son of the Rotuman god Tagaroa (Kanaloa*), personified by a turtle. (Gardiner 1898:467.)

TOKA, an ancestral spirit who tattooed the Māori chief Tamanui-araki* so that he would not be recognized by his relatives. (Tregear 1891:525.)

TOKAIRAMBE, the god of all Katumbalevu, Lau Islands, (Polynesian outliers in Fiji), whose temple is called Mauthori. Tokairambe's earthly representation is the sacred hawk, and his name is most likely Melanesian in origin. (Hocart 1929:189.) See also **Tui Lakemba.**

TOKA-I-VEVAU, a Marquesan god of the creation, son of Papa-Uka and Papa-Ao. (Christian 1895:188–189.)

TOKANIUA, a legendary figure of Rotuma, the first man. Anciently, before there were any mortal men on Rotuma, two women, Sientafitukrou and Sienjarolol (goddesses ?), set about creating female children from water and tumeric in coconut shells. One day, however, a male child named Tui Savarara was born, and he went to live with his sister, Sientakvou, who gave birth to a son, Tokaitoateniua (later shortened to Tokaniua). Ashamed of their act, Sientakvou left the child on a rock to die and fled into the bush where she became a wild woman named Honitemous. Ever since, the rock supposed has its menstrual periods with blood oozing up from a crack in it.

Tui Savarara unsuccessfully attempted to get rid of his son, but on each occasion he was miraculously saved. Tokaniua eventually settled in Niuafoou, but before he died, he returned to Rotuma where he had a son called Pilhofu who was stone except one eye and one big toe. (This same lava stone supposedly lies in Soukata today, oval shaped, about nine feet long, six feet wide, and three feet high.) Another legend relates that Pilhofu's son, also known as Tokaniua, came to Rotuma to find his stone father. They two were eventually reconciled, but only after several near disastrous events. (Gardiner 1898: 506–510.)

TOKE-I-MOANA, a Tongan god of Uiha in Ha'apai, worshipped by the royal family before conversion to Christianity. His intercession cures sickness. (Collocott 1921:234.)

TOKILAGAFANUA, anciently sent from heaven to be the ruler of 'Eua, Tonga, he can take the form of a shark in water or of a man on earth. The legend tells of the unsuspecting, incestuous relations between members of Tokilagafanua's family. First of all he slept with his sister, Hinatua-fuaga, and she gave birth to twin daughters, Topukulu and Nafanua* (rain goddesses). In disgrace he fled to Samoa, only to have his daughters visit him there, and he had children, Hemoanauliuli and Tafakula,* by them. They in turn cohabitated and have a son Lofia. As a result, all members of the family were turned into volcanic stone. (Reiter 1907:743–754; Collocott 1921:236.)

TOKO, one of the Māori props of heaven used by the god Tāne (Kāne*) to separate Rangi* (sky father) from Papa* (earth mother). Others were Haronga, Ruatipua, Toko-maunga, Toko-pā, Toko-roto, Rangi-pōtiki,* Tūrangi.*(Shortland 1882:12, 20; Tregear 1891:528–529; White 1887a:41, 52.) See also **Heavens.**

TOKOHITI, a Marquesan god, ruler of Hawaiki,* son of Papa-Uka and Papa-Ao. (Christian 1895:187–202.)

TOKO-MARU, name of one of the celebrated Māori canoes that brought the first Polynesians from Hawaiki* to New Zealand, commanded by chief Manaia* and Rakeora. (Grey 1970:108, 176–181; Tregear 1891:21–22, 529; White 1887b: 177.) See also **Canoes, Māori Migration.**

TOKOTOKO-URI, one of the gods of the Tuamotuan underworld.* (Stimson 1964:550.)

TOLIOATUA, a god of thieves on Niue Island. (Loeb 1926:163.)

TONGA, the Tuamotuan god of forests and uncultivated land (Stimson 1964:543); the Māori god of the south and the god of the forehead (Tregear 1891:531; White 1887a:App); the name of a whale belonging to the hero Tinirau (Kinilau*) in Tongan legend (Gifford 1924:139–152); also a principal god of Aitutaki, Cook Islands (Pakoti 1895:65–70).

TONGAHAKE, a division of the Tuamotuan underworld.* (Stimson 1964:543.)

TŌNGĀHITI, Māori god of headaches, mentioned in the story of Tāwhaki (Kaha'i*). (Tregear 1891: 531; White 1887a: 101.)

TONGAITI, a Cook Island god, responsible for guiding the navigator Uenga from Avaiki (Hawaiki*) to the Cook Islands. (Gill 1911:141.)

TONGA-ITI, the third son born to the great god Vātea (Wākea*) in Mangaian legends, whose earthly representation is the spotted lizard, worshipped under the name Mata-rau. (Buck 1934:165; Gill 1876:10–11.)

See also **Tangiia; Tane-papa-kai.**

TONGAMATAMOANA, a Tongan god whose magical fishhook was used by his twin grandchildren in fishing up the Tongan Islands. (Gifford 1924: 20.)

TONGA-MAULU'AU, a beautiful maiden, born to a heavenly couple, Aofitoki and his wife Aouli, in Tonga. In due course, a mortal man, Kulakehahau, heard of her beauty, stole to heaven, and kidnapped the young maiden. Eventually the parents were reconciled to their loss and allowed her to remain on earth. Not long afterwards, Kulakehahau was seduced in leaving his family and in living with his niece. When time came, Tonga-maulu'au gave birth to a daughter, Fakakanaoelangi, and when her husband did not return, she grew angry and decided to return to her heavenly home. Kulakehahau ran after her, and only because of the cries of her daughter did Tonga-maulu'au become reconciled with her husband and remain on earth. (Collocott 1928:41–43.)

TŌNGĀMEHA, Māori god of the eye (White 1887a: App.). Also the name of an ogre in the legend of Tāwhaki (Kaha'i*) who tore the eye out of one of Tāwhaki's slaves who happened to look upon his fortress.

(Grey 1970:53; Tregear 1891: 532.)

TONGAMULI, an ancestral god worshipped on Futuna. (Burrows 1936:105–108.)

TONGA-NUI, a Māori sea god, grandson of the god Tangaroa (Kanaloa*). Māui's* fishhook caught hold of Tonga-nui's house at the bottom of the sea. He pulled it up, and dry land appeared. (Grey 1970:31–32; Tregear 1891:532.) Also name of the land in Tuamotuan legends in which Hiro (Hilo*) lived when king Puna* sent for Hiro's son Tauta to serve him. (Stimson 1957.)

TONGAU, one of the four ancient Easter Island gods brought to the island by the voyager Hotu-Matua. (Alpers 1970:237–241; Métraux 1940:58–69.) See also **Kuaha; Kuihi; Opapako.**

TONGO, a Samoan war god, whose earthly representation is the owl. (Turner 1884:60–61, 74–75.)

TONGOTONGO, the mother of the sun god Rā* and the moon goddess Marama* by her husband Haronga* in Māori legends. (Shortland 1882:17; Tregear 1891:532.) Also the name of the wife of the Māori hero Tāwhaki (Kaha'i*), sometimes known as Hapai.* (Grey 1970:52–61; Tregear 1891:47; White 1887a:129.)

TONUAILANGI, a god of Fakaofu, Tokelau Islands, having the ability of prophesy through his earthly priests. (Macgregor 1937:60.)

TONUITENGENGA, one of many district gods of the Kaitu'u clan on Bellona Island, the son of the principal god Tehu'aingabenga.* (Monberg 1966:67.)

TONU-MĀ-NAHA, a Tahitian fish god. (Henry 1928:612.)

TONU-TAI, Tongan goddess of the creation, tortuous-water, daughter of the goddess Touiafutuna (metallic stone), twin to Tonu-uta* (tortuous-earth) with whom she married and became the parents of Vale-sii, (small-desire, mother of the famous demigod Māui*). (Reiter 1907:230–240.) See also **Creation.**

TONU-UTA, Tongan god of the creation, tortuous-earth, son of the goddess Touiafutuna (metallic stone), twin to Tonu-tai* (tortuous-water) with whom he married and became the parents of Vale-sii,* (small-desire, mother of the famous demigod Māui). (Reiter 1907: 230–240.) See also **Creation.**

TOPUKULU, a Tongan rain goddess on the island of 'Eua, daughter of Tokilagafanua* and his sister Hina-tuafuaga,* and twin to the goddess Nafanua.* Both were turned into volcanic stones because of their incestuous relations with their father. (Reiter 1907:743–754.)

TOROA, name of one of the canoes that brought the first Polynesians to New Zealand. (Tregear 1891:22; White 1887b: 179.)

TOROAKI, a major god of the island of Anuta. (Feinberg 1988.)

TŌTARA-KERIA, name of a celebrated canoe used by Māori warriors from New Zealand to return to their homeland of Hawaiki* to avenge the curse laid upon them by Manaia.* (Grey 1970:128–142; Tregear 1891:537.)

TOTE, the Māori god of sudden death. (Tregear 1891:537.)

TOTO, father-in-law to the Māori hero Turi.* He constructed two canoes, one he gave *Matahōrua** to Reti and *Aotea** to Turi to use in their migration to New Zealand. He had a son, Tuau, a daughter, Rongorongo* (wife to Turi), and a daughter, Kuramarotine (wife to Hoturapa*). (Grey 1970:161; Tregear 1891:537.)

TŌTORO-PŌ-TA'A, Tahitian god of hairdressing. (Henry 1928:379.)

TOUFA, a Tongan god who can take possession of a person (priest), a shark, or a gecko. (Beckwith 1948: 128; Gifford 1929:288.)

TOUIAFUTUNA or **TOUIA-A-FUTUNA**, the Tongan goddess of all creation, born to Limu* and Kele* in the form of a large metallic stone that belched forth four different sets of twins— Piki* and Kele,* Atugaki* and Maimoa-alogna,* Tonu-uta* and Tonu-tai,* Lupe* and Tukuhali*—all of whom brought forth new generations of deities. (Collocott 1921:152; Reiter 1907:230–240.) See also **Creation.**

TU, Tuamotuan name of the land through which Hina* traveled in her attempts to find another lover. She became the mistress of Māui,* and her previous lover, Tuna* (the eel), was killed, his head planted, and from it grew the first coconut tree. (Stimson 1934:28–32.) For the god Tū, see **Kū.**

TUA, a Tuamotuan god with extraordinary powers. (Stimson 1964:560.)

TUA-NUI-A-TE-RA, a member of the crew aboard the *Aotea** canoe in the Māori migration from Hawai'i* to New Zealand. He became insolent to Turi,* the chief of the canoe, and was throw overboard. When the canoe landed, the crew discovered the foot prints of Tua-nui, which they recognized because of a deformity in one of his feet. (Grey 1970:169–171; Tregear 1891:543.)

TUANUI-KA-RERE, a Mangaian demon from the east, who, in a fit of rage, swallowed the moon and caused lunar eclipses. (Gill 1876:47.) See also **Tangiia-ka-rere**.

TUAPIKO, one of the two guardians of the gate to the Māori underworld.* Mortals whose spirits are light fly quickly through; if heavy, they are caught and destroyed. (Tregear 1891:496; Wohlers 1876:111.) See also **Tawhaitiri**.

TUAPU'U, a Marquesan demon wife who could store her fish catch in an opening in her back. Her children gave her eels to eat which killed her, but she came back to life, pursued them, but they killed her once more. (Handy 1930:37–45.)

TUA-RA'A-TAI, a Tahitian god of the sea, servant to Tino-rua* (lord of the ocean). (Henry 1928:359.)

TUARAKI, name of that portion of the Tuamotuan underworld* where the adventures of demigods and heroes occurred. (Stimson 1964:562.)

TŪ-A-ROTO-RUA, the ancient Māori chief who first settled the

area called Rotorua, New Zealand, but who was dispossessed by his rival, Ihenga. (Grey 1970:123–125; Tregear 1891:554.)

TUĀTARA, a Māori lizard god, the son of Tū-te-wanawana* and Tupari. (Tregear 1891:544.)

TUA-TE-AHU-TAPU, the Marquesan god who guards the door to the underworld,* similar to Cerberus, the dog of Hades, in classical mythology. (Christian 1895:190.)

TUAU, son of the ancient Māori chief Toto* who was tricked to come aboard the *Aotea** canoe by his brother-in-law, Turi,* in their emigration from Hawaiki* to New Zealand. (Grey 1970:165–166; Tregear 1891: 544.) See also **Canoes, Māori Migration**.

TŪ-'ETE, the Tahitian god of licentiousness. (Henry 1928: 380.)

TŪ-FENUA, a Tahitian god created by Ta'aroa (Kanaloa*) during the creation.* (Henry 1928:344.)

TŪ-FE'UFE'U-MAI-I-TE-RA'I, wife of the Tahitian warrior god 'Oro,* formed by the great creator god Ta'aroa, and pushed out of heaven by her husband. She landed upon the earth and became a heap of sand where she ever remained. (Henry 1928:231, 375.)

TUFI, a Samoan war god whose earthly representation is in the form of a ten-foot long coconut spear. (Turner 1884:61–62.)

TUFULA, a god of Niue Island. (Loeb 1926:162.)

TUHAITENGENGA, one of the many district gods of the Kaitu'u clan on Bellona Island, the son of the principal god Tehu'aingabenga.* (Monberg 1966:67.)

TŪ-HAKAPŪIA, a Tuamotuan god of the sky world, the Rangi-pō. (Stimson 1964:565.)

TŪ-HINA-PŌ, an ocean god who guarded the Māoris in their migration to New Zealand. Seaweed is the offering made to him. (Tregear 1891:545; White 1887a:40.)

TŪ-HORO-PUGA, the supreme ruler of the ocean in Tuamotuan legends to whom prayers and sacrifices of food are made. (Stimson 1964:566, 620.) Also, a Tuamotuan chief who became the king of Havaiki (Hawaiki*) upon the death of the glutton king Mahu in the Tahaki (Kaha'i*) legend. (Stimson 1937:96–146.)

TŪ-HOU-RANGI, a Māori chief of historic times whose bones were revered by the people because of his large stature (nine feet tall). They were displayed on sacred occasions, especially at harvest time when fishing season commenced and when an enemy would attack. They were eventually carried off by the Ngā-Puhi tribe and seen no more. (Grey 1970:119–120; Tregear 1891:546.)

TŪHURUHURU, Māori name for the fairies Turehu* and Patupaerehe.* (Tregear 1891:546.) See also **Elves and Fairies.**

TŪ-HURUHURU, the son of the Māori goddess Hina and her husband, Irawaru,* who was born while Hina was living with the great hero Tinirau (Kinilau*). When Hina abandoned the child, he was reared by his foster father, Tinirau. When Tū-huruhuru was old enough Tinirau sent him out to find his mother who returned home to witness his baptism. After Tinirau's encounter with the sorcerer Kae* over his two pet whales, the followers of Kae attacked Tinirau's fortress and killed his son, Tū-huruhuru. (Grey 1970:69–76; Tregear 1891:546; White 1887b:142–146.)

TUI ALII, a benevolent household god in Samoa who bestows good health and a long life. Baldness is a sign of his punishment. (Turner 1884:75–76, 145.)

TUI ATUA, an ancient Samoan chiefly title, one of the three highest ranking titles in its history. Tui Atua was at one time the name of an ancient demon or god. (Krämer 1902:291.) See also **Tui Manu'a**. Also the name of a Samoan war god worshipped at Leone and Pago Pago. (Stair 1896:41.)

TUIFITI, a Samoan god or malevolent spirit especially venerated at Matautu, Savai'i. He can appear in the form of a woman, man, or dog. He dwells in ironwood trees. (Krämer 1902:23, 58; Turner 1884:62–63.) Also a Samoan war god worshipped at Matautu. (Stair 1896:41.) A god from the island of Fakaofo, Tokelau, who lives in the heavens with his daughter. Once when she came to earth to find food, she met two brothers, Moenī and Tafaki (Kaha'i*), and their sisters, Papua and Sigano. and married Moenī. (Burrows 1923:166–172.)

TUI-HAAFAKAFONUA, a Tongan sea god, identified with the Samoan god Moso,* who lives in the village of Maofanga near Nuku'alofa and who appears to mortals in the form of a lizard. (Collocott 1921:227.)

TU'I HAATALA, a mortal in Tongan legend whose spirit still wanders from one island to another. The legend relates that Tu'i Haatala (named after his father) was the sixth of nine sons. One by one, each of the sons began to die. Being the next in line, Tu'i Haatala decided to visit the underworld* (Pulotu*) in spirit to see why his brothers were being carried off. He instructed his family not to bury his body while he was gone so that he could return to it after his voyage.

Arriving in Pulotu and the house of Hikuleo,* the god of the underworld, Tu'i Haatala stole six pieces of a yam that were baking on the hearth. When Hikuleo discovered Tu'i Haatala's presence, he inquired why he had come to visit him. Tu'i Haatala told him of his family's losses on earth, and Hikuleo replied that the brothers had been taken because of the poverty on earth.

Because of Tu'i Haatala's visit, however, Hikuleo swore that he would never take another mortal. Satisfied, Tu'i Haatala returned to earth, but because his family had already buried his body, he was unable to return to life. Therefore, his spirit was forced to roam the islands where he is known in Tonga as the god Fehunui* and in Samoa as the god Moso.* (Gifford 1924:153–155.)

TŪ-I-HAWAIKI, a god of the Chatham Islands. (Shand 1894:90.)

TUI LAKEMBA, a primary god of Valelailai, Lau Islands

(Polynesian outliers in Fiji), also called Sereivalu because he unfolds war and all things. His temple was located at a sacred spot called Nautuutu, established anciently by immigrants from Tonga, therefore, he is regarded as a foreign god who came down from heaven (Thakaundrove), whereas Tokairambe* is a local god. Tui Lakemba is the title of the ruling chief. (Hocart 1929:190.) See also **Tokairambe.**

TUI MANU'A, highest-ranking chiefly title in all of Samoa, traditionally established by the sun god Tagaloa (Kanaloa*) or Lā* through his half-mortal son Pili,* who became the first Tui Manu'a. His three sons Ana, Tua, and Tuamasaga divided the island of 'Upolu and became the founders of the high-ranking titles in the Western Samoa islands (Tui Manu'a, Tui Atua* and Tui A'ana). They were awarded sacred reverence because of their divine origin, and many laws and taboos were created to protect their persons. (Craig 1981:298; Krämer 1902: 8–9.)

According to legend, the goddess Nafanua* revoked the chiefly titles shortly after they had been allotted, and they were not returned until the time of the famous chiefess Salamasina* (ca. A. D. 1500). (Krämer 1902:222.) See also **Malietoa.**

TUI-OLOTAU, a Tongan god of Olotau, located near the trilithon, the Ha'amonga-a-Māui, in east Tongatapu (similar to Stonehenge). His earth representation is the sea snake. (Collocott 1921:233.)

TUI ONEATA, the god of Oneata, Lau islands (Polynesian outliers in Fiji), incarnate as part snake, part eel. He has two nephews, known as Vasu i Tui Oneata, who live in stones in the village and who steal peoples' souls. (Hocart 1929:198–199.)

TUIOPULOTU, a Samoan war god identified with the district of Fagaloa, 'Upolu, Samoa, and the warriors from here take the image of their god into battle in a war chest aboard their canoes. (Krämer 1902:278–279.) Tuiopulotu is also a Samoan war god worshipped at Fagaloa and Atua. (Stair 1896:41.)

TU'I-ORA, a great, learned artisan for the Tahitian god Tāne (Kāne*). (Henry 1928:370.)

TUIPANGOTA, an inferior household god of Samoa who guards against thievery. (Turner 1884:76.)

TU'I-PULOTU, a minor Tongan sea god, patron god of chief Finau (Mariner 2:107). Also a god of the underworld* (Pulotu*) who invited several mortal sisters to his abode to slay them.

They were saved through the intervention of his brother, Vaipepe, but not before Tu'ipulotu had slept with the youngest on a special woven mat, hence the origin of the marriage mat of virginity (*kie tangavai*) in Tongan customs. (Collocott 1928:16–17.)

TU'ITATUI, the eleventh Tu'i Tonga* (king of Tonga), son of king Momo and his wife Nua (daughter of chief Lo'au*). Tu'itatui built the great tombs near the village of Heketa, east of Tongatapu, and the great trilithon called Ha'amonga-a-Māui (similar to Stonehenge) with the aid of his two sons, Talatama and Talaiha'apepe. He did not complete the work because he raped his half-sister Latuama, and her brothers chased him out of Heketa. He fled to 'Eua where he died. (Rutherford 1977:33–34.)

TU'I TOFUA, a Tongan shark god, originally the mortal son of Vakafuhu and Langitaetaea. Once when Vakafuhu was napping, Tu'i Tofua and his companions decided to play the game of *sika* (throwing cane spears along the ground). Their noise irritated Vakafuhu so much that he severely chastised the boys, whereupon Tu'i Tofua and his companions decided to set sail, never to return to land. Once out on the open ocean, each of his companions jumped into the water and was turned into a shark. Tu'i Tofua jumped last and turned into a great man-eating shark. Since then Tu'i Tofua has been worshipped as a god, and in Tonga the shark is sacred and is not to be eaten. (Gifford 1924:77–81.) See also **Fakapatu.**

TUI TOKELAU or **TUI TOKELAU SILI**, the principal god on Fakaofu, Tokelau Islands, who resides in the sky, and his appearance is accompanied by thunder and lightning. Fire is also sacred to him. He is a cannibal god who snares the spirits of mortals during the night and thus causes their death. He is associated with the god Tangaloa in the other Polynesian islands. (Macgregor 1937: 59–60; Turner 1884:268–269.)

TU'I TONGA, refers to the ancient kings of Tonga, who claimed divine descent from the great god Tangaloa (Kanaloa*). According to Tongan tradition, humans emerged from worm-like creatures who inhabited the earth. Once, the god Tagaloa 'Eitumatupua descended to earth by climbing down a huge ironwood tree which grew on the island of Toonangakava. He became enchanted with the mortal woman 'Ilaheva (sometimes called Vaepopua, the daughter of Seketoa*) and on several occasions cohabited with her. From this union was born a male child, 'Aho'eitu.*

Upon reached maturity, he asked his mother about his father. She informed him that he dwelt in the heavens, where-upon, 'Aho'eitu set out and found him. They rejoiced seeing each other, and then Tagaloa introduced 'Aho'eitu to his half-brothers who were very jealous of their handsome brother. In a rage, they sprang upon him, hacked him to pieces, and then ate him. When Tagaloa came home looking for his mortal son and not finding him, he sus-pected foul play. He demanded that each of his other sons vomit into a huge bowl. After 'Aho'eitu's bones and head were found, Tagaloa added water and leaves from the *nonufiaifa* tree (*Eugenia malaccensis* or Malay apple) to the mixture, and 'Aho'eitu was thus brought back to life.

When the brothers learned that he was really their blood brother, they rejoiced and pleaded with their father to al-low them to accompany 'Aho-'eitu to earth. When 'Aho'eitu returned to earth, he became the first Tu'i Tonga, and from him descends the royal rulers of Tonga (thirty-nine in direct descent—'Aho'eitu, Lolofaka-ngalo, Fangaoneone, Lihau, Kofutu, Kaloa, Mauhau, Apua-nea, Afulunga, Momo, Tu'ita-tui, etc.). (Gifford 1924: 25–70; Reiter 1933:355–362.)

TUI VAKANO, the chief god of Vakano, Lau Islands (Polyne-sian outliers in Fiji). (Hocart 1929:198.)

TUI VUTU, the god of Tuware, Lau Islands (Polynesian outliers in Fiji), who lives in the banyan tree and blows his whistle. (Hocart 1929:193.)

TŪKAHEROA, a Tuamotuan demon who can bend or stretch any part of its body to immense size in order to frighten hu-mans. (Stimson 1964:567.)

TUKAITAUA, a benevolent god of Aitutaki who presides over the good land (heaven) called Iva. On Mangaia, however, Tukaitaua is a malevolent god who brings violent death. (Gill 1876:175.)

TUKUTUKURAHO-NUI, great spider, name of the magical net used by the Tuamotuan hero Tahaki (Kaha'i*) in capturing the goblins who held his father. (Stimson 1937:86–89.)

TULAGAMOMOLE, a god of Niue Island invoked to make an opponent slip. (Loeb 1926:162.)

TULAU'ENA, a handsome Sa-moan, son of Tafitofau and Ogafau, who married the beautiful Sina (Hina*). His el-der brother, Tulifauiave, was jealous and killed him at sea. When Sina learned of the tragedy, she set out to find the sorceress Matamolali who could help bring her lover back to life. On the way, Sina met several birds whom she rewarded or cursed because of their instructions to her. She finally reached Matamolali who searched down into the waters of life, seized the spirit of the young husband, and returned with him to Samoa. Sina and Tulau'ena were reunited, and they lived happily ever after. (Krämer 1902:124–127.)

TULI, a plover, a bird messenger for the Samoan creator god Tagaloa (Kanaloa*), sent to earth to search for dry land on which to create plants, animals, and eventually humans. Because Tuli could not find dry land, Tagaloa threw stones down from heaven, and they became the islands of the sea. Sometimes Tuli (Turi) is regarded as Hina,* the daughter of Tagaloa. (Fraser 1890: 207–211; Krämer 1902: 394; Stair 1896:35.) See also **Tongo-noa**.

TULI-LEO-NU'U, a Samoan war god worshipped at A'ana and Tuamasaga. (Stair 1896: 41.)

TULIVAEPUPULA, a Samoan demon killed by two brothers, Laupanini and Laupanana, reminiscent of the European story of Hansel and Gretel. Laupanini and Laupanana were run out of their home by their parents because of their dis-

obedience. To spite their parents, they ran away to the demon Tulivaepupula where they were captured and served as his delousers until they were fat enough for the oven. The two boys tricked the demon into getting into the oven where he almost lost his life. The two boys escaped, the demon pursued, but in the end the two boys were able to kill him. (Krämer 1902:143–145.)

TŪ-MAKAVA-TAI, guard god of the rocks, Mangaia, Cook Islands. (Buck 1934:168.)

TŪ-MĀ-TAHI, a sea monster in Tahitian legend. (Henry 1928: 524.)

TŪ-MATAUENGA, son of the west wind according to Chatham Island mythology, gives strength to trees, fish, and birds in order to harm mortals. (Shand 1894:122.)

TŪ-MATUA, the sixth and last creation of the goddess Vari-ma-te-takere* in the Mangaian story of creation. She lives with her mother in the bottom depths of the universe called Avaiki (Hawaiki*) which is shaped in the form of a coconut. (Gill 1876:5–6.) See also **Kū**.

TŪ-METUA, a Mangaian goddess, daughter of the great goddess Vari-ma-te-takere,* whose name means straight-speech because she spoke no evil. (Buck 1934:13.)

TŪ-MOANA-'URIFA, the traditional father of turtles, chickens, and pigs according to Tahitian belief. Anciently, Tû-moana-'urifa and his wife Rifarifa from the island of Havai'i visited the island of Pupua in the Tuamotus. While there, turtles were born to them. When they returned home, they produced a family of chickens. Finally a human son, Metua-pua'a, was born. When grown, he was taken to Bora-Bora where he settled down and married. For a while the couple was happy, but soon the wife began teasing Metua-pua'a that he owned no land on Bora-Bora.

Tearfully, he returned home and told his mother his sad story. She told him to retire to the woods the following morning, open his mouth, and from it would rush a number of small animals which he was to secure into a pen until nightfall. They then would be mature animals. These he should present to his wife and family on Bora-Bora. Metua-pua'a followed his mother's instructions, and his wife's family was delighted with the fascinating new animals. From them, sprang all the other pigs on the earth, and they became food for both gods and humans. (Henry 1928:381–382.)

TUMEI-O-RANGI, a god of the Chatham Islands. (Shand 1894:90.)

TUMU, the Tuamotuan god of life who rewards spirits according to their earthly deeds. (Henry 1928: 349.)

TUMU-AO, Tuamotuan name of one region of the sky world, the Rangi-pō. (Stimson 1964: 572.)

TUMUE, the god of evil on Mangareva (French Polynesia). (Caillot 1914:154.)

TUMU-HARURU, Tuamotuan name of one region of the sky world, the Rangi-pō. (Stimson 1964:572.) See also **Heavens.**

TUMU-NUI, a major Tahitian god during the creation.* Tumu-nui and his wife Papa-raharaha* were responsible for creating the pillars that hold up the sky (Rumia*). Another name for the Tahitian creator god Ta'aroa (Kanaloa*). Also the name of the uncle to the Tahitian hero Rata (Laka*). When he and his relatives were lost at sea, Rata became king. (Henry 1928:342–343, 356, 358, 395, 419.)

TUMU-O-TE'OTE'O, the Tahitian god of springtime. (Henry 1928:378.)

TUMU-PŌ, Tuamotuan name of one region of the sky world,

the Rangi-pō. (Stimson 1964: 572.) See also **Heavens.**

TUMU-RA'I-FENUA, the name of the great octopus in Tahitian mythology that firmly held the sky and land together during the early creation. It was the god Tū (Kū*) that killed him in order that the separation could take place. The great octopus fell to earth and became the island of Tubuai. (Henry 1928: 356, 441.)

TUMURŪIA, supreme lord of the sky world, the Rangi-pō, according to Tuamotuan legends. (Stimson 1964:572.)

TUMU-RUPERUPE, the Tahitian god of summer and of wind. (Henry 1928:378, 395.)

TUMUTEANAOA, the fourth deity (goddess), named Echo, brought forth in the Mangaian story of creation by the goddess Vari-ma-te-takere.* (Gill 1876: 5.)

TUMU-TE-OVE, a minor god of the Manaune tribe, Mangaia, Cook Islands. (Buck 1934: 168.)

TUMU-TE-VAROVARO, one of the first gods of Rarotonga, Cook Islands. His son, Mo'o-kura, married Kaua and migrated to the west side of the island. Once Tumu-te-varovaro visited his son, and while he was away, the god Tangaroa

(Kanaloa*) came to Rarotonga and with his warrior Au-make leveled the land all around with his walking stick. When Tumu-te-varovaro returned, all that he found was his house standing, now known as Mount Raemaru, the flat top mountain of the village of Arorangi. (Brown 1897:1–10.)

TUMUTUMU-WHENUA, a divine ancestor of the Māori people, often referred to as Tupu-tupu-whenua. (Tregear 1891:552.) See also **Kumu-honua.**

TUMU-WHAKAIRIHIA, a Māori chief of ancient Hawaiki* who instructed chief Rua-whārō* of the famous *Taki-tumu* canoe in incantations and spells he needed for revenge against his enemies. (Tregear 1891:552; White 1887c:43–47.)

TUMU-WHENUA, the Māori patron god of rats, son of Ati-nguku. (Tregear 1891:552; White 1887a: App.)

TŪNA, a giant eel, the husband of the goddess Hina* in the Tuamotuan story, who lived with her at the bottom of the sea. When Hina became tired of him, she sought a lover elsewhere. When she found Māui,* Tūna became enraged, contested with Māui on the beach, and Māui won. Tūna's head was cut off and planted from whence sprouted the first coconut tree. (Stimson 1934:28–33; Stimson 1964:573.)

Several variant stories of Tuna exist in **New Zealand**. One refers to him as a god, the son of Manga-wai-roa, who descended to earth because of a drought in heaven (Wohlers 1874:19, 44). Another suggests that he raped Hina, wife to the demigod Māui, and that he was hacked to pieces by the hero. From the various parts of his body came monsters, various plants, as well as the eel family (White 1887b:83–84). The last maintains that Hina was the daughter of Tuna and Repo and the wife to Māui. When Tuna violated his daughter, Māui killed his father-in-law, and the parts of his body became eels and certain land trees and plants (White 1887b:76).

TUNA-RANGI, the Māori god of the fern root and flax plants. (Tregear 1891:552; White 1887a: App.)

TUNARUA, name of the water monster slain by the Māori hero Māui.* (Tregear 1891:552.) See also **Tuna**.

TUNA-TE-VAI-ROA, the Tuamotuan name of the giant eel who lives in the land of Kautu and who once became Hina's lover after the death of Tiki. (Stimson 1937:8.)

TUOHEA, a Tuamotuan giant and cannibal who ruled the southern part of the Hao atoll. He was born with four eyes and was, therefore, abandoned by his parents. He ate all humans who dared come near his islets of Opokara and Onikau. He was finally captured and slain by his younger brothers and sister by deception. The sister seduced Tuohea into eating some forbidden food (shark and tuna), whereupon he died. After his death, humans were free to venture near the southern part of the island once again. (Caillot 1914:43–50.) See also **Giants.**

TŪ-O-TE-TO'I-'OI, a powerful Tahitian wind god who drives away invading armies. His earthly representation is the cricket. (Henry 1928:393.)

TUPA, an ancient hero of Mangareva (French Polynesia). During the reign of kings Tavere and Taroi, Tupa and his brother Noa (sons of Ahipiki-ragi) came with their companions from the west to Mangareva. They had been exiled from their homeland because of a religious war. On Mangareva, they taught the people how to fish and farm more effectively, and they established the worship of the powerful god Tū (Kū*) throughout the surrounding islands. Eventually the party set sail to return to their native land of Havaiki (Hawaiki*) and were never seen again. (Caillot 1914:173–174.)

In the **Marquesas**, Tupa is identified with the introduction of kava* to mortals. Tupa died in heaven and his body fell to earth. A mortal by the name of Kaukau ate the food and died. From his body grew the first kava plant from which Kaukau's younger brother Feitu derived the sacred drink. (Steinen 1934:227–228.)

In **New Zealand**, Tupa is a sister to the Māori chief Tūtānekai* (lover and later husband to the beautiful Hinemoa*). (Grey 1970:183, 191.)

TUPA-I-HAKAAVA, a Marquesan god of the creation, son of Papa-Uka and Papa-Ao. (Christian 1895:188–189.)

TŪ-PAPA, wife of the Tahitian god Ra'a* (sacredness). (Henry 1928:357.) See also **Papa**.

TŪPARA-HAKI, ancestress of the principal chiefs of the Ngāti-Paoa tribe in New Zealand, the daughter of Takakopiri* and Kahu-rere-moa,* supposedly having lived some eleven generations (275 years) before A.D. 1853. (Grey 1970:210; Tregear 1891:555.)

TŪ-PARAU-NUI, an ancient Māori god who assumed the form of a fly and buzzed over the grave of Tū-te-nganahau, the slain son of chief Manaia*

of Hawaiki.* (Tregear 1891:555; White 1887b:187.)

TŪ-PARI, mother of the Māori lizard gods Moko-i-kuwharu, Tuatara, Kaweau, Mokomoko, and others by her husband, Tū-te-wanawana.* (Tregear 1891:555; White 1887a:App.)

TUPARIMAEWA, the Māori god who presides over the liver. (Tregear 1891:555; White 1887a:App.)

TUPE, the Māori god who presides over the calf of the leg. (Tregear 1891:555; White 1887a:App.)

TUPE-'I'O-AHU, one of the great demons of the sea in the Tahitian Rata (Laka*) legend. (Henry 1928:470–495.)

TUPENGUSU, an obscure snake goddess from Bellona Island, not related to the other gods. (Monberg 1958:46–49.)

TŪ-PENU, a Māori chief of ancient Hawaiki* who was slain in a war brought about by his rape of Rongo-tiki,* the wife of chief Manaia.* As a result of the bad blood between the two tribes, Mangaia and his people boarded the *Toko-maru* canoe and emigrated to New Zealand. (Grey 1970:173–176; Tregear 1891:555.)

TŪPERE-KAUAHA-ROA, a Tuamotuan name for the lower

jaw of the universe; the upper jaw is Kokohu-i-matangi. (Stimson 1964:574.)

TŪPERE-TEKI, a Tuamotuan tossing game or contest supposedly occurring between heroes and demigods. (Stimson 1964:574.)

TUPETUPE-I-FARE-ONE, an ingenious Tahitian goddess who dwells with Tāne (Kāne*) in the sky. (Henry 1928:371.)

TŪ-PORO-MAI, one of the daughters of the Tahitian creator god Ta'aroa (Kanaloa*) and his wife Papa-raharaha,* goddess to proclaim upon the mountains for Ta'aroa. (Henry 1928:374.) See also **Tū-poro-tū.**

TŪ-PORO-TŪ, daughter of the Tahitian creator god Ta'aroa (Kanaloa*) who proclaimed him upon the mountains. She also helped create the first *marae** (temple) for her father Ta'aroa. It was formed from Ta'aroa himself. His backbone became the ridgepole, his breast bone was the capping of the roof, and his thighbone became the carved ornaments around the house. This *marae* became a model for all subsequent temples for the gods. (Henry 1928: 374, 426.) See also **Tū-poro-mai.**

TUPUA, a Māori name for a goblin, a monster, a demon, a fairy, or the spirit of a deceased sorcerer. (Tregear 1891:557;

White 1887a:48, 2:9.) Also one of the descendants of Rangi* (sky father) and Papa* (earth mother) that became stars in the heavens after their separation. (Tregear 1891:500; White 1887a: 48.)

The name of one of the original **Tuamotuan** creator gods, believed to have been the first sorcerer, frequently identified with the god Tahito.* (Stimson 1964:575.)

A **Samoan** word to designate the deified spirits of chiefs who are supposed to dwell in the underworld,* Pulotu. (Stair 1897:34.) A star god of Futuna. (Burrows 1936:105–108.)

TUPUALEGASE, a Samoan god, patron deity of the district of Falefā, 'Upolu, Samoa, an important district for being a distinguished seat of government as well as rich in ancient history. (Krämer 1902:277.)

TUPUFUA, the first man according to the Samoan genealogy of the Tui A'ana chiefs, the son of Salasala and Tagaloanimonimo (Tagaloa-the-immeasurable). (Krämer 1902: 168.) See also **Creation; Ma'ata'anoa.**

TUPUIMANUKATU'U, after Tehu'aingabenga,* the second major god of Bellona Island. (Monberg 1966:58–74.)

TUPUIMATANGI, one of the many district gods of the

Kaitu'u clan on Bellona Island, the son of the principal god Tehu'aingabenga.* (Monberg 1966:67.)

TUPUITENGENGA, one of the many district gods of the Kaitu'u clan on Bellona Island, the son of the principal god Tehu'aingabenga.* (Monberg 1966:67.)

TUPUNUI-A-UTA, a Māori chief who lived at the time of the great deluge* and who attempted to teach the people the true doctrines regarding the separation of Rangi* (sky father) and Papa* (earth mother). He and his companion, Para-whenua-mea, built a large canoe which saved them from the flood. Perhaps the same person as Tupu-tupu-whenua.* (Tregear 1891:558; White 1887a:172–180.)

TUPU-O-TE-MOANA, a Tahitian god of the rocks in the ocean during the time of creation.* (Henry 1928:344.)

TUPU-O-TE-RANGI, the dwelling place of the Māori god Rehua,* the tenth or highest division of heaven. (Taylor 1870:283; White 1887a:App.)

TUPURANGA-O-TE-AO, the name of the path traveled by the Māori goddess Hine-nui-te-pō* on her journey to the underworld.* (White 1887a:131.) Also the name of the doorkeeper to the underworld who opened the doors to allow the god Tāne (Kāne*) to enter to seek his wife, Hine-nui-te-pō. When Tāne saw the darkness therein, he drew back terrified and would not enter. (White 1887a: 132.)

TURA, an ancient Māori chief of Hawaiki* who is famous for having accompanied his friend, Whiro (Hilo*), the great voyager, on his travels of discovery. When they reached the shores of a land called O-tea, Tura left Whiro and set out on his own. He met a group of fairies (elves*) called Aitanga-a-nuku-mai-tore and married one of them (Turaki-hau) and lived happily for a while. He taught them to make fire by friction and to cook their food.

When Turaki-hau came time to deliver their first child, she lamented that she soon would die because it was their practice of performing Caesarian operation, a certain death for the mother. Tura drove off the midwives and delivered the child the natural way. One day Turaki-hau discovered white hairs growing from her husband's head and asked what they were. He informed her that it was a sign of old age and death. Tura bid farewell to his wife and son, and set up residence some distance away from the group.

Here he spent his remaining years, reminiscing of his

younger years and his travels with Whiro. He often cried out in his sleep for his son Ira-tū-roto whom he had left behind in Hawaiki. Ira-tū-roto heard his father in his dream, and was determined to set out to find him. He found him in a most destitute state, washed him, and carried him back to his own land to his first wife, Rau-kura-matua, where he died. (White 1887b:6–19.)

In the **Cook Islands**, Tura was a mortal man who came from the island of Atiu to marry Tara-matie-toro, daughter of the god of the underworld,* Uke, and they became the progenitors of the Mauke islanders. (Gill 1911:136.)

TŪ-RAHU-NUI, Tū-the-great-conjurer, one of the many epithets of the Tahitian god Tū (Kū*). The island of Tahiti was anciently believed to have been attached to the sacred island of Ra'iātea (Hawaiki*). When the separation of the islands occurred, Tahiti floated as a fish south and eastward to its present location guided by the god Tū-rahu-nui, who still guards its position in the island chain. (Henry 1928:355, 438.)

TŪ-RA'I-PŌ, the patron god of tattooing. According to Tahitian legend, tattooing originated in the chaotic period of the creation* (called the *pō*). It was invented by the god Matamata-arahu* (printer-in-charcoal),

aided by his assistant Tū-ra'i-pō (Tū-of-the-dark-sky). They were the artisan gods of Ta'ere,* the god of skill who dwells at the center of the earth (Rua-papa). (Henry 1928:287, 374, 406.) See also **Tattoo.**

TŪ-RAKI, ancestor of the moon goddess in Māori legends. (Tregear 1891:561; White 1887b: 87.)

TURAKI-HAU, the fairy wife to the Māori hero Tura* whom he met and fell in love with during his voyage from Hawaiki* to New Zealand. (Tregear 1891: 561; White 1887b:12–13.)

TURANGA, a tribal god of the Tongaiti, Mangaia, Cook Islands, also known as Matarau (two-hundred-eyes), the spotted lizard. (Buck 1934:165–166.)

TŪRANGA-I-MUA, son of the Māori chief Turi,* born to him in ancient Hawaiki* before his emigration to New Zealand. (Grey 1970:160; Tregear 1891: 561.)

TŪRANGI, one of the props of heaven according to Māori belief, the child of Rangi-pōtiki* and his wife Hine-ahu-papa.* (Tregear 1891: 561.) See also **Heavens; Toko.**

TURI, an ancient Māori chief of Hawaiki* responsible for the emigration of the first Polynesians to New Zealand. In

Hawaiki, a relative of Turi sent his young son, Pōtiki-roroa, with some burnt offerings for food to the high priest Ue-nuku.* The young boy tripped and lost the food, whereupon the angry Ue-nuku killed and ate the boy. In revenge Turi killed Ue-nuku's son, cut out his heart, baked it, and sent it to Ue-nuku for food. When he learned of the terrible deed, Ue-nuku swore revenge upon Turi and his family. Meanwhile, Turi's father-in-law, Toto, gave his daughter Rongo-rongo a specially-constructed canoe named *Aotea* in which they could flee Hawaiki. Turi and his family gathered together their belongings and set out to discover a new home, a land described to them by another famous voyager Kupe.*

In mid-ocean, the *Ao-tea* developed a leak, and they had to stop at a small island, Rangitahua, for repairs and to offer sacrifice for their future success. After an argument regarding their course of direction, the crews were on their way once more. The accompanying *Ririno* canoe became lost and was ultimately destroyed on a reef. Turi and his party aboard the *Ao-tea* finally landed in the harbor called *Aotea* in New Zealand, and then made their way along the coast to the Patea river where they settled. Turi and his wife had several children, and they became the progenitors of the Whanganui and Ngāti-Ruanui tribes of New Zealand. (Grey 1970:158–172; Tregear 1891:563.)

TURIA, a Samoan god of war, peace, and weather. (Turner 1884:62.)

TURIHONO, Tuamotuan name of a sky region in the underworld* (Rangi-pō). (Stimson 1964:578.)

TŪRIKIRIKI, Tuamotuan name of a sky region in the underworld* (Rangi-pō). (Stimson 1964:578.)

TURI-TUA, a Samoan war god worshipped at Falealili. (Stair 1896:41.)

TURTLES, a story from Bora-Bora tells that turtles were first born to a mortal couple, Tū-moana-'urifa* and his wife, Rifarifa, from Ra'iātea who became the parents of turtles while they were visiting the Tuamotuan island of Pupua. From here, the turtles spread throughout the other islands. Turtles are sacred food for the gods to be consumed only by kings and priests in the *marae** (temple). (Henry 1928:380–381.)

TŪTAE-'ĀVAE-TO'ETO'E, a Tahitian god to whom warriors' clothes are dedicated. Tattered and blood stained clothing are stored in the temple (*marae**) dedicated specifically to this god. He is also the god of the underworld* (Hades) and the god who guards the buried victims from the battlefield for the war god 'Oro. (Henry 1928: 314, 318–319, 375.)

TŪ-TAE-POROPORO, a water monster supposedly having lived in the Wanganui river of New Zealand, killed by Aokehu,* who, having been swallowed by the monster, hacked it to death. (Kauika 1904:94–98; Tregear 1891:566.)

TŪ-TĀ-HORO'A, a Tahitian god who guards the fork in the road on the island of Ra'iātea leading to the underworld* called Rohutu-noanoa (fragrant Rohutu). Sometimes he directs spirits to return to earth for a while, others he directs either to the right to paradise (Rohutu-noanoa) or to the left to the region of utter darkness (pō). (Henry 1928:201–202, 564; Moerenhout 1837:434.) See also **Ta'ere.**

TŪ-TAKA-HINAHINA, an ancient Māori (god ?) without father or mother who traversed the face of the oceans. Just before his death, he instructed his son, Roiroi-whenua, to bury him face down beside his house because darkness would spread upon the face of the earth. He also instructed his son to cook a large maggot which would emerge from the grave. (According to this legend, this was the first fire to be created by fiction and to be introduced among humans.) While the worm was cooking, Roiroiwhenua struck the oven, and light emerged once again upon the face of the earth. Since that time, the morning dawn has been dedicated to to the god Tamatea* rather than to Tangaroa (Kanaloa*). (Tregear 1891:566; White 1887b:48–51.)

TŪTĀNEKAI, the celebrated lover of the beautiful Māori heroine Hine-moa.* (Grey 1970:183–191; Tregear 1891: 566.)

TŪTANGATAKINO, a Māori reptile god, the son of Tū-tewanawana and Mairangi,* who presides over the human stomach, and who dwells with Miru (Milu,* the goddess of the underworld*). (Tregear 1891: 566; White 1887a:App.)

TUTAU, a war god of Niue Island. (Loeb 1926:162.)

TŪTAWA, son of the Māori chief Turi* and his wife Rongorongo, born in the canoe *Aotea*,* on their journey from Hawaiki* to New Zealand. (Grey 1970:169; Tregear 1891: 566.)

TŪ-TAWAKE, an ancient Māori god, born from the loins of the goddess Haumea,* who preached to the evil nations of the world. They would not listen, therefore, he destroyed thousands of them in a battle called Tai-pari-pari (flowing-tide), and drove many others into the forests. (White 1887a:166; Tregear 1891:566–567.) Another story of Tū-taw(h)ake refers to him as being evil, but the extant legend is garbled and unintelligible. (White 1887b:172.)

TŪTEA-ITI, an elder brother of the Māori hero Tūtānekai* (lover to the heroine Hine-moa*). (Grey 1970:83; Tregear 1891:567.)

TŪ-TE-HAHI-RANGI, a Tua-motuan god associated with the gods Kiho, Rongo, and Tāne-tū-tira. (Stimson 1964:580.)

TŪ-TE-KORO-PANGA, a Māori chief who eloped with Ruku-tia,* the wife of Tama-nui-a-raki.* (Grey 1970:35–47; Tregear 1891:567; White 1887a:42.)

TŪ-TE-NGANAHAU, son of the Māori chief Manaia* of ancient Hawaiki.* (Tregear 1891:567; White 1887b:187.)

TŪ-TE-PAE-RANGI, name of the canoe of the Māori chief Ruatapu* who drowned 140 elder sons of his enemies. (Tregear 1891:567; White 1887c: 10.)

TUTEPOGANUI, the name of the Tuamotuan sea god whose chief attendant is Tohoropuga. They both live in Ruahatu (Hawaiki*). (Caillot 1914:95–109.)

TŪ-TE-WANAWANA, the patron god of reptiles according to Māori tradition, the son of Punga* and grandson of Tangaroa (Kanaloa*). During the war in heaven, the children of Punga deserted Tangaroa and fled to the earth for safety. Ikatere* fled to the sea and became lord of the fishes, Tū-te-wanawana fled to the forests where he became lord and pro-genitor of the reptiles. His wives were Whaitiri and Tu-pari. (Grey 1970:6; Tregear 1891:567; White 1887a: App.) See also **Tū-te-wehiwehi**.

TŪ-TE-WEHIWEHI, the patron god of reptiles according to Māori tradition, the son of Punga,* and grandson of Tan-garoa (Kanaloa*). During the war in heaven, the children of Punga deserted Tangaroa and fled to the earth for safety. Ikatere* fled to the sea and became lord of the fishes, Tū-te-wanawana fled to the forests where he became lord and pro-genitor of the reptiles. (Grey 1970:6; Tregear 1891:567; White 1887a:App.) See also **Tū-te-wanawana**.

TŪ-TONO, an artisan for the Tahitian god Ta'ere* who dwells in the center of the earth and who is the source of all knowledge and skill. (Henry 1928:374, 406.)

TUTU-MAI-AO, an extinct people who supposedly inhabited the islands of New Zealand before the arrival of the Polynesians. They were invaded by the Turehu people (elves* or fairies) who intermarried with them and who assimilated them into their culture. The Turehu also became extinct before the Māoris arrived. (Tregear 1891: 568; White 1887c:188–189, 191.) See also **Hiti; Moriori; Mū People.**

TUTUMATUA, the god of Naitombo, Lau Islands (Polynesian outliers in Fiji), of Polynesian origin, and extremely popular. He lives on the shore and is often visible by the islanders. Stories are told of his sexual exploits with his long penis. (Hocart 1929:191.) Also the god of Yawalevu in Yandrana, Lau Islands (Polynesian outliers in Fiji), who fell from heaven to earth and whose earthly form is the white crane. He is a brave god and extremely fond of women. (Hocart 1929:196–197.)

TUTU-NUI, a monster whale, son of Tini-rau and Putu-rua, in the Tuamotuan story of Rata (Laka*). He guards the entrances to the lands belonging to the king of Puna. (Stimson 1937:126–129.) Also the name of a pet whale belonging to the Māori hero Tinirau (Kinilau*). (Grey 1970:69–76; Tregear 1891: 568.) See Also **Kae.**

TŪ-TŪ-RAHU-NUI, a big spider, the shadow (messenger) of the Tahitian god Tū (Kū*), responsible for guiding the island of Tahiti to its final resting place during the breakup of the islands during the creation. (Henry 1928:392.) See also **Terehe.**

TUTUROROA, the Māori god of mists. (Tregear 1891:568.)

TUUHITI, a Marquesan god of the creation, son of Papa-Uka and Papa-Ao, principally worshipped at Hiva Oa. (Christian 1895:188–189.)

TU'UITEIKA, one of the many district gods of the Kaitu'u clan on Bellona Island, the son of the principal god Tehu'aingabenga.* (Monberg 1966:67.)

TU'UKITEIKA, one of many many district gods on Bellona Island. (Monberg 1966:71.)

TU'U-KO-IHU, the first priest on Easter Island who introduced the carving of images with prominent rib cages. He fashioned them after two spirits, Hitirau and Ha-uriuri, whose ribs he saw showing. Afterwards, he caused the images to walk. (Alpers 1970:243–246.)

TU'UOLA, a minor god of Futuna who lives in the sea. (Burrows 1936: 105–108.)

TU'URA, a Rotuman word to indicate a person's ghost (*'atua*) which has taken up residence in a certain animal. (Churchward 1938:471.)

TŪ-URE-NUI, son of the Māori chief Manaia* of ancient Hawaiki* who accompanied his father to New Zealand. The Urenui River is named after him. (Grey 1970:107–110; Tregear 1891:568.)

TUVAIUA, a god of peace of Tuapa, Niue Island. (Loeb 1926: 160.)

TUVUVOTA, a Samoan god, who conspired with Sisi* and Faingaa* to steal the island of Tofua, Tonga. They were prevented from doing so by the Tongan god Tafakula.* (Gifford 1924:89.)

TŪ-WAE-RORE, one of the many wives of the Māori god Tāne (Kāne*), patron goddess of the seaweed, the *Tanekaha*, (*Phyllocladus trichomanoides*), and the *kahika-tea* (white pine). (Tregear 1891:568; White 1887a: 143.) See also **Kuraki.**

TŪ-WHAKARARO, a Māori chief of ancient Hawaiki* whose murder caused the civil strife that lead to the Māoris leaving Hawaiki to settle New Zealand. Tū-whakararo, son of Tū-huruhuru and Apakura and grandson of Hina* and Irawaru,* once visited his sister Mairatea and her husband. While there, he engaged in a friendly wrestling match, but his defeated opponent became angry and clubbed him to death.

When the news of the event reached the ears of his brother, he raised a select army, and set sail in their canoes under the leadership of Whakatau-pōtiki. Having secured the safety of his sister, Whakatau-pōtiki avenged his brother's death, burned down the tribal meeting house, the Te Uru-o-manono, with all those within, and then returned home. The subsequent intertribal conflict caused a large group of Māoris to set out for New Zealand. (Grey 1970:77–83, 90; Tregear 1891:568–569; White 1887b: 147–150.) Also the name given to the son of the Māori hero Rata (Laka*) and his wife Tonga-rautawhiri. (Grey 1970:90.)

TŪ-WHARE-TOA, an ancient Māori chief, father to Tūtānekai* (the husband of the beautiful Hine-moa*). (Grey 1970:183; Tregear 1891:569.)

TŪ-WHENUA, ancestor to the Māori chief Tama-nui-araki,* who met him in his travels to the underworld.* (Tregear 1891:569.)

–U–

UAHEA, goddess in the Tahitian creation, born to the god Rū and his wife Rua-papa, wife to Hiki-Rā (sun), and mother to the demigod Māui.* In the Tuamotus, she is the mortal wife to the god Tangaroa-i-te-pō and thus the mother of Māui. (Henry 1928:348, 352, 408.)

UA-NANA-NEI, a Marquesan god mentioned in the story of Ta'a-pō* and her journey to the underworld.* (Handy 1930:85.)

UATAI, a Māori lizard god of inferior status. (Tregear 1891: 571; White 1887a:App.)

UĒNGĀNUKU, a Tuamotuan god. (Stimson 1964:583.)

UENGAPUAARIKI, the Māori chief who captained the *Horouta* canoe in the Polynesian migration to New Zealand. (Tregear 1891:572.) See also **Canoes, Māori Migration**.

UE-NUKU, a name of several Māori gods, heroes, and ancient chiefs. He is the god of the rainbow, referred to as Kahukura,* and hawk feathers are sacred to him. (Davies 1885:164; Tregear 1891:572.) Another Ue-nuku is a minor reptile god, the son of Tū-te-wanawana* and Mairangi, and a descendant of the fire goddess Mahuika.* (White 1887a:App.) One mortal Ue-nuku is a deified ancestor of the Māoris, a descendant of the war god Tū-mata-uenga, and father to Ru-atapu* (responsible for the great deluge*). (Grey 1970:90–108.)

The high priest Ue-nuku was responsible for the emigration of the hero Turi* from Hawaiki to New Zealand. (Grey 1970: 158–172; Tregear 1891:563.) Another Ue-nuku was the Māori chief of Hawaiki,* responsible for the Māori migration to New Zealand. He and his friend, Toi-te-hautahi, killed and ate the dog Pōtaka-tāwhiti, which belonged to chief Haumai-tāwhiti. In revenge, Haumai-tāwhiti's two sons, Tama-te-kapua* and Whaka-turia, stole fruit from Ue-nuku's *poporo* tree, and, as a result, war broke out between their two villages. Haumia-tāwhiti and his son Whakaturia were killed, but Tama-te-kapua emigrated from Hawaiki to New Zealand, but not before they cut off Ue-nuku's head. (Grey 1970: 99–104; Tregear 1891:459.)

UE-NUKU-KŌPAKO, a Māori rainbow god. (Tregear 1891: 572.)

UETONGA, patron god of Māori tattoo,* the grandson of Rū (the earthquake god), who dwells in the underworld* (the *pō*). He taught the art of tattooing to Mataora* (his son-in-law) who then taught it to other humans. Uetonga was responsible for tattooing the great demigod Māui.* (Grey 1970:44; Tregear 1891:574; White 1887b: 4.)

ŪHO, the Tuamotuan name for the first living matter, the primeval force, or the creative powers of divinity. (Stimson 1964:585.)

UHU-MAKAIKAI, the parent of all fish according to Hawaiian legends (Beckwith 1948:24); a parrot fish; name of the fish which dodged the spears of Kawelo,* a popular Hawaiian warrior. (Beckwith 1948:48, 406–407, 410.)

UI, meaning darkness in Samoan, a female personage in the creation who was responsible for the slowing of the sun, Tagaloa (Kanaloa*), and for preventing him from continuing his cannibalistic ways. Once, a young chief by the name of Tufugauli overheard the women in the sun's household shaming him, and as a result, he went and told him about it. The sun swore that he would rise slowly in the morning and slay all humankind. Luama'a and his sister Ui heard about it and planned what they should do. The next morning, Ui set out toward the east, and when the sun arose, she straddle him, and he agreed to slow his course to allow more light, but not enough to destroy the human race.

The son of the union of Ui and Tagaloa was named Tagaloaui. After the death of his mother and uncle, Tagaloaui went to find other mortals on the islands. He came upon the home of Pava* (a demon and war god of 'Upolu) and his two sons Telemū and Maifa'i. They drank kava* and conversed together for two days. He continued his journey until he reached Lefaga where he lived until he died. He supposedly married the goddess Sināsa'umani* and through his lineage gave rise to the high chiefly title Tui Manu'a.* (Fraser 1892:121– 132; Krämer 1902:403–409.) Another legend says that Ui (Luaui) and Luama'a were children of Fiso and Ufi. (Krämer 1902: 409–410.)

UIKA, a demon, a dark colored centipede, encountered by the first Cook Island explorers, Te Erui and his brother Matareka, from Avaiki (Hawaiki*). (Gill 1911:150.) See also **Katotiae; Mokoroa.**

UI-KOVARO, a god worshipped by the great voyager Iro (Hilo*) from the island of Aitutaki. (Large 1903:133–144.)

UIRA, a Māori god, descendant of Rangi* (sky father) through Rehua* (the god of kindness) and who was the progenitor of Whaitiri* (god of thunder and lightning). See also the Hawaiian god of thunder and lightning Kahuila-maka-keha'i-i-ka-lani.* (Beckwith 1948:492–495; Tregear 1891:574.)

UKE-UMU, god the underworld,* according to Cook Island legends, who came to earth and married the woman Puai-angauta, and their descendants populated the islands of Mauke and Aitu in the Cook group. (Gill 1911:136.)

ULAVAI, an inferior household god of Samoa, incarnate in the crayfish. (Turner 1884:77.)

ULI, the supreme goddess of sorcery in Hawaiian legend with the power to heal and the power to kill. The goddess Hi'iaka* invoked Uli when she brought chief Lohi'au* back to life for her sister Pele.* (Beckwith 1948:144–147; Emerson 1915:144–146; Pukui 1971:397.) Also a spirit god of Atua, Samoa, son of Folasa. (Fraser 1897:34.)

ULI-LA'A, the Hawaiian god of medicine, invoked in order to bring death to an enemy. (Beckwith 1948:114–115; Malo 1903:145.) See also **Maka-kū-koa'e**.

ULUKIHE-LUPE, a beautiful Tongan girl, born with the head of a bird after her mother, Finemee, had eaten her pigeon god. She was abandoned, but another couple, Ahe and Tofue, found and nurtured her to ma-turity. Takalaua, the Tui Tonga,* heard of her beauty and sent his men to bring her to him. She and Takalaua were married, and then their first-born son, Kauulu-fonua, became the next ruling chief. (Gifford 1924:62–65.)

ULUNAWALE, head-only, the god of Tarukua, Lakemba, Lau Islands (Polynesian outliers in Fiji), identified with Ulupoko in Tumbou. (Hocart 1929:198.)

ULU-NUI, a Hawaiian god of crop growing. Also the name of a chief on Maui under whom agriculture greatly flourished. (Emerson 1915:79.)

ULUPOKO, a god of Tanggalevu, Lau Islands (Polynesian outliers in Fiji), who is all head and no body. His presence portends death, and his earthly representation is the crab. (Hocart 1929:192–193.)

ULUTUPUA, a god of Niue Island. (Loeb 1926:162.)

ULUVALU, an eight-headed demon (*nifoloa*) in Tongan legend who captured a beautiful maiden and took her to Pulotu* (underworld*). Her lover followed them, tricked the demon into going to sleep, and then the pair returned to the upper world of mortals. (Collocott 1928:14.)

'UMI, a popular Hawaiian chief from the Big Island who lived ca. A. D. 1500 (Fornander 1920:324). He was the illegitimate son of Līloa, the high chief of the island, and Akahīakuleana, a woman of lower status. When 'Umi became a young man, he set out with his mother's institutions to find his father. He entered Līloa's house and produced the symbols his father had given his mother before he was born. Līloa recognized the implements and declared 'Umi one of his heirs. When Līloa died, 'Umi gathered his forces, dethroned, and murdered his elder brother who had proven to be wicked and incompetent.

As sole ruler of Hawai'i, 'Umi spent his remaining years developing and refining his administration. He encouraged fishing and agriculture and constructed sacred temples as well as new houses. He lead his people in peace and prosperity. When he died, his bones were concealed away according to tradition, and only the birds know where 'Umi, son of Līloa, lies buried. (Beckwith 1948:330–331, 389–392; Fornander 1880: 74–78, 96–108.)

UMU-KARIA, a Māori chief and father to the beautiful Hine-moa* by his wife Hinemaru. (Grey 1970:184; Tregear 1891:576.)

UNDERWORLD. There are many unresolved variations and contractions regarding the Polynesians' concept of the state of the soul after death. There are enough similar beliefs that can be singled out, however, to group them around a central theme that can be called the journey of the soul. Since Māui* failed to gain immortality for man, mortals have undergone death wherein the soul leaves the body and journeys to a leaping off place, a point on every island from which the spirits enter the underworld called the Pō or Pulotu.*

If a spirit survives the pitfalls encountered on its journey to the leaping place, two or three places await it. Law breakers and those who showed lack of respect to the gods and priests enter into a wasteland presided over by the god or goddess) Milu* (Miru) where they are annihilated in Milu's ovens or where they become servants to the gods and goddesses. Ancient Polynesian religion was not an ethical one–there was no concept of reward or punishment for one's behavior in this life. Nor did Polynesians believe in reincarnation. Commoners and wrongdoers could only look forward to Milu's world of misery and harshness.

The upper members of the privileged class, however, inherited a sort of paradise, an Elysium, where the air is salubrious, where food is abundant, women beautiful, and where there is no sickness or aging. The Tahitians believed their paradise (called Rohutu-noa-noa* or Ta'ere*) to be on the north side of the island of Ra'iātea; in Hawai'i, Kāne-hūnā-moku is beneath of the ocean in the west; in Samoa, Bulotu is on the western point of the island of Savai'i and ruled over by Saveasi'uleo.* In this underworld, spirits carry on life much as they had on earth. To reach paradise, one's soul has to have a powerful guardian spirit ('aumakua in Hawai'i) as well as relatives (deceased as well as living) to assist it on its journey. Proper burial by the living is a necessity. For example, it is imperative in the Laka* and Kaha'i* legends for these two heroes to regain the bones of their fathers and to give them a proper burial.

On Rurutu, Cook Islands, the great evil spirit Vaerua Kino comes and swallow's the dead person's spirit into his belly and after a time evacuates the spirit into a mixture of coconut in a bowl. This causes the spirit to become an evil Vaurua-rikiriki (little spirit) who works as a servant for his master. (Gill 1911:218.)

Many stories tell of moral adventurers who visit the underworld. Tafa'i (Tahiti), for example, recovers his wife's spirit; Sina's spirit (Samoa) is recovered from heaven; Hina's brother (Tonga) brings back her son-in-law from *pulotu* ; Hutu (New Zealand) descends into the *pō* to rescue his beloved Pare who has just hung herself; Kina (Marquesas) rescues his wife Tefio from the underworld twice before he is able to restore her to life; and Hi'iaka (Hawai'i) regains the spirit of chief Lohi'au twice in the Pele* legend; numerous others could be cited.

Spirits who are unsuccessful in their journey as well as warriors who are slain in battle frequently remain on earth. These malevolent spirits inhabit the wild places and frighten humans who dare come near their domain. Polynesians rarely visit this taboo places when alone or at night. See also **Ghosts.**

UNUMIATEKORE, a Māori god, one of the powers of night and darkness. (Tregear 1891: 576; Wohlers 1875:32.)

UPE-OUOHO, principal god of Taipi Valley, Nuku Hiva, Marquesas Islands, worshipped in the form of a stingray. (Christian 1895:202.)

UPOKOTOEA, one of the Māori names of the original inhabitants of New Zealand before the arrival of the Polynesians. (Tregear 1891:577.)

URANGA-O-TE-RA, the fifth lowest level of the Māori

underworld* presided over by Rohe,* the wife of Māui.* (Tregear 1891:578; White 1887a: App.)

'URA-TAETAE, the Tahitian god of music, entertainment, and merrymaking. (Henry 1928:378.) See also **Arioi Society**.

URE, a minor god of Easter Island responsible for the first bone fishhook made on the island. (Métraux 1940:317.)

UREIA, a water monster (*tāniwha*) who once dwelt at Hauraki, New Zealand, but who was slain by another water monster named Haumia.* (Shortland 1882:76.) Another account maintains that he was slain by the crew aboard the *Tainui* * canoe at Puponga, Manukau. (White 5:76, 78.)

'URU, conjured forth by Ta'aroa to be his canoe bailer in Tahitian legend. (Henry 1928: 356, 405, 415.)

URU, a legendary ancestor of the Polynesians who appears on both the Māori and Hawaiian genealogies as the son of Tiki* and the father of Nganana. (Tregear 1891:579.)

'URU-O-TE-'OA-TI'A, son of the Tahitian goddess Hina* and her husband, the first mortal man Ti'i (Tiki*). (Henry 1928: 403.)

URUTAHI, patron goddess of the Tui bird in New Zealand. (White 1887a:142; Tregear 1891: 581.)

'URU-TE-TEFA, one of the two sons of 'Oro,* the god of war, and his mortal wife Vai-rau-mati who were turned into the sacred pigs honored by the Arioi Society* in Tahiti. (Henry 1928: 232.)

URUTIRA, a shark god in Māori legends. (Tregear 1891: 581; White 1887a:App.)

URUTONGA, mother of the famous Māori hero Tāwhaki (Kaha'i*) by her husband Hema.* Both were captured by the Ponaturi;* Hema was slain, and Urutonga was kept as a door stop. She assisted her two sons, Tāwhaki and Karihi, in locating her husband's bones and in slaying the Ponaturi. (Grey 1970:46–51; Tregear 1891: 581.)

UTA, husband to the Māori ogress Hou-mea.* (Tregear 1891:582.)

UTAKEA, a god of Mangaia, Cook Islands, introduced from Rarotonga, a brother to Motoro.* (Buck 1934:166; Gill 1876: 12.)

'UTAMA'UNGI, one of the many district gods of the Kaitu'u clan on Bellona Island, the son of the principal god Tehu'aingabenga.* (Monberg 1966:67.)

UTA-TE-'ĀU, the messenger of Rua-hatu* in Tahitian legends. (Henry 1928:358.)

UTI, a female fairy of Mangaia who stalks the earth in search of food. She and her daughters taught mortal women the art of night fishing by torch light. (Gill 1876:124–125.)

UUHOA, the Marquesan god of the coconut palm. (Christian 1895:190.)

UWĒUWĒ-LEKEHAU, an ancient high chief on Hawai'i, the son of Kū* and Hina.* One day he went to play in the ocean where he was transformed into a fish. He swam to Kaua'i and became the secret lover of Lu'u-kia, daughter of high chief 'Olopana. When 'Olopana found out, he banished them to a desolate land called Mana. 'Olopana finally discovered Uwēuwē-lekehau's true identity, and made him the ruling chief of Kaua'i. (Beckwith 1948:515; Fornander 1917:192–199.)

–V–

VAENUKU, a Tongan who killed his brother because he was jealous of the beauty given to him by the gods Eikimotua,* Eikitufunga,* and Vaeuku. (Collocott 1928:50–51.)

VAERUA KINO, the great evil spirit on the island of Rurutu, Cook Islands, which comes and swallow's the dead person's spirit into his belly. After a time, he evacuates the spirit into a mixture of coconut in a bowl. This causes the spirit to become an evil Vaurua-rikiriki (little spirit) who works as a servant for his master. (Gill 1911:218.)

VAERUARAU, a deified chief of Mangaia, Cook Islands, later generally abandoned because his followers were cannibals and sickly. (Buck 1934:167.)

VAEUKU, a Tongan god. See Eikimotua.

VAHATAI, a Tuamotuan demon. (Stimson 1964:596.)

VAHIEROA, see Wahieloa.

VAHINE-'AI-TA'ATA, the cannibalistic great-grandmother of the legendary Tahitian demigod Tafa'i (Kaha'i*). (Henry 1928:552,566.) See also No-na.

VAHINE-HUI-RORI, daughter and the second child of Hina* and Māui,* according to

Tuamotuan legends. (Stimson 1934:46–49.)

VAHINE-MAU-NI'A, the Tahitian goddess responsible for holding everything together. (Henry 1928:378.)

VAHINE-NAUTAHU, the Tuamotuan goddess who molded the god Ātea (Wākea*) into a recognized form. (Henry 1928: 349.)

VAHINE-NUI-TAHU-RA'I, the Tahitian goddess who protects fire walkers from becoming burned when they invoke their prayer: "O Vahine-nui-tahu-ra'i, hold the fan and let us go into the oven for a while!" She is also the friend of the goddess Hina,* benevolent, and protects her follow creatures. She has at her command the lightning which comes at her bidding. (Henry 1928:216, 464.)

VAHI-VERO, the son of Kui* and princess Puhehuehue, the father of the famous Tuamotuan hero Rata (Laka*) by his water-nymph wife Tahiti-tokerau.* Rata named his canoe Vahi-vero after his father. (Stimson 1937:99–103, 1964: 597.)

VAIARI, name of the first region of the Tuamotuan underworld,* a paradise located just below the earth's surface. (Stimson 1964:598.)

VAI'EA, the Tahitian god of comedy, the son of 'Oro-tāua.* (Henry 1928:375.)

VAIHAU, the Tuamotuan expression meaning ancient homeland. Similar to Hawaiki.* (Stimson 1964:598.) See also **Vavau**.

VAIHĪ, a legendary land in Tuamotuan stories where the first coconuts originated. (Stimson 1964:598.)

VAIOLA, the water-of -life or bathing place in the Samoan underworld* where departed spirits refresh themselves. (Turner 1884:258–259.) See also **Leosia; Luao**.

VAI-TU-MĀRIE, the tragic wife of the Tahitian god Hiro (Hilo*). (Henry 1928:543–544.)

VAI-UKA, a Tongan god worshipped in Niutoua. Volcanic stones are sacred to him. (Collocott 1921:233.)

VALEVALENOA, space, a child of the Samoan god Tagaloa (Kanaloa*) and the queen of earth. (Turner 1884:5.)

VANA'ANA'A, daughter of the Tahitian god Ra'a,* the goddess of eloquence, one of the old female goddess who guard the world. (Henry 1928:357, 416.)

VAORAKA, Tuamotuan name of the ceiling of the earth sphere and floor of the sky sphere. The god Tāne (Kāne*) rules here. (Stimson 1964:600.)

VARI-MA-TE-TAKERE, the great mother, a primary being (female) in Mangaian mythology, who resides at the lowest depths of the universe (shaped in the form of a coconut) where she must rest in the fetal position. In the creation, she plucked a piece from her right side, and it, Avatea or Vātea (Wakea*), half male and half fish, became the first god. Afterwards, she plucked off another piece from the right side and it became Tinirau (Kinilau*), lord of fishes. She continued her creation of numerous progeny. (Gill 1876:3–5.)

VASEFANUA, the first man according to legends on Fakaofo, Tokelau. He originated from stone, and the first women originated from earth. (Turner 1884:267.)

VĀTEA, see **Wākea.**

VATEA-NUKU-MAUATUA, the supreme god of the Tuamotus who created the heavens and the earth (Havaiki). (Caillot 1914:7–10.)

VATOA, god of the Mbaumbunia clan in Yandrana, Lau Islands (Polynesian outliers in Fiji). (Hocart 1929:197.)

VAVAU, the ancient one, son of the Samoan god Tagaloa (Kanaloa*), who was sent from heaven to bring peace to humans. He failed, and as a result, was exiled from heaven. He became the progenitor of the Samoan race. (Fraser 1897:19–36.) Also Vavau in the Tuamotuan language means ancient homeland, similar to Hawaiki.* The island of Ra'iātea in the Society Islands was formerly called Vavau. (Stimson 1964:603.) See also **Vaihau.**

VAVAU-NUI, Tuamotuan name for the birth place of Rata (Laka*), the great hero in Polynesia, a land located in Havaiki-te-a-raro (Havaiki below). In the Rata cycle, it is identified as the island of Mangareva. In the Society Islands, it is known as Bora-Bora. (Stimson 1937:96.)

VAVE, a Samoan war god sometimes appearing in the form of a sultan hen, pigeon, or rail bird. Some traditions say he came originally from Tonga. (Krämer 1902:23, 58; Turner 1884:64–66.) See also **Nafanua.**

VĀVE'A, a Tahitian god who causes waves to break on the reefs and shore. (Henry 1928:377.)

VAVENGA, a malevolent god of Bellona Island who tried to seduce the wife of Tamoa. (Bradley 1956:334–335.)

VE'ETINA, the first mortal on Mangaia to experience a natural death, the only son of Tueva and his wife Manga. The elaborate ceremonies associated with death were instituted by his mourners. (Gill 1876:181–189.) See also **Matoetoeā**.

VELE-LAHI, Tongan goddess, daughter of Atugaki* and Maimoa-alogona,* wife to Tau-fuli-fonua, and thus mother to the sky god Tagaloa (Kanaloa*) and all his descendants. (Reiter 1907:230–240.) See also **Creation; Heavens**.

VELE-SII, according to one Tongan tradition, mother to the demigod Māui,* daughter of Tonu-uta* and Tonu-tai,* wife to Tau-fuli-fonua.* (Reiter 1907:234.) See also **Creation**.

VERI, a minor god of Putai, Mangaia, Cook Islands. (Buck 1934:168.)

VEROHIA, a Tuamotuan demon or demigod. (Stimson 1964:607.)

VĒVĒ, a mortal woman from Aitutaki, Cook Islands, who first introduced mosquitoes to Mangaia. On leaving Aitutaki, she filled her pierced ear with mosquitoes to have their hum travel with her. Upon landing in Mangaia, she took them out when bathing, and they flew away and populated Mangaia. (Gill 1876:126–128.)

VEVEA, a demigod of Fakaofu, Tokelau, Islands, who lost a wrestling match to the god Toikia.* (Macgregor 1937:60.)

VIE MOKO and **VIE KENA**, two fraternal gods of Easter Island responsible for the introduction of tattooing* among the islanders. (Métraux 1940:316–317.)

VIE-MOKO, a popular god or goddess on Easter Island in the form of a lizard associated with her daughter Vie-kena. (Métraux 1940:322.)

VINAKA, good, a young goddess of Thekena, Lau Islands (Polynesian outliers in Fiji), sister to Tha, "bad," and daughter to Tui Vakano (god of Vakano), identified with birds who fly in and out of houses foretelling fate. The two are regarded as war goddesses and are identified as children of the Two Ladies (*koirau na marama*), or the winds, who cause mortal death. (Hocart 1929:191–192.)

VIVI-TE-RUA-EHU, a shark god belonging to high chief Moe in Tahiti that inhabits the coral reef outside the district in Tai'arapu. (Henry 1928:389.)

VUHI-ATUA, a goddess of Easter Island, wife of Atua-metua,* who produces the green leaves. (Métraux 1940: 322.)

– W –

WAHIAO, elder sister to the Māori heroine Hine-moe.*

WAHIELOA (FAFIELOA, VA-HIEOA, VAIAROA, VAHIE-ROA, WAHIE-ROA), a Polynesian figure associated with the Kaha'i* and Laka* epics. In Hawai'i, Wahieloa was one of the husbands of the volcano goddess Pele* by whom she had two children, Laka and Mene-hune. Her husband was kidnapped, and Pele migrated to Hawai'i to search for him. Wahieloa was also the name of the son of chief Kaha'i and Hina-'ulu-'ōhi'a. He took to wife Hina-hawea (daughter of Hina-howana). After the birth of their son Laka, he set sail to the Big Island to offer birth gifts to the child's grandmother. When he landed at Punalu'u (Ka-ū), he was seized and sacrificed, and his bones hid in a cave at Kaualehu. Laka's voyage took him to the Big Island where he rescued his father's bones and returned them to Maui where they were given a proper chief's burial. (Beckwith 1948:259; Fornander 1917:524; Thrum 1907:36; Westervelt 1916: 7.)

In New Zealand, variations exist regarding the legend of Wahie-roa. He is generally regarded as the first born son to the Māori demigod Tāwhaki (Kaha'i) and his wife Hine-priri,* and is named after the long piece of firewood carried by his pregnant mother to aid her wounded husband. When he reached manhood, Wahie-roa married Kura (also referred to as Matoka-rau-tāwhiri, Hawea, or Hine-tū-a-haka) who gave birth to the famous hero Rata (Laka*). Soon after Rata's birth, Wahie-roa was murdered by Matuku-takotako, a supernatural being from the underworld,* and his bones carried off by the Ponaturi* fairies. Rata set out on his famous voyage to avenge the death and indignity of his father. He recovered his father's bones and killed Matuku-takotako. (Grey 1970:47, 84–90, 107; Tregear 1891:587–588.) Another legend says that Wahie-roa was slain in attempting to get some exotic parson birds for his pregnant wife in lands belonging to Matuku-takotako (White 1887a: 36).

Vahieroa, the son of the **Tahitian** chief Tafa'i (Kaha'i) by his wife Hina,* married Maemae-a-rohi,* a sister to Tumunui, the ruling chief of North Tahiti. When Maemae-a-rohi's niece, Hau-vana'a, and her fiancé were lost a sea by being swallowed up by a great clam, Vahieroa and his brother-in-law set out to find them. They too became lost, and consequently, Maemae-a-rohi left her son Rata as regent and set out to find her husband. Just as she was being drawn down into the great didactna, Rata came

to their rescue and restored the bones of the other voyages. (Henry 1928:468–476.)

In the **Tuamotus**, Vahieroa is the father to the famous Rata. He and his wife Matamata-taua (or Tahiti To'erau) were snatched away by a demon bird belonging to king Puna of Hitimarama. The bird bit off the head of Vahieroa and used his wife as a food holder in Puna's home. Another story states that Vahi-vero was the son of Kui, a demigod of Hawaiki*, and the goblin woman Rima-roa.* They became the parents of the great hero Rata. (Stimson 1937:96–147.)

In the **Cook Islands**, Vaieroa is the son of Taaki and Ina-uru-orunga, and he and his wife Tairiiri-tokerau lived in Avaiki (Hawaiki*). When his wife became pregnant, Vaieroa was sent to search for some delicious eels that when eaten produced a rash in their young child. In searching for seaweed to cure the rash, Vaieroa was swallowed by the sons of Puna (octopus or great clam) and his mother captured. (Savage 1910: 143–146.)

The **Marquesan** story tells of Vehie-oa who lived in Northern Tahiti with his wife, Tahi'itokoau, and six children, four sons and two daughters. Vehie-oa was kidnapped, and Tahi'i-rokoau went to live with Teiki-o-te-pō in Hawaiki* (the underworld*). On each day of her journey, she left tokens along the way (a broken leaf, spittle, tears, etc.) by which her husband eventually found her. (Steinen 1933:38–41.)

In **Samoa**, Fafieloa is the son of Tafa'i (Kaha'i*) and his second wife Hine-piripiri. Tula is his wife and Lata their son. (Krämer 1902:1:456.)

WAHIEROA, see **Wahieloa**.

WAHIMU, see **Ahimu**.

WAHINE-KAPU, a relative of the Hawaiian goddess Pele,* who sits on a sacred place atop Kī-lau-ea crater on the Big Island. (Emerson 1915:172.)

WAHINE-'ŌMA'O, a female companion (green-woman) who accompanied the Hawaiian goddess Hi'iaka* to Kaua'i to fetch chief Lohi'au for her sister Pele.* (Pukui 1971:397–398; Emerson 1915:26.)

WAIA, an evil and corrupt chief of ancient Hawai'i, surprisingly the son of the good chief Hāloa.* He failed to observe religious observances (prayers, etc.), cared little for the poor and needy, and ruled for his own pleasure. (Malo 1903:244–246, 320–322; Pukui 1971:398.)

WAI-AKUA-A-KĀNE, the sacred or holy water of Kāne,* a Hawaiian reference to the place where the first human pair was created, a stream of crystal water that can restore life to the dead, a water of life. (Beckwith 1948:73–77; Malo 1903:208; Fornander 1920:266–268, 273–275; Fornander 1878:77–78.) Wai-ora-a-tāne is the Māori equivalent. The moon bathes monthly in the Lake of Waiora to renew herself. (White 1887b:13; Tregear 1891:591; White 1887a:141–142.) Lake Vaiola in Tongan legends is situated in paradise or underworld* (Pulotu*), the residence of the god Hikuleo,* and has the same restorative characteristics as in other Polynesian legends. (Fison 1904:16–17; Turner 1884:258–259.) Vai-ora-a-tāne in Tahiti is the Milky Way, the water for the gods to lap up into their mouths. (Henry 1928:356.)

WAIHINANO, a Hawaiian sorceress on Maui, encountered by the goddess Hi'iaka* in her journey to Kaua'i. (Emerson 1915:75.)

WAIHONUKU, a Māori teacher in ancient Hawaiki* who taught the proper ceremonies and incantations. (White 1887a:170; Tregear 1891:590.)

WAIHOU, a Māori water monster, the son of Āraiteuru.* With one full sweep, he created Omapere Lake in New Zealand with his tail. (Tregear 1891:590.)

WAIHUKU, a prominent Māori chief whose elder brother, Tūteamoamo, attempted to kill him in order to marry his wife, Hine-te-kākara. Waihuku was saved from the depths of the sea by an ancestral water monster who carried him to shore just in time to prevent his brother from forcing himself upon Hine-te-kakara. (Tregear 1891:590.)

WAIMA, a Māori water monster, son of Āraiteuru.* (Tregear 1891:590.)

WAIRUA, the ninth heaven according to Māori tradition, presided over by the god Rehua.* (Tregear 1891:592; White 1887a: App.)

WAIRUARANGI, a god of the Chatham Islands. (Shand 1894: 90.)

WAITAHA, name of a group of Māoris whose ancestor Tamate-kapua* captained the famous *Arawa** canoe. They first settled in the north, but through the centuries, they were gradually pushed further south to the South Island of New Zealand. (Tregear 1891:592; White 1887c: 288–289.)

WAKA, a Hawaiian lizard (*mo'o*) goddess worshipped by female chiefs. In the Ha'inakolo* romance, she was sent in the form of an eel to prevent Lono-kai from approaching the land called Kū'ai-he-lani.* When he caught the eel and cut it open, out stepped a beautiful woman who attempted to se-

duce him. (Beckwith 1948:286–287; Westervelt 1915a:213–214.) In the Lā'ie-i-ka-wai* romance, Waka acts as guardian for the beautiful young girl until she can find an appropriate husband for her. (Beckwith 1919; Beckwith 1948:526–528.)

WAKAMARU, the second Māori heaven, the realm of sunshine and rain, the realm of the god Maru.* (Tregear 1891: 593; White 1887a:App.)

WAKAOTI-RANGI, a prominent ancestor of the Māori chiefs in their descent from Toko-mua* (one of the props of heaven). (Shortland 1882:14: Tregear 1891:593.)

WAKARINGARINGA, name of one of the canoes that brought the first Polynesians to New Zealand, captained by chief Mawakeroa. (Tregear 1891:22.) See also **Canoes**, **Māori Migration**.

WAKA-TŪ-WHENUA, one of the famous canoes that brought the first Māoris to New Zealand. See also **Canoes, Māori Migration**.

WĀKEA (AKEA, ĀTEA, VĀTEA), vast space, personified as a supreme god in several Polynesian groups. In one **Hawaiian** legend, Wākea and Papa* appear as the creators of the island of Kahiki (Tahiti ?) and of the Hawaiian islands.

(Beckwith 1948:301–302.) Papa is personified as a gourd from which Wākea created the universe. The calabash becomes the land, its lid becomes the heavens, its juice becomes the rain, and its seeds become the sun, the moon, and the stars. (Beckwith 1948:304–305; Fornander 1920:322.) Some time later, Wākea seduces the goddess Hina* who gives birth to the island of Moloka'i in the Hawaiian chain. (Beckwith 1948:302; Tregear 1891:28–29.) In other Hawaiian legends, however, Wākea is mortal, the eldest son of Kahiko-lua-mea* (Tawhito*), the ancient one, and his wife Kūpūlanakēhau. From Wākea and his wife Papa*-hanau-moku descend the high chiefs of Hawai'i, the *ali'i*. From his two brothers, Lī-hau-'ula and Maku'u, descend the priests and commoners.

In **Tahiti,** Ātea* is personified by the vast space created by the god Ta'aroa (Kanaloa*), and the extension of Ātea provided living space (homes) for the other powerful gods. (Henry 1928:342–343.) According to their creation chant, Ātea was first masculine and then became feminine. (Henry 1928: 571.) One story tells of the powerful god Tāne (Kāne*) who once sailed through the heavens, but was stopped by the power of Ātea. Tāne mustered all the forces from one end of the universe to another, but they all failed to defeat Ātea;

and, as a result, Ātea has stood unmoved in his place to this day. Another tradition tells that Ātea looked upon his wife Hotu (fruitfulness) and Rû, the first man, was born (Henry 1928: 407).

In the **Marquesas** and **Tuamotus,** Ātea takes the place of the god Tāne, and his wife, Fa'ahotu, gives birth to birds, butterflies, and all kinds of creeping things (Henry 1928: 349). The Tuamotuans have a similar story as the one in Tahiti regarding the conflict between Tāne and Ātea. In it, the defeated Tāne flees to earth where he learns to dwell with human beings. After many years, Tāne decides to attempt his conquest of slaying Ātea again. This time, he uses his magical thunderbolts and all the other powers he controls, and this time he slays Ātea; but Ātea's power cannot die, for it still remains great in the islands. From Ātea, also, descends the ruling family of Tahiti which had its origins in the Tuamotus. (Henry 1928: 352.)

The **Cook Islanders** regard Ātea as the son of Vari-ma-te-takere (the very beginning), a goddess who plucked him from her right side. Ātea became the father of gods and men. He is a fish god but half human, and his brothers are Tinirau (Kinilau*), Tango,* Tumuteanaoa, Raka (Laka*), and Tū-metua. Atea's wife is Papa, and they gave birth to five sons, Tangaroa (Kanaloa*), Rongo (Lono*), Ta)ne (Kane*), Tongaiti, and Tangiia. (Buck 1934:162; Gill 1876:3.)

WAKIRERE, name of one of the canoes that was to bring the first Polynesians to New Zealand. It did not arrive, but went to Matetera and then returned to Hawaiki.* (Tregear 1891:22.)

WAKULIKULI, ancestor god of Oneata, Lau Islands (Polynesian outliers in Fiji), who allowed mosquitoes to be introduced on the island by the god Mberewalaki.* (Hocart 1929: 199.)

WALINU'U, a Hawaiian lizard (*mo'o*) goddess whose beneficence brings about stable governments. Memorials in the form of pillars were erected to her in the temples (*heiau*). (Beckwith 1948:126–127.) Also she is mentioned in one chant as the wife of the god Wākea.* (Fornander 1916:12–19.) The name of the goddess Haumea* when she becomes mortal and lives in Kalihi valley on O'ahu. (Beckwith 1948:281–282.) Also known as Wali-manoanoa.

WĀNANGA, the eleventh age of the universe according to the Māori creation.* See also **Kore**.

WARENGA, son of the Māori chief Tū-horo, and grandson of the hero Tama-te-kapua.* (Grey 1970:99; Tregear 1891: 595.)

WAWAU, one of the descendants of Rangi* (sky father) and Papa* (earth mother) that became stars in the heavens after their separation. (Tregear 1891: 500; White 1887a:48.)

WĀWAU, a Māori god, the son of Tū (Kū*), in the creation, used by the god Tāne (Kāne*) to beautify and decorate Rangi* (sky father) after his separation from Papa* (earth mother). (Tregear 1891:598; White 1887a: 49.) He and his relatives (Tupua, Tāwhiti, Te-kū, Te-para-kū-wai, Para-koka, and Te-pora-pora) became the eyes of heaven, the first glimmer of light.

Wāwau (Vavau) is also an ancient island mentioned in many Polynesian legends. In the Māori legend of the travels of Tura* and Whiro,* it is the destination of Whiro. In French Polynesia, it is the ancient name of the island of Bora-Bora. In Hawai'i, Wāwao figures in the Pele* legend while the Marquesans consider it as the outer limits of the physical world, sometimes an epithet for the legendary Hawaiki.* An island called Vavau stills exists in the Tongan group today; and the Samoan word *vavae* means ancient times. (Tregear 1891: 597–598.)

WEHI-NUI-A-MAMAU, a Māori god who supplied the god Tāne (Kāne*) in the creation with stars to beautify Rangi* (sky father). (Tregear 1891:599.)

WEKA, a Māori sea god, ancestor of the great demigod Māui,* who nourished him in infancy when he had been thrown into the sea by his mother Taranga.* (White 1887b:63, 71; Tregear 1891:599.)

WEROWERO, wife of the Māori god Rangi* (sky father) and mother to the sun god Rā.* (Tregear 1891:601; White 1887a: App.)

WHAIĀ, the fourth age of the universe according to the Māori creation.* See also **Kore**.

WHAINGA-ARIKI a Māori sea god, progenitor of the sea monster Paikea.* (Tregear 1891:605; White 1887c:56.)

WHAITIRI, an ancient Māori goddess of the *pō** whose chant separated Rangi* (sky father) and Papa* (earth mother). (White 1887a:51.) She is also the god or goddess of thunder and lightning, the cannibalistic grandmother to the demigod Tāwhaki (Kaha'i*) through her son Hema,* known also as Mataerepō.* She was smitten by blindness by the sacrilegious acts of her husband Kaitangata,* and her grandsons Tāwhaki and Karihi* restored her sight. (White 1887a:119–132.) One legends lists Whaitiri as the father to Tāwhaki (White 1887a:56) and the son of Tāwhaki in another (Shortland 1882:24).

WHAKAOTI-RANGI, the chiefess whom the Māori voyager, Tama-te-kapua,* abducted aboard his canoe, the *Arawa*,* on his planned migration from Hawaiki* to New Zealand. Whakaoti-rangi was the wife of chief Ruaeo* of the *Tainui** canoe. (Grey 1970:110–118; Tregear 1891:606–607.) Also the name of the wife of the Māori chief Ue-nuku-mai-rarotonga,* son of Tāwhaki (Kaha'i*). (Tregear 1891:606–607.)

WHAKA-RINGARINGA, name of one of the canoes that brought the first Māoris to New Zealand. (Tregear 1891:607.) See also **Canoes, Māori Migration**.

WHAKATAU, born in a miraculous manner to Tū-whaka-raro* and Apakura,* and thus grandson to the famous Māori hero Rata (Laka*). One day, his mother, Apakura, threw her apron into the ocean, and the god Rango-takawiu took it and gave it form and being. Whakatau was, thus, instructed in the magic and the use of all kinds of enchantments. As a child he ran across the ocean floor flying his kite above the water.

Once he came ashore and was chased by all the people. He would only let his mother catch him, and after that remained with her and grew up to be a renown hero. He set sail to avenge his father's death by the hands of the Ngāti-hapai tribe. His huge expeditionary force surrounded the Uru-o-manono temple where his enemies had gathered, and they burned it to the ground. He and his men returned to their own village. (Grey 1970:93–98; Tregear 1891: 607.)

WHAKATAUIHU, an ancient and highly revered Māori chief who lived in Hawaiki* before the Polynesian migration to New Zealand. (Grey 1970:99, 126.)

WHAKATURIA, a Māori chief of ancient Hawaiki,* son of Houmai-tawhiti and brother to Tama-te-kapua.* When he and his brother went to steal the fruit of Ue-nuku,* Whakaturia was captured and hung from the rafters to suffocate. Tama-te-kapua rescued him, and war was declared between the two tribes. The dissention lead to the migration of the Māori people to New Zealand. (Grey 1970: 99–105; Tregear 1891:607.)

WHAKAUE-KAIPAPA, famed ancestor of the Māori Ngāti-whakaue tribe of New Zealand, married to Rangiuru,* who presented her husband with an illegitimate son Tūtānekai* (famed for his romance with the lovely Hine-moa*). (Grey 1970: 183; Tregear 1891:607.)

WHAKAWAHA-TAUPATA, the name of the famous canoe used by the Māori hero Turi* in his voyage of discovery and settlement of New Zealand. (Grey 1970:158–172; Tregear 1891:607; White 1887d:12.)

WHALES, see **Kae**.

WHANAUMOANA, the son of the Māori hero Turi,* born mid-ocean between Hawaiki* and New Zealand, also known as Tutawa.* (Grey 1970:169; Tregear 1891:609.)

WHANA-WHANA, an ancient fairy chief mentioned in Māori incantations. (Shortland 1882: 50; Tregear 1891:609.)

WHANUI, brother to the Māori god Rongo-ma-tāne,* and resides in the heavens. Rongo-ma-tāne once visited his brother, stole sweet potatoes (*kumara*) from him, and brought them to earth where his wife Pani* introduced them as food to humans. (Tregear 1891:610; White 1887c:98–117.)

WHAOA, a Māori chief of the *Arawa** canoe that brought the first Polynesians to New Zealand. (Shortland 1882:51;

Tregear 1891:611.) See also **Ca-noes, Māori Migration**.

WHARE-KURA, an ancient Māori house of sacred learning or instruction where the high priests taught mythology, history, genealogy, agriculture, astronomy, etc., to select novices (sons of priests) through repeated recitations and memorization techniques. Schooling was rigorous, usually lasting from sunrise to midnight, five months a year, for five years. During teaching sessions, teachers and pupils were *tapu* (sacred), and no one could approach the whare-kura except designated female servants. (White 1887a:8–16; Tregear 1891:613.) Also, Māori name for the door leading to the underworld* presided over by the goddess Miru.* Also known as Tatau-o-te-pō. (Tregear 1891:613.)

Similar schools existed throughout the Society Islands where they were divided into priests' schools (mainly for men called *fare-'ai-ra'a-upu*) and teachers' schools (men and women, called *fare-ha'a pi'ira'a*). The instruction in the teachers' schools consisted of practical knowledge of astronomy, navigation, geography, numbers (math), genealogies, and pastime activities. The priests' schools were more intense, and not until the novice passed an oral examination before the priestly fraternity could he be accepted as a full-fledged priest. (Henry 1928: 154–155.)

WHĀ-TINO, son of the Māori chief Whena,* who was captured for stealing food from the home of Ue-nuku.* In revenge, Whena murdered Ue-nuku's children and war broke out. Whena and his men were defeated. (Tregear 1891:616; White 1887c:5–13.)

WHATITIRI-MĀTAKATAKA, ancestor to the Māori demigod Māui,* who sent down a deluge of water to save Māui from the fires set by the goddess Mahu-ika.* (Grey 1970:38.)

WHEKA-I-TE-ATA-NUKU, a Māori sea god who guided and protected the Polynesians in their migration from Hawaiki* to New Zealand. Seaweed is the offering made to him. (Tregear 1891:620; White 1887a:40.)

WHEKE, an ancient Māori god of shell fish, the son of Tū-wanawana and Whaitiri,* also an unseen air goddess whose voice can be heard singing. (Tregear 1891:620; White 1887a: App.)

WHEKE-O-MUTURANGI, a giant cuttlefish or sea monster slain by the Māori hero Kupe* in his voyage to New Zealand. (Grey 1970:102; Tregear 1891: 620.)

WHEKE-TORO, an ancient Māori chief who navigated the *Manga-rara* canoe from Hawaiki* to New Zealand. (Tregear 1891:620; White 1887b: 189.) See also **Canoes, Māori Migration**.

WHENA, an ancient Māori chief of Hawaiki* whose two sons, Whā-tino* and Wharo, were captured as they attempted to steal food from the home of chief Ue-nuku.* In revenge, Whena slew Ue-nuku's four children and, as a result, war broke out between the chiefs. Whena and his men were defeated. (Tregear 1891:620; White 1887c:5–13.)

WHETĒ, a Māori goddess, ancestress to the god Tāne (Kāne*), who supplied him with the necessary parts to create the first man, Ti'i (Tiki*). (Tregear 1891:627.)

WHIRITOA, name of the canoe belonging to the Māori demi-god Whakatau* in his revenge of his father's murder. (Grey 1970:93–98; Tregear 1891:624.)

WHIRO, see **Hilo**.

WHITI, a minor Māori reptile god. (White 1887a:App.)

WHIWHIA, the fourteenth age of the existence of the universe according to Māori tradition. (Tregear 1891:628.) See also **Kore**.

WHIWHIA-TE-RANGI-ORA, husband to the Māori goddess Papa* (earth mother), father of Tū-whare-nikau and Hawaiki.* (Tregear 1891:628; White 1887a: App.)

WĪ, an ancient Māori preacher of righteousness whose words were disregarded, and as a result, the great deluge* was brought forth. (Tregear 1891: 602; White 1887a:167–168.)

APPENDIX: CATEGORIES OF GODS AND GODDESSES

CANNIBAL DEITIES
Aku-aku (Easter Island & Tuvalu)
Atuasolopunga (Tuvalu)
Haumea (Tahiti)
Haumei (Marquesas)
Kaikapu (Hawai'i)
Kūkl-waha-ilo (Hawai'i)
Maniloa (Samoa)
Miru-kura (Mangareva)
Nō-na (Tahiti)
Oroi (Rotuma)
Sama (Samoa)
Satia (Samoa)
Tagaloa (Samoa)
Tāne (Tuamotus)
Tapuitea (Samoa)
Tauiti (Tuamotus)
Tui Tokelau (Tokelaus)
Vahine-'ai-ta'ata (Tahiti)
Whaitiri(New Zealand)

CANOE DEITIES
'Elepaio (Hawai'i)
Ka'ā (Hawai'i)
Ka-pū-o-alaka'i (Hawai'i)
Kū-'ālana-wao (Hawai'i)
Kū-holoholo-pali (Hawai'i)
Kū-ka-ōhi'a-laka (Hawai'i)
Kū-moku-hāli'i (Hawai'i)
Kūpā-'ai-ke'e (Hawai'i)
Kū-pepeiao-loa (Hawai'i)
Lata (Samoa)
Manufili (Samoa)
Rongo-ma-ruanuku (New Zealand)

Ta'ere (Tahiti)
Te-fatu (Tahiti)
Tīfai-o-te-peho (Tahiti)

CREATION DEITIES
(MAJOR ONES ONLY)
Ahātea (Tuamotus)
Ātea (several groups)
Ātea-rangi (Tuamotus)
Eitumatupua (Tonga)
Fāo (Niue)
Feke (Tikopia)
Gai'o (Samoa)
Havea-lolo-fonua (Samoa)
He (Niue)
Kāne (Hawai'i)
Kele (Tonga)
Kore (New Zealand)
Kū (Hawai'i)
Lagatea (Rotuma)
Limu (Tonga)
Lono (Hawai'i)
Maimoa'alogona (Samoa)
Makemake (Easter Island)
Mataoa (Marquesas)
Māui (several groups)
Mihitoka (Marquesas)
Nareau (Tarawa)
Pahi (Marquesas)
Papa (several)
Paparoa-i-te-itanga (Cook Islands)
Papatea (Rotuma)
Papa-tu'oi (Tahiti)
Piki (Tonga)
Rangi (New Zealand)
Rongo (New Zealand)
Ro'o (Tahiti)
Rū (several)
Salevao (Samoa)
Ta'aroa (Tahiti)
Ta'ere (Tahiti)

Takaroa (Tuamotus)
Tagaloa (Tonga, New Zealand)
Tangaloa
Tangaloaui (Samoa)
Tama-pouli-ala-mafoa (Tonga)
Tau-ne'e (Tahiti)
Te-aka-ia-roē (Mangaia)
Tekoputu-aue (Marquesas)
Te-manava-roa (Mangaia)
Te-papa (Tahiti)
Te-tangaengae (Mangaia)
Te-tupu'o'ai'ai (Tahiti)
Tītī-mā-tai-fa'aroa (Tahiti)
Toka-i-vevau (Marquesas)
Tonu-tai (Tonga)
Tonu-uta (Tonga)
Touiafutuna (Tonga)
Tū (several)
Tumu-nui (Tahiti)
Tupu-i-hakaava (Marquesas)
Tuuhiti (Marquesas)
Ui (Samoa)
Vari-ma-te-tahere (Mangaia)
Vātea (several)
Wākea (Hawai'i)
Wehi-nui-a-mamau (New Zealand)

EEL DEITIES
Alii-o-fiti (Samoa)
Fataa-koka (Marquesas)
Faumea (Tuamotus)
Fuailagi (Samoa)
Heimoana (Tonga)
Ia (Rotuma)
Kaloafu (Tonga)
Kani-loloū (Hawai'i)

Koiro (New Zealand)
Kuma (Hawa'i)
Matirohe (Tuamotus)
Nganaheke
    (Tuamotus)
Pili (Samoa)
Puhi-nalo (Hawai'i)
Pusi (Samoa)
Rerekiekie (Tuamotus)
Rongo-mai-tauira
    (Chatham Islands)
Ruahine (New
    Zealand)
Samani (Samoa)
Saveasi'uleo (Samoa)
Soesai (Samoa)
Taisumalie (Samoa)
Te-puhi-nui-o-autoo
    (Marquesas)
Te Pusi (Tokelau)
Teuhie (Tonga)
Tui-oneata (Lau
    Islands)
Tuna (New Zealand,
    Tuamotus)
Tuna-te-vai-roa
    (Tuamotus)
Waka (Hawai'i)

FIRE DEITIES
'Ai-lā'au (Hawai'i)
Hina-nui-te-'ara'ara
    (Hawai'i)
Kāne-i-kaulana-'ula
    (Hawai'i)
Ke-ua-a-ke-pō
    (Hawai'i)
Kuru-mehameha
    (Tuamotus)
Mafui'e (Samoa)
Mahuika (New
    Zealand)
Māhuike (Tuamotus)
Matuku (New Zealand)
Nā-maka-o-kaha'i
    (Hawai'i)
Ngātoro-i-rangi (New
    Zealand)
Pele (Hawai'i)

Pere (Tahiti)
Tama-'ehu (Tahiti)
Tamatea (Tahiti, New
    Zealand)
(Te) Vahine-nui-tahu-
    ra'i (Tahiti)
Tui Tokelau (Tokelau
    Islands)

FISH DEITIES
(SEE ALSO SHARK
    DEITIES)
'Ai'ai (Hawai'i)
Aketoa (Mangaia)
Ātea (Cook Islands)
Faamalu (Samoa)
Fe'e (Samoa)
Gutufolo (Niue)
Hapuku (New Zealand)
Haumakapu'u
    (Hawai'i)
Hina-hele (Hawai'i,
    Tahiti)
Hina-'ōpū-hala-ko'a
    (Hawai'i)
Hina-puku-i'a
    (Hawai'i)
Hine-hēhēheirangi
    (New Zealand)
Ika-tere (New Zealand)
Kahi-kona (Hawai'i)
Kāne-'āpua (Hawai'i)
Kāne-'ukai (Hawai'i)
Kāne-koa (Hawai'i)
Kāne-kokala (Hawai'i)
Kāne-lau-'āpua
    (Hawai'i)
Kāne-makua (Hawai'i)
Kinilau (Hawai'i)
Kū-'ula-kai (Hawai'i)
Lagitaitaia (Niue)
Liavaha (Niue)
Mālei (Hawai'i)
Makona (Mangaia)
Mata-tina (Tahiti)
Matutu (Mangaia)
Mautaki (Mangaia)
Moe-hakaava
    (Marquesas)

Muriwhakaroto (New
    Zealand)
Pou (Chatham Islands)
Pounama (New
    Zealand)
Rio (Tahiti)
Roli (Niue)
Rongo (Chatham
    Islands)
Rua-atu (Mangaia)
Rua-hatu (Tahiti)
Rua-hatu-tinirau
    (Tahiti)
Rua-tamaine (Mangaia)
Seketoa (Samoa)
Si'uleo (Samoa)
Ta'aroa (Tahiti)
Ta'aroa-'ōfa'i-i-te-pari
    (Tahiti)
Tagaloa
Tagaloa-puipui-maka
    (Niue)
Tagaroa (New Zealand)
Tangaroa (Chatham
    Islands)
Tango (Mangaia)
Taufatahi (Tonga)
Tiki-kapakapa (New
    Zealand)
Tinirau (New Zealand)
Tonu-mā-naha (Tahiti)
Tutu-mai-tokerau
    (Mangaia)
Tutu-mai-tonga
    (Mangaia)
Uhu-makaikai
    (Hawai'i)
Whatukura (New
    Zealand)
Wheke (New Zealand)

LIZARD DEITIES
Ahīmu (Hawai'i)
Finau-tau-iku (Tongan)
Hau-wahine (Hawai'i)
Hotu-puku (New
    Zealand)
Kaipaku (Hawai'i)

Ka-lama-i-nu'u
  (Hawai'i)
Kalama-'ula (Hawai'i)
Ka-mo'o-'inanea
  (Hawai'i)
Kāne-kua'ana
  (Hawai'i)
Kaweau (New Zealand)
Kiha (Hawai'i)
Kiha-nui-lulu-moku
  (Hawai'i)
Kiha-wahine (Hawai'i)
Kiki-pua (Hawai'i)
Kiore (Tuamotus)
Koronaki (New
  Zealand)
Lani-loa (Hawai'i)
Lani-wahine (Hawai'i)
Lesā (Samoa)
Makali'i (Hawai'i)
Makiki (Hawai'i)
Mārongorongo (New
  Zealand)
Matarau (Cook Islands)
Matipou (New
  Zealand)
Moke-hae (Marquesas)
Moko (Tuamotus)
Mokomoko (New
  Zealand)
Mokongārara
  (Tuamotus)
Mokoroa (New
  Zealand)
Mokotiti (New
  Zealand)
Moku-hinia (Hawai'i)
Mo'o (Tahiti)
(Ka) Mo'o-'inanea
  (Hawai'i)
Ngārara-huarau (New
  Zealand)
Pi'i-ka-lalau (Hawai'i)
Pili (Samoa)
Pun(g)a (Tuamotus)
Samani (Samoa)
Te-ohiu-māeva (Tahiti)
Te-rehu-o-tainui (New
  Zealand)

Tipa (Tahiti)
Tonga-iti (Mangaia)
Tuātara (New Zealand)
Tui-haafakafonua
  (Tonga)
Tū-pari (New Zealand)
Turanga (Mangaia)
Uatai (New Zealand)
Vie-moko (Easter
  Island)
Wahīmu (Hawai'i)
Waka (Hawai'i)
Walinu'u (Hawai'i)

MOON DEITIES

Ali'i-wahine-o-ka-
  malu (Hawai'i)
Aloimasina (Samoa)
Hina (Tahiti, Hawai'i)
Kura-e-hā (Tuamotus)
Mahinatumai (Niue)
Marama (New
  Zealand)
Rona (New Zealand)
Tapirinoko (Tuamotus)
Te-hei'ura (Tahiti)
Titi-usi (Samoa)

OCEAN DEITIES OR
MONSTERS

(See also Eel Deities
  and Shark Deities)
'Ahifa-tū-moana
  (Tahiti)
Aihu-moana (New
  Zealand)
Akua-peha-'ale
  (Hawai'i)
Ama-tai-ātea (Tahiti)
Ana'e-moe-oho
  (Tahiti)
'Are-mata-pōpoto
  (Tahiti)
'Are-mata-roroa
  (Tahiti)
Fafie (Tokelau)
Fai (Tahiti)
Fakapatu (Tonga)
Fuailagi (Samoa)

Hai-puka (Marquesas)
Hale-lehua (Hawai'i)
Hā-u'i (Hawai'i)
Hemoana (Tonga)
Hikueru (Tuamotus)
Hina-lau-limu-kala
  (Hawai'i)
Hina-'ōpū-hala-ko'a
  (Hawai'i)
Hine-hēhēheirangi
  (New Zealand)
Hine-huauru (New
  Zealand)
Hine-tokura (New
  Zealand)
Huanaki (Niue)
Huru-mānu-ariki
  (New Zealand)
Kanae (New Zealand)
Kanaloa (Hawai'i)
Kāne
Kāne-lu-honua
  (Hawai'i)
Ke-au-kā (Hawai'i)
Kinilau
Koroimbo (Lau)
Ku-moana (Marquesas)
Lima-loa (Hawai'i)
Luafakakana (Niue)
Luatotolo (Niue)
Luatupua (Niue)
Ma'a-tahi (Tahiti)
Mafola (Tokelau)
Matarua (New
  Zealand)
Moana-nui-ka-lehu
  (Hawai'i)
Moso (Tonga)
Mū (New Zealand)
Mupere (Tuamotus)
Nganaheke
  (Tuamotus)
Nine-tokura (New
  Zealand)
Nuku-te-rā-tai
  (Tuamotus)
Nuku-te-rā-uta
  (Tuamotus)
'Oro-pa'a (Tahiti)

Paikea (New Zealand)
Para-hia (New Zealand)
Parata (New Zealand)
Petipeti (New Zelaand)
Ponaturi (New
    Zealand)
Punga (New Zealand)
Pusi (Samoa)
Rauaika-nui (Mangaia)
Raumati (New
    Zealand)
Roi-vaha-nui
    (Tuamotus)
Rongo-ma-rua-nuku
    (Tuamotus)
Rongo-takawiu (New
    Zealand)
Rongo-tumu-here
    (Tuamotus)
Rori-mata-popoko
    (Tuamotus)
Rori-tau (Tuamotus)
Rua-hatu (Tahiti)
Rua-hatu-tinirau
    (Tahiti)
Ruamano (New
    Zealand)
Rua-puna (Tahiti)
Rua-ra'a-tai (Tahiti)
Samani (Samoa)
Sinā-sa'umani (Samoa)
Talimainuku (Niue)
Tama-nui-te-rangi
    (New Zealand)
Tamauanuu (Samoa)
Tāne (Tahiti, New
    Zealand)
Tangaroa (New
    Zealand)
Taufa (Tonga)
Taungeri (New
    Zealand)
Te-a'u-roa (Tahiti)
Te-anu-ti-ananua
    (Marquesas)
Te-fatu (Tahiti)
Tefehemoana (Niue)
Te Moana (Tokelau)

Te Wheke-a-
    muturangi (New
    Zealand)
Tinirau
Tino-rua (Tahiti)
Tohu (Tahiti)
Tonga-nui (New
    Zealand)
Tongo-takawiu (New
    Zealand)
Tua-ra'a-tai (Tahiti)
Tū-hina-pō (New
    Zealand)
Tū-horo-puga
    (Tuamotus)
Tui-haafakafonua
    (Tonga)
Tui-olotau (Tonga)
Tu'i-pulotu (Tonga)
Tū-mā-tahi (Tahiti)
Tūna (Tuamotus)
Tupe-'i'o-ahu (Tahiti)
Tutepoganui
    (Tuamotus)
Tu'uola (Futuna)
Weka (New Zealand)
Whainga-ariki (New
    Zealand)
Wheka-i-te-ata-nuku
    (New Zealand)
Wheke-o-muturangi
    (New Zealand)

PEACE DEITIES

Āparangi (New
    Zealand)
Hau (Tahiti)
Maleloa (Niue)
Ta'i-vārua (Tahiti)
Te-hau (Tahiti)
Tū (Mangareva
Turia (Samoa)
Tuvaiua (Niue)

RAIN DEITIES

Foge (Samoa)
Hiro (Easter Island)
Kama-ua (Hawai'i)
Kāne-pua'a (Hawai'i)

Ka-o-mea-lani
    (Hawai'i)
Ka-ua-ka-āhiwa
    (Hawai'i)
Ke-olo-'ewa (Hawai'i)
Kū (Hawai'i)
Kū-ka-'ōhi'a-laka
    (Hawai'i)
Kū-ke-olo'ewa
    (Hawai'i)
Kū -mauna (Hawai'i)
Lesā (Samoa)
Lono (Hawai'i)
Mata-vara-vara (Easter
    Island)
Nafanua (Samoa)
Pūnua-mo'e-vai
    (Tahiti)
Rogo (Mangareva)
Saato (Samoa)
Ta'ū (Samoa)
Toafa (Samoa
Toho-tika (Marquesas)
Topukulu (Samoa)
Ua (Samoa)

RAINBOW DEITIES

Āheahea (New
    Zealand)
'Ānuenue (Hawai'i)
Atuatoro (New
    Zealand)
Haere (New Zealand)
Haluluko'ako'a
    (Hawai'i)
Hine-kōrako (New
    Zealand)
Ka-hala-o-puna
    (Hawai'i)
Kāhukura (New
    Zealand)
La'ama'oma'o (Samoa)
Lono (Hawai'i)
Nuku (New Zealand)
Tagaloa Fafao (Niue)
Tagaloa Fakaolo (Niue)
Tohaerereoa (New
    Zealand)

Ue-nuku (New
  Zealand)
Ue-nuku-kōpako (New
  Zealand)

SHARK DEITIES
'Ai-kanaka (Hawai'i)
Baabenga (Bellona)
Fa'arava'i-te-ra'i
  (Tahiti)
Ha'i-wahine (Hawai'i)
Ire (Tahiti)
Ka-'ahu-pāhau
  (Hawai'i)
Ka-'ehu-iki-manō-o-
  pu'u-loa (Hawai'i)
Ka-holi-a-kāne
  (Hawai'i)
Kama-i-ka-'āhui
  (Hawai'i)
Ka-moho-ali'i
  (Hawai'i)
Kāne-hūnā-moku
  (Hawai'i)
Kāne-i-kō-kala
  (Hawai'i)
Kauhuhu (Hawai'i)
Ka-welo-mahamaha-i'a
  (Hawai'i)
Ke-ali'i-kaua-o-ka'ū
  (Hawai'i
Kua (Hawai'i)
Kū-hai-moana
  (Hawai'i)
Maka'u-kiu (Hawai'i)
Mako (Marquesan)
Mami (Lau Islands)
Mano-ka-lani-pō
  (Hawai'i)
Mano-niho-kahi
  (Hawai'i)
Ma'o-purotu (Tahiti)
Mātuku-tagotago
  (Tuamotus)
Nanaue (Hawai'i)
Nenewe (Hawai'i)
Pau-walu (Hawai'i)
Pehu (Hawai'i)

Rangi-hiki-waho
  (Chatham Islands)
Seketoa (Tonga)
Tae-hau-moana
  (Tahiti)
Tā-hui (Tahiti)
Tama-'ōpū-rua (Tahiti)
Tamarau-ariki
  (Chatham Islands)
Tāne-ma'o (Tahiti)
Tanifa (Rotuma)
Te-a'u-moana (Tahiti)
Te-autā (Tahiti)
Te-hiuta (Tahiti)
Tekea (Mangaia)
Tere-māhiamā-hiva
  (Tahiti)
Tino-rua (Tahiti)
Tohu (Tahiti)
Tokilagafanua (Tonga)
Toufa (Tonga)
Tui-tofua (Tonga)
Urutira (Marquesan)
Vivi-te-rua-ehu
  (Tahiti)

SORCERERS OR
  WITCHES
Fataa-koka (Marquesas)
Hākawau (New
  Zealand)
Hama (Tonga)
Hine-tū-a-hōanga
  (New Zealand)
Ka'alae-nui-a-hina
  (Hawai'i)
Kae (New Zealand)
Ka-hala-o-māpuana
  (Hawai'i)
Kālai-pāhoa (Hawai'i)
Ka-maka-nui-
  'aha'ilono (Hawai'i)
Ka-maunu-a-niho
  (Hawai'i)
Kāne-i-kaulana-'ula
  (Hawai'i)
Kapo (Hawai'i)
Kaulana-iki-pōki'i
  (Hawai'i)

Kaunati (Tuamotus)
Ke-ao-'ōpua-loa
Ke-olo'ewa (Hawai'i)
Kiki (New Zealand)
Kiki-pua (Hawai'i)
Kuhi (Tuamotus)
Kū-waha-ilo (Hawai'i)
La'a-mai-kahiki
  (Hawai'i)
Laenihi (Hawai'i)
Leti (Tuvalu)
Lō-lupe (Hawai'i)
Mākutu (New Zealand)
Maliu (Hawai'i)
Matamolali (Samoa)
Merēhau (Tahiti)
Miru (Easter Island)
Mongihere (Tuamotus)
Ngārara-hua-rau (New
  Zealand)
Noho-a-mo'o (Hawai'i)
Nua (Tahiti)
Pahulu (Hawai'i)
Pili-a-mo'o (Hawai'i)
Pōti'i-tā-rire (Tahiti)
Pua (Hawai'i)
Purata (New Zealand)
Ruāhinē (Tuamotus)
Ruahine-kai-piha
  (New Zealand)
Sina-sengi (Samoa)
Tāmure (New
  Zealand)
Tapatapafona (Tuvalu)
Tautōhito (New
  Zealand)
Tavā (Tuamotus)
Tupua (New Zealand,
  Tuamotus)
Uli (Hawai'i)
Waihinano (Hawai'i)
Whakatau (New
  Zealand)

SUN DEITIES
Hiki-rā (Tahiti)
Hita-rā (Tahiti)
Ka'ōnohi-o-ka-lā
  (Hawai'i)

Lā (Samoa)
Laa (Tonga)
Ngana (New Zealand)
Rā (New Zealand)
Ra'a (Tahiti)
Rā-tā-nui (Tuamotus)
Rā-ta'iri (Tahiti)
Tagaloa (Samoa)
Tama-nui-te-rā (New
  Zealand and Tahiti)
Tami-ta-ra (Chatham
  Islands)
Te-hei'ura (Tahiti)

THUNDER AND
LIGHTNING DEITIES
Fakakonaatua (Niue)
Fatu-tiri (Tahiti)
Ihi-awaawa (Hawai'i)
Ihi-lani (Hawai'i)
Ka-huila-maka-keha'i-
  i-ka-lani (Hawai'i)
Kāne (Hawai'i)
Kāne-hekili (Hawai'i)
Kāne-wawahi-lani
  (Hawi'i)
Kū-waha-ilo (Hawai'i)
Lono (Hawai'i)
Nā-kolo-lani (Hawai'i)
Rakiteua (Samoa)
Rangiwhenua (New
  Zealand)
Rongo-mai-tauira
  (Chatham Islands)
Tairi (Mangareva)
Tagaloa (Tonga)
Tāne (Tahiti)
Tapuariki (Samoa)
Te-fatu-tiri (Tonga)
Tāwhaki (New
  Zealand)
Tāwhiri-matea (New
  Zealand)
Tili-tili (Samoa)
Toho-tika (Marquesas)
Tui Tokelau (Tokelau
  Islands)
Vahine-nui-tahu-ra'i
  (Tahiti)

Whaitiri (New
  Zealand)

UNDERWORLD
DEITIES OR SPIRITS
Atua-mangumangu
  (Futuna)
Atua-matalua (Futuna)
Elo (Samoa)
Hānau-a-rangi
  (Tuamotus)
Hikuleo (Tonga)
Hina (Mangareva)
Hina-nui-te-pō (New
  Zealand)
Ihungata (Tuamotus)
Io (Tuamotus)
Ka-hō-'āli'i (Hawai'i)
Kāina (Tuamotus)
Kaitoa (New Zealand)
Karagfono (Rotuma)
Kiho (Tuamotus)
Kobine (Tarawa)
Leosi (Samoa)
Mafui'e (Samoa)
Mahuika (Tokelau,
  Tuamotus)
Māhu-tū-tāranga
  (Tuamotus)
Mairihau-o-rongo
  (Tuamotus)
Mākutu (New Zealand)
Māruki-ao (Tuamotus)
Matirohe (Tuamotus)
Mātuku-tagotago
  (Tuamotus)
Mero (New Zealand)
Milo (New Zealand)
Milu (Hawai'i)
Miru (Mangaia, New
  Zealand)
Mofuta-ae-ta'u (Tonga)
Mokorea (Tuamotus)
Mu-e-o (Tuamotus)
Muru (Rarotonga)
Mutu (New Zealand)
Nganahau (Tuamotus)
Ngā-ariki (Tuamotus)
Ngāti-nau (Tuamotus)

Nuku-te-rā-tai
  (Tuamotus)
Nuku-te-rā-uta
  (Tuamotus)
Pakiraho-nui
  (Tuamotus)
Pō-tangotango (New
  Zealand)
Pua-kai-mahuki
  (Tuamotus)
Rima-hora (Tuamotus)
Rohe (New Zeland)
Rōi-iti (Tuamotus)
Rongo-ma-tāne (New
  Zealand)
Saveasi'uleo (Samoa)
Tahito-henua
  (Tuamotus)
Tamatū-hau
  (Tuamotus)
Tāne (Tuamotus)
Tāwhaitiri (New
  Zealand)
Te-ailoilo (Futuna)
Te-tareva (Mangaia)
Tiki (Marquesas)
Tokotoko-uri
  (Tuamotus)
Tuapiko (New
  Zealand)
Tua-te-ahu-tapu
  (Marquesas)
Tukaitaua (Mangaia)
Tupuranga-o-te-ao
  (New Zealand)
Tūtae-'āvae-to'eto'e
  (Tahiti)
Uetonga (New
  Zealand)
Uke (Cook Islands)
Uke-umu (Cook
  Islands)

REGIONS OF THE
UNDERWORLD
Anaunau (Tuamotus)
Ao-o-milu (Hawai'i)
Apanoa (Tuamotus)
Apapa-nui (Hawai'i)

Apatahi (Tuamotus)
Atuā (Tuamotus)
Avatele (Niue)
Bulotu (Samoa)
Fu'e-aloa (Samoa)
Hanakāmālu (Hawai'i)
Havaiki (several)
Hawaiki (several)
Hikutoia (New
  Zealand)
Kapi-raro (Tuamotus)
Kātaka (Tuamotus)
Kio-taetae-ho
  (Tuamotus)
Kororūpō (Tuamaotus)
Kūwatawata (New
  Zealand)
Luao (Samoa)
Mātua-papa
  (Tuamotus)
Meto (New Zealand)
Mōrianuku (New
  Zealand)
Niutakouhua
  (Tuamotus)
'Oroi-ta (Rotuma)
Orovaru (Tuamotus)
Paerau (New Zealand)
Pipirau (New Zealand)
Pō (New Zealand)
Pouturi (New Zealand)
Pulotu (Samoa, Tonga)
Rangi-pō (Tuamotus)
Rarotonga (New
  Zealand)
Rohutu (Tuamotus)
Rohutu-noanoa
  (Tahiti)
Rōiata (Taumotus)
Rōvaru (Tuamotus)
Ta'ere (Tahiti)
Tai-haruru-tauaro
  (Tuamotus)
Tai-haruru-tautūa
  (Tuamotus)
Tākohua (Tuamotus)
Tātaka (Tuamotus)
Tia (Tuvalu)
Tongahake (Tuamotus)

Tuaraki (Tuamotus)
Vai-tea (Tuamotus)
Vaiari (Tuamotus)
Vaiola (Samoa)

WAR DEITIES
Aitu-i-pava (Samoa)
'Ere'ere-fenua (Tahiti)
Faamalu (Samoa)
Faaola (Samoa)
Fakahoko (Niue)
Fakalagalaga (Niue)
Fakatafetau (Niue)
Fanonga (Samoa)
Fe'e (Samoa)
Fitikili (Niue)
Fuailagi (Samoa)
Ga'e (Samoa)
Heauoro (Chatham
  Islands)
Ka-hinihini (Hawai'i)
Kā-'ili (Hawai'i)
Ka-maiau (Hawai'i)
Kauakahi (Hawai'i)
Kekauakahi (Hawai'i)
Kū (Hawai'i, New
  Zealand)
Kū-ho'one'e-nu'u
  (Hawai'i)
Kū-'ili-kaua (Hawai'i)
Kū-kā'ili-moku
  (Hawai'i)
Kū-ke-olo'ewa
  (Hawai'i)
Kū-lili-'ai-kaua
  (Hawai'i)
La'ama'oma'o
  (Hawai'i)
Lagiofa (Niue)
Lefanonga (Samoa)
Lesa (Samoa)
Lua (Niue)
Manataefetau (Niue)
Mao-ma-uli (Samoa)
Māpu (Hawai'i)
Maru (New Zealand)
Matu'u (Samoa)
Moso (Samoa)
Nafanua (Samoa)

Namuefi (Niue)
Nanduruvesi (Lau
  Islands)
Ndauthina (Lau
  Islands)
Ndimailangi (Lau
  Islands)
Nifoloa (Smoa)
'Oro (Tahiti)
'Oro-taua (Tahiti)
Pava (Samoa)
Rima-roa (Tahiti)
Rongo (Mangaia)
Rongomai (New
  Zealand)
Sa-fulu-sa (Samoa)
Salevao (Samoa)
Sepo-malosi (Samoa)
Sili Vaai (Samoa)
Taafanua (Samoa)
Taemā (Samoa)
Taisumalie (Samoa)
Tama-faigā (Samoa)
Taomaga (Niue)
Tapaai (Samoa)
Tapatu (Niue)
Tapatulele (Niue)
Tapatutau (Niue)
Taufeleleaki (Niue)
Te-agiagi (Mangareva)
Teele (Niue)
Te-rehu-o-tainui (New
  Zealand)
Tilifaigā (Samoa)
Tili-tili (Samoa)
Toho-tika (Marquesas)
Tongo (Samoa)
Tū (Marquesas,
  Samoa)
Tufi (Samoa)
Tui Atua (Samoa)
Tuifiti (Samoa)
Tuiopulotu (Samoa)
Tuli-leo-nu'u (Samoa)
Tū-mata-uenga (New
  Zealand)
Turia (Samoa)
Turi-tua (Samoa)
Tutau (Niue)

Vave (Samoa)
Vinaka (Lau Islands)

WIND DEITIES
Aka (Marquesas)
Āwhiowhio (New
    Zealand)
Haluluko'ako'a
    (Hawai'i)
Hau-ngangana (New
    Zealand)
Hau-Whenua (New
    Zealand)
Hōkeo (Hawai'i)
Hono-a-lele (Hawai'i)
Kū-waha-ilo (Hawai'i)
La'ama'oma'o
    (Hawai'i)
Lau-kapalili (Hawai'i)
Leomatagi (Niue)
Makani-ke-oe (Hawai'i)
Mata'i-fe'etietie
    (Tahiti)
Ngana (New Zealand)
Pu-'āhiuhiu (Hawai'i)
Pungawere (New
    Zealand)
Ra'a (Tahiti)
Raka (Mangareva)
Rangimaomaō
    (Chatham Islands)
Rā-tā-'iri (Tahiti)
Tango (Mangareva)
Tapakaumatagi (Niue)
Tāwhiri-mangatē
    (Chatham Islands)
Tāwhiri-matea (New
    Zealand)
Te-muri (Tahiti)
Tipa (Tahiti)
Tumu-ruperupe
    (Tahiti)
Tū-o-te-to'i-'oi (Tahiti)
Vinaka (Lau Island)

INDEX

The following comprensive index includes all references to mythological characters. Those page numbers in bold print indicate the pages on which a full citation exists for that particular character or subject. The Appendix (pp. 331–338) contains a select listing of various categories of gods and goddesses.

Fish Deities, List of, 311
Fishing tools, 3, 6, 7, 8, 47, 68, 92, 128, 136
FITI, fishing god of Avetele, Niue, Island, 39
FITIAUMUA, Samoan conqueror, 40
FITIHULUGIA, god of Niue Island, 40
FITI-KAI-KERE, Tikopian building gods, 40
FITIKILA, war god of Hakupu, Niue Island, 40
FITU, Futunan ancestral god, 40, 155
Flood, see Deluge
Flute, Nose, 70, 105, 211
FOGE, Samoan rain god, 40, 240, 284
FOILAPE, god of Nukufetau, Tuvalu, 40
FO'ISIA, Samoan chief, the Tui'ofu, 40
FOLAHA, principal god on Nanumea, Tuvalu, 41
FOLASA, Samoan father of demons, 241, 312
FONO-KI-TANGATA, Tongan god, 40
FONOLAPE, stone god of Tuvalu, 40-41
FONU, turtle god of Futuna, 41
FONUAGALO, Niuean underworld, 78
Fornander, Abraham, Hawaiian scholar, xxi, xxv–xxvi, 34
FOTOGFURU, malevolent god of Rotuma, 41
FOTOKIA, reef god of Niue Island, 41
FOUMA, Rotuma's greatest ancient warrior, 41
Fraser, John, Samoan scholar, xxvii
FUAILAGI, Samoan creator of the heavens, 41
FUE, Samoan goddess, 206
FU'E-ALOA, Samoan underworld, 146
FUIALAIŌ, brother of Pili, 211
FULUFULUITOLO, Samoan who visited heaven, 137
FULUHIMAKA, Niue god, 8
FULU-ULAALEMATATO, Samoan cannibal goddess, 164

FUNEFE'AI, husband to Sinaalāua, 100
FUOGA, son of Souragpol, 247
FUTIFONUA, god of Niue Island, 8, 41
FUTIMOTU, god of Niue Island, 8, 41

G

GA'E, Samoan war god, 42
GAGULUĒ, father of Lautī, 136
GAGULUŌ, mother of Lautī, 136
GAI'O, Samoan creation god, 42
GAISINA, Samoan sailor, 178
GAITOSI, Samoan god, 42
GAITUA, mother to Rogo-tau-hia, 231
GAIULI, Samoan sailor, 178
GAIVA'AVA'AI, Samoan god, 42
GALUMALEMANA, Samoan chief, 42
GAUGANO, primeval god of Bellona Island, 42
GAUGATOLO, 186, (same as Nifoloa)
GAUTEAKI, primeval goddess of Bellona Island, 42
GEGĒ, Samoan god who killed demons, 42
Genealogies, 26, 39, 120, 126
Ghosts, 1, 7, 13, 42-43, 106, 240, 309
Giants, 43-44, 74, 100, 103, 118, 269
Gifford, Edward, Tongan scholar, xxvii
Gill, William Wyatt, Cook Island scholar, xxiii
GOFU, king of Rotuma, 223
Grasshopper, 102, 152, 214, 244
Greenstone, see Jade
Grey, Sir George, Māori scholar, xxi–xxii
GUTUFOLO, fishing god of Niue Island, 44

HANA'AUMOE, malevolent spirit of Hawai'i, 49

HĀNAI-IA-KA-MALAMA, Hawaiian goddess Hina, 47, 49

HANA-KAHI, peaceful Hawaiian chief, 49

HANAKĀMĀLU, Hawaiian underworld, 49–50

HANAKE or NIHO-OA, malevolent Marquesan god, 50

HĀNAU-A-RANGI, supernatural beings in the Tuamotus, 50

Handy, E. S. Craighill, Marquesan scholar, xxiv

HĀNEO'O, fish pond on Mau'i, 50

HANGAROA, Māori god, 50

HANITEMAU, goddess of Rotuma, 50

HĀ-NUI, brother to the Māori hero Hatupatu, 51

HĀ'OA'OA, sister to the Tahitian god 'Oro, 50

HAOTU, first mortal man, 73, 163

HĀPAI, heavenly Māori goddess, 50–51, 88, 89, 209, 260, 289

HĀPOPO, Māori god, 51

HA-PU'U, Hawaiian goddess of necromancy, 51

HARATAUNGA, daughter of Mangamangai-atua, 51, 76, 155

HĀ-ROA, brother to the young Māori chief Hatupatu, 51

HARONGA, Māori prop of heaven, 51, 57, 158, 222, 287, 289

HATONA, Marquesan god, 51

HATUMANOKO, god of Bellona Island, 51

HATUPATU, Māori hero, 51-52, 128

HAU, Tahitian god of peace, 52

HAUA, Easter Island god, 151

HAU-ATA, child to Tiki and Hina, 280

HAUHAU-TE-RANGI, Māori jade axe, 52

HAU-HUNGA, Māori god of bitter cold, 52

HĀ-U'I, Hawaiian sea dragon, 52

HAU-LANI, Hawaiian plant goddess, 52, 54

HA'ULILI, Hawaiian god of speech, 52

HAULIPARUA, Rotuman goddess, 223

HAUMAI-TĀWHITI, Māori chief, 214, 286, 310

HAUMAKAPU'U, Hawaiian god of fish ponds, 52

HAU-MĀ-RINGIRINGI, Māori god of mists, 53

HAU-MARO-TŌ-ROTO, Māori god of mists, 53

HAUMEA, Hawaiian fertility goddess, 48, 49, 53, 59, 75, 98, 103, 106, 108, 109, 123, 129, 150, 181, 190, 202, 207, 219, 233, 241, 306, 325

HAUMEI, Marquesan cannibal goddess, 53

HAUMIA, Māori water monster, 53, 315

HAUMIA-TIKITIKI or HAUMIA-TIKETIKE, Māori god of vegetable foods, 27, 53, 214, 257, 270

HAU-NGANGANA, Māori god of blistering winds, 54, 183

HAUNGA-ROA, daughter of Manaia, 54, 84, 154, 160, 232

HAUNU'U, Hawaiian plant goddess, 52, 54

HAU-ORA, Māori universe age, 54, 56, 225

HAURAROTUIA, Māui's canoe, 54

HAU-TI'A, Tahitian god, 54

HAU-TUIA, daughter to Parorotea, 204

HAUTUPATU, Māori chief, 259

HA-URIURI, Easter Island spirit, 308

HAUVANA'A, wife of king Tui-i-hiti, 133, 321

HAU-WAHINE, Hawaiian lizard goddess, 54

HAU-WHENUA, Māori god of gentle breezes, 54

HAVA, wife of Ataraga, 16, 54, 77

HAVAIKI, 54, 62, 177, 191, 200, (see also Hawaiki)

HAVAIKI-NOHI-KARAKARA, Tuamotuan god, 54

HAVAIKI-NUI-A-NA-EA, sacred Tuamotuan land, 54

J

K

L

LAFAISAOTELE, father to Sinaalāua, 100

LAGATEA, Rotuman creation god, 130, 195, 203

LAGE-IKI, principal god of Niue, 130, 131

LAGEIKIUA, god of Niue Island, 130

LAGI, Rotuman heaven, 130–131, 195

LAGI-ATEA, principal god of Niue, 78, 131

LAGIHALULU, malevolent god of Niue Island, 131

LAGIHULUGIA, god of Niue Island, 131

LAGILOA, god of Niue Island, 131

LAGIMAFOLA, wife to the Samoan god Tagaloa, 100

LAGIOFA, war god of Niue Island, 131

LAGITAITAIA, fish god of Niue Island, 131

LĀ'IE-I-KA-WAI, popular Hawaiian heroine, 5, 47, 90, 91, 106, 112, 113, 131, 135, 136, 149, 151, 323

LĀ'IE-LOHELOHE, sister to Lā'ie-i-ka-wai, 131

LA'ILA'I, first Hawaiian woman, 111, 114

LAKA, popular Polynesian hero, 3, 4, 7, 33, 46, 106, 126, 127, 131–135, 144, 149, 314, 320, (known also as Aka, Lasa, Lata, Rata)

LALATĀVĀKE, wife to Tinirau, 135

LALO-HĀNA, wife of the first man, 135

LALO-HONUA, wife of the first man, 1, 135

LANGI, (heavens), primeval Samoan creation, 28; Tuvalu heavenly god, 245

LANGITAETAEA, mother of Tu'i Tofua, 295

LANI-KĀULA, Hawaiian prophet, 135, 197

LANI-LOA, Hawaiian lizard goddess, 135

LANI-WAHINE, Hawaiian lizard goddess, 135

LANO, Hawaiian chief, 43

LASA, 134, (see also Laka)

LATA, benevolent god of Niue Island, 135; son of Fafiola and Tula, 322

LATE, same as Topolei, 153,

LATUAMA, sister to Tu'itatui, 295

LAUAMATOTO, Samoan servant to Tafa'i, 89

LAUHUKI, goddess of tapa makers, 149

LAU-KA-'IE'IE, Hawaiian forest goddess, 61, 135, 136

LAU-KAPALILI, sacred heavenly gourd, 135

LAU-KIA-MANU-I-KAHIKI, Hawaiian maiden, 136

LAU-KIELE-'ULA, Hawaiian sweet-scented goddess, 135, 136

LAUKITI, principal god on Nanumea, Tuvalu, 136

LAULAU-A-LE-FOLASA, wife of the god Tagaloa, 251

LA'ULU, Samoan fisherman, 8, 136

LAUPANANA, Samoan warrior, 297

LAUPANINI, Samoan warrior, 297

LAUTHALA, god of Lau Islands, 136

LAUTĪ, a servant of Sina, 136

LAVAKIMATA, god of Niue Island, 136

LAVANIA, Samoan chief, 136

LAVASII, chief ruler at Lefanga, Samoa, 136–137

Lavonès, Henri, Marquesan scholar, xxiv

LAWEKEAO, mother of the Hawaiian hero Kinilau, 118

LEA, Hawaiian goddess of canoe makers, 126, 137

LE ALALI, Samoan warrior, son of Atiogie, 17

LEASIASILOGI, son of the Samoan god Tagaloaui, 100

LEATAAOFITI, son of Muiu'uleapai, 178

LEATUALOA, household god of Samoa, 137

LE-FALE-I-LE-LANGI, Samoan goddess, 137, 267

O

P

S

U

Y

About the Author

ROBERT D. CRAIG is Professor of History and Chairman of the Social Sciences Department at the Alaska Pacific University, Anchorage. He is editor of *Pacifica: A Journal of Pacific and Asian Studies* and he coauthored the *Historical Dictionary of Oceania* (Greenwood Press, 1981). Craig is currently writing a history of Tahiti and compiling a Tahitian-English, English-Tahitian Dictionary.